R. from M.
25 January 1995

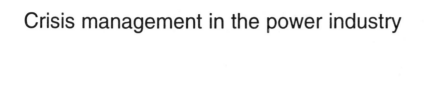

Crisis management in the power industry

Crisis management in the power industry

An inside story

Frank Ledger and Howard Sallis

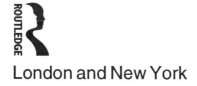

London and New York

First published 1995
by Routledge
11 New Fetter Lane, London EC4P 4EE

Simultaneously published in the USA and Canada
by Routledge
29 West 35th Street, New York, NY 10001

Typeset in Times by LaserScript, Mitcham, Surrey
Printed and bound in Great Britain by
Biddles Ltd, Guildford and King's Lynn

British Library Cataloguing in Publication Data
A catalogue record for this book is available from the British Library

Library of Congress Cataloging in Publication Data
A catalogue record for this book has been requested

ISBN 0–415–11876–X

*To Alma and Joan
for their
unstinting support
and
to all those in
electricity supply
who sought always to
keep the lights on*

Contents

Illustrations   ix
Glossary of terms   xi
Foreword   xiii
D. G. Jefferies CBE
Introduction   xv

1 Britain's most vulnerable industry in perspective   1

Part I Trials of strength

2 1926: Electricity supply and the General Strike   11

3 1949: Reds under the bed?   23

4 1970: Working to whose rules?   34

5 1971–2: The edge of darkness   43

6 1973–4: Heath and the miners   59

7 1977: No work, no pay   74

Part II The miners' strike 1984–5

8 Conflict in context   87

9 Preparations for the inevitable?   95

10 Overtime ban   104

11 Strike   111

12 Facing up to the long haul   125

13 Can we get through the winter?   143

14 Winter   159

15 Back to normal and counting the cost   170

Part III Resource management in the 1984–5 miners' strike

16 Coal on the move   181

17 Oil: the £4 billion story   195

18 The power system: innovation and flexibility   210

19 Essential supplies: from helicopters to CO_2 221

20 Generating plant: problems and opportunities   230

21 The managers, the unions and the staff   241

22 Who is my brother?   246

23 Partners: the distribution boards   256

24 Information: handle with care   261

Part IV The future

25 Keeping the lights on in the 1990s and beyond   271

Appendices

  I Electricity generation: a brief history   287
 II The miners' strike, 1984–5   294
III The CEGB organisation 1984–5   301
     Notes   306
     Index   326

Illustrations

PLATES

1 Bomb-proof war-time accommodation for grid control
2 Stray barrage balloons caused many war-time electrical faults
3 The Central Electricity Board meet by candlelight: February 1947
4 Darkened Piccadilly Circus: December 1970
5 Transmission teams repair overhead lines: winter 1962-3
6 Miners' pickets: Battersea Power Station
7 A 'merry-go-round' coal train at a larger power station
8 Essential supplies by helicopter
9 Grain Power Station achieved record output: the 1984-5 miners' strike
10 Trawsfyndd Nuclear Power Station saved coal: the 1984-5 miners' strike
11 Kingsnorth oil jetty for Kingsnorth and Grain Power Stations
12 Some CEGB members and staff in the 1984-5 miners' strike

FIGURES

8.1 Location of power stations 1984–5	93
8.2 Transmission network 1984–5	94
11.1 Colliery to power station railway connections	117
16.1 Coal stocks at CEGB power stations	183
17.1 Spot fuel oil price	209
18.1 System endurance assessment	214
18.2 Have-not stations coal burn: example for week 47 (end November)	215
18.3 Winter power flow pattern (daytime)	217
20.1 Oil and gas generation capability over 1984–5 miners' strike	231
AIII.1 The CEGB organisation at March 1984	302
AIII.2 Typical CEGB regional organisation 1984-5	304
AIII.3 CEGB Operations Department organisation	305

TABLES

6.1 Miners' pay claim and settlement 1974	72
7.1 Terms of agreement on travel allowances, 3 November 1977	80
15.1 Fuel consumption and costs	177
16.1 Coal stock distribution	184
16.2 Weekly coal deliveries	188
17.1 Oil burn increase	199
17.2 Oil burn – consumption 1984–5	201–2
17.3 Coal-fired stations with oil burn capability	203
19.1 Weekly consumption of essential commodities at power stations	223
20.1 Oil and gas generation capability at peak demand period during January 1985	234
AIII.1 CEGB March 1984	303

Glossary of terms

AC:	Alternating current: a current which alternates its direction of flow at very short intervals of time.
DC:	Direct current: in contrast to alternating current DC is a unidirectional current.
Coal-equivalent:	The weight of coal with a similar heat content: a means of expressing the quantity of primary fuels in a common way. At the time of the 1984–5 miners' strike 1 million tonnes of heavy fuel oil was approximately 1.75 million tonnes of coal equivalent.
Frequency:	The rate at which direction reversal cycles take place for an AC supply, normally expressed as cycles per second or Herz (Hz). The standard frequency in Europe including the UK is 50 cycles per second or 50 Hz.
Have and have-not power stations:	*Have* power stations were those in the 1984–5 miners' strike that were receiving coal supplies. *Have-not* power stations were those that were not. They were terms which emerged naturally at planning and operational meetings and served their purpose well.
Loading regime:	The pattern of daily loading of electricity generation at a power station.

Base-load is a loading regime of full load 24 hours per day.

Two-shifting is a loading regime in which the power station or generating unit is used for only two of the three eight-hour shifts in each day.

Peaking is a loading regime in which the power station or generating unit is only run to supply electricity over the time of the heaviest daily demand.

Tons and Tonnes: Units of weight: ton was the old imperial unit and tonne the metric unit of 1000 kilogrammes that succeeded it. 1 ton = 1.01605 tonnes. The CEGB went over to the metric system in the early 1970s.

Volt: Unit of electrical pressure that causes a flow of current. *KV* is kilovolt: thousands of volts (e.g. the original grid system voltage of 132 000 volts or 132KV).

Watts: A unit of power: the rate of doing work.
KW kilowatt: one thousand watts.
MW megawatt: one million watts or one thousand KWs.
GW gigawatt: one thousand million watts or one thousand MWs.
One horsepower is the equivalent of 746 watts or 0.746 KWs

Watt-hour: A measure of energy production or consumption. The most widely used version of this measure is the *KWH* kilowatt-hour or in other words one kilowatt for *one hour*, normally referred to as a 'unit' of electricity.
MWH, *GWH* and *TWH* are respectively megawatt-hour, gigawatt-hour and terawatt-hour. The unit of electrical energy used most frequently in the text is the TWH, which is one thousand million KWHs. At the time of the 1984–5 strike 1TWH was generated by burning just under half a million tonnes of coal-equivalent.

Note: Should the reader need further help in understanding some of these definitions a standard dictionary may, in some cases, give longer explanations.

Foreword

D.G. Jefferies CBE
Chairman, The National Grid Company plc

Most of us take our electricity supply for granted. This is a major tribute to the professionalism of those who work in the electricity industry and to the technical facility with which supplies are maintained.

This book is about those occasions in the past seventy years when our day-to-day certainties were replaced by an unaccustomed uncertainty and when supplies were threatened.

Frank Ledger and Howard Sallis recollect how the industry maintained supplies through times of crisis – most recently during the miners' strike in 1984–5 – and how it managed during the blackouts in the 1970s and in the more distant past. With the electricity industry sitting centre stage during these various crises the authors address the historically complex interactions of politics, industrial relations, fuel supplies and the actual workings of the industry.

In the past the industry has not always been good at telling its customers and the population at large what it does, how it does it and the risks to continuity of supply that it has had to deal with. For historians, students of the industry and professional managers alike, this book will be essential reading. It pulls together for the first time a wealth of information and demonstrates the technical flexibility of the UK power system and the resourcefulness of its analytical tools for dealing with extreme situations. The book serves as an important contribution to the study of crisis management in a large and vital infrastructure industry.

As a key player within the operations functions of the CEGB during the 1970s and 1980s and as one of those at the very centre of policy during the mid-1980s, Frank Ledger lived at first hand many of the events described in this book. His colleague and co-writer, Howard Sallis, was also at the centre of decision-making – in the industrial relations area – first at the CEGB and latterly at the Electricity Council. Their combined perceptions provide a unique insight into the history of the power industry into the mid-1980s and beyond.

However, as the last chapter of this book makes clear, the restructuring and privatisation of the UK electricity industry in the late 1980s has dramatically changed the situation. The Electricity Act of 1989 introduced a more competitive market and at the same time, through new legal arrangements for the operating companies, has ensured that a range of public service obligations are met and that fuel security provisions are in place.

The CEGB has been replaced by several independent generation companies each now with separate negotiating machineries – thus reducing the threat from any single employee group. In addition, the introduction of significant amounts of gas into primary energy supplies for power plants has brought a much greater fuel diversity – thus reducing the threat of interruption from any one fuel source such as coal. The unique historic relationship between the UK coal and power industries has changed fundamentally.

The new companies also clearly understand the importance of giving a high quality service and continuity of electricity supply within a competitive market-place. This changing culture is supported by mechanisms that provide an over-view of the whole electricity system – through the National Grid's Seven Year Statement – and increasingly sophisticated energy management centres, which ensure the very best use of the generation and transmission system at any time. Having said that, however, there can never be any cut and dried certainty about supply in the future – the impact of events both within and outside the industry is unpredictable. It is with this in mind that the observations in the final chapter are particularly appropriate.

The passage of time often lends a welcome perspective. Frank Ledger and Howard Sallis make a huge contribution to that perspective. Their attention to detail and the mass of documentation they have assembled, together with the personal judgement they have brought to bear, make this book essential reading and a very important addition to our current understanding of the industry as well as of its past.

Introduction

This book is a study of crisis management in the electricity supply industry over about seventy years. The successive crises were all serious because of the industry's extreme vulnerability. The most serious were a result of the coal strikes of 1972, 1974 and 1984–5 because they were organised by the National Union of Mineworkers, one of the most powerful trade unions at the time, and because that union sought to win its conflicts with the Coal Board by stopping electricity supply. The last of these strikes is inevitably attracting public attention this year, its tenth anniversary, but the book extends much further, revealing an electricity supply industry that, through changing times and forms of organisation, planned, adapted and improvised to fulfil its statutory responsibility to keep the lights on.

Our position as co-authors is this. One of us, Frank Ledger, was the Central Electricity Generating Board's System Operation Engineer during the miners' strikes of the early 1970s and Director of Operations during the year-long miners' strike of 1984–5. He writes from direct experience, having played an important part in managing these crises on behalf of the Board. Howard Sallis was Head of Industrial Relations at the CEGB during the disputes of the 1970s and Central Director for Industrial Relations at the Electricity Council in the 1980s.

We have written the book now for a number of reasons. First, we think the subject is of wide public interest, in particular to people in politics, business, the universities and trade unions. Second, it has only been in the last two years or so that the industry has felt sufficiently free from the sorts of threats it faced in the 1970s and 1980s to tell in full the story of past conflicts; it has taken us this time to plan, research and write the book. Third, we wanted to give an account of the electricity supply industry as it exists now, after three to four years of privatisation and reorganisation, and to be able to raise in the last chapter the compelling questions: could there be another serious threat to continuity of supply, and if so could the 'new' industry cope?

We cannot list here all the companies and individuals who have helped us in preparing this book since they are too many. We have, however, named many in the notes to the chapters. Among the companies we must mention are the CEGB successor companies, East Midlands Electricity PLC and Yorkshire Electricity

PLC. Among the individuals we must mention are Lord Marshall, Sir Philip Jones, James Cowan, David Prendergast, John Wooley, Ed Wallis, Roger Farrance, Granville Camsey, Bill Kerss, David Hill and Mike Wickham. All these have made essential contributions of various kinds. We also wish to thank Philip Way who has processed and assembled the photographs.

We wish to thank the staff of the Public Record Office who gave us access to their files on the 1926 General Strike and governmental references to industrial relations in 1945–51. Many publishers have allowed us to quote from books that they have published; these are acknowledged in the notes to the chapters. Among authors our indebtedness is especially deep to Martin Adeney and John Lloyd, Keith Jeffery and Peter Hennessy, and Eric Wigham. We apologise to those whom, in spite of our efforts, we have not been able to contact.

Finally we thank Nuclear Electric plc for their practical support throughout. In their London office Liz Washford dealt efficiently with our meeting arrangements and correspondence. At the company's Barnwood office Rex Melville, Company Secretary, gave us access to necessary help from his staff. There Alan Tugwell established and sustained the office services that we needed. Anne Fincher received our manuscripts and did much skilful and painstaking editorial work on them. She also worked closely with the typing centre, especially Dominique Shaw, who did the bulk of the preliminary typing, and with Lynn Reade who did most of the later typing and revisions of the manuscript speedily and accurately. We are extremely grateful to this group, not least for their constructive comments on our work and their interest in its progress. We could not have managed without them.

In spite of all the guidance we have received there are no doubt errors of fact and judgement. These belong exclusively to us.

Frank Ledger CBE
Howard Sallis

Chapter 1

Britain's most vulnerable industry in perspective

Many ordinary people know more about plastics and computers than they do about electricity supply. Many scarcely ever think about it, even though a moment's thought would yield a stark picture of life without it.

THE VULNERABILITY OF ELECTRICITY SUPPLY

Electricity supply is infinitely more fundamental to the economy, to transport, to life itself than the source of the TV that enlivens our evening, the light to find our way to bed and the kettle to make our morning tea. The full implications of its loss would begin to dawn when travel to work was affected by the absence of street lighting, the crippling of petrol pumps and the cessation of electric trains and signals. The next stage would be no work to go to, with factory plant out of action, tills and typewriters silent, computers blank. Gas ceases to flow. Telephone and postal services collapse. Water supplies and sewage disposal cease. Food shortage is accelerated by lack of refrigeration. But the seriousness of the situation would stun us even more if we had sickness in our home or a member of the family on dialysis. The fact that electricity cannot be stored adds to its vulnerability.

Few people know how close we have come on more than one occasion to a disaster of this kind. From 1948 the publicly owned electricity supply industry had a statutory obligation to maintain public supplies. Despite serious temporary inconveniences endured by consumers during successive crises, especially in the 1970s, the public never seemed to believe that the ultimate nightmare could become wide-awake reality.

THREATS AND TREMORS

For this reason and others this book needed to be written; it recounts the threats to electricity supply that occurred well within one lifetime, and the industry's response. The book appears, as it happens, during the tenth anniversary of the 1984–5 miners' strike, which brought the unthinkable nearer than trembling distance. Strange that in the spate of political memoirs published by leading political figures of the 1980s, culminating in those of Baroness Thatcher, little has been written about how electricity supply, specifically the Central Electricity Generating Board, responded to this threat. Yet failure on the part of the CEGB would have changed the course of history.

As we imply, there is more than one dramatic story in this book. It is true that the miners' strike of 1984–5 brought into use all the crisis management skills learnt in previous episodes; that its risks in political terms and the implications of failure both for the mining industry and the government were dramatic; that its human and community aspects called for immense sensitivity; and that its media interest was high and sustained. It is also true that, as the tenth anniversary recalls memories, the strike could well seem the most important event recounted in this chronicle of years of managing crises in power supply. It should be seen rather as a major but not isolated experience in meeting threats to a vital industry, all with common dangers and challenges. In fact other episodes displayed single even more dramatic features: political dangers shown to be more than rhetoric; the public severely inconvenienced, though never on a wide enough scale or for long enough to bring home the nightmare possibilities; industry seriously disrupted, and so on.

The chapters that follow relate the story of a succession of major disputes from the 1926 strike onwards. All demonstrate how the importance and inherent vulnerability of the industry have several times led groups of people either inside or outside to use this to bring pressure to bear on employers or the government. The objectives have been higher pay, better working conditions or the abandonment of plans for change.

WHAT CRISIS MANAGEMENT MEANS IN A BASIC INDUSTRY

The industry's responses demonstrate crisis management at its most demanding. Any undertaking may at some time have to confront events that, whether or not foreseen, whether or not possible to prepare for, are outside its daily experience. They are hostile. They threaten, either from inside or outside the undertaking, its ability to meet its objectives, the public confidence it commands, its very survival. They tax its resources and the skills of its managers, who know that failure to cope will have serious consequences for the organisation, its employees and its customers.

In extreme cases failure could threaten the stability of the community. Sometimes failure can be prevented by the application of well-tried techniques. More often the task will need exceptional measures and stratagems. This is the interest of the events recorded here for all those who might at some time be involved in crisis management.

Crises must, if possible, be foreseen. This is the first task of those responsible for management information, whose writ extends beyond its own markets and production problems to events and conditions in other industries, economic intelligence, raw material supplies and prices, national and local politics, the law, and the preoccupations of organised labour. There must be structures in place to chart and predict the course of events and the appropriate responses.

Plans must include the maximum flexibility of access to raw materials and other essential supplies and transport. Well in advance the roles and responsibilities of managers in a crisis must be clearly delineated, combining firm strategy at the centre with scope for rapid responses at local level where appropriate. Flexibility at operational unit level in organising responses, safe-guarding supplies, and monitoring events is crucial. This makes communication between the centre and operating units all important, if the crisis is to be managed always at the appropriate level. Management information services remain crucial as the crisis develops.

It follows that relationships assume vital significance if well-informed and highly motivated responses at various levels are expected: industrial relations must be well managed for remedial actions to be understood and supported by employees. If a basic industry is involved it is essential to manage the media presentation of the crisis well and to ensure that consumers are informed of developments and dealt with as far as possible on a basis of equality in any necessary restrictions of supply. If the crisis has originated in one's own enterprise, management must be seen to be seeking a solution with a proper sense of urgency. If the trouble arises elsewhere great sensitivity is needed to avoid appearing to become a participant in someone else's dispute or to provoke those involved. Finally management must never forget that when the crisis is over it will be necessary to resume normal operations and restore effective working relationships within and between undertakings.

A STORY WAITING TO BE WRITTEN

Much of the material used in this narrative has been drawn from the industry's own archives and those of the Public Record Office, from consultation with others directly involved and from direct personal experience. Much of it has not been published before and this is particularly true in the case of the miners' disputes of the early 1970s and 1984–5. Indeed it could not have been told before, for a number of reasons.

At the time, and for some years afterwards, there were strong tactical reasons for keeping quiet about the dangers to electricity supply and the strategies for overcoming them. There was also sensitivity to the feelings of many CEGB employees who lived in mining communities and mining homes. The CEGB did not want to be or appear to be a participant in the government's and the National Coal Board's fight against the National Union of Mineworkers and the striking miners, and it played its statutory responsibility straight down the middle. In recent years, however, the threat of a strike of the same kind to electricity supplies has for various reasons become small. The electricity supply industry has changed its structure through privatisation in ways that would make any future crisis significantly different. There is no reason now to hold back a story of great public interest and importance.

COULD IT HAPPEN AGAIN?

In the wake of the privatisation of the electricity supply industry, we can now ask challenging and controversial questions that have not been asked before and that are of fundamental importance to the economy, the quality of life and even the political stability of the country. Is the privatised industry more or less vulnerable to internal or external assaults on its capacity to maintain a public electricity supply than it was under public ownership and other forms of organisation? Where if anywhere could those assaults possibly come from? Do changes in the strength of other related industries and in trade union law have a decisive influence? Are the government's and the industry's crisis management arrangements capable of meeting any new threats effectively in the future?

These questions are examined in the final chapter of the book, but their importance here is that knowing them in advance as each crisis is recounted gives the reader a chance to ask what bearing the organisation of the industry at the time and the structures in place to manage the crisis had on the outcome. Seeing the narrative in this organic way will provide some of the material to answer those final questions.

The events described took place under different forms of ownership and organisation, at different stages in the advance of technology, and with different policies, practices and constraints in industrial relations and the relevant law, changes not all perhaps as dramatic as nationalisation in 1948 or privatisation in 1990, but significant. A full account of the changes in structure, technology and industrial relations is given in Appendix 1. Here we attempt only a brief guide, one long enough to make what follows intelligible but not so long that it impedes the flow of the story.

ELECTRICITY GENERATION OVER THE YEARS[1]

Before World War I

Electricity generation began in small sheds and basements in the late 1870s, grew rapidly, and came under legislative regulation in the 1880s and 1900s. Technological developments by such pioneers as Ferranti and Parsons enabled generators to increase in size from a few kilowatts to several megawatts. By 1914 hundreds of independent undertakings, private and public, had been established, with sales of electricity for power exceeding those for lighting and traction. The main limitation was that there were few connections between local undertakings, and many technical differences.

By 1907 there were about 20 000 people wholly or mainly employed in generation and supply, with about 5 per cent of them in trade unions, mainly Electrical Trades Union craftsmen. There was no collective bargaining.

World War I

In World War I demand increased from 1.96 TWHs to 3.57, the demands of munitions factories providing a great fillip. Power stations remained unlinked, however, and it was not until 1919 that there was legislation aimed, among other things, at correcting this. Trade unions in the industry also grew, with some elements of collective bargaining including, in 1918, a famous arbitration award – No 2772 – establishing a standard rate for electricians in London and later beyond. The Electrical Power Engineers' Association, representing technical and scientific staff, was formed towards the end of the war.

The inter-war years

Electricity Commissioners, established by legislation in 1919, had a useful regulatory role but did not get far with co-ordinated developments through the joint electricity authorities that the law had envisaged.

There was much industrial disturbance at the time and the government extended the Conspiracy and Protection of Property Act of 1875 to cover electricity supply.[2] In 1920 came the Emergency Powers Act.[3] In 1919 negotiating machinery was established for manual workers (the National Joint Industrial Council) and in 1920 for technical and scientific staff (the National Joint Board). The EPEA and the ETU, the two strongest unions, were at logger-heads, otherwise the EPEA would have joined the NJIC. The industry suffered for many years from this division.

The manual workers' trade unions in the industry were involved in the 1926 General Strike (see Chapter 2) This set back relationships, but the manual workers did not do as badly in the Depression as many elsewhere.

At the time of the General Strike total sales of electricity were 5.8 TWHs, generated by 478 power stations with a total capacity of 4422 MW. Local authorities owned 264 stations and companies owned 215, the biggest of which had more than 100 MW of plant installed.

In 1926 legislation established a public body, the Central Electricity Board (CEB), with powers among other things to control power stations' operations and to establish a 'grid-iron' of high voltage transmission lines. By 1935 this was complete, with 148 power stations under the CEB's direction. In 1939 it became a nationally integrated network with a National Control Centre.

Inter-war expansion was rapid. In 1914 sales per head of population had been 77 KWHs; by 1939 they were 486. Then the installed capacity of power stations was 9712 MW, most new generators being 30 or 50 MW capacity. The pay of the manual workers fell behind that generally prevailing as the economy recovered in the later 1930s, and this remained the case until 1948 and beyond. In other ways conditions of employment were relatively good.

World War II and nationalisation

The industry suffered bomb damage and other disruptions during World War II, while construction, repair and maintenance of power stations fell behind. As the economy adjusted to peacetime conditions there was a serious shortage of power, made worse by a shortage of coal, extensive use of electric fires, and the terrible weather of the 1946–7 winter.

The whole industry in Great Britain (except the North of Scotland Hydro-Electric Board, already a public board) was nationalised from 1 April 1948 when the assets of 200 companies, 369 local authority undertakings and the CEB were brought together under the British Electricity Authority (Central Electricity Authority from 1954) and 14 area distribution boards. Within the BEA a Central Authority ran the power stations and transmission systems.

Gradually post-war difficulties were overcome and there was rapid growth. Bigger, more efficient, generating sets were installed and the building of a 275 KV supergrid was started. On 1 April 1949 there were 197 power stations and about 156 000 employees all told, about 41 000 of them working for the Central Authority.

On 1 April 1948, and in the next two or three years, the industry's machinery for determining pay and conditions and for joint consultation was extended to cover the employers and all employees except a handful at the top and a few industrial relations specialists.[4]

Progress in industrial relations was limited, quite apart from the industrial dispute in 1949 dealt with in Chapter 3. The manual workers were heavily dependent on overtime to keep their earnings competitive, and labour productivity was low. There was progress on joint consultation.

On 1 January 1958, following examination of the industry by the Herbert Committee[5] and legislation, the main changes introduced were: (i) the establishment, in place of the CEA, of an Electricity Council to act as a central policy-making body for the whole industry in England and Wales, and to carry some specific responsibilities such as maintaining the industrial relations machinery; and (ii) a Central Electricity Generating Board (CEGB) which was to be responsible for generation and main transmission in England and Wales, owning such assets as the power stations and the grid.

The CEGB in the 1960s

The CEGB established five regions to operate the power stations and the grid. It inherited 262 power stations with a capacity of 24.34 GW, and annual sales of 40.3 TWHs.

Output increased rapidly in the 1960s and was catered for by a huge programme of power station and transmission line construction, including eight Magnox nuclear power stations. The Board had its problems, particularly in getting the big new stations to work properly. In 1971 the Board owned 187 power stations with a capacity of 49.28 GW and annual sales of 184 TWH. The 1960s (continuing into the early 1970s) were also a time of extensive bargaining with the NJIC trade unions on staff status for manual workers (subsequently called industrial staff), pay and productivity. Much was achieved including, for manual workers, a substantial move towards full staff status, the elimination of heavy overtime work, the introduction of staggered work patterns and a commitment to eliminate restrictive practices and to spread best practices. Parallel, though less far-reaching, agreements were made with the non-industrial staff unions.

In 1967 and 1968 came NJIC national agreements governing work-study-based incentive schemes to be introduced locally. This took time and the unions and many employees became impatient. There was industrial action in December 1970 (see Chapter 4). The Court of Inquiry[6] that followed set the industry on the right road. In March 1967 the number of industrial staff had been 53 915. By March 1973, when 77 per cent were working under incentive schemes, most at standard performance, the number was 38 893. Earnings had been raised and regular heavy overtime eliminated.

CEGB developments to 1984

In the 1970s, the big coal- and oil-fired stations began working well, and the 400 KV supergrid was completed. In the early 1980s the Monopolies and Mergers Commission[7] made a generally favourable report on the Board. The 2000 MW cross-Channel link was started and the first steps taken towards a pressurised water reactor at Sizewell. Dinorwig's great pumped storage scheme was officially opened.

Growth in units sold was much slower than in the 1960s. In 1973 the war in the Middle East and the associated oil shortage created problems for the world economy and in 1975–6 the Board had to close 5000 MW of plant with 5000 job losses. In the early 1980s 9000 MW of plant were closed and that number of jobs lost. By March 1984, the start of the year-long miners' strike, the Board had 90 power stations, a capacity of 51 028 MW, and annual sales of £7146 million.

The two miners' strikes of the early 1970s, with internal industrial action in 1973 and 1977, caused serious problems described in later chapters. Hard bargaining took place from time to time but some sound agreements were reached, not least in the NJIC in 1980.

Between 1967 and 1984 CEGB staff numbers fell from 80 189 to 50 250, the industrial staff bearing most of the losses. The figures reflected improved labour productivity, but the fall in numbers since privatisation shows that there was scope for more. Over-centralised negotiations and multiple negotiating bodies were impediments.

Nevertheless, by 1984 the Board was a coherent, purposeful and competent organisation by the standards of the time. The following twelve months were to put it to the test as it faced the greatest challenge in its own and the whole industry's history.

Part I

Trials of strength

Part I describes the six industrial disputes that most threatened electricity supplies before 1984–5. It sets them in their wider political, economic and industrial relations framework. Three disputes, in 1926, 1971–2 and 1973–4, primarily concerned the coal industry. Three, in 1949, 1970 and 1977, directly involved electricity supply employees. Each had its own dramatic features, which included rationing of electricity, intimidation on picket lines and suggestions of communist subversion. One precipitated a general election and the fall of a government.

Chapter 2

1926: Electricity supply and the General Strike

The General Strike of 1926 was the first occasion on which large numbers of power station workers took concerted strike action. It was also the first occasion on which such action threatened to interfere seriously with the nation's essential supplies. The story therefore exemplifies the central theme of this book.

EVENTS LEADING TO THE GENERAL STRIKE

In June 1924 a new wage agreement was reached in the mining industry; it was more favourable to the miners than the previous one. Shortly afterwards, however, mining moved into recession with a particularly serious fall in exports. This was exacerbated by the 1925 Budget in which the Chancellor of the Exchequer, Winston Churchill, put the pound back on the gold standard at the pre-war rate, making coal much more difficult to sell abroad.

In July 1925 the coal owners gave notice to the Miners' Federation of Great Britain (precursor of the National Union of Mineworkers) of their intention to end the 1924 wage agreement, offering new terms at lower rates. The Federation rejected this offer and prepared for strike action.

A strike in such a huge basic industry, employing 1 000 000 people, would clearly affect the whole economy, especially as there would be a degree of support from some other unions such as rail. The government therefore stepped in. However, as in 1981, it was not ready to take on the miners and on 30 July 1925 (Red Friday as it became generally known) the government decided to subsidise miners' wages for a period of nine months at a cost of £23 million. It also established a Royal Commission, chaired by Sir Herbert Samuel, to look into the coal industry's problems and to make recommendations.

The Commission reported on 10 March 1926. Its recommendations were complex but essentially stated that the industry was not efficient, needed to be reorganised and that thereafter the national minimum wage would have to fall, at least temporarily. The government subsidy should not continue beyond the end of April 1926.

Each side rejected various key recommendations in the report. In April the government, chaired by the Prime Minister, Stanley Baldwin, held lengthy discussions with the parties, but to no avail. The TUC affirmed its support for the miners.

On Friday 30 April the coal owners imposed a lockout, while negotiations, primarily between the government and the TUC's Industrial Committee, intensified.[1]

Meanwhile the government had not left the security of the nation to chance. In the war, *ad hoc* arrangements had been made to deal with civil and industrial disturbances and these arrangements were later further developed. Make-shift arrangements made in February 1919 to keep the power stations working were refined into the 'London Electric Power Scheme' under which, among other things, skilled volunteer labour was organised. The Admiralty also agreed to provide skilled stokers. Immediately following the rail strike of early October 1919 the government established its Supply and Transport Committee (STC), a Cabinet Committee with the Minister of Transport in the chair. This was to supervise arrangements for meeting civil contingencies. It created a sub-committee of senior civil servants, which in turn created several more specialist committees. This complex became the Supply and Transport Organisation (STO). In March 1920 the Prime Minister, Lloyd George, appointed eleven civil commissioners in England and Wales, plus a chief civil commissioner, to organise essential services, to maintain law and order and to recruit special constables. This whole structure, said Jeffery and Hennessy (1983), was to underpin the government's policy towards major strikes for the next twenty years.[2]

When the 1919 and 1920 strikes in rail and coal were over, the STC, but not the STO, became inactive. However, it was revived in late 1924, met again in February 1925, and met every day during the General Strike. It established an Organisation for the Maintenance of Supplies (OMS) and it was this body that arranged for naval stokers and other members of the military to be trained for essential services. It also prepared lists of civilian volunteers, skilled people to take up specific positions if required, and people willing and able to help generally.

The weekend before the strike began was hectic. At the TUC's request the executives of affiliated unions assembled on Thursday 29 April in London to back the TUC's Industrial Committee in its final negotiations. Although the miners were being locked out on 30 April, discussions between TUC representatives, the miners, the government and the owners went on through that day; but they got nowhere. The miners and the Industrial Committee reported back at midnight to the miners' delegate conference and union executives respectively. As they dispersed the executives took with them copies of instructions issued by the General Council's Ways and Means Committee for conducting the General Strike.

On the following day, Saturday 1 May, the conference of union executives endorsed 'proposals for co-ordinated action by trade unions'. The scope of the strike was to include all transport (including the docks), printing trades, iron and steel, metal and heavy chemicals and building (except houses and hospitals). The trade unions in gas and electricity supply were recommended to co-operate with the object of ceasing to supply power. The actual calling out of workers was to be left to the unions. The executives then voted to place their powers in the hands of the General Council and to carry out the Council's instructions during the dispute (the voting represented a membership of 3 653 527 in favour and 49 511 against).

The Industrial Committee, despite the lockout of the miners and the preparations for action, had further meetings with the Prime Minister on the evening of Saturday 1 May, after the miners and the union executives had gone home. This meeting went on into the Sunday and concluded with a statement to the effect that, if negotiations continued, there was a possibility of a settlement within a fortnight. The miners' representatives had not been present but at the General Council meeting on the following day (Sunday) they repudiated the statement. At a further meeting in Downing Street the Prime Minister and his colleagues tried to persuade the unions' negotiating team to support a reduction in miners' pay. While the union team were reporting back to the General Council in No 11 and the miners' representatives were joining them, the Prime Minister, Stanley Baldwin, called the unions' four negotiators out to meet him and his colleagues. The PM told them that the printers at the *Daily Mail* had refused to print a leading article, that this was a direct challenge to the government and that no government could go on negotiating in these circumstances. Baldwin gave the four negotiators a letter (also given to the press) stating that the General Strike notices must be withdrawn before negotiations could go on.

Acting TUC General Secretary, Walter Citrine, who recorded some of these event in his diary,[3] added that on Monday 3 May there were parliamentary debates but no new developments. The General Council stayed together until well after midnight but by that time a State of Emergency had been declared and the civil commissioners were taking up their posts. The first workers were coming out on strike.

THE GENERAL STRIKE

According to the official notes of the meeting of the STC held on 4 May, most railway, dock, tramway and bus workers ceased work, although goods transport by road was not seriously affected.[4] According to Citrine, who relied on daily reports from the TUC's Strike Organisation Committee, 'the strike is complete. The reports are simply marvellous'.[5] On that day, only 849 trains ran. In London all the dockers came out and the underground railway workers. The London newspapers (not the provincial) stopped, although *The Times* appeared in shortened form. The BBC increased its news coverage, sought to fulfil its responsibilities impartially, but tended to support the government line. Safety men remained in the mines. Special constables were recruited in large numbers; in London alone the number rose from 3035 on 4 May to 51 807 on 11 May.

On 5 May, 2127 trains ran; there was no lack of road transport. Volunteers were coming forward in large numbers: on 11 May, 487 124 workers had volunteered for work. According to Phillips[6] the OMS had handed over 100 000 names to the Voluntary Service Committees spread around the country. Just over 5000 were employed in essential occupations, most in transport. Of these 5000, 1194 were employed in power stations. The STC were informed that 1 000 000 miners and between 1 580 000 and 2 000 000 other workers were on strike. Other participants and commentators agree with these figures.[7]

The British Gazette, a government news-sheet, was published on 6 May and, from the *Daily Herald* offices, the TUC's *British Worker*. The government repeated assurances that people remaining at or returning to work would be protected, while the TUC insisted that the strike was industrial, not political.

By Friday 7 May the number of trains running had increased to 2778. The TUC had given assurances about food supplies and although there were odd local cases of these being held up there were no serious shortages. Citrine recorded in his diary that the Strike Organisation Committee had reported 'the position throughout the country to be as solid as a rock'.[8]

On the following day, Saturday, the government called for recruits to a Civil Constabulary Reserve to be made up of territorials and ex-military men, 9000 were recruited but they were never used. Throughout the weekend 3176 trains had run and things generally were quiet. The Manchester Ship Canal was idle.

On Monday 10 May 4253 trains ran. According to the STC, workers were slowly returning throughout the country and various undertakings that had closed down initially had reopened. Behind the scenes, the TUC were trying to establish a negotiating position through the good offices of Sir Herbert Samuel. Citrine was recording his view that, 'while the position of our forces was strong, we could not count upon a continuance of the dispute without serious dangers of breakaways. We must get a settlement as soon as we could'.[9] The miners were standing firm.

On the following day 5079 trains ran and there were 850 buses on London's streets. Mr Justice Astbury gave a judgement that the strike was illegal, that members of trade unions could not lose benefits by refusing to obey an illegal order and that the funds of the unions could not be used or depleted by strike pay.[10] Citrine recorded in his diary 'the men are as firm as a rock. What then can be the cause of apprehension? I think it is because most of us know that no matter how determined our men are now, once the strike has reached its highest point and the maximum of members have been called out, a gradual decline in economic power must ensue. Then we shall have dribblings back to work here and there, and possibly large desertions'.[11] Citrine quotes Ernest Bevin as telling the General Council on this day: 'I don't think it is right to go on asking men to make sacrifices if we can get justice in some other way. The other side does not want to fight this matter out to a finish'.[12]

On Wednesday 12 May men were reported to be returning to work in small numbers. It appeared that only 20 per cent of members of the Shipbuilding and

Engineering Unions had responded to the strike call. At 1pm the General Council of the TUC met the Prime Minister and some of his Cabinet colleagues to inform them that they were calling off the strike, although they were not speaking for the miners.

The immediate response to the strike call had been overwhelming and the return to work quite small even according to a government source.[13] Such events always produce simple, or even simplistic, indicators of how events are moving and the daily movement of trains had served that purpose. Yet information from the 4 main railway companies, quoted by an STC sub-committee, showed that the number of railwaymen available for work at the start of the strike was between 13 and 20 per cent in the different companies and at the end between 14 and 22 per cent. There had been no widespread violence, little or no sabotage, few arrests, stocks remained good and there were plenty of offers to help with transport.

If strikers generally returned without having achieved anything for the miners, the miners themselves were to continue their strike for a total of six months. There were some defectors however: in Nottinghamshire George Spencer negotiated local deals that led to men returning to work; in October 1926 the Nottinghamshire miners left the Federation.

THE INVOLVEMENT OF POWER STATIONS

In 1926, there were 479 power stations in statutory undertakings with a total capacity of 4422 MW (twice the 1920 capacity). There were 264 power stations owned by the local authorities and 215 owned by private companies,[14] Greater London alone had 75. There were some large stations like Barking (137.5 MW installed and 100 MW under construction) and Manchester (two stations of 107 MW and 90 MW owned by the local authority). Over 84 per cent of this plant was in 125 stations having installed capacities of 10 000 KW or more. Most power stations were coal-fired. A few local authorities and companies linked their own stations (e.g. Newcastle-upon-Tyne and the London Power Companies) but most stations stood alone serving only their immediate localities. There were no inter-connections between neighbouring undertakings, and this strike, unlike all later industrial action affecting this industry, did not have a national power system connotation.

On Saturday 1 May the instructions to specific trade unions about strike action requested the electricity supply unions to 'co-operate with the object of ceasing to supply *power*' [our italics]. The General Council request that the executives of the trade unions concerned shall meet at once with a view to formulating a common policy'. By this time the NJIC had been suspended.

The trade unions in the industry were divided. In particular there was hostility between the two strongest unions, the Electrical Power Engineers' Association and the Electrical Trades Union. The main reason was recruitment: both unions, for example, competed for representation of sub-station attendants and switchboard attendants. Further, the EPEA were not then affiliated to the TUC and this was held against them by the other unions.

The EPEA had held discussions with the government before the strike[15] at which they had been told the government's plans; the EPEA had promised co-operation. The Association's General Purposes Committee held an emergency session on Sunday 2 May at which it was stated that two possible courses were open. First, the normal position in a trade dispute could be taken 'not to perform any of the duties usually carried out by the men on strike or supervise any labour utilised in substitution for such men'. Secondly, 'in accordance with its oft-declared policy, the Association could refuse to allow the electricity supply industry to be involved seeing the present dispute arose outside the industry'. Instead it relied on the TUC General Council's instructions quoted above, interpreting them to mean that the General Council wished to maintain essential electricity services during the dispute. The EPEA also made the point that, under its constitution, it could, in any case, only authorise strike action after a ballot of the membership and it was too late for that. The EPEA's General Purposes Committee then resolved:

(1) That the essential public services in connection with the supply of electrical energy should be maintained.

(2) The Association deprecates the introduction of volunteer workers in the Electricity Supply Industry, but in the present emergency this Executive Committee agrees that to maintain the essential public services it hereby instructs its members to co-operate in the government scheme for the maintenance of such services.

(3) That to prevent a situation arising which may operate to the detriment of the foregoing resolutions, it is advisable for instructions to be given by His Majesty's government to all Electricity Supply Undertakings that to maintain the supply of energy for such essential public services care shall be exercised that a supply of power shall not be given to an industrial works engaged in work of a non-essential character.

(4) That the aforementioned resolutions be officially communicated to H M government at the earliest opportunity, and that copies of such resolutions be sent to the National Joint Board and all the District Joint Boards.[16]

On 3 May Bob Prain, Assistant General Secretary of the ETU, sent down the union line the General Council's document, already quoted, at the same time telling the members to await union instructions. However, the relations between the Union's national executive and the London (No 10) District Committee were not good, London being the most militant of the union's districts. The District Secretary, Bill Webb, on the same day wrote pre-emptively to every branch secretary and shop steward in London calling for immediate strike action. His letter (endorsed on the following day by his committee) stated:

On the instructions of the General Council of the TUC and your Executive

Council every member of the ETU must cease work at 12 midnight tonight Monday May 3, 1926 . . . . No member of the ETU must remain at work unless he has the written consent of the London District Committee to do so. The London District Committee rely upon the loyalty of its members upon this momentous occasion. Everyone must cease work.[17]

There was no mention here of waiting for union instructions.[18] John Lloyd states[19] that in the following few days reports came in of an enthusiastic response around the country in spite of the initial confusion from the gas and electricity leaderships. According to Phillips[20] and Farman[21] there were in all perhaps 15,000 workers on strike part or all of the time in the electricity supply industry and according to Hannah,[22] who used these figures, this constituted slightly more than half the industry's manual workers.

The distribution of this number throughout the country and the effect of their absence from duty on the ability of the stations to continue to generate is difficult to assess precisely. Account needs to be taken of the fact that EPEA members, along with most other non-manual power station employees, continued to work and that there was widespread use of naval stokers and civilian volunteers. The *Electrical Review* of 28 May 1926 gave a detailed, although not comprehensive, account of the impact of the strike on power stations, although it is not entirely clear when references are being made to power stations and when to distribution undertakings. The article refers to the 'comparative ease with which supplies of electricity were maintained. This, and the normality, apart from reduced loads, with which very many undertakings . . . in all parts of the country were able to carry on were the outstanding features of the situation'. But what were the particular implications of those 'reduced loads'?

The *Electrical Review*[23] gave a list of big provisional cities in many parts of the country. This included every permutation between those stations at which all the employees remained at work and those which for short periods at least were shut down. By the end of the article the initial impression of business as usual is somewhat vitiated, especially in London.

The Supply and Transport Sub-Committee records that no planning for the maintenance of provincial stations in emergencies had been undertaken and that generally speaking provincial stations maintained an adequate supply. But London was a different matter: there the plans were said to have been well laid.

The parent committee, the STC, was told on 3 May that by 4.30pm that day the movement of naval ratings to London would be complete. After the strike, the STC sub-committee stated that 34 London power stations had been identified as being of vital importance and estimates had been made that (presumably apart from EPEA members) 499 naval ratings and 2120 civil volunteers would be needed to man them. In fact during the whole course of the strike assistance was given to 33 London stations, with 434 naval ratings and 737 civil volunteers being employed in all.[24]

Meanwhile the ETU's London District Committee and specifically Bill Webb, the District Secretary, were creating serious problems for those attempting to optimise action in the stations. Lloyd states[25] that on 5 May Webb informed the municipalities and companies in London that all power stations would stop at 3pm that day if they did not agree to isolate the public lighting and prevent the supply of power to industry and commerce. This was technically a difficult thing to do (certainly it was impossible to do it completely). However the Labour-controlled authorities in East and South London, except Stepney, agreed to supply only 'essential services'. This alarmed the General Council and Farman says[26] that on 6 May they revised this policy and told strike committees to meet the local authorities 'and offer to supply light and power for such services as house, street and shop lighting, social services, power for food, bakeries, laundries and domestic purposes'. Although a refusal by most to negotiate led to an almost total withdrawal of manual union labour the government was well able to cope.

On 7 May Webb reaffirmed his instructions to stations in London to stop work, despite the General Council's instruction. According to Bob Prain, as quoted by Lloyd, 'immediately this was done, naval ratings were brought into the stations, and these ratings, along with the EPEA, have managed to carry on as if nothing had happened'. On 9 May the ETU's sub-executive wrote to the London Committee requesting that it 'loyally carry out the decisions arrived at and the instructions issued by the TUC General Council'. But it made no difference to Webb and his Committee whose attitude ultimately reduced the effectiveness of the strike and caused great embarrassment to Jimmy Rowan, the Union's General Secretary, in his dealings with the General Council.[27]

The daily proceedings of the STC, under the chairmanship of the Home Secretary, do not suggest that, except in two individual cases, they spent much time on power station issues, even though an item on the 'London Electric Power Scheme' continued to appear on their agenda.

Meetings of the Committee on the 4, 5 and 6 May received details of naval ratings and volunteers sent to London stations.[28] The situation was said to be satisfactory except in the Labour boroughs of Battersea, Bermondsey, Poplar, Stepney and West Ham. On 6 May continuous supplies were being maintained from stations in these boroughs (except for Stepney) for lighting but not for industrial power. However, at the meeting the following day (after the General Council's instructions) it was reported that these same stations were normally supplying light and power for hospitals and other essential services, including bakeries. With more naval ratings being moved that day into the stations the proceedings of 8 May had a ring of complacency about them, contrasting with the baleful interpretation of the same events by Bob Prain, which we have quoted.

The two issues that took up considerable time at meetings of the STC concerned Stepney and St Helens Power Stations, the latter the only reference in the proceedings of the Committee to any action in power stations outside London. On 4 May the Committee's record states, referring to Stepney, that 'the Borough Council had given instructions that no power or light was to be provided by the stations under their control between sunrise and sunset and that after sunset power should be provided only to hospitals'. The STC decided not to take precipitate action because they were extremely concerned not to cause EPEA members to walk out with possible knock-on effects in other stations. Clement Attlee was the Chairman of the Borough Electricity Committee and, according to Lloyd,[29] he 'handed over to the workers the responsibility for making sure no unauthorised electricity was used outside the lighting and hospital service'.

The local action continued in spite of the attention of the STC and it was not until 11 May that the government served notices on the Town Clerk and each member of the Stepney Borough Council directing them to supply power for all purposes. Otherwise they would be summonsed. Next day it was reported that the Borough Council had complied.

On 9 May, at the STC, the Chief Civil Commissioner reported on a problem at St Helens Power Station. On the previous day the Chairman of the local Trades and Labour Council (who was also Chairman of the Watch Committee) had threatened that, unless the members of the EPEA were withdrawn from the station and replaced by members of the ETU, the station and the gas works would be stopped. He had then brought forward a motion at the Town Council that the members of the EPEA should be dismissed. The motion had been defeated by a majority of two, but the Council had passed a resolution that 'we place the machinery of the Electricity Department in the hands of the ETU and that the ETU be responsible to find the labour necessary to work these machines, on the understanding that the members of the EPEA continue to do the supervising only and that vital services be maintained'.

The main concern of the Commissioner was that the power supply for industrial purposes might be cut off since if that happened mines would be flooded and the furnaces at the glass works so choked up that they would have to be rebuilt, with 1700 people thrown out of work. The EPEA, in their official history,[30] state that the significance of this whole episode was that there were no ETU members at the station and that the Union were trying to use the emergency to get them there. The Civil Commissioner had suggested to the STC that he should take over the station and the gas works under existing powers and following further representations through the District Joint Board the Commissioner took control. Shortly afterwards he handed over responsibility for controlling and running the station to the District Joint Board for the duration of the strike.

AN ASSESSMENT OF THE STRIKE IN THE POWER STATIONS

It is difficult to assess accurately the extent of the strike action taken by power station manual workers and the effect that it had on the wider scene. The *Electrical Review* had referred to the ease with which electricity supplies were maintained but nevertheless also referred, in unspecific terms, to reduced outputs. Commentators refer to rather more than half the manual workers being on strike for part or the whole of the time, but the government, in their STC and STC sub-committee reports, give the impression that power station problems were mainly confined to London.

The difference between the number on strike and the number of naval ratings and volunteers employed might suggest that power station outputs dropped by a greater amount than was generally admitted, but we would judge from our more recent experience that, for such a short period as ten days, stations could be kept going by the high skills of the technical staff combined with a small number of support staff working long hours and by foregoing normal maintenance work.[31]

It has to be added that from the point of view of the TUC and the Miners' Federation the division within the power station trade union ranks – especially between the EPEA and the ETU – was a serious impediment and that the maverick behaviour of the ETU in London was a disaster.

As to the effect of strike action on electricity supplies, the most authoritative source of information, the Electricity Commissioners' annual report, does not refer to the General Strike at all. What it does is to refer to the effect of the six months' miners' strike. It refers to the adverse effects of that strike on the output and operating results of the power stations. It quotes[32] the percentage increase in output annually since 1921, explaining that, while an actual increase in output in 1926–7 of less than 3 per cent was recorded, this rate of growth was much below the figures in earlier years.[33] Operating results were also affected by the inferior quality of much of the coal available: instead of the increased output involving a smaller pro-rata increase in the consumption of fuel, as in former years, the amount of coal and coke consumed (8 711 027 tons) 'was upwards of 3 per cent higher than in 1925–6. Fuel oil consumption was up to 145 911 tons compared with 38 810 tons in 1925–6'.

AFTERMATH

The General Council's meeting on 12 May with the Prime Minister and his colleagues amounted to unconditional surrender. 'The General Strike' Mr Pugh (Chairman of the Trade Union side) told the government 'is to be terminated herewith in order that negotiations may proceed'.[34] His colleagues asked for a government statement against victimisation and an initiative on the continuing mining disputes, but it was not at that stage forthcoming.

There was a speedy general return to work except in the mines and for those who were refused reinstatement as strike activists. Many strikers lost entitlements to sickness and holiday pay and some who remained at work received loyalty bonuses. A year later a new Trade Disputes Act placed a legal ban on sympathetic strikes.

In electricity supply the EPEA were obviously in favour with the government and the employers. As to the manual workers' unions, all were probably weakened financially[35] and some members undoubtedly suffered the sort of penalties and rewards experienced by the workforce generally.

The NJIC for the industry resumed its activities on 15 October 1926, five months after the general strike ended. A new procedure for the settlement of differences was agreed by a committee of the two sides and the NJIC unanimously approved its report. Under this there was to be no stoppage of work until the cause of the difference had been referred to the district and/or National Councils and any breach of this was to entitle 'the side of the Council not in default to give notice to dissolve the Council and abrogate all agreements'. Employers could require each employee to sign an agreement that his contract of service was in accordance with the terms agreed by the National and district councils.

Some electricity companies, pre-eminently the County of London Company, left the NJIC and DJIC, but they mostly paid the NJIC/DJIC rates. Indeed some companies paid a bonus. The County of London Company, for example, paid 7 per cent and the irony is that the attempt by the British Electricity Authority 23 years later to consolidate this bonus led to the next significant strike in the industry.

LONG SHADOWS

The 1926 General Strike, organised by the TUC, was the first and last of its kind in British industrial history. The TUC attempted to put pressure both on the mine owners and the government, one way being to cut off the movement of coal, the basic fuel for the whole economy. The TUC required the staff of the power stations to play their part, although it cannot be said that they clearly envisaged a total cessation of power supplies. They wanted to make selective use of this potentially powerful weapon, but in common with the manual workers' unions in the industry they failed to organise themselves effectively to that end.

What happened to electricity supply employers and employees was unprecedented, and a few of these happenings cast long shadows into the future. For instance the NJIC agreed before being reconstituted after the strike, to a statement aimed at reducing the risk of unconstitutional action, and something similar was written into the NJIC constitution after the industry's 1970 dispute (See Chapter 4). While the earlier terms were imposed on the trade union side, the latter were freely entered into.

Another recurring theme was whether the electricity supply unions should lend their strength to help unions in other industries to fight their battles. As we have seen the EPEA had a clear policy on this in 1926 and before, but not the NJIC unions. The issue was to arise in each successive miners' strike, most critically in September 1984. A parallel of a different kind was the withdrawal of the Nottinghamshire miners from the MFGB in October 1926. They formed their own union and did not rejoin the Miners' Federation until September 1937. The Nottinghamshire miners were to exercise a similarly independent role in 1984.

It would be tempting for a zealous researcher to exaggerate the significance of these parallels, and also the increased burning of oil in the power stations in 1926, which was in fact only a marginal substitution for coal compared with 1984–5. We have, however, gone as far as we think we reasonably should to identify interesting parallels between 1926 and the miners' strikes of more recent years.

Chapter 3

1949: Reds under the bed?

On 12 December 1949 workers in three power stations in Greater London went on unofficial strike, followed next day by workers at a fourth. The strike lasted a week. In the conditions in electricity supply since the early 1950s such a strike, while it would have been taken seriously within the industry, would not have caused more than a ripple on the surface of the country's affairs. However, in 1949 political, economic and industrial conditions were such that the strike became a *cause célèbre*. Why this should have been is the subject of this chapter. The full story has not been told before; it is intriguing and highly relevant to the central theme of the book.

THE FORTUNES OF THE LABOUR GOVERNMENT

The Labour government under Clement Attlee had come to power in July 1945 at the end of a world war that had used up many of the country's home and overseas resources. The government, continuing in the wartime interventionist mode, gave the lead in the rebuilding of the economy, but while the country, from 1948 on, benefited from the Marshall Plan,[1] the people of Britain had to be denied the economic benefits of victory so as to build up the exports needed to pay for imported food and industrial materials. It was a hand-to-mouth existence for some years.

In a remarkably short time millions of men and women were brought back into the industrial labour force from the armed services and, except during the 1946–7 fuel crisis, full employment prevailed. The TUC and most of the big unions strongly supported government policies, including the retention of the July 1940 Conditions of Employment and National Arbitration Order, 1305 which prohibited strikes and lockouts and placed an obligation on the parties to submit unsettled disputes to binding arbitration. This was the period when many basic industries and services, including electricity supply, were brought into centralised public ownership. The government also established national and local institutions like the Ministry of Labour's National Joint Advisory Council and the British Productivity Council through which it sought to involve employers, unions and workers in macro-economic decision-making. Food rationing was more onerous than in wartime; there was also a chronic shortage of many industrial essentials, especially coal, timber and steel. In the 1946–7 winter a combination of appalling weather and a coal shortage brought great deprivation, disorganisation and misery, made worse by failures of electricity supply.

In mid-1947 there was a sterling crisis, culminating in the suspension of convertibility in August. There was serious talk of wage controls and in February 1948 a White Paper[2] declared that 'in present circumstances and until more goods and services are available for the home market there is no justification for any general increase in individual money incomes'. The government sought voluntary wage restraint and this brought some marginal short-term benefits.

The economy enjoyed a good year in 1948 with a substantial revival of industry and an improvement in exports so great that by the end of the year there was a small current account balance-of-payments surplus. However, the improvement was shortlived, the economic situation deteriorated rapidly in 1949, and on 18 September 1949, after 'trauma which disorientated the government'[3] the Chancellor, Sir Stafford Cripps, was forced to devalue the pound. He demanded more effective support from the unions and the TUC agreed that wage rates should be held stable for at least a year so long as the retail price index did not rise by five points or more. With import prices rising after devaluation TUC leaders found it impossible to hold the line.

Although they were illegal there were a number of strikes, mostly unofficial, in the period between 1945 and 1950,[4] but involving nothing like the number of workers as in many later years. In 1947 the government had established the Dock Labour Board, which decasualised dock labour, thus fulfilling the dockers' dreams of a century. Yet the worst strikes experienced in these post-war years were in the docks. There were serious strikes – sometimes more than one – in the docks during every year between 1945 and 1951, except 1946, and in all of these strikes, except in 1951, the troops were brought in to discharge cargoes. States of Emergency were declared in both the 1948 and 1949 strikes.

THE FEAR OF SUBVERSION

A feature of the two Attlee administrations was their fear of Communist subversion first in the unions, then in industry and then, perhaps, in the political and constitutional structure. It is difficult for us, forty to fifty years on, to grasp the intensity of this fear until we remember that the Communist Party of Great Britain had built up a strong membership during the war, which it held on to in the early post-war years, and that the Cold War was at its height at this time. The Soviets sought to weaken the West by every means short of war itself. In 1948 the seige of West Berlin led to direct confrontation through the airlift of supplies to that beleaguered city. In 1949 the North Atlantic Treaty Organisation for the defence of the West was established, while in the summer of 1950 the Great Powers' proxy conflict in Korea reached the shooting stage. In Britain there were constant calls for the rooting out of Communists and fellow-travellers from positions of power and in the USA anti-Communist hysteria reached its apogee in 1950 with the start of the McCarthy witch-hunt.[5]

The government's response to threats, real and imagined, to the country's security was firm. It inherited the Supply and Transport Organisation set up after World War I. It had unfortunate connotations for Labour however and in February 1947, using as an excuse the need for an emergency organisation to deal with a repeat of the recent coal and weather crisis, the government established an Emergencies Committee of the Cabinet, a co-ordinating committee of civil servants and a number of sub-committees. It was a case of *plus ça change*. One of the sub-committees, on fuel and power, made similar plans to its predecessor to prepare for power station strikes. It was, however, a sign of the times that it added the caveat that 'a close scrutiny of all volunteers would be desirable in order to ensure that subversive elements do not gain access into power stations with the intention of carrying out acts of sabotage'.[6]

POWER STATION PLANT SHORTAGES

From 1 April 1948 the power stations in Great Britain (other than the North of Scotland) were owned and operated by the British Electricity Authority under the chairmanship of Lord Citrine.[7] By March 1950 there were 293 power stations within the Authority's 14 operating divisions; their installed capacity was 13 784 MW, although not all that plant was available at any one time. There was a national grid with 5424 route miles of main transmission lines of which 3753 operated at 132 000 volts; the capacity was not enough to give significant inter-area support. At that time 43 power stations and 27 extensions were under construction, the size of turbines, to speed up manufacture, being restricted to 30 and 60 MW. Coal consumed that year was 29 240 000 tons with coke and oil negligible by comparison. 42 338 men and women worked in the operating divisions, 32 906 of them manual workers.[8]

The most significant facts of life in the industry in those early post-war years were the plant shortage and the concerted efforts being made to overcome it. In 1948 the government had predicted[9] that there would be load spreading and load shedding for the following three years, and how right they turned out to be. The shortage arose from the virtual halt to power station construction during the war, the shortage of skilled men and materials in the construction business, the fact that it took four years to build a power station and that demand was increasing at an inordinate pace.[10]

The plant shortage in the winter of 1949–50 was grave. At the time of maximum demand that winter the shortage was estimated at 1518 MW (sent out), which was the equivalent of about one-eighth of the capacity of the total plant available at that time. In the year to March 1950 load shedding was necessary on 124 occasions, the maximum reduction called for in any one of the 7 grid control areas being 25 per cent. British industry, in December 1949, was required on Monday to Friday to reduce its maximum demand by 20 per cent between 8am and 10am and by 10 per cent from 10am to noon compared with the maximum demand in 1946–7. In addition, at the discretion of the regional boards for industry, there could be a reduction of 20 per cent between 4pm and 5.40pm Monday to Friday.[11]

INDUSTRIAL RELATIONS IN THE POWER STATIONS

In the early post-war period there were signs of restlessness in some power stations, particularly in London. In the summer of 1946 the London Electricity Shop Stewards Committee had organised disputes over non-unionism at Barking and Littlebrook Power Stations in East London and Dartford respectively and an unofficial central body of shop stewards called the Combined Works Committee, with representatives from twenty or more stations around the country, but mainly London, started to hold meetings and to produce a news sheet *The Power Worker*. The ETU had Communist leaders and this worried the government, the Emergencies Committee and the industry's top managers.[12]

The newly reconstituted NJIC had many problems to deal with, especially since many of the pre-nationalisation undertakings had paid their manual workers bonuses to help attract and retain staff, for work in abnormal conditions or as a share of the profits. These bonuses, commonly 7½ per cent of wage rates, could not simply be taken away from employees in order to introduce uniform national pay scales and BEA's attempts to reduce and eliminate them led to disturbances in a number of power stations. Late in 1949 these were at their worst.

POWER STATION STRIKES AND GOVERNMENT INVOLVEMENT

Citrine wrote[13] about the concern he felt at this time about the activity of the Combined Works Committee, particularly its attempts to build up its own organisation inside the stations. 'I was thoroughly familiar', he wrote 'with the Communist tactics of creating disruption in industry and I knew that power stations were the most vulnerable to attacks. The members of the central committee for the most part were not Communists. But there was the inevitable nucleus of active Communists, inspiring, organising and stimulating its activities'.

In December 1948 Citrine confided his anxieties to Hugh Gaitskell, Minister of Fuel and Power, and George Isaacs, Minister of Labour, and they informed the Cabinet. In the spring of 1949 Citrine was assured by the government of its support in dealing with politically motivated strikes.[14]

Through the late spring and summer of that year the government was seriously involved in further strikes in the docks, the first, in London, mainly being a reaction to the sacking of thirty-three 'ineffective workers', and the second, mainly in Avonmouth, Liverpool and London, over attempts by employers to work Canadian ships in British ports against the wishes of the striking Canadian Seamen's Union. The government was convinced that Communists lay behind these difficult and damaging strikes and it is of great interest that it published its long promised White Paper[15] on these strikes six months after they were over and right in the middle of the December power station strike. In his foreword the Minister of Labour stated that 'preparations for the strike began as early as the latter part of last year, although the first strike did not take place until May of this year. The evidence shows that there was throughout a cold and deliberate plan and that the unofficial leaders were completely indifferent to the loss and suffering that might result. They had one aim – and one aim only – to restore the fortunes of the Communist-dominated Canadian Seamen's Union'. On the day before the White Paper was published the Minister, in answer to a question in the House about the power station strike stated that 'there is dynamite lying about. It is piling up. I would ask the House not to press me in view of the difficult situation.'[16] Publication of the White Paper at this time and this statement to the House strongly suggest that the government considered the Communists to be behind the power station strike as well as the dock strikes.

On 31 May 1949 the NJIC had agreed on an increase of $1\frac{1}{2}$d per hour in the wage rates for the industry's 109 000 manual workers in Great Britain (this figure includes the distribution boards) adding that, where excess payments were being made beyond those provided for in the National Agreement, these should merge to the extent of the $1\frac{1}{2}$d per hour. It was later agreed by the NJIC that the excess payments should not merge where they were being genuinely made for abnormal working conditions in a particular place.

The NJIC set up a sub-committee to look at working conditions in the stations where merging was likely to be challenged. But before these could be completed 337 employees at Tir John Power Station in Swansea (147.75 MW capacity) came out on strike for 4 days in October. The sub-committee decided that at Barking A & B Power Stations (522.25 MW capacity) the $1\frac{1}{2}$d should not merge in the bonus, but that it should in Brimsdown A & B Power Stations (220.5 MW capacity), Taylors' Lane, Willesden Power Station (76.5 MW capacity) and Littlebrook A & B Power Stations (240 MW capacity) where working conditions were judged to be normal.[17]

It was obvious to everyone that strike action at those last three stations was likely. In view of the acute plant shortage, the risk of such a strike spreading, and the fear of Communist activity in the stations, the Cabinet's Emergencies Committee, under the Home Secretary's Chairmanship, met on 2 December and reaffirmed that servicemen would be moved into striking stations. The Committee met again on 12 December[18] and this time Citrine and EW Bussey, the BEA's member responsible for industrial relations, were present.[19] During the meeting it became known that the employees at the three stations had walked out without notice.

Citrine explained the background, describing the strike as 'part of an organised movement and that it had to be met as such'. He added that, assuming the technical staff remained on duty, 480 servicemen (as stated on 2 December) would be needed at the stations and 1300 if the strike spread. He concluded that 'there might have to be some reduction of supplies, but it should be possible to maintain the service at 80 per cent of normal'.

All told 1140 workers ceased work at the 3 stations and by the evening of the first day, Monday 12 December, 131 naval men were working, with a small number of RAF men and soldiers, bringing the figure up to 180 the following morning. As expected the technical staff stayed at their posts; despite this however output was only one-third to half of normal. Power cuts occurred over a wide area although, on the first day, how many were attributable to the action we cannot judge. Frank Foulkes publicly expressed regret over the strike and with his colleagues arranged to meet representatives of the workers on Thursday 15 December to discuss their claims.

Next day, 13 December, the 1610 manual workers at the A & B stations at Barking joined the strike in sympathy and at this stage the BEA judged that the strike would spread, especially to Battersea and Deptford Power Stations. Power cuts occurred in London in the afternoon, and in the evening there were widespread blackouts, reaching 20 per cent in London as a whole, the highest figure since the previous winter.

On Wednesday 14 December mass meetings were held at all four stations at which the workers heard reports of meetings of strike leaders with union officials. They were told that the trade unions' members of the NJIC would discuss their grievances on the following day if they returned to work. In the evening the Combined Works Committee met in a public house in Farrington Street in London. They issued a statement supporting the strike and opposing 'the use of troops and blacklegs'.

Much happened on Thursday 15 December. The long-suffering British public woke up to read a press that was largely hostile to the strikers. *The Times*, in its leader,[20] referred to delays by the NJIC Sub-committee in consulting aggrieved groups and of the failure of the trade unions' side on one occasion to produce a quorum. It saved most of its wrath however for 'wilful men' who, 'for the sake of a grievance about a few shillings', had 'launched this attack on the whole community'. The Cabinet urged the BEA to take civil proceedings against the strikers that would help extinguish 'the political forces which were at the root of the present strike'.[21] The advice was not followed.

The strikers, having received the assurances from their union leaders, were on the point of returning to work but were deterred at three of the stations (excluding Barking) by notices that all men returning to work must do so unconditionally. Some were actually required to sign a statement to this effect. On reading the notices they decided that this was in effect a lockout and victimisation and decided to stay out. Frank Foulkes was contacted. He agreed that the strikers should not take up employment unconditionally but only on conditions laid down in the NJIC agreement. The staff at Barking had returned to work at 10.45am but when, later, the same notice was posted they came out again. However they returned later in the day probably having by then seen the BEA's new notice. This stated that the Authority fully intended to observe the terms of the NJIC agreement, implying that the whole thing had been a misunderstanding. This was reinforced the following day by a statement, also posted in the stations, by George Isaacs.[22]

The NJIC union leaders, as promised, met the local leaders of the shop stewards, and the press reported that Frank Foulkes had told them that their grievances could not be considered until they returned to work. He had assured them of no victimisation and of early discussions of their grievances. In the evening the Combined Works Committee met, this time to support the Union leaders' efforts to get a return to work.

The public continued to suffer, in spite of mild weather and voluntary economies in the use of electricity. Alf Robens, Parliamentary Secretary at the Ministry of Fuel and Power, told the House that there was something like one quarter less electricity being generated than was required. Load shedding was necessary in many parts of the country in the morning and evening peak periods. Electricity failed for a time at Kingston-Upon-Thames and Palmers Green and the Enfield and Barking areas were particularly hard hit.

On the following day, Friday, mass meetings of the strikers were told of the reassuring meetings with national trade union leaders and of the withdrawal of the original BEA notice of Thursday 15 December. The men decided to resume work on the night shift on Saturday morning. The servicemen were withdrawn.

A CONTINUING CONSPIRACY?

The government, with so many other difficulties closing in on them, and with the Prime Minister having to decide the date of a General Election, must have felt relief to be able to turn away from the threat of widening disturbances in electricity supply. Yet such a threat remained uppermost in the mind of Citrine. On 23 December he wrote as follows to Hugh Gaitskell.[23]

Dear Gaitskell,

London Power Stations Strike

I have given a good deal of thought to the recent strike in the London Power Stations and I cannot help expressing the feeling that we have not seen the end of the trouble. As you are aware, a body known as the Combined Works Committee has for long been at work fomenting dissension in the stations, and I am under the impression that it was with this body that the trade unions entered into discussion when urging a return to work. It seems to me that the trade unions, in substance, acted as intermediaries between the men on strike and the Central Authority, and I have as yet seen no signs of any inclination on the part of the trade unions to recognise the strike as what it really was, namely, an attack upon the community by disorganising a vital public service. In my opinion unofficial strikes in the electricity supply industry are in quite a different category from normal trade disputes, and should be so regarded by the government, the trade unions and the British Electricity Authority.

I repeat that we have not seen the end of the trouble and I am satisfied that the same forces which provoked the recent strike are still at work. I have had preliminary information that at Brimsdown the recent strike is regarded as a victory for the men, and I have heard that attempts are being made to bring about another stoppage during the third week in January unless the bonus issue is decided to the satisfaction of the men. I have arranged for an examination into the happenings of the recent strike to take place on the 5 January, when the Divisional Controllers and others will be brought into consultation by the Central Authority, as I am anxious to ensure that all reasonable steps should be taken to avoid a recurrence. I want equally to ensure that if a strike does occur, we have taken all appropriate steps to ensure a continuance of supply.

I intend to meet the trade unions subsequently to see whether they are prepared to face up to the issue of disciplining their members who take part in unofficial strikes, but I have little confidence that anything really effective will be done in that direction.

The purpose of this letter is to acquaint you with the possibilities of a recurrence of the strike in the third week in January and to express my opinion that the trouble is not at an end. Indeed, I fear that the recent strike may be little more than a rehearsal for something bigger.

Yours sincerely,

(Sgd) Citrine

Chairman

Gaitskell immediately informed the Prime Minister. His response, made on 3 January 1950, was to ask Sir Edward Bridges, Permanent Secretary of the Treasury, to examine various points concerning strikes in power stations. Bridges did this in consultation with the permanent secretaries of other departments primarily concerned. His ten-page report,[24] sent to Attlee on 18 January, covered questions which had been raised by Gaitskell. The Bridges report was discussed at a meeting of senior ministers on 24 January,[25] although first they discussed the immediate situation in the power stations.

Gaitskell said that an NJIC committee of inquiry was investigating matters further at Brimsdown Power Station on 1 February and speculated that when their report was known there might be a further stoppage. The meeting decided that, in that event, service personnel would be made available to assist in maintaining electricity supplies. In spite of its length the Bridges report was modest both in its content and its main conclusion. This was that there was little difference between strikes in electricity generating stations and other industrial disputes. Gaitskell, in the debate, stated that he did not share this view. He added however that 'there was perhaps no need to take this point further at the present time; but in due course the government ought thoroughly to review the principles involved'.

There was at the same meeting discussion of the need to train servicemen for work in the power stations. Obviously the men could not be trained within the stations and the rather throw-away conclusion was reached that 'something might, however, be accomplished by including in the service education programme lectures on electricity generation'. More to the point, the meeting discussed the possible use, in a future power station strike, of the criminal provisions of the Conspiracy and Protection of Property Act. The Attorney General wanted to know whether this was a real possibility because the Director of Public Prosecutions and the police would have to be warned. The decision was against this since action could only be taken against a few people 'on whose behalf there would then be raised a cry of victimisation, with the possibility of further strikes on that account'. Members were more inclined to favour civil proceedings. 'If the matter could be taken up when things were quiet, there seemed a reasonable possibility that it could be put in such a way as to be acceptable to the trade unions'. This did not seem to have a ring of conviction about it and indeed the whole proceedings read like the deliberations of men who had other things on their minds.

At the General Election on 23 February 1950 Labour were returned to office with an overall majority of five seats. Gaitskell became Minister of Economic Affairs and Philip Noel-Baker Minister of Fuel and Power. In April the government became embroiled in a strike in the London docks followed in June and July by an extremely difficult meat transport strike based on Smithfield meat market. In June war broke out in Korea.

On 3 August 1950 Noel-Baker met Citrine and in a note[26] to Attlee told him that Citrine had expressed the view that 'the Russians regarded our power stations as the nerve centre of British industry and that they would make special efforts to get influence among workers in power stations'. Citrine 'was convinced that . . . there were between twenty and thirty men, mainly in London power stations, who were active and dangerous communists. He had always felt that the strikes last winter were only a dress rehearsal. . . . The right thing would be to get the twenty or so communists out of the power stations into jobs in industry where they could not do so much harm'. Citrine wanted a lead from the government on this and an assurance that they would be prepared to face the strikes which would probably follow the removal or transfer of such men.

Attlee ordered an investigation by the Security Service into possible subversion in power stations. This was conducted by R H (later Sir Roger) Hollis and P A Osborne of MI5,[27] and on 16 August the Home Secretary told the Cabinet that 'there was no reason to believe that any organised outbreak of sabotage was imminent' and that for the BEA to move the twenty or so men out of the stations would be 'almost certain to provoke a widespread strike in the electricity industry on the ground that the men transferred had been victimised'.[28]

Citrine was informed and an examination of Cabinet and Emergencies Committee records, the minutes of BEA meetings and the second volume of his biography suggests that Citrine accepted this finding. Nor is there any evidence that the MI5 findings found their way into the press.

CONCLUSIONS

Central control over strikes

In 1949, in contrast with 1926, the grid system covered most of Great Britain. Without the strike the country had about 12 000 MW of plant available at the time of maximum demand in the winter of 1949–50. This was about 1500 MW short of needs. The installed capacity of plant at the 4 stations on strike was 1058 MW and assuming that about 1000 MW of this would normally have been available the shortfall must have increased from roughly 12 to roughly 20 per cent. This difference could be said to be a measure of the BEA's failure to keep the lights on, although in the circumstances whether they could properly be blamed it is hard for us to say. The industry certainly learnt from the experience.

The old Central Electricity Board, in the twenty-two years of its existence, 1926 to 1948, had had experience of controlling an expanding transmission system and the output of the major power stations, and during the war this control had been intensified. CEB did not, however, own and operate the stations and the December 1949 strikes were the first in which the centre made the critical day-to-day operational decisions, albeit with the divisional controllers. In the forty years that followed there were a number of strikes involving one or two stations, which were handled locally, but essentially, from 1949, strikes of any significance simply had to be responded to from the centre. The reasons were the nature of the BEA's accountability to the government and the consumers, the fact that the power system had much greater interconnection capacity, and the statutory provisions on industrial relations. This was certainly to be the pattern for the future.

Limits to the use of troops

Much was learnt about the use of troops. Before the strike Citrine, who would have been carefully briefed on this, told the Cabinet that with the technical staff at their posts and the necessary help from servicemen, supplies from the stations could be maintained at 80 per cent of normal. But this proved false. At a meeting on 23 January 1950, convened by the Ministry of Fuel and Power and attended by senior armed service and BEA officers, experience with the way troops in the December strike were used was examined in detail.[29] The main conclusions were that reasonable results for station output when operated by volunteers and service people (plus the engineers in post) were: (a) by the end of the first week 50 per cent of the generating plant in operation and 20 per cent efficiency of the coal plant; and (b) by the end of the second week, 75 per cent of the generating plant in operation and 60 per cent efficiency of coal handling plant (50 per cent at riverside stations). The services had no crane drivers of the kind required and this, said the report, would be the factor preventing maximum station output.

In future emergencies the industry's senior management, although they considered using troops, always decided against, for various reasons – particularly the sensitivity of the technical staff, fear of spreading the strike, the limited availability of troops at short notice and the fact that plant became so technically advanced that servicemen could not be expected to cope without effective training on the plant.

The threat of subversion

As to the threat of Communist subversion in the power stations, with the continuation of the Cold War management had to be vigilant about who they recruited into the power stations, but they did this without excess. From time to time unofficial shop steward committees emerged but, whether Communist-inspired or not, they were never again regarded as quite the major subversive threat that they were thought to be in 1949 even though, in 1970 and 1977, they created some difficulties. One reassuring change was the overthrow of the ETU's Communist leadership in the early 1960s which opened the way not only to a more constructive relationship by managers with that union but with all the industry's manual workers' unions.[30]

The government, as we have seen, considered using the Conspiracy and Protection of Property Act but decided against it. The industry's management shared this view: it seemed too insensitive an instrument to use in hyper-sensitive power station situations.

The problem of bonus payments

In time the problem of pre-nationalisation bonus payments was solved, although commutation of one sort or another was untidy and protracted. It does seem from this distance that the BEA and the national trade unions might have spent more time improving communications with the power stations[31] on pay and conditions and passing more decision-making down the line. We have to remember, however, that in the first few years of nationalisation the BEA were trying to create a coherent organisation of 1 central body and 14 area boards (including 2 in Scotland) out of over 500 undertakings. So far only Janus has succeeded in facing in two opposite directions at the same time and there were few Roman gods to be found in the electricity supply industry at the time.

Chapter 4

1970: Working to whose rules?

In December 1970 industrial action, in the form of a ban on overtime and working to rule, called for by the leaders of the four industrial staff unions, took place in many parts of the industry, especially the power stations. This was the first official industrial action on a national scale since 1964, and only the second since 1926. Including the Electrical Power Engineers' Association's industrial action in 1973 (see Chapter 6) there were, all told, three such events in the industry's forty years of public ownership. The December 1970 action is interesting in itself but more so because it led to some decisions that were to be important in the difficult three years immediately ahead. This chapter is a short account of the main events.[1]

INDUSTRIAL RELATIONS UNDER LABOUR

The Labour governments of 1964 to 1970 and the Conservative government of 1970 to 1974 attempted more changes in the institutional and legal framework of industrial relations than ever before. These efforts were combined with policies of direct intervention aimed at reducing pay settlements and price increases.

In July 1966 the Labour government introduced 'comprehensive and tough' measures to deal with the country's economic problems, including an immediate prices and incomes standstill until the end of the year to be followed by a period of severe restraint. A National Board for Prices and Income (NBPI) was established under the chairmanship of Aubrey Jones to consider and report on wage claims and settlements and related questions referred to it by the government. The government's policies were backed by Prices and Incomes Acts in 1966 and 1967.

In the first two years the government's policies, applied by a highly efficient NBPI, were remarkably successful, but as the economic situation improved and application of the policies created new problems (particularly over pay differentials) the restraints of the policies were relaxed. In September 1969 the TUC called on the government to abandon wage control legislation and to end the NBPI as a statutory body. The government nevertheless, in December 1969, gave the NBPI guidelines for a norm for wage settlements in the 2.5 – 4.5 per cent range. However pay settlements continued to rise and by June 1970 the annual average rate of increase in all earnings was about 12 per cent. The RPI in the six months to June 1970 rose by 4.4 per cent, while the number of days lost through strikes in the same period, at about 5 000 000 working days, was greater than in the corresponding period in any of the previous nine years.[2]

In 1965 the government had set up a Royal Commission on Trade Unions and Employers' Associations under Lord Donovan. It reported in June 1968.[3] Donovan stated that while 'the first task in the reform of British industrial relations is to bring greater order into collective bargaining in the company and plant, the second is to extend the coverage of collective bargaining and the organisation of workers on which it depends'. After a detailed analysis[4] the Commission advocated an industrial relations act under which companies of a certain size would be obliged to register their collective agreements. A Commission on Industrial Relations would be set up to investigate and report on problems disclosed. It would also deal with trade union recognition problems although there would be no penalties for refusing to carry out its recommendations.

In January 1969 the government produced their White Paper 'In Place of Strife', with provisions among other things for setting up the Commission. It also made provision for a discretionary reserve power: (i) to require a 'conciliation pause' of 28 days in certain defined conditions relating to a dispute: and (ii) where a major official strike was threatened to require a union to hold a secret ballot. Breach of orders issued by the Secretary of State[5] were liable to result in fines on trade unions or individuals.

The TUC expressed concern over the last two conditions and there was a long debate. In June 1969 the government dropped them, together with the penal sanctions, in return for a 'solemn and binding undertaking' from the TUC to deal with strikes in breach of negotiating procedures. The government went ahead with a truncated Bill, but although the Commission on Industrial Relations was *de facto* established the Bill never reached the Statute Book because of Labour's defeat in the June 1970 General Election.

INDUSTRIAL RELATIONS UNDER THE CONSERVATIVES

Edward Heath became Prime Minister in a Conservative government with a small overall majority. As soon as possible the government dismantled the NBPI, making it clear that prices and incomes should largely be left to find their own level in the market-place. The government proposed to introduce an Industrial Relations Bill based on the 1968 Conservative party pamphlet 'Fair Deal at Work'.

Robert Carr was appointed Secretary of State for Employment and Productivity and he and his government were in difficulties almost immediately over a national dock strike on pay. A State of Emergency was declared on 16 July and a Court of Inquiry established under Lord Pearson. The Court recommended terms that improved on those offered by the employers. Work restarted in early August and the State of Emergency ended on 4 August.

Round about this time wage claims were presented on behalf of a total of 2 500 000–3 000 000 workers who were demanding pay increases from 15 to 38 per cent. Two of these claims led to strikes, namely in local government and in coal. The first was given much publicity and the outcome influenced negotiations in electricity supply. The second influenced the conduct of future coal strikes and an important change in the NUM constitution.

Local government manual workers were demanding increases of 55 shillings (£2.75) a week. At the end of September, following a breakdown in negotiations on pay, some local authority workers in London went on strike and were followed by others elsewhere until a total of about 125 000 men and women were involved and many local services disrupted. The local government employers asked for a government inquiry but this was refused. The employers finally appointed Sir Jack Scamp, very experienced in these matters, to chair an inquiry. In November his three-man committee recommended an increase of 50 shillings (£2.50) and Scamp and his colleagues incurred the wrath of the government for what was thought to be an inflationary offer and a set-back for the government's policy of steadily reducing pay settlements in the public sector – what was known as the N-1 policy.

In 1969 and 1970 there were industrial relations difficulties in the coalfields. In October 1969 there was a strike (not supported nationally) in the Yorkshire coalfield. Ostensibly this was to secure a reduction in hours of work of surface workers, but in fact it was over wider issues than that. Arthur Scargill was not in office as Yorkshire president (that came in 1973) but he was a strong militant influence and played a leading part in organising the so-called flying pickets of striking Yorkshire miners who moved into other coalfields where initially they gained support on a considerable scale. However, the strike petered out within two weeks during which time the Coal Board had conceded the NUM's 1969 pay claim in full. Nevertheless Scargill did not share the view that the strike had been beside the point, saying in 1975 that ' '69 was responsible for producing all the victories that were to come'.[6]

The new militancy of the Yorkshire miners was next seen at the 1970 NUM annual conference when a motion by Scargill, originating in his own pit Woolley, called for a basic wage of £30 for face workers, £22 for other underground workers and £20 for surface workers. The motion was supported by Peter Heathfield and Mick McGahey who were to be Scargill's close colleagues in later strikes, especially 1984–5. The motion was approved, together with a motion for strike action if the claim was not met. In the subsequent ballot the voting was 55 per cent for and 45 per cent against a strike. This did not meet the two-thirds majority requirement of the NUM constitution and the National Executive was forced to accept a slightly improved pay offer. Most of the Yorkshire pits, supported by at least two other areas, responded by strike action. However, this ended in a week or so with men drifting back to work.

In the last few months of 1970 there were two major political events at home. First, a gloomy economic atmosphere led the new Chancellor of the Exchequer, Anthony Barber, on 27 October 1970, to introduce a mini-Budget, which while it reduced income tax and corporation tax provided for cuts in public expenditure. There were highly controversial increases in health charges and school meals, the abolition of free school milk for the seven–eleven age group and the end of cheap milk for the under fives. Second, at the end of October the government published its consultative document on industrial relations and in early December introduced its Industrial Relations Bill.

This Bill was a far-reaching measure. Its main provisions were the legal enforceability of all collective agreements unless specifically stated otherwise, the right of a worker to join or not to join a trade union, the right of a worker not to be unfairly dismissed, the abolition of the closed shop and the establishment of the agency shop, subject to a ballot of eligible employees, the establishment of bargaining units, a register to examine the rules and conduct of trade unions and employers' associations, definitions of 'unfair industrial practice', the establishment of new industrial relations courts and an emergency procedure containing provisions for a cooling-off period.

Both measures were attacked by the TUC. They described the mini-Budget as an exercise in regressive redistribution of income, which would also inflate the cost of living for most ordinary families. But the full wrath of the TUC and the unions was directed against the Industrial Relations Bill whose central provision on union registration was anathema to them. On 8 December there was a huge demonstration by trade unionists against the Bill with further demonstrations in the following months. In the 12 months ending in December the RPI had risen by 6.4 per cent and basic hourly rates by 13.8 per cent. The number of days lost in strikes in the year was 10 980 000.[7]

THREATS OF INDUSTRIAL ACTION, 1969 AND 1970

A number of these external factors influenced events within electricity supply, particularly in the power stations: the collapse of incomes policy in 1969, 1969 settlements around 10 per cent for firemen, dustmen, miners and others, and in 1970 industrial action followed by substantial settlements for dockers and local government manual workers. Between October and December the mini-Budget, rising wage rates elsewhere and the Industrial Relations Bill were even more influential.

In the autumn of 1969 the CEGB had experienced industrial relations difficulties through the action of an unofficial shop stewards' committee drawn from a limited number of local management units, especially power stations, spread around the country. Their basic demands were as they had always been: higher pay and the involvement of shop stewards in national negotiations. On 7 November the NJIC produced an agreement which gave an average wage increase of 10 per cent plus other improvements, but this was not enough for the shop stewards. They called for strike action and thirteen power stations and some area board units indicated some degree of support with bans on overtime and working-to-rule.

The shop stewards then met again and decided to call on industrial staff throughout the industry to give twenty-one days' notice of a seven-day strike from Monday 5 January 1970, preceded by a one-week ban on overtime and working to rule. The declared aim was to re-open pay negotiations to get a better settlement. The shop stewards were soon claiming widespread support but the national union leadership fought back strongly and effectively, both publicly and through their own channels. Nevertheless, a week before the strike was due to start, unofficial working-to-rule or an overtime ban or both were operating in 29 power stations and strike notices had been handed in at 38 power stations in England and Wales having an installed capacity of about 13 000 MW out of 44 000.

As the last days before 5 January went by successive reports showed a falling-off in support for the strike, the efforts of the national trade unions' officers having been reinforced by a strong letter in the CEGB newspaper from its Chairman. The unofficial leaders met on 3 January and called the action off. However, the influence of the shop stewards could not be completely written off. They were again in evidence in putting pressure on power station employees and national union leaders in the weeks and months before the December 1970 industrial action. They made capital not only out of the collapse of incomes policy but out of the comparatively low earnings of electricity workers before the November 1969 settlement, the many changes affecting industrial staff which had taken place in recent years, the substantial fall in their numbers, the slowness of some boards, at least as some employees saw it, to introduce bonus schemes, and the general expectation of employees to be more involved in industrial relations decision-making.

On 10 September the official unions presented claims to the NJIC for a substantial pay increase and specified improvements in conditions. The electricity boards' representatives offered 35 shillings (£1.75) (they had construed the unions' claim as being for £5) and offered to look at the unions' other claims.[8] The national leadership of the unions came under increased pressure from the unofficial group and many of their members as the weeks went on. The complaint that was being highlighted was that employees were being put on to work-study-based incentive schemes, with the associated bonuses, far too slowly.

The boards' representatives refused to make any real improvement in their offer and with all the pressures that they were under the NJIC trade union leaders felt that they had to call for industrial action. Indeed they were convinced that if they did not give a strong lead it would be given by others. They rejected the boards' offer and called for a ban on overtime and a work to rule from midnight on Sunday, 6 December. They refused to take the issue to arbitration. In about a dozen power stations the action started before the deadline.

INDUSTRIAL ACTION

Industrial action began in many area board depots and power stations on the Monday morning. Interpretations of what was meant by working-to-rule varied from one workplace to another. Mainly, however, it meant that industrial staff would no longer accept temporary transfers or temporary work at higher and lower levels (with pay protection); they also refused to operate shift rotas flexibly and withdrew other forms of co-operation with management. They refused to work overtime and to respond to call-outs from home. The EPEA issued instructions to their members not to take over industrial staff duties except to prevent injuries or damage to plant, which was a blow to the boards.

The effect of the industrial action on electricity supplies was immediate and substantial. In many power stations employees enthusiastically devised 'rules' to work to. There was not a detailed rule book. However, the safety of people and plant required some rules and procedures and these were suddenly interpreted so as to justify shutting down plant. From the early hours of that first Monday morning, 7 December, plant in many stations was being shut down or not started up to meet the morning peak demand.

The work-to-rule also meant that managers were not able to move staff around to cover for absences, while the ban on overtime meant that staff could not be called in for this purpose. This again led to plant having to be shut down. During that first day it was necessary to apply voltage reductions. A reduction of 6 per cent in consumers' supply voltage at that time resulted in about a 6 per cent reduction in the demand for electricity. It was also necessary to disconnect consumers during the evening peak to reduce demand by a further 20 per cent to a level which could be met by the reduced generating capacity. Lesser disconnections had also been necessary throughout the day.

The established arrangements for this sort of contingency were based on disconnecting consumers in 5 per cent load steps. This was done by area board engineers working to CEGB instructions. Back in 1970, unlike now, area board engineers had to visit substations to open switches to telephone instructions although the London Electricity network, which was underground, operated with greater remote control.

What threatened to make matters worse was that on the afternoon of the first day the EPEA, with whom the employers were negotiating a revised salary structure, called for industrial action because of alleged lack of progress. Later in the week they called it off but the threat, while it lasted, added considerably to the industry's concerns.

On Tuesday 8 December, a day on which workers throughout the country demonstrated against the Industrial Relations Bill, loss of supply was again serious. In the evening peak the CEGB called for voltage reductions with 25 per cent of all load disconnected. The disconnections again continued for most of the day with a brief respite overnight. The area boards started to change the planned disconnection stages each day to spread the misery as fairly as possible. This was an ad hoc start to rota disconnection arrangements that were organised in advance for future emergencies. They involved rotating the disconnections of over 20 000 000 consumers. Despite an attempt to disconnect in a discriminating way some large industries were halted or slowed down, shops were forced to close early and homes were without electricity for various periods of time.

On Wednesday 9 December the supply position was much the same with the maximum voltage reduction and 25 per cent disconnections again in the power needed to cover the morning peak. On that day Robert Carr, Secretary of State for Employment ('Productivity' had just been dropped from the title) saw the union leaders who told him that they were still not willing to go to arbitration. Major cuts in supplies continued on Thursday at the same level as on the previous day.

By this time all area boards were receiving reports of mounting press and public hostility to the industry and its employees. Critical articles and letters appeared in some sections of the press. Signatures were collected from people in the street protesting at the unions' action, employees' cars were damaged, some showroom windows belonging to electricity boards were smashed, and manure, dead chickens and tropical fish were dumped on board premises in a few cases. In an unfair world some of those staff who had their cars and vans damaged were actually working extremely hard to minimise the effects of disconnections. It was impossible to judge accurately what effect all this was having on employees, but many managers expressed the view that it caused anxiety to many.

On the Thursday there was also considerable 'diplomatic' activity. The Chairman of the Electricity Council and Bob Roberts, the Member for Industrial Relations, saw Robert Carr. Vic Feather, General Secretary of the TUC, met some of the union leaders and subsequently Robert Carr and Electricity Council leaders. As a result representatives of the two sides agreed to meet on the following day.

On Friday 11 December the reduction in power called for involved 20 per cent disconnections, a reduction compared with mid-week at least partly explained by milder weather. No formula for renewed negotiations was found at the informal meeting, but the unions asked for facilities at the Electricity Council for a Sunday meeting, requesting that representatives of the employers should be available.

Meanwhile on Saturday the government had declared a State of Emergency; on that day the country was virtually free from power cuts, although there were voltage reductions. Following the Sunday morning meeting the trade union leaders indicated their support for a public inquiry saying that, if this was acceptable, they would instruct their members to resume normal working forthwith. After discussions with the two sides in the afternoon the government agreed, although they had an extremely lengthy debate with the unions on whether the terms of reference should include a reference to the Court having to take into account the public and national interest.

On Monday 14 December loss of supply amounted to 20 per cent disconnections. The unions called off their industrial action, although the government had not shifted their ground on the issue relating to the terms of reference. On Tuesday supplies were rapidly returning to normal and the emergency powers were allowed to lapse.

THE PLANT/DEMAND SITUATION IN PERSPECTIVE

During the week of the industrial action the industry was fortunate that temperatures were higher than average for that time of the year, reducing the estimated national peak demand to 34 500 MW, a saving of some 5 000 MW on average cold-spell conditions, the weather standard used for operational planning. As the week went on consumers made voluntary economies during the morning and evening peaks amounting to between 2000 and 2500 MW. These two factors greatly helped in confining load disconnections to a maximum, on various working days, of between 20 and 26 per cent (on the Sunday the estimated figure was 6 per cent, i.e. voltage reductions only and on the Saturday nil).

Loss of capacity directly from the industrial action peaked in mid-week between 8000 and 9000 MW, the highest losses being in the South East and the lowest in the North West.[9] It was apparent that the plant loss and the depth of the emergency that resulted were greater than the unions had expected. There was a strong public reaction and the unions tried to moderate the effects of what they had started. At some stations employees worked overtime to return plant to service so as to obviate further stages of disconnection.

THE WILBERFORCE INQUIRY AND SETTLEMENT OF THE DISPUTE

The Wilberforce Court of Inquiry was in session throughout the week beginning Monday 18 January 1971. Their report was published on 10 February.[10] The report surveyed the intense and far-reaching developments in productivity bargaining in the industry, which had started in 1964. The introduction of work-study-based incentive schemes was a central part, the approach being to bring local groups into schemes within the terms of the national agreement as measurement was completed and the correct manning levels achieved. According to Edwards and Roberts:[11]

> in the Court's view the great majority of workers in the industry had not, between 1964 and 1969, been adequately compensated for the changes they had willingly accepted. Nor would the offer made by the boards in 1970 have substantially improved the position. For these reasons the industrial staff had begun to develop a sense of grievance, made more acute by the slow rate at which productivity schemes had been introduced.

The Court recommended pay increases from 21 September 1970 (the annual round date) of £105 a year with an extra £35 a year for craftsmen and foremen, plus improved shift payments and three additional days' holiday. They also recommended that groups of staff not already working under incentive scheme conditions because local schemes had not been prepared in the detail required should, with certain safeguards, receive weekly 'lead-in payments' of £1 from 1 April 1971, £1.50 from 4 October 1971 and £2 from 3 January 1972.[12]

These recommendations were incorporated in an agreement between the two sides on 22 March. The terms appear to be comparatively straightforward and predictable, but as Edwards and Roberts said:[13]

> The essential role of the Court of Inquiry, like so many others, was not to propose solutions which could not have been thought of by others but, through its independent membership, its public proceedings and its report, to create a climate of opinion in government, among the public and between the parties which would enable a fresh start to be made.

CONCLUSION

Both sides learnt much from this experience. The trade unions learnt that it was easier to start industrial action than to control it once started. After the 1969 experience they had recognised the need to improve communications with their members down the line and both before and after the 1970 dispute they worked hard on this both as a negotiating team and as individual unions. They were also made aware, as were many of their members, particularly in area boards, that the active hostility of some of the millions of people who were suffering the effects of disconnection was a powerful force in helping to bring the action to an end.

The Electricity Council and the boards learnt at least as much. They needed to improve their own communications with their staff and set out to achieve this. It cannot be said that the industry recognised the potential threat to electricity supply in the NUM's 1969 militancy and the use in Yorkshire of the so-called flying pickets, but certainly from the industrial action in December 1970 the boards learnt about the need for and the possibilities of rota disconnections of 20 000 000 consumers. This work, co-ordinated by the Electricity Council, was carried out by the area boards. It was a demanding job done in the limelight of media and public attention and was well done. Even more to the point, the Council and the boards provided themselves with experience that was to stand them in good stead in the national miners' strike, which was only thirteen months away.

The agreement, made possible by Wilberforce, led to a marked improvement in industrial relations, a measured improvement in labour productivity, increased earnings and a speedy and sustained reduction in manpower through voluntary selective severance. All this was a much more attractive outcome than had been predictable in the dark days of early December.

Chapter 5

1971–2: The edge of darkness

From 1 November 1971 the NUM imposed a ban on overtime and between 9 January and 28 February 1972 the country experienced the first official national miners' strike since 1926. In the coal industry over 10 500 000 working days were lost while in industry at large well over 1 500 000 workers worked short time with many others laid off. It was one of the declared policies of the NUM to win the strike by depriving the nation of its power supply. The resulting picketing at the power stations and elsewhere was on an unprecedented scale and ferocity and the Generating Board had the utmost difficulty in maintaining supply even at a much reduced level. The government introduced a State of Emergency on 9 February and the Secretary of State for Trade and Industry ordered restrictions on the use of electricity through a system of rota disconnections operated primarily by the twelve area electricity boards.

Despite improved offers to the miners the strike continued even beyond the stage at which the government set up a Court of Inquiry under the chairmanship of Lord Wilberforce. The NUM did not accept the findings of the Court until they had been further improved by the Coal Board. When eventually the strike came to an end the CEGB was rapidly running out of coal and other essential stocks, particularly lighting-up oil, and the country could, without excessive drama, be said to have been living at that time on the edge of darkness. Douglas Hurd, at the time Political Secretary to the Prime Minister, Edward Heath, described the outcome of the strike as disastrous for the government, although it was to be another two years before the disaster could be seen in its full magnitude.[1] The CEGB was to experience a major energy emergency requiring a new method of managing the power system and very much involving the area electricity boards.

THE GOVERNMENTAL BACKGROUND

The government and the country did not have a particularly good year in 1971, although two or three of the economic indicators were encouraging. GDP for the year was up 1.7 per cent and the balance of payments on current account was in credit by £1051 million; average wage rates increased by 12.6 per cent over the year, a marginally smaller increase than in the previous year. However the RPI rose from 6.4 to 9.4 per cent and unemployment (GB seasonally adjusted) from 589 300 to 940 022, the worst figure since 1940. Days lost in strikes were 13 551 000, a high figure compared with the average of the previous 10 years.

The preoccupation of the government during the year appeared to be with three matters: the negotiations leading to the UK's entry into the European Economic Community (the Treaty was signed on 22 January 1972); the mounting death toll in Northern Ireland and the intense negotiations for a settlement there; and the passage through Parliament of the Industrial Relations Bill, which received the Royal Assent in August 1971. There was at the time a tacit government policy to try to keep pay settlements below 8 per cent.

Even before the miners' dispute there were in 1971 some serious industrial disturbances. 180 000 postal staff stopped work in support of a claim for a 15 to 20 per cent pay increase and returned to work on 8 March with a 9 per cent settlement, as recommended by the Hardman Committee. On 5 February a strike at Ford's over pay lasted until early March and led to the loss of 2 000 000 days' work and a compromise solution. The most visual industrial event – apart from the miners' strike – took the form of trade unionists' protests against the Industrial Relations Bill. There was a demonstration in Trafalgar Square on 21 February in which 140 000 people took part. There were also one-day protest strikes involving 350 000 workers on 8 December 1970, between 170 000 and 180 000 on 12 January and about 1 250 000 on both 1 March and 18 March.[2] What has to be added is that neither the government, the media, the public, nor the electricity supply industry appeared to pay much attention to the threat of a miners' strike even when, in the second half of the year, the signs were increasingly there to be read. The NUM in those days was not regarded as a threat. There had not been an official strike of any size since 1926 and, under the seemingly benign NCB chairmanship of Lord Robens in the 1960s, successive pay settlements had been moderate, with large numbers of coal mines closed with minimum disturbance. The election of Joe Gormley as President of the NUM from June 1971 may have seemed equally reassuring.

THE NUM BACKGROUND

When we refer to the signs being there to be read we are referring partly to militant activities in parts of the mining industry, especially Yorkshire in 1969 and 1970, and the first example on a sizeable scale of 'flying pickets' organised in Yorkshire by Arthur Scargill and his colleagues.

A further sign came in April 1971. Gormley, then candidate for the post of NUM President, demanded in his election address that the government commit itself to the maximum use of indigenous coal and to the miners being made the highest paid industrial workers in Britain. At the Union's annual conference in July a pay claim was formulated involving increases of up to 47 per cent at an extra cost of £120 million a year: from £18 to £26 a week for surface workers, from £19 to £28 for underground workers and from £26.37 to £35 for face workers covered by the national power loading agreement. In July Gormley privately warned Derek Ezra, NCB Chairman, that 'the figure you will have to settle at is in the region of three and a half quid'.[3]

In October the Coal Board offered an average rise of 7.1 per cent, costing £25 million a year. This was rejected by the NUM, which shortly afterwards decided on a ballot in support of a national strike. On 1 November an overtime ban was imposed and on 16 December the NUM rejected a further offer of £2 a week for face and surface workers and £1.90 a week for others (7½ per cent, £28 million). They did the same on 5 January to a marginally increased pay offer plus additional holidays and special productivity arrangements (7.75 per cent, £32 million). The result of the ballot, announced on 2 December, was 58.8 per cent in favour of a national strike, which was a sufficient percentage under the union's revised rules. The East Midlands coalfields voted marginally against and Yorkshire three to one in favour. The NUM executive, a week later, decided unanimously on a national strike.[4]

THE CEGB BACKGROUND

For the CEGB 1971–2 was a year in which electricity sales increased by 2.4 per cent and income went up 12.8 per cent, despite the miners' strike. The Board operated 183 power stations with a maximum output capacity of 54 322 MW. New plant commissioned, 5895 MW, was a record, although the Board was having teething problems with many of its 42 recently commissioned 500 MW units. Fuel burnt in the power stations amounted to 94 900 000 tons of coal equivalent, mostly coal. Because of acute problems in the stations caused by the strike thermal efficiency was down and units actually produced were more expensive than usual. Total employees fell from 70 288 to 65 410 (-6.9 per cent); among these were the industrial staff whose numbers fell from 45 142 to 40 226, a reduction of 10.9 per cent. During the year much attention was paid, quite independently of the miners' strike, to fuel diversity and flexibility. In particular the Board began modifying some of its coal-fired plant so that existing boilers could be operated on natural gas or oil instead of coal. There was a shift in emphasis from coal to nuclear power and oil in the power station construction programme.

In the light of what was to happen thirteen years later it is important to remember that in 1971, in spite of what had happened in 1969, the Generating Board had never had grounds to believe that picketing could take place on the scale and intensity that it did; nor had it judged that the NUM would turn their attention more directly to supplies moving into power stations than to picketing the movement of coal from NCB stocks. The likelihood of a strike starting or being of long duration was not considered such as to warrant massive and uneconomic precautionary measures.

However, at the end of September, a month before the start of the NUM's ban on overtime, stocks of coal at the power stations were 15 600 000 tons, 2 400 000 tons above planned requirements. Five days after the start of the ban CEGB coal stocks, at 16 900 000 tons, were the highest ever. The explanation was that earlier in the year the government and the Coal Board had requested the CEGB to take excessive coal into their stocks and that is what they had done.

The delivery rate soon began to fall, in spite of the Board taking stocks from NCB depots, licensed mines and imports, and when the strike started coal stocks were 12 300 000 tons, which represented 6.1 weeks' fossil fuel burn or 7.9 weeks' coal consumption. In December the CEGB had judged that it would be able to fulfil its target of having in stock sufficient coal for six average winter weeks' burn with enough left over by the end of March for the equivalent of four winter weeks' burn. However, as it turned out, these endurance targets failed to take account of the effects of the miners' picketing of the stations and the difficulty of getting other essential supplies commensurately with the build-up of coal stocks.

The Board had another worry with the rejection on 16 December by the NJIC trade unions of the electricity boards' offer of base rate increases of £1.30 to £1.60 a week. This would have given an average increase of 7.2 per cent, which compared with the current offer to the miners of a 7.5 per cent increase of £1.90 to £2 a week. The ESI unions began to talk of industrial action to back their claim and behind them the unofficial shop stewards' committee was also exerting pressure.

THE BEGINNING OF THE STRIKE

In the light of later events it is remarkable how little attention the government, the media, industry and the public paid to the overtime ban, leaving it to the NCB to make their successive offers and civil servants at the Department of Trade and Industry (DTI), on 6 January, to invite NUM leaders to come to see them, an invitation which was declined. The Secretary of State for Employment did not (as by now in law he could have done) ask the new National Industrial Relations Court to order a sixty-day cooling-off period, clearly judging that it was unlikely that it would work.

On 9 January 280 000 miners in 289 pits stopped work, to be joined on 17 January by 12 000 NCB clerical staff. On the first day the NCB withdrew their pay offer and the government called for maximum economy in the use of coal. On the next day the Finance and General Purposes Committee of the TUC decided to leave it to the NUM to plan pickets where they were needed, while other unions were requested not to cross official picket lines. The NUR had already instructed its members not to move coal during the strike and the four NJIC unions in electricity supply instructed their members not to handle new coal supplies. Also on 10 January Joe Gormley stated that the unions would make sure that the pickets were in the right place and this turned out to be, above all, the power stations. He considered that this, together with picketing of the ports, coal depots and steelworks, was the way 'to make the battle as short and sharp as possible'. He reckoned that shortly after the start of the strike 60 000 men were on the picket lines.[5]

However, while Gormley's objective was to 'freeze' domestic and industrial coal supplies, so hoping to force NCB into a wage settlement acceptable to his members, some NUM militants appeared to have different objectives. Thus Arthur Scargill, now a pit delegate to the Barnsley area of the NUM, described his objectives and his use of flying pickets in a recorded interview given in 1975 about the 1972 strike:[6]

'In Yorkshire we had every pit picketed on the first morning to get out the weekly paid industrial staff members . . . . After this we immediately switched our attack to every major coal depot and power station in the region . . . . You see, we took the view that we were in a class war . . . . We were out to defeat Heath and Heath's policies . . . . We had to declare war on them and the only way you could declare war was to attack the vulnerable points. They were the points of *energy*: the power stations, the coke depots, the points of supply. Now the same week as we launched our attack on the power stations, the NEC decided to deploy pickets all over Britain at the power stations . . . . Just before the battle of Saltley (4–10 February) we thought we had nearly every picketing point covered, we had sewn it up, and we had a permit system operating.'

GOVERNMENT INACTION

One of the few public actions by the government in the first month of the strike was the effort of the Secretary of State for Employment, Robert Carr, on 21 January, to bring the parties together. This failed. Behind the scenes, on 19 January, the DTI requested the Electricity Council and the CEGB to submit a paper estimating the extent and duration of electricity rationing that would be required from various start dates. The response was plain: 'the longer restrictions are delayed, the more severe they will have to be'. The DTI certainly got on with preparations for statutory restrictions on the use of electricity including the determination of priority categories.[7] Douglas Hurd reflected at the time the mood within government. He referred[8] to the other serious problems assailing the government but added that 'these weeks of the 1972 miners' strike were the worst of all. There seemed no way through'.

PICKETING

At the time of the strike peaceful picketing *per se* was not illegal, even peaceful secondary picketing.[9] During the strike much of the picketing of the power stations was far from peaceful. Picketing of stations started almost straight away and rapidly grew in intensity and spread. No coal came into the stations from the Coal Board and supplies from non-vested sources (small pits privately owned and licensed by NCB) and imports rapidly dwindled to a trickle. Interference with supplies extended to commodities such as lighting-up oil and hydrogen, which were as important as coal and had not been stocked in exceptional quantities.

In all of its five operational regions the CEGB's big coal-fired stations were picketed most of the time with varying degrees of rigour but great effectiveness. It took a little more time for the pickets to get around to the oil-fired stations while there was no discernible pattern of picketing at the nuclear power stations. By 1 February a round-the-clock picketing vigil had been established at the stations. In a few stations the CEGB's own staff threatened to take industrial action if coal was brought in from unusual sources, but most staff just got on with their work as well as they could, in several cases co-operating with exceptional methods of getting supplies past the pickets.

In various stations attempts were made to bring in supplies by night but the NUM got wise to this and reinforced night picketing. At many big stations the numbers on picket lines ebbed and flowed between 40 and 80. In some cases pickets were reinforced by students, for example Essex University students joined picket lines at Ipswich. When fifteen MPs joined the Battersea Power Station picket lines this sent up the numbers. The shortage of lighting-up oil became acute in some stations and in some of these cases small oil tanker firms gave constant help to the Board where the big companies had failed. Various other forms of ingenuity were used. West Burton Power Station on the Trent installed a pipeline to convey oil delivered by barge to the station boilers. Transformer and circuit breaker tanks delivered to stations seemingly as substantial engineering items unconnected with the strike were filled with lighting-up oil or diesel to keep the stations going. At West Thurrock Power Station oil was taken from the service tanks of a docked coal ship in 40 gallon drums and manhandled into the station. There were some deliveries by helicopter, which influenced preparations for the 1984–5 strike. At another station a piece of perimeter fencing was made detachable so that convoys of vehicles could avoid pickets. Picketing was particularly strong and intimidating in the South Yorkshire stations, but it was at Keadby, near Scunthorpe, where the only death on a picket line occurred: a lorry leaving the station crushed a picketer. At Thorpe Marsh Power Station near Doncaster hydrogen supplies were brought in by helicopter.

So how, more evocatively, may the human reality of picketing in the power stations be conveyed? There was always at least one picket, sometimes referred to as 'token'. His presence was, however, much more than that. He was in himself a picket line that road transport and rail trade unionists 'respected' by not crossing. At any time, but especially at night, he was in a position to warn striking miners elsewhere if 'advantage' was being taken of a small picketing presence to 'smuggle' supplies in (this was the language of the picket line).

At power stations in the mining areas there were usually more than a handful of pickets and in the militant areas such as South Yorkshire the numbers were often 40 and more, most of the time just standing there stamping their feet, drinking tea, and waiting for something to happen. Then quite suddenly numbers would increase to a hundred or many more. The strikers, reinforced perhaps by members of other unions and students, might simply have decided or been instructed by the NUM's picketing committee to make a show of strength. Or word might have been got to them that supplies were to go into a station at a specified time. The news might, for example, have originated at a hydrogen and oxygen gas or oil depot. So large numbers, many of them strong and exuberant young miners, might arrive ready for whatever action was demanded of them. The police, who were normally at the power station gates in ones and twos, might have known what was planned and have called in reinforcements. So the scene would be set for at least a certain amount of catcalling, stone throwing and, above all, pushing and shoving. Often this sort of behaviour on both sides was something of a ritual, but sometimes something would happen that would change the mood. It might be the arrival of further police reinforcements, or the rumour might have been well-founded and loaded lorries might arrive set on getting through the picket lines into the station.

It was in such circumstances as these that the stone throwing would begin in earnest, the police pressing the strikers back off the station entrance, the odd picketer breaking through and being brought down by the police, greatly intensified pushing and shoving, sometimes attempts made to overturn vehicles and police batons raised and lowered in anger. In some cases it would be seen that the pickets were being led by one or more people standing in prominent positions directing or more often attempting to direct their followers above the turmoil. At some stage the strikers might withdraw and regroup and the police would then do the same. This might then be followed by a further engagement or police officers and strike leaders might join forces to try to stop things getting completely out of control. Sometimes vehicles carrying supplies would withdraw and this would take a lot of heat out of the situation, being regarded by the strikers as a tactical triumph.

Such confrontations often ended as quickly as they started with individual strikers and their supporters fanning out into the countryside or, like the police, returning to their buses and cars. Then would come the counting – or perhaps even the double counting – of the wounded on both sides, with perhaps the sight and sound of ambulances approaching to deal with them. Considering the size, the sound and the fury of the encounter, the injuries were mostly few and not too serious. Some strikers would then be taken off to be cautioned and charged with obstruction or assault and usually released on bail.

Within a short time all that would be left on the scene would be battered fences, sticks, stones and nails scattered over the road and the original small group of pickets reliving the encounter, shouting good-naturedly to the small group of policemen across the road. Some days later the same scene might be played out again and perhaps this time even more violently.

The role played by the police would have varied with and depended on the chief constable. This description exemplifies the type of confrontation that took place when the police supported normal deliveries. Their object was to protect people and property and to preserve law and order. But secondary picketing was not illegal and police objectives, as seen by some chief constables, would be served by the CEGB stopping deliveries and thus avoiding provoking the pickets. That request was made on a number of occasions.[10]

Meanwhile the CEGB had another problem. Pay negotiations for the industry's industrial staff had run into trouble and on 17 January the trade unions were threatening an overtime ban from the end of the month, with London shop stewards threatening to start it earlier. Later the unions changed the date of the ban to 8 February, the day after the next NJIC meeting. At that meeting, after many hours of bargaining, the claim was settled, although not before there had been unofficial overtime bans, working to rule and the blocking of fuel movements within a few stations. The settlement, from 21 September 1971, gave increases from £1.65 a week to unskilled staff to £2.05 to craftsmen. These were increases of up to 9 per cent on the basic rates, although only 7.5 per cent on the wage bill – within the prevailing 8 per cent government limit.

AN UPHILL STRUGGLE

At the beginning of the strike the Board's operating arrangements had aimed at reducing output to protect coal stocks at stations with less than 35 days' supplies at the existing rate of consumption. There were 45 stations with an aggregate capacity of 7473 MW in this category. During the second week the effect of picketing was increasingly serious because it was causing the loss of oil supplies to coal-fired stations. This affected the CEGB's ability to preserve its dwindling coal stocks. The explanation is that lighting-up oil has to be burnt in coal-fired boilers to stabilise combustion during start-up and low load operation. Without it there is a high risk of an explosion. A shortage of lighting-up oil also prevents generating units being used flexibly. In particular it prevents those stations with low coal stocks being used for only part of each day. In addition stations burning poor quality coal could only be used with a continuous oil burn to maintain stable combustion. These stations could not be used safely without lighting-up oil, even though some had good coal stocks. These factors made control of the power system difficult; the control of electrical frequency became a particular problem.

The shortage of hydrogen also caused problems. Hydrogen gas is used as a coolant in electricity generators. Slight leakage is normal and is made good from bottled storage facilities. Without fresh supplies some stations were having to shut down generators.

By the end of the third week the total coal stock had been reduced to 7 600 000 tons of which 6 120 000 million were effective. This was equivalent to 27 average winter days' supply; 71 stations, with a total capacity of 12 687 MW, were now in the protected category, that is they had less than 30 days' supply. The total loss of plant readily available had now risen to 3538 MW, 1120 MW being due to lack of coal or very low stocks. Some stations with low outputs lifted their availability through forcing supplies into the stations, but the losses were consistently greater than the gains. On 30 January the first voltage reductions of the emergency were necessary when up to two stages of load reduction were applied over the Sunday lunch-time peak.

Yet on the following day, with day-time temperatures nearing freezing point, the loads on the system were the highest yet experienced and at 6pm a demand of 39 925 MW was met at normal frequency and without any load reduction. This involved power station staff using only coal reclaimed from stock, this coal being wet and therefore difficult to handle and to burn.

On 1 February a higher unrestricted demand of 40 812 MW occurred, but the demand met was only 38 123 MW. At the peak time two stages of load reduction were necessary and the frequency was below normal, which had the effect of reducing demand. On 4 February the CEGB publicly warned that essential supplies were being badly affected by the 'unrelenting blockade' of the stations. It was clear by then that the declaration of a state of emergency was not far off.

Voltage reductions were necessary on 6, 8 and 9 February and on this last date the press carried reports that the area electricity boards were preparing to administer systematic cuts. On the following day, Thursday 10 February (the thirty-third day of the strike), the first disconnections took place when four stages of load reductions were necessary. By this time the effective coal stock had become 3 680 000 tons, the equivalent of 16 days' average winter burn; 84 stations, with a capacity of 16 009 MW, were in the protected category (less than 30 days' supply) while a further 6936 MW of output capacity had been lost, 2561 MW through shortage of lighting-up oil, 3715 MW from a shortage of primary fuel and 660 MW from lack of other essential supplies.

CRISIS POINTS

On 11 February Douglas Hurd wrote in his diary:[11] 'The government now wandering vainly over battlefield looking for someone to surrender to – and being massacred all the time'. This was, however, a bit hard since on the previous day the government had started to stir itself. The Secretary of State for Employment brought the NUM and NCB together. The NCB, with government backing, made an offer, to cover an 18-month period from 1 November 1971, of £3 extra for surface workers, £3.50 for underground and £2.75 for those at the coal face working under the Power Loading Agreement. The NUM countered on the following day demanding £6, £7 and £4 extra, plus an additional week's holiday – an average rise, if conceded (which it was not) of 25 per cent. The government must have expected a negative response because, on 9 February, they had declared a State of Emergency, which the CEGB had been seeking for some time.

Very low stocks at the power stations were certainly the main reason but they must also have been influenced by the self-confidence of the NUM and the striking miners, which at the time was being displayed not only at the power station gates and at the negotiating table but at what was referred to as the Battle of Saltley.[12]

Saltley was a West Midlands Gas Board coke depot near Nechells Power Station, Birmingham. It had in stock what *The Times* on 9 February called 'a monstrous mountain of coke, 100 000 tons of it',[13] which served Midlands industries, particularly the foundries. It had a normal outflow of 400 lorries of coke a day, which by the end of January had allegedly risen to 650–700. Picketing of the main gate by hundreds of striking miners, many of them from South Wales, had started in earnest on 4 February. Scuffles with lorry drivers began, reinforcements of pickets and police arrived and Scargill took charge.

In the following days more and more police and pickets had descended on the depot, disorder grew with violence, personal injury and arrests. On the day that the State of Emergency was declared there were 2000 pickets, only 43 lorries were loaded and each one had to be forced through. The Birmingham engineering and transport unions called sympathy strikes for Thursday 10 February and soon after 10am there was a crowd of 15 000 at the coke works. At 11am the gates were closed and later it was agreed by all concerned that the depot would admit only vehicles carrying trade union permits to collect coke for hospitals, schools, old people and other special cases. During the 6 active days at Saltley 30 people had been injured, 16 of them police, 76 arrests had been made, 61 of them miners. Scargill called Saltley a great victory and overnight he became a national figure.

Further evidence of the government's concern over the mounting crisis was their decision, announced on 10 February, to set up a Court of Inquiry into the dispute and the following day they announced that Lord Wilberforce, who had presided over the inquiry in electricity supply a year earlier, would be the chairman.[14] The Secretary of State suggested to the NUM that they return to work pending the outcome, but they refused.

Under the emergency powers now available to them the government immediately made a number of far-reaching orders rationing electricity and conserving coal and other essential commodities: (i) they relieved the CEGB and the area electricity boards of their statutory responsibility to supply electricity to all consumers (from 11 February); (ii) they restricted the use of electricity for advertising and display purposes and for floodlighting (from 10–11 February); (iii) they banned the use of electricity for the heating of offices, shops, public halls, catering establishments and premises used for recreation, entertainment and sport (from 12 February); (iv) they required most industrial consumers with an estimated maximum demand of 100 KW or more not to use any electricity on Sundays or on three other days in the week, while large users on separate circuits operating continuous processes were required to cut their consumption by 50 per cent (from 14 February). These were draconian provisions but excluded such critical services as water, sewage, gas, bakeries and hospitals.[15]

From 11 February the area electricity boards had their first experience of operating power cuts on a rota basis coordinated by the Electricity Council's Contingency Review Panel. The territory covered by each board was divided into up to eighteen areas, each allocated a three- or four-hour period each week under which they were at high, medium or low risk of disconnections. In those days the boards, except London, had few remote control means of opening switches to disconnect consumers and this task was done by the boards' technical staff between 6am and midnight. The CEGB's National Control managers instructed the start of the disconnections each morning and restoration of supplies in the evening.[16]

On 11 February there were on average 10 per cent rota disconnections in the country as a whole. But the disconnections were uneven; for example, in the Midlands and the South supplies were reduced in the afternoon by 21 per cent. The CEGB emphasised the grimness of it all by stating that some power stations were 'having to practically sweep up the last remnants of their coal stock'. By Monday 14 February 800 000 people had been laid off work and many thousands more were on short time. On the railways one rush-hour train out of ten was cancelled and one in five of other services, the latter figure later becoming three in five. The Secretary of State for Trade and Industry, John Davies, announced that at the weekend the amount of coal at the power stations had been 4 000 000–8 000 000 tons but that, of this, 2 200 000 tons could not be used because of picketing and other factors. Later, in the House, he made one of the most dramatic statements ever about the threat to normal everyday life in this country. He said that if the response to the government's appeals for economy were really satisfactory stocks of coal would give the CEGB an endurance of two more weeks at the present rate of consumption. But at the end of that time there was no certainty of being able to provide even for essential services. There was no experience, he added, of handling electricity at these low levels of load. CEGB's capacity would be down to about 20 to 25 per cent of normal load. There would be electricity for neither industry nor the home.[17]

From 15 February the sense of drama was intensified by the government publishing a list of those services that they regarded as essential to life and health, by the street lights being switched off,[18] and by CEGB stating that every high risk area on the area board rotas would, the next day, get a cut instead of standing the customary one-in-three chances of escaping a switch off. Indeed from 16 February the number of stages of rota disconnections was increased to 3, giving a 15 per cent level of disconnection at any one time. Also on 16 February 10 power stations with low coal stocks were closed, to give the stations a longer potential life; many more were operating at reduced capacity. The NUM leaders on this day 'recommended' that in future there should only be token picketing of power stations, but this did not particularly help since the road and rail unions acknowledged token pickets as fully as large numbers. By now 1 400 000 workers were idle and by 18 February the official figure was 1 600 000, with large numbers on short time.

The energy situation went on deteriorating. John Davies, speaking on television on the day before, had been extraordinarily frank. The government, he said, had not realised that picketing could restrain the capacity of the electricity supply industry to such a degree, adding that if the crisis continued for another ten days industry would virtually come to a halt. The low point was reached on

Friday 18 February. Planned rota disconnections of fifteen per cent plus six per cent voltage reductions were imposed at 11.15am and continued through the evening peak. High risk consumers suffered nine hours of blackout. The restricted demand at the peak, the lowest weekday figure of the emergency, was 24 093 MW. This meant that the plant readily usable figure had dropped by some 16 000 MW in the 18 days from 31 January when the winter peak had actually been met.[19]

At this time coal stocks at the stations were 4 100 000 tons while, for the reasons we have given, the effective coal stocks were 2 080 000 tons. This figure was equivalent to 9 average winter days' supply, the range of regional figures being 6 to 18 days; 84 stations with a total capacity of 9198 MW were now in the protected category and a further 19 767 MW were not readily usable through primary fuel or lighting-up oil shortages. It was clear that even the greatly reduced level of supply could not be sustained for more than a few days. The situation could hardly have been more grave.

THE END OF THE STRIKE

On that critical day – 18 February – the Wilberforce Report was published. It supported the miners' claim for an 'exceptional increase', if necessary paid for by the government. The main recommendations were for a £5 increase to £23 in the minimum weekly wage for surface workers, a £6 increase to £25 for underground workers and a £4.50 a week increase to £34.50 for men at the coal face covered by the National Power Loading Agreement. Wilberforce also recommended that the agreement should run from 1 November 1971 for sixteen months. Following immediate discussions between NCB and the three senior NUM officers the NUM Executive, on a vote, narrowly rejected the Wilberforce terms that were offered to them, but in discussions at No 10 Downing Street later that night first with the Prime Minister and then with NCB representatives, further concessions were made and agreement reached, subject to ballot.[20] These further concessions put the Coal Board's salary bill up by a further £5 million over the costs of the Wilberforce recommendations, which themselves were estimated to be £85 million.[21]

The NUM called off its pickets, the NCB's final offer was put to the NUM's membership in a ballot and the result, on 25 February, showed overwhelming acceptance.[22] The miners returned to work on 28 February. In order to give some relief to consumers and to obtain a higher minimum load the government, on 23 February, removed restrictions on commercial space heating and the industrial load and in the following two weeks further relaxations were made. Rota cuts were reduced and by 1–2 March were ended.

By 28 February recovery within the Board had already gained momentum using NCB coal stocks, imported coal, increased oil burn and overburn. Figures for plant not readily usable had risen to 29 936 MW, compared with an average cold spell demand for the time of year of 36 100 MW. At the end of March all restrictions (except on display and floodlighting) were removed, even though the plant readily usable figure was only 33 436 MW so that there was some risk involved. The Board then had an effective coal stock of 6 420 000 tons, which represented 29 days' stock. On 8 March the government had officially ended the State of Emergency.

A CLOSE-RUN THING

A survey of press coverage in the period of the 1972 strike shows an emphasis on picketing and particularly on the violence experienced at some power stations, but more especially at Saltley. There was however little awareness of how close to calamity the country was on 25 February – the day when the NUM members accepted the Coal Board's terms for a settlement.

On 10 February, as we have seen, the miners achieved a victory of sorts at Saltley: certainly they and their supporters confronted the police in huge numbers and forced the closure of the main depot gate. This may not have greatly affected supplies of coal to power stations, but it certainly gave a huge fillip to the morale of striking miners all over the country and probably forced the government (which established the Wilberforce inquiry on that day) to recognise that NCB were going to have to concede generous terms to the miners.

On the same date effective coal stocks at the stations were down to 3 680 000 tons, the equivalent of only 16 days' average winter burn. Just over a week later, on 18 February, the date on which the Wilberforce Report became available, these figures had dropped calamitously to 2 080 000 tons, the equivalent of only 9 average winter days' supply. If the NUM had rejected the Coal Board's offer, a few days later, they would have had no difficulty in persuading their members to continue the strike. If those in power in the Union had been bent on bringing down the government and causing the imminent collapse of the country's electricity supplies this probably would have been achieved.[23]

CONDITIONS FOR SURVIVAL: THEN AND NEXT TIME

Managers and staff in the power stations, and those in charge of generation in the CEGB, needed the commitment and involvement of three main groupings of people and institutions in their efforts to keep the lights on. First the government, second those working in the grid control and transmission network of the CEGB, and third the Electricity Council and the area electricity boards (plus the Scottish electricity boards).

The government

The government did not do well at any stage. It was a case of doing too little too late at the political level although, when the government eventually took emergency action, the Department of Trade and Industry and its regional set-up did well in advising industry and commerce on how to survive in the crisis and in drafting and getting out the necessary emergency orders.

Douglas Hurd, who was at or near the centre of political power, admits that for weeks the government gave little attention to the dispute. No analysis seems to have been made of the political, economic and social forces at work in the NUM and the mining communities or consideration given to whether the miners could be regarded as a special case to whom pay concessions could be made.

If the government thought of the NUM at all they seem to have assumed that since the Union had not taken national strike action since 1926, had been eminently restrained through most of the 1960s when pits were being closed all over the place, and now had elected the moderate Joe Gormley as their President, the dispute could be expected to run an unexciting and diminishing course.

The Generating Board, as we have seen, failed to predict the assault on the power stations and the need to build up essential supplies other than coal; but being at the sharp end of events it learnt rapidly and, with the Electricity Council, repeatedly warned the government of the need for action. Eventually, on 9 and 10 February, the government stirred itself with the State of Emergency and the Court of Inquiry. If these steps had been taken at least two weeks earlier not only would the impact of the crisis have been much less but also the price paid for a settlement.

Where was the government's emergency organisation during this time? After the crisis was over this is the question which the Prime Minister asked. Not only did he express dissatisfaction with the role of that organisation during the strike, but commissioned a thorough review of the civil planning machine. The outcome was the establishment of the Civil Contingencies Unit under the chairmanship of the Home Secretary with the status of a standing Cabinet committee. It was this body that from then on was the government's principal formal weapon for dealing with stoppages in essential industries, including the 1973–4 crisis.[24]

The National Grid

During the strike the CEGB's grid control and transmission system, which delivered bulk supplies of electricity to the area boards' bulk supply points and directly to large consumers, were exposed to some operational difficulties. Serious frequency control problems arose as the strike went on. Between 30 January and 11 February there were 175 occasions when frequency control was outside operational limits. When, on the latter date, the Board was released from its statutory responsibilities, the objective was to have a target frequency of 50 Hz kept within $\pm$ 0.2 Hz limits by load shedding at near normal frequency. Achieving this took much skill and patience and required radical changes in a number of attitudes and practices.

The strength of the 400 KV system enabled the super-grid to deal with abnormal power flows and unbalanced generation patterns, and to exploit this potential flexibility required much staff resourcefulness. The transmission system had been built and used mainly to carry high voltage power from the north and the East Midlands to the south. However, for long periods during the strike the flow was the other way, which required careful analysis of the consequences to ensure that system stability could be maintained. There were also examples of transmission initiatives in reducing the effects of low coal stocks: in one 275 KV management group this was done by physical modifications, which had the effect of converting one circuit into another, thus enabling two instead of one 400/275 KV transformer to support the group.

Studies were undertaken to assess operating conditions in the primary trans-mission system with drastically reduced levels of coal-fired plant available – the disaster scenario. Among other things, the CEGB learnt from these studies that an interconnected system, albeit with many circuits switched out, could be maintained at all coal stock levels down to almost complete exhaustion of coal. The snag was, however, that although gas and oil plant availability amounted to 12 000 MW, supplies of other essential materials were simply not available for such a level of generation.

Distribution

From the time of the State of Emergency the Board's grid control managers worked even more closely than usual with their area board colleagues managing the implications of the reduced electricity supplies. Indeed, in its 1971-2 annual report the CEGB acknowledged that dealing with this crisis of supply had been a job for the whole industry and that the wider team could always be relied on in an emergency.

The Electricity Council and all the boards (including the CEGB), following the experience of December 1970, had been preparing for a time when electricity supplies might have to be rationed and on 11 February the area boards began disconnecting all but essential consumers for periods of three to four hours at a time in accordance with a widely published plan. Disconnections were generally confined to two days each week, plus one period on Sunday.

The switching off of consumers mostly had to be done manually in the field except, as explained earlier, in London. In quantitative terms, in the three weeks of the crisis, about 20 000 switching operations had to be conducted in London alone with each consumer, on average, being disconnected for 44 hours. Outside London the North Eastern Board was fairly representative of all the boards. Supplies there were disconnected for three-hour periods between 6am and midnight each day. Consumers were placed in eighteen different blocks for switching purposes and disconnected on pre-determined, well-publicised rotas. They operated on a three-day cycle, each block having a high-risk day on which there were up to three periods of disconnections. These were followed by medium- and low-risk days when disconnections were few if any.[25]

It is impossible to generalise accurately about consumer reactions to all this inconvenience. There were some displays of hostility, particularly by some commuters stuck on darkened, inactive railway platforms, but all area boards recorded that many consumers had thanked them for their efforts to spread the misery as fairly as possible. One marked difference with the December 1970 dispute in electricity supply was that this time public opinion made little impact on the attitudes of those taking the industrial action.

PREPARING FOR THE NEXT TIME

The CEGB with the area boards (and not least the two Scottish boards) had done their utmost to keep the lights on. They were not entirely successful, but with the help of government regulations and consumer co-operation they had prevented the collapse of the system, with something to spare. It was obvious that the settlement brought no guarantee that the NUM would not before too long turn again to industrial action. The CEGB began its preparations for the next time almost immediately, which is just as well for as it turned out the next time was not too long in coming.

Chapter 6

1973–4: Heath and the miners

By selecting some of the basic indicators 1973 could, in retrospect, be regarded as a good year for Edward Heath's Conservative government and for the people of this country. It was a time of virtually full employment, the seasonally adjusted unemployment figure (GB) for December 1973 being 2.1 per cent of the insured population, round about half a million. The gross domestic product in 1973 increased by 7.4 per cent, the highest increase for any year since recovery from World War II, the product of a deliberately expansionist budget in the spring of 1972 and of certain supporting measures that came later. The balance of payments on current account was only modestly in the red at minus £1113 million and the Retail Price Index, in spite of growing pressure on resources, remained in single figures (9.2 per cent). Perhaps the biggest governmental sigh of relief was over the fall in the number of days lost in strikes. In 1972 there had been the loss of 23 909 000 man days, an enormous figure, but in 1973, while the number of strikes – 2873 – was not much changed, the number of days lost was down to 7 197 000.

Yet well before the year was out the government was having to deal with a fuel crisis precipitated by war in the Middle East and the second November overtime ban in two years by the National Union of Mineworkers and the prospect of worse. The CEGB itself was having to face up to a crisis of fuel supply, which threatened its ability to keep the lights on to a degree which equalled the crisis induced by the miners' strike of 1972. The CEGB was hit by four occurrences of enormous weight: the oil shortage and the trebling of the cost of oil; the miners' overtime ban; industrial action by their technical and scientific staff in the power stations and on the transmission system (and for that matter in the area boards); and interference with rail-borne coal supplies by industrial action by members of the Amalgamated Society of Locomotive Engineers and Firemen's Union (ASLEF).

No-one could, however, have predicted that by February 1974 a miners' strike would have led the Prime Minister to call a General Election in which he would be defeated. It is a remarkable story and one in which the operations of the Generating Board were central.

PAY POLICY AND THE INDUSTRIAL RELATIONS BACKGROUND

On 6 November 1972 the government had announced a three months' freeze on pay and prices as Phase One of their new counter-inflationary policy; this was later extended to the end of March 1973 for pay and the end of April for prices. Phase Two followed. On 17 January 1973 a White Paper and draft bill (later the Counter-Inflation Act) led to the government gaining powers to control pay and prices for three years. Under Phase Two, from April 1973, pay rises were to be calculated on a group basis, the negotiators deciding on their distribution. Annual rises were not to exceed £1 a week, plus 4 per cent on the current pay bill of the group (excluding overtime), with a maximum of £250 a year. There was to be no further increase for twelve months. A Pay Board and a Prices Commission were established to regulate pay and price increases. Anomalies under the pay freeze were to be adjusted in Phase Three in the autumn and the Pay Board was asked to prepare a report on anomalies and a report on relativities generally.

There were protests against this statutory policy. In early 1973 a number of groups took limited forms of industrial action, including gas, parts of the civil service, and ancillary hospital staff. The issues were resolved although the civil servants had to wait some time for a report by the Relativities Board (as described later). On May Day nearly 2 000 000 workers came out on strike. What might have led to the ruin of Phase Two was another miners' strike. But although the left within the NUM forced a ballot on strike action over pay this was defeated by 143 006 to 82 631. In April 1973 the pay claim was settled within the terms of Phase Two, bringing the minimum pay of surface workers to £25.29, underground to £27.29 and face workers under the National Power Loading Agreement to £36.79. The agreement was to run for eleven months.

THE EMERGING OIL CRISIS

In April 1973 the Generating Board estimated that their fuel consumption in 1973–4 would be 105 000 000 tonnes of coal equivalent, including estimated consumption of about 61 000 000 tonnes of NCB coal, the balance being oil (29Mtce), nuclear fuel, gas and non-NCB coal. In the same month, however, at the government's request, the CEGB signed a 'Support for Coal' Agreement with the Coal Board to promote the consumption of NCB coal by applying a rebate to all NCB coal consumed above a datum of 59 000 000 tonnes. By the late autumn some 7 000 000 extra tonnes of coal had been burned. Deliveries were above the programme level and by the start of October the CEGB had coal stocks of 18 700 000 tonnes, the highest ever. With its large, efficient stations in good order the Board was ready to meet the winter demands of its consumers. But then things started to get more complex.

As promised the government produced its White Paper on Phase Three on 8 October 1973. Phase Three was to run from 1 November 1973 to July 1974. It allowed for a norm of £2.25 a week or 7 per cent, whichever was the higher, plus a 1 per cent flexibility margin, with an individual maximum of £350. Two new provisions were for extra pay for those who had to work 'unsocial hours' and for threshold payments when the RPI rose by more than 1 per cent – 40p a week for every 1 per cent rise above 6 per cent. With unemployment at 2.5 per cent and wages still ahead of prices there were some grounds for thinking that the new policy might hold.

On 6 October war broke out between certain Arab states and Israel – the so-called Yom Kippur War – and on 17 October the Arab oil states, acting under the umbrella of the Organisation of Petroleum Exporting Countries (OPEC), declared a 25 per cent reduction in oil deliveries to the West, with a massive increase in oil prices. Richard Clutterbuck states[1] that the posted price of crude oil had been US$2.40 a barrel and that on 16 October it rose to US$5.11 and on 1 January 1974 to US$11.65. On that date in the UK the price was US$11.30 and this was estimated to add £1800 million to the UK's current balance of payments deficit.

Deliveries of heavy fuel oil to the power stations were seriously affected: by December 1973 they were 26 per cent down on December 1972. The Oil Industries Emergency Committee (OIEC) (made up of representatives of the oil industry) had the role of allocating the oil products that were available and co-ordinating the oil industries' response to the difficult position that the shortage of crude oil had placed suppliers and consumers in. The CEGB required various oil products for normal operation and many of these were more important because of coal supply difficulties arising from action by the miners (see later). As we have seen, lighting-up and flame stabilisation oil for coal-fired boilers is important to permit coal-fired power stations to be used flexibly to conserve coal stocks. Diesel fuel was required for mobile coal-handling plant to reclaim coal from the power station coal stocks. Oil was required for gas turbine generators to help the peak lopping of consumer demand. However, the main requirement was for heavy fuel oil for main generating plant to enable coal to be conserved. All oil was short and the OIEC had to decide what they could allow the CEGB to have.

CEGB TECHNICAL AND SCIENTIFIC STAFF WORK-TO-RULE

To add to the difficulties of the government and the CEGB, on 1 November the Electrical Power Engineers' Association (EPEA), the union representing technical and scientific staff in the power stations and transmission networks (and elsewhere in the industry) placed a ban on out-of-hours work, a term which covers call-outs from home to deal with operational emergencies as well as conventional overtime. Their antagonists were not the electricity boards but the government for refusing to allow application of an agreement reached in December 1972 that allegedly conflicted with pay policy. The union had a case, reinforced by strongly based concern over recent pay increases relative to those received by their colleagues the industrial staff.

This action by the technical staff was serious. At that time – over twenty years ago – load reduction by consumer supply disconnection because of generating capacity shortage had to be applied (except in London) by area board technical staff posted out in the field at substations to carry out discriminatory switching to avoid switching out hospitals and other vital electricity users. Since they were not available – because of their industrial action – to do that work over the winter darkness peak, 4.30pm to 5.30pm, load disconnections had to be done from normally manned points that permitted little or no discrimination. The shortage of generating capacity came from the loss of adequate engineering presence outside normal hours at power stations as a result of the EPEA's action. It amounted to about 5000 MW of additional plant being shut down. The EPEA managed the situation carefully so that, although their action caused much difficulty, it fell just short of causing disconnections. Load shedding by voltage reduction was necessary at just about all the evening peaks while the action lasted. In addition, generating plant was late returning to service and the resultant operation of less efficient stations caused more coal to be burned than normally, and coal stocks to become badly distributed between power stations. To add to all these difficulties, about 400 000 tonnes of extra coal were burned because the technical staff's action reduced nuclear power station output.

THE MINERS' OVERTIME BAN

Superimposed on all these problems was the NUM's ban on overtime, to take effect from 12 November, in support of a pay claim, and at this time Douglas Hurd[2] wrote in his diary:

> During November 1973 the earth began to move under the government's feet. Our oil supplies were going to be cut by the producers. . . . At the same time the government was being drawn into a struggle with the miners on incomes policy. The Conservative Party, its Leader, its ministers, its back benchers and its supporters in the country had already been beaten on this very ground in 1972. We have most of us dreaded, beyond anything else, a further engagement with the miners. Yet here we were being manoeuvred once again towards the same fatal field, still littered with relics of the last defeat.

It is necessary to go back a few months to look at how this situation had developed. In the NUM Joe Gormley, the President, with a reputation for being a moderate but wily negotiator, believed that he could negotiate an acceptable pay rise for his 270 000 members under Phase Three. At the NUM conference in Inverness in early July he was forced to accept as NUM policy the Scottish miners' demands of minimum rates of £35 (surface), £40 (underground) and £45 (NPLA), increases of around 35 per cent. A few days later, on 16 July, he secretly met the Prime Minister, at which meeting he dropped a hint that the way out of a dispute might be a provision in the Phase Three White Paper of a payment to the miners for unsocial hours work.[3] According to Fay and Young in their *Sunday Times* review, Gormley told a press man that the special payment 'would be there, under the table, to be produced at a suitable moment in the autumn to settle the miners' strike, as if by magic'.[4]

On 10 October, four days after the outbreak of the Middle East War and two days after publication of the Phase Three White Paper, the NCB met the NUM. The Board's Deputy Chairman, Norman Siddall, made an offer that lumped together the 7 per cent allowed by the forthcoming Phase Three with a shift allowance (the unsocial hours payment), which amounted to 4.5 per cent, and an extra 1.5 per cent of odds and ends. This amounted all told to 13 per cent on average. Further, if the miners accepted the Board's productivity scheme they would get 3.5 per cent more straight away. This offer was the maximum that Siddall could offer under Phase Three, but the NUM turned most of it down, leaving the Board and the government with hardly anywhere to turn.[5]

The Prime Minister received an NUM delegation on 23 October, but made no concession. On 25 October a national delegate conference authorised an overtime ban to be applied if and when necessary, a decision strongly supported in area ballots. On 30 October the NCB improved their offer slightly but to no avail. When the overtime ban started on 12 November the NUM added extra sickness and holiday pay and retirement lump sums to their demands.

The overtime ban seriously affected coal production. Despite an increased uptake of coal from pithead stocks, coal supplies to power stations were quickly reduced by 25 to 30 per cent. For some time the CEGB had been expressing great concern to the government about the effect of this expected ban and the government, advised now by a revitalised Civil Contingencies Unit,[6] and taking heed also of the uncertainties over oil deliveries, declared a State of Emergency on 13 November. This imposed various direct and indirect restrictions on the use of electricity, although the effect was limited. With the shortages of both oil and coal the CEGB abandoned normal economic operation from 22 November and operated its power stations in order of the efficiency with which they could convert fuel into electricity in order to maximise the amount of electricity produced from the available fuel. It negotiated a gas supply for its two large stations, which had a gas-burning capacity giving a potential coal saving of around 5 000 000 tonnes of coal a year.

In November various unsuccessful searches for a way through were conducted by the NUM with the Pay Board, NCB and the Secretaries of State. On 21 November the NUM rejected an offer said to be worth £44 million. On 28 November the Prime Minister told the NUM that if they accepted the maximum settlement under Phase Three the government would start a wide-ranging review of the coal industry and the position of the miners, but this was not accepted. It was at this meeting that Mick McGahey, Vice President of the NUM, said: 'Of course I want to change the government, but I want to do it by democratic means through the ballot box'. Gormley distanced himself from the remark but the damage was done.[7] The remark was leaked from the meeting, inaccurately and out of context, so that it looked as though he was saying that the strike was about bringing down the government.

RESPONSE TO THE CRISIS

By the first week in December the outlook for the winter electricity supplies was grave. Coal deliveries to power stations were now nearly 35 per cent below programme. Coal stocks were dropping by some 800 000 tonnes each week and on 9 December stood at 14 700 000 tonnes, some 3 700 000 tonnes less than programmed. Both the NCB and British Railways Board advised that few or no coal deliveries could be expected during a two-and-a-half to three-week period covering Christmas and the New Year. Supplies of both heavy fuel oil and light oils were being cut by more than 20 per cent compared with the previous year.

By early December the CEGB's oil supply position had become sufficiently serious to be brought to the attention of the government. The CEGB and the OIEC were faced with the consequences of both an oil and a coal shortage. There were differences of opinion about the requirements of the CEGB in this complex situation. However, the Secretary of State did authorise heavy fuel oil to be diverted to power stations as the emergency became more serious. It took some time before the results of this decision became apparent and the CEGB became very anxious about its own ability to improve the oil supply situation. The supply of the other categories of oil seemed to be much more satisfactory. However, much effort was required by all those involved to keep the situation satisfactory. At the best the heavy fuel oil supply was less than 90 per cent of the previous year's burn.

On Wednesday 12 December, against this background, the train drivers' union ASLEF began a ban on overtime and Sunday work, the dispute being over their unwillingness to accept an offer on pay that the other rail unions had accepted. Their action had a severe effect on commuter services, especially in the South East, while the restricted movement of coal meant not only that stocks fell more quickly but that there was further maldistribution of coal between stations, compounding the effect of the EPEA's action.

On the same day, and as the news of rail dislocation was coming through, senior members of the Electricity Council, the CEGB and the twelve area boards met to survey the supply situation. They decided to ask the government to impose controls on electricity consumption enabling coal and oil supplies to be conserved. What the industry advised the government was that on the basis of the position early in December coal stocks would continue to decline and would reach the critical level of 6 000 000 tonnes by the end of January or early February. With cold winter weather or further deterioration in deliveries of coal, this level might be reached even earlier. Below the critical stock level, many of the Board's 117 coal-fired power stations would have stocks which were so low that only limited generation would be possible and progressive unplanned disconnections of electricity supplies would be unavoidable. Services essential to the life and health of the community would be in peril.[8]

At the same time the Electricity Council told the media that the industry's rota plans for disconnections, devised before the 1971–2 miners' strike, had been modified for energy saving purposes and that details would be completed by the area boards for publication at the weekend. The system was based on a six-day cycle, giving the advantage of informing all consumers of fixed days of the week on which they could be at high risk. It would also help commerce and industry to plan should load disconnections became necessary.

Work between the Department of Trade and Industry[9] and the industry (guided by the Electricity Council's Contingency Review Panel) had of course been going on for some time in anticipation of these developments and of a major response by the government. The leading players were Philip Jones, Under Secretary in charge of the Electricity Division in the Department, Dr Trevor Broom, CEGB Director of Operations, and Harry Shepherd, Head of Engineering at the Electricity Council.

The basic question for them was of course how could energy consumption be reduced sufficiently, effectively, and for the necessary period. In the 1971–2 strike rota disconnections had been the means of reducing the energy demands on the system. They were very blunt instruments. Industry and commerce could merely change the pattern of work and use the same quantity of electricity and for those consumers whose supply was on the same feeders as recipients of essential supplies there were no constraints. In addition the interruption of domestic supplies had made the public critical not only of the NUM but of the government and the electricity supply industry.

Jones, Broom and Shepherd and their staff realised that what was needed in the present crisis was a means of curtailing consumption by reducing energy demand at the industrial and commercial consumers' premises. In order to determine the likely size of the reductions needed, judgements had to be made on how long the crisis was likely to last (including the ASLEF and the technical staff's actions), what level of coal stocks was critical and the detailed methods by which the reductions might be achieved. They were clear from the start that this was going to be a complex administrative and operational enterprise, which had to be planned at high speed and which had to produce, at the first stage, a system intelligible and acceptable to the government and the nation. Philip Jones was the architect of the government policy that followed.

By 13 December the Prime Minister was briefed and ready to make a statement in the House. He said that, to ensure the industrial and economic survival of the nation, industrial and commercial premises other than continuous process users and certain essential services would be limited to a three-day working week from 31 December. From the following Monday, 17 December, and until the three-day week began, industry and commerce would be limited to a total of any five days during those two weeks. Also from Monday continuous process users would be limited to 65 per cent of their normal supply. Orders would be issued to exempt certain essential business. From 17 December BBC and ITV services would close not later than 10.30 each evening except over Christmas and New Year's Eve. All domestic consumers were being asked to restrict the use of electricity for space heating in the home to one room and then only if the householder had no other form of heating available. The new restrictions amounted to an additional 20 per cent cut in electricity consumption above the 20 per cent already in effect. The Prime Minister did not consider that rota cuts would be necessary on top of all this but that they would be applied if the necessary savings were not achieved. The three working days each week would be consecutive and selected on the basis of schedules drawn up for each electricity board area.

The Secretary of State for Trade and Industry, Peter Walker, authorised the CEGB under the emergency legislation to disregard certain of their statutory and contractual duties relating to the supply of electricity. The government also took the necessary powers to impose the restrictions announced by the Prime Minister and within a few days had issued those orders which were to apply from Monday 17 December.[10] These came into operation none too early because, in the hour or two before midnight on Friday 14 December, all parts of the country suffered from the power crisis with over a million homes suffering blackouts. The CEGB imposed 5 per cent cuts on all 12 area boards, rising to 10 per cent in parts of London and the South East. The Board explained that the cuts were due to the technical staff's dispute, sudden cold weather and the public's unwillingness to take the need for economies seriously enough. Even before the cuts the Electricity Council's Deputy Chairman, Ronald Richardson, in apocalyptic mood, had warned that in the next few weeks entire cities could lose their supply of electricity 'at a stroke', including hospitals and essential services.

In the next ten days activity was at a hectic pitch in Downing Street, Whitehall and all parts of electricity supply. On 17 December the Chancellor of the Exchequer introduced a supplementary Budget aimed at cutting public expenditure by £1200 million in a full year. On 19 December the Prime Minister and William Whitelaw (who had been appointed Secretary of State for Employment at the beginning of the month) met Len Murray, TUC General Secretary, and other trade union leaders. Murray urged the government to allow the Minister to breach Phase Three, arguing that such a concession would not necessarily lead to similar inflationary settlements elsewhere. Next day Whitelaw met the Executive of the NUM when it was formally raised that more money might be found for the miners under Phase Three to cover time spent by miners cleaning up at the end of each shift and also preparing to start work at the coal face. The Secretary of State also said that, following a settlement with the Coal Board within the provisions of Phase Three, the NUM would be able to sit down with ministers and the Coal Board to examine pay arrangements appropriate to a modernised industry in the longer term. The Coal Board did its research on 'washing and waiting' and submitted its evidence to the Pay Board who had been asked to examine the issue. On 3 January they ruled that 'waiting time' payments to miners would not conform to the requirements of Phase Three. Before this the miners' leaders had anyway dismissed the money to be gained by this device, based on the NCB's appraisal of the time involved, as derisory.[11]

In Whitehall a number of government departments, co-ordinated by Philip Jones at DTI, continued with the task of preparing Orders controlling electricity consumption to apply from 17 December and a further Order governing operation from 31 December of the three-day week.[12] This work was incredibly detailed and complex and was done at great speed. The orders were published in the press on the 20 and 24 December respectively and involved the area electricity boards in a major job of work in dealing, in collaboration with the government departments, with the large consumers who were struggling to come to terms with the new operating regimes. The job was going to last for the coming three months although there were two immediate sources of relief: the reduction of the non-domestic load over the holiday period and the fact that the EPEA called off their industrial action and, from 2 January, the technical staff returned to normal work.[13]

On Friday 21 December, the CEGB summed up its position. Stocks of coal and oil were sufficient for six-and-a-half weeks of normal consumption, but little if any coal would be delivered over the next two weeks because of the holiday. At this time of year it was usual for the Board to burn 1 600 000 tonnes of coal a week. The actual burn now was about 1 700 000 tonnes, mainly because of the oil shortage but also because of reduced output from nuclear power stations. The shortfall in coal deliveries through the miners' overtime ban and the train drivers' dispute was estimated to have reached 2 300 000 tonnes so far. The shortfall had risen from 20 per cent in the first week of the miners' action to 36 per cent in the fifth week. Coal stocks earlier in the month had been put at 13 300 000 tonnes.

AN IMPROVING SUPPLY POSITION

During January the electricity supply position improved. The resumption of normal working by the technical staff from 2 January led to an improved availability of all plant, particularly nuclear. The Coal Board, as things turned out, were able to deliver much more coal – 1 700 000 tonnes – over the Christmas and New Year period than had been expected and the weather in January was turning out to be milder than in any winter since 1932. Above all the cut in consumption associated with the three-day week and other restrictive measures were an enormous help. Together these factors practically halted the expected decline in coal stocks at the power stations, which in mid-January stood at about 13 000 000 tonnes. Indeed the CEGB Chairman, Arthur Hawkins, told *The Times* on 16 January that, with 60 per cent of normal coal deliveries, oil supplies at 87 per cent of last winter and other reasonable conditions, which he defined, electricity supply could be maintained throughout the winter period. As if to emphasise the independent standing of his Board he added: 'we would support all means necessary to give the miners an adequate reward for the difficult and dangerous job they do'.[14]

So how did the government and the NUM react to this changing situation? On 9 January, at a meeting of the National Economic Development Council, the Chancellor of the Exchequer, Anthony Barber, rejected a further offer by Len Murray, TUC General Secretary, to use his organisation's prestige with other unions to prevent their using a coal industry settlement made under a relaxation of incomes policy as an argument in support of their own claim. The offer was repeated to the Prime Minister and William Whitelaw on 14 January and this time rejection seemed to be less than whole-hearted. Murray said that the offer remained on the table and the TUC leaders were given full backing for this stance at a conference of union leaders on 16 January.

Also on 16 January Lord Carrington, newly appointed Secretary of State in the newly established Department of Energy, stated that with only a small drop in coal stocks, the prospect of more oil from the Middle East, mild weather and the railway situation not worsening, the government were to have talks with the CBI, TUC and the retail trade on the possibility of introducing a four-day week, or even a five-day week with certain restrictions. Full electricity supplies were being restored immediately to the steel industry. On 21 January, for the last time, the government rejected the TUC's offer of restraint by other unions if the government made Phase Three concessions to the miners.

Clearly the NUM had to react to these developments and on the same day Joe Gormley said, according to *The Times*, 'the government have had no intention of settling the dispute. . . . They cannot blame our executive. If the executive in considering this decision take a tougher line, the government can blame nobody but themselves'.[15] And a tougher line is exactly what the NUM executive did take. On 23 January they decided to increase the pressure by taking a ballot of the members on strike action to which the immediate government reaction was not to go ahead with any relaxation of the three-day week and other restrictive measures. On 28 January ASLEF announced that their present ban on overtime and rest-day working would be intensified by a series of one-day strikes in each of British Rail's five regions starting on 7 February. On 24 January the Pay Board's relativities report was published. It proposed the establishment of new procedures for examining wage relativities. The report covered anomalies under the pay standstill of November 1972 as well as later pay anomalies. In particular a procedure was recommended for examining cases in which special treatment was claimed. Its relevance to the current dispute was obvious. The Prime Minister offered talks to the TUC and CBI on the basis of acceptance of the Phase Three offer and immediate talks on long term pay arrangements or alternatively for the miners' case for relative improvement in their position to be examined through the operation of the Pay Board's relativities report. Talks were held at Downing Street on Monday 4 February, but no progress was reported. This was hardly surprising since the TUC representatives would not have wanted to pre-empt the NUM executive's decision on strike action to be made the following day. Later that day Whitelaw tried to get Gormley to a meeting with him before the start of his executive meeting, but Gormley responded that there would be no return to the conference table without a promise of more pay.

At the executive meeting it was reported that the ballot had produced a vote of 188 393 in favour of a strike and 44 222 against. The NUM called an all-out strike from midnight on 9 February. The TUC assured the NUM that all affiliated unions would be asked to ensure that their members did not cross miners' picket lines. The NUM were bent on immobilising coal stocks and the movement of oil into the power stations. They agreed, however, to set up a national strike committee of nine to control picketing operations, including relaxation of industrial action where necessary to supply fuel to schools, hospitals and old people.

A GENERAL ELECTION IS CALLED

On 7 February, three days before the strike was to begin, the Prime Minister called a General Election for 28 February. He was not, however, abandoning all efforts to settle the miners' dispute. He asked William Whitelaw to set up immediate standing arrangements for the examination of the main relativity claim. 'At its first meeting', the Prime Minister said, 'this new machinery will conduct a full examination of the miners' case. It will be conducted in accordance with the principles of the relativities report' and whatever recommendations the new body made in the miners' case they would be backdated to 1 March.[16]

This book is about the ability of the Generating Board – and its predecessors – to keep the lights on, not about the vagaries of British politics but this was one of those moments in history when electricity supply and politics became interlocked. In calling the election was the Prime Minister motivated mainly by the position reached in the miners' strike? Did he think that in some way the result of the election would bring it to an end? Did he think that 'Who Governs Britain?' would be an irresistible vote winner? Did he think, after the experience of 1971–2, that the Generating Board would fail, in the face of the forthcoming strike, to maintain supplies even at a level to sustain a three-day working week? Douglas Hurd says that Edward Heath had been mulling over an election date for weeks and that 'the government needed a chance to discuss the changed economic situation with the electorate, and gain a new mandate from the electorate for harsh measures'.[17] Yet the main theme of the Conservative Party's manifesto was that 'the choice before the nation today, as never before, is a clear choice between moderation and extremism'.[18]

William Ashworth certainly saw the coal strike and therefore the electricity supply position as the central issue. He nevertheless thought that this was odd because 'the government had already set in train alternative moves towards a settlement thus making an electoral verdict on the strike superfluous' – a reference to the inquiry into relativities.[19] What the CEGB had to do was to prepare itself once more to keep the lights on in face of whatever the NUM, the striking miners and their allies chose to throw at it. The thought that its success or failure in the coming weeks might decide the fate of the government was hardly uppermost in the minds of its managers and staff. It was nevertheless true.

THE STRIKE

At the start of the strike the Generating Board, having learnt from the 1971–2 miners' action, had installed with government support additional plant and facilities to enable greater stocks of lighting-up oil and other essential materials to be stored at their stations and all such materials were at their maximum, allowing about six weeks' operation without further supplies. Deliveries of fuel oil had increased markedly during January and in the week before the strike exceeded the previous year's level. However, this was well short of the oil supply necessary to support the maximum oil burn that would normally have been used during a coal strike. Coal stocks at the power stations stood at 11 400 000 tonnes which, with the government's restrictions on electricity consumption and voluntary economies producing a saving of about 20 per cent, and assuming average weather conditions, was estimated to enable the generating system to carry on for six weeks before disconnection of supplies became inevitable. However, beyond that time a rapidly deteriorating electricity supply situation would develop. It was likely that before six weeks the government would find it necessary to reduce consumer demand further by a 30 to 35 per cent saving. That would make it necessary to limit industry to a two-and-a-half to two-day week. That level and the rota disconnections that would have to accompany it would be approaching the point when there were risks to essential supplies. It would be necessary to by-pass some sewage plants, telephone services would be difficult to maintain fully, food production generally and milk and bread in particular would have to be focused on 'nucleus' plants and cold storage facilities. There was virtually no prospect of any further coal supplies for the duration of the strike: the national officers of the industrial staff unions in the industry had, on 11 February, instructed their members to ban all deliveries of coal from any source, including imports, to power stations and to resist any abnormal movement of oil likely to be used to replace coal. Further, the long-term weather forecast was for a cold spell, and there was no guarantee that present economies in electricity use could be sustained.

Obviously throughout the strike the Generating Board made maximum use of the nuclear stations, and of the oil-fired stations to the extent that the constrained oil supplies allowed. As for coal, the objective was to make the best use of the coal-fired stations' coal stocks. This was far from being as simple as it sounds because of the issue of critical stock levels already referred to. With the onset of the strike, with the attitudes and behaviour that it engendered, and the effect of ASLEF's industrial action, it became impossible for the Generating Board to control the equalisation of coal stocks between stations. As a result, the measures to concentrate generation on high efficiency plant quickly caused the stocks at the high merit stations to fall. Some relief was obtained by not running some of the plant, made possible because electricity demands were below the available plant capacity. However, this did not provide good control of the situation. On 14 February the merit order, that is the order in which stations are brought into operation to meet the demand, was, therefore, further modified for coal-fired stations to reflect the coal stocks, the merit order for stations using other fuels remaining unchanged. The regime was intended to enable the reduced demand for electricity to be met for as long as possible. It was found, however, that stocks at the large high efficiency stations continued to fall because their inflexibility prevented effective operation to take advantage of the revised operating regime. Hence their generating units had progressively to be withdrawn from service. These large conventional units were newly commissioned and a flexible method of operation had not yet been developed. This caused large and abnormal power flows on the system and a dangerous threat to the Board's ability to meet demands. It not only illustrated the CEGB's contention that a minimum stock level of an appreciable size was necessary, but explains why, during the strike, daily peak demands had to be eased by reducing voltages.

The Generating Board, after its appalling experience of picketing during the 1971–2 miners' strike, had made its anxieties about a repetition clear at a meeting on 29 January between senior representatives of the Electricity Council, the Generating Board and of the Department of Energy and the Home Office. The CEGB Chairman stated what protection was needed for the movement of staff and materials into the stations and these requirements were passed on to the police authorities.

However, as things turned out, from the start of the strike the NUM made every effort to discourage mass picketing and violence. They instructed that picketing of power stations and elsewhere should be limited to six men and in general this level was not exceeded and cases of unrestrained action by individual pickets were few. Scargill said that more pickets were not needed because 'in the main the unions responded magnificently – wherever we produced a picket line the unions refused to cross it'. He added that the second reason for modest picketing was that the 'Tories were trying to use mass pickets as a lever on the British electorate'.[20] What astonished the CEGB was the fact that on 22 February the NUM actually withdrew even token pickets from all of the Board's oil-fired power stations.

As the days of the strike passed, the Generating Board's managers and staff continued to cope with the problems of steadily reducing coal stocks and their increasingly uneven distribution. As the date of the General Election drew nearer every issue relating to the strike was examined by the political parties to see what capital could be made out of it. On 21 February an event took place, which according to Fay and Young in *The Sunday Times* seriously undermined the government in the middle of the election campaign. The Pay Board, during their hearings on the dispute, released new statistical evidence suggesting that the Coal Board's figures for miners' average earnings had consistently overstated the position by including holiday money, whereas other industries with which miners' pay is compared did not. This meant that the differential between average earnings in manufacturing industries and miners' wages was £3 a week greater than previously supposed. Fay and Young state[21] that this interpretation of the figures was challenged, but by then the damage had been done. Harold Wilson thought that this was a crucial turning point in the dispute while the Prime minister, according to Fay and Young, thought that the Pay Board had conspired against him. Gormley described it as a body blow to Heath.[22]

The General Election result in terms of House of Commons seats was Labour 301, Conservatives 297, Liberal 14 and Others 23. On the day of the election, the Pay Board published its report on the dispute which recommended exceptional payments to the miners. Heath then started his negotiations with the Liberals to see if he could carry on as Prime Minister. He failed. It was 4 March before Harold Wilson became Prime Minister with Liberal support. Michael Foot became Secretary of State for Employment and, the day after, the NUM and NCB received copies of the Pay Board report. The two sides were authorised to negotiate freely and the day after the report was published the NUM accepted the NCB's offer on pay and certain other improvements which the NCB had added. The claim and settlement, as summarised by Ashworth, was as shown in Table 6.1.

Ashworth adds that 'the settlement restored the gains in external relativities obtained from the Wilberforce settlement and did a little more for face workers and a lot more for surface workers'.[23]

After this the strike was virtually all over; on 11 March the miners returned to work and the State of Emergency was formally ended. Coal-fired power stations reverted to thermal efficiency merit order with coal stocks of 7 400 000 tonnes. The five-day week was restored from 9 March. The Chairman of the CEGB wrote to the chairmen of area boards expressing confidence that the CEGB would be able to meet the full load. He recalled that the industry had been in a state of emergency since the beginning of November 1973 and that operating the electrical system in face of the actions of the EPEA (up to the end of December), the NUM and ASLEF, plus the hazards of the Middle East oil crisis, had been fraught with difficulty. He paid a tribute to the area boards, saying that they had always been ready to respond without delay to the call from the CEGB's National Control. By being able to depend on this the Board had been able to maintain supplies with the minimum of reserve capacity. The CEGB had also been able to save a substantial quantity of fuel by relying on the area boards' ready response to voltage control over peak periods. The whole operation had been an industry-wide enterprise.

On 23 March all remaining restrictions on electricity consumption were lifted, and after nearly three months the area boards could put down the heavy burden

Table 6.1 Miners' pay claim and settlement 1974

Mineworkers' pay claim and settlement 1974 £ per week (basic)			
	1973 Actual	Claim	Settlement
Minimum surface	25.3	35	32
Minimum underground	27.3	40	36
Coal face (NPLA)	36.8	45	45

Source: Ashworth (1986)

they had borne in helping to administer and operate the government's Orders on the three-day week.

CONCLUSIONS

The CEGB reviewed its experience in the dispute, but while it set about rebuilding coal, oil and other stocks it certainly did not, as it was to do in the early 1980s, assume that it would be faced with another miners' strike in the following year or two and that it should prepare to operate again under seige conditions.

It has to be remembered that a Labour government had come to office and that, as is made clear in Chapter 8, it set about working closely with the trade unions and introducing pro-union legislation. The NCB at that time had a relatively new Chairman in Derek Ezra and the NUM a relatively new President in Joe Gormley. With strong support from the government, they were clearly resolved to keep the peace in the coal industry and as the clearest public demonstration of this they produced a plan for coal[24].

The CEGB had other problems to deal with such as a lack of growth in demand for electricity, nuclear power policy and problems on power station construction sites. It was not until the early 1980s that the Board needed to turn its attention again to militancy in the coalfields.

Chapter 7

1977: No work, no pay

In September 1977 briefly, and in October–November 1977 at length, there was unofficial action in many CEGB power stations in the form of a ban on overtime and a work-to-rule. This action proved awkward to handle for the CEGB, serious in its consequences for consumers and when it was over of distressing significance for many power station staff. It also had its influence on future industrial relations.

Ostensibly the action, promoted by a group of shop stewards acting unofficially and mostly based on the big coal-fired stations in South Yorkshire and the East Midlands, was intended to achieve three things: concessionary staff rates for electricity staff in parallel with the free coal supplies to miners (which were to a maximum value of £230 a year, less delivery charges), travel to work allowances (again to parallel those in the mining industry which were so arranged that no miner paid more than 52.5p a week), and improved rates for shift workers. There were a number of relevant factors in the background that need to be briefly described.

LABOUR GOVERNMENT AND ITS INCOMES POLICY

The Labour party had been in office since March 1974, but from 1976 without its own majority in the House.[1] Before coming into office Labour and the TUC had committed themselves to a social contract under which, to put it simply, the Party would produce pro-union legislation in return for restraint on pay. This was a strong challenge to Labour since it had inherited many economic and industrial difficulties and was almost immediately faced with strikes in local government, the motor industry and among teachers, civil servants and bank employees.

Labour repealed the 1971 Industrial Relations Act[2] but the threshold increases under stage three of the previous government's pay code inevitably led, in 1974, to inflationary settlements. By the end of 1974 the economic indicators were grim.[3]

However, the TUC were beginning to play their part. The September 1974 Congress had approved guidelines for negotiators: settlements should no more than offset rises in the cost of living and claims for increases should be made at no less than twelve monthly intervals.[4] However, by mid-1975 prices on the year were up by about 25 per cent and weekly earnings by about 28 per cent.[5] More was required of the trade unions, especially after the government, in 1975, had delivered legislative improvements in employment protection, health and safety and sex discrimination and provided a statutory base for the Advisory, Conciliation and Arbitration Service (ACAS).

At the September 1975 Congress the unions endorsed government proposals for a flat rate limit on pay increases of £6 a week (equivalent to 10 per cent on average) and an upper limit on pay increases at £8500 a year. The policy was widely observed and industrial action remarkably reduced. With other fiscal and monetary policies in place some of the main indicators, by the end of 1975, showed at least some improvement over 1974.[6]

Nevertheless 1976 was a difficult year with a sterling crisis in the summer accurately forecast by many. In the March Budget the Chancellor, Denis Healey, offered tax cuts if the TUC delivered effective support on pay. This was forthcoming in June, the new policy providing for a cash limit on increases of a minimum of £2.50 a week to a maximum of £4 (all pay elements to be included). In April James Callaghan had succeeded Harold Wilson as Prime Minister. Following the summer sterling crisis the Chancellor negotiated overseas credits and loans, although at the price of a severe mini-Budget in December, which was bound to increase unemployment.

Union members were getting restless over high inflation and low settlements, with craftsmen particularly concerned over narrowing differentials. Early in 1977 British Leyland tool room workers took strike action and in June 18 000 trade unionists demonstrated in support of strikers at the Grunwick film processing laboratory in Willesden, a further symptom of general restlessness.[7] The TUC's General Council stated in July that the pressures could only be relieved by a return to free collective bargaining. In the same month the Chancellor stated the government's own policy, namely settlements in single figures. The Prime Minister reinforced this at the September TUC, but Congress overwhelmingly reiterated its support for free collective bargaining while retaining the 'twelve-month rule'. At the time increases in weekly earnings over the year were down to 5.8 per cent[8] and the other indicators (except unemployment, which was increasing rapidly) were also moving in the right direction.[9]

DEVELOPMENTS WITHIN THE CEGB

The period 1 April 1974 to 31 March 1977 saw a growth in electricity sold by the CEGB of only 2.4 per cent, with an actual reduction of 3.3 per cent in 1975–6. There had been nothing like it in CEGB history. In 1976 and 1977 3400 MW of plant was closed down in 48 power stations with 5000 jobs lost. Staff either retired early, accepted redundancy terms or were redeployed. Total staff fell by 5.4 per cent with a fall of 10 per cent in the industrial staff. On the other hand thermal efficiency had improved and the new 500 MW machines were beginning to work well. There were serious labour problems on a number of power station construction sites, especially the Isle of Grain; CEGB staff were not involved. The price of coal went up substantially, including a 15 per cent rise on 1 March 1977.

On 4 July 1974 the NJIC trade union members presented a claim for travelling allowances to and from work for staff working in remote power stations. This demand had originated in 1973 at Ratcliffe Power Station and had been supported by four other Trent Valley stations. The response of the NJIC boards' members, including those from the CEGB, was that the solution should be for the CEGB to arrange for the equivalent of public transport to the five power stations with the employees contributing the equivalent of public transport fares. The CEGB arranged this by 15 July, as promised, but the services were not used and all but two of the contracts were terminated by the end of October. What the industrial staff had wanted all along, as everyone knew, was a travel allowance and in August staff took unofficial industrial action at three of the stations, although it did not last long. The issue of travel allowances was not pursued again until 1977 because of the constraints of incomes policy. There was also a limited form of industrial action by clerical and administrative staff in 1975 over London allowances, but a Pay Board report provided a way out.

The mid-1970s saw the establishment of a new, unrecognised trade union that indicated its aspirations in its title: the Electricity Supply Union. It gained a curtain amount of support in a number of power stations and caused the NJIC unions and the CEGB some irritation until it petered out a few years later. Meanwhile the unions representing the three main groups of staff were making annual pay settlements within the terms of government and TUC pay policies. The NJIC unions had made their latest agreement with the boards from March 1977 and the average weekly earnings position of the CEGB's industrial staff in October 1977 compared with manual workers in all industries and services and in mining were: the CEGB £79, all industries £73.27, and miners £75.10 (an average of surface, coal face and other underground workers). Average weekly hours worked in the three groupings were much the same but unsocial hours worked in the form of shift and staggered day patterns were much higher in the CEGB.[10]

Conditions for unofficial strike action

Clearly certain facts and circumstances could, in the late summer of 1977, be exploited by shop stewards acting unofficially and bent on stirring up trouble in the stations. They could quote three years of high inflation, combined with relatively low pay settlements, a narrowing of differentials between skilled and unskilled workers, the return to free collective bargaining, the irritant of the 'twelve-month rule', power station closures, a fall in numbers of industrial staff and a perceived remoteness of the industry's negotiators who made their national settlements without, it was alleged, reference to the staff in the stations. The shop stewards would, however, have to be careful about some things: earnings and general conditions were good, nearly all staff were now on work-study-based incentive schemes, there were no compulsory redundancies, and it was getting increasingly cold outside.

The unofficial leaders were mostly employed in the big new baseload coal-fired power stations in South Yorkshire and the East Midlands. A high proportion of the industrial staff in those stations lived in the mining villages with family members and friends working in the pits. In coming into the new power stations over the previous ten years, many from the mines, these staff had become aware that there was nothing available to them to be compared with the miners' concessionary coal. They regarded the achievement of concessionary electricity rates a highly desirable target. The miners were also now getting substantial help with travel to work just at the time when, with the return to free collective bargaining, the industrial staff at the Trent Valley stations were thinking that the issue needed to be taken out of cold storage.

This was the background against which the unofficial shop stewards, now recruiting supporters elsewhere and meeting as a quasi-national committee, formulated their plans. As they prepared the ground for a ban on overtime and work-to-rule, they found that little was being done by managers or unions to deter them and that they were getting some rank and file response. Their aim, so they stated publicly, was to persuade the NJIC trade union leaders to take over and pursue their three claims. In private they hoped in time to create a single electricity supply union and, in the short term, to be involved in pay negotiations and to be recognised.

INDUSTRIAL ACTION, 6–7 SEPTEMBER 1977

In August the unofficial shop stewards called for an overtime ban and work-to-rule to start on 6 September on much the same basis as in December 1970.[11] On 31 August the NJIC unions told the boards that they would be acting on the unofficial claims. Since the dispute was unofficial the EPEA responded positively to an appeal by the CEGB to support technical and scientific staff in running as much plant as possible.

On 2 September the CEGB's judgement was that there was likely to be a plant shortage of 20 per cent against a likely peak demand of around 28 000 MW. The public were informed.

On the afternoon of 5 September the Board was well aware of the likely extent of the industrial action and it was able to make a more sanguine judgement. With power available from Scotland (whose workers were not yet involved), higher CEGB plant availability and improving weather, the Board thought that the next day they might avoid disconnections by relying on voltage reductions.

With these favourable factors, during 6 and 7 September the technical staff achieved remarkable results in running the 46 power stations at which some 14 000 industrial staff were taking industrial action or, to be accurate, in many cases inaction. On 6 September one stage of voltage reduction of 3 per cent was called for to last 1 hour 45 minutes in the north and 1 hour 12 minutes in the south. The next day a voltage reduction covering all areas lasted an hour. Such voltage reductions were hardly perceptible. The highest demand met was 27 000 MW at 5.30pm on 6 September. The unofficial leaders of the industrial action and their followers must have realised that things were not going according to plan and, on 7 September, men started working normally on the night shift. The unofficial action had come to an abrupt end.

Early consequences

The use of the technical staff,the great majority of whom were members of the EPEA, to run stations on their own created a good deal of anguish among the industrial staff. Some managers also had difficulty in persuading the technical staff that their action had genuinely been needed to avoid widespread disconnections.

Surprising as it seemed to many managers the action was claimed as a success by some of the unofficial leaders because the NJIC unions had picked up the three claims and raised them at an NJIC meeting. At the meeting the unions stated that the claims related to all NJIC staff, not just power station staff. The boards' representatives were prepared to discuss the claims, progress was made and a working party continued discussion on 13 October, the day before the next full NJIC meeting.

The unofficial shop stewards' committee had met on 24 September when they decided to await the outcome of that meeting before deciding on the next step. It was clear that if nothing was settled there would be further industrial action.

CONFRONTATION: 24 OCTOBER–11 NOVEMBER

At the NJIC meeting on 14 October, following discussions on the previous day, agreement in principle was reached to meet some of the travel expenses of all industrial staff. However, details needed to be agreed, including the application date. At the same meeting there was agreement on improved shift pay, although from March 1978, 12 months from the previous settlement.

On 17 October the unofficial shop stewards' committee met, expressed dissatisfaction with most of this, and called for a work-to-rule and overtime ban in the power stations from Monday 24 October.

The CEGB recognised that if the action went much further than in September there would be serious problems of communication with unofficial groups in the stations, especially with great variations from one station to another over what was meant by the self-imposed 'rules' to which the staff were working. The EPEA were concerned about relations between technical and industrial staff, which had been damaged in the earlier dispute. They nevertheless indicated that their members could be relied on to run the plant if supply was threatened.

Industrial staff not working normally would have to have left the plant before the technical staff could operate it, which turned out in some stations to be nothing like so easy as it might sound.

On 25 October, the first full day of the industrial action, there were 5 per cent disconnections in supply in each area board, with cuts lasting from 11 to 25 minutes, starting at 5.30pm. On that day, 4500 MW of usable output was lost and this figure rose within a few days until a loss of nearly 11 000 MW was being sustained. Load reductions at peak times were over 20 per cent.

Also on the same day, the Electricity Council and the CEGB made an important decision. With the possibility of a conditional agreement being reached at the NJIC meeting on 3 November, nine days ahead, it was agreed that CEGB management should avoid action that might be provocative and lead to intensified action. The CEGB hoped the pressures from local managers and the unions, and the prospect of an NJIC settlement, would lead to a resumption of normal working. But if, within a week, disruption of supplies continued, firmer action would be taken.

In that week disruption continued and on 31 October the CEGB took action. They warned the industrial staff that if their action continued beyond the NJIC meeting on 3 November any employee who refused to work normally would be in breach of contract and would not be paid.[12] The EPEA supported this policy and called on their members to maintain supplies.

At the NJIC meeting on Thursday 3 November agreement was reached on travel allowances. Because of the constraints of incomes policy, it would however be necessary to seek government agreement on implementation, which would not be until the staff returned to normal working. The agreement on travel allowances to NJIC staff was:

> in recognition of the unusual nature of many of the patterns of work required of employees and . . . the remote nature of many of the sites. . . . The payments were in recognition of the *differential* rate of increase in the cost of travel over movements in salary levels and movements of the RPI in recent years and any further adjustments . . . will take into account this relationship. [authors' emphasis]

The terms set out in Table 7.1 show that it would not be an expensive deal, although it did breach the long-standing principle that staff should find their own means of getting to work and pay for it themselves.

The industrial action continued, reinforced by evidence of growing militancy in the mines, especially in South Yorkshire.[13] After formal warnings staff refusing to work normally were not paid. In some power stations this policy intensified the action. On 5 November industrial staff at several power stations stopped work. These included Ratcliffe, Rugeley, Drakelow, Cottam and West Burton in the East Midlands and Drax, Ferrybridge, Eggborough and Thorpe Marsh in South Yorkshire. In South Wales staff at Aberthaw A Power Station changed from working-to-rule to doing nothing. One of the unofficial leaders said that the effect of a confrontation might be to 'close down every power station

Table 7.1 Terms of agreement on travel allowances, 3 November 1977

Distance travelled	Rates of allowance per week
Less than three miles	NIL
Three or more miles but less than six	£0.80
Six or more miles but less than ten	£1.30
Ten or more miles	£2.00

Source: The Electricity Council

in the country'. But six other stations in the North East accepted the ultimatum and returned to normal working.

EPEA members at Ratcliffe, Rugeley and Drakelow Power Stations continued to operate the stations without NJIC staff. On Sunday 6 November the EPEA agreed, in an attempt to avoid power cuts, to request their members to restart some of the stations which by now the CEGB had been forced to close. A senior CEGB spokesman said that cuts were getting beyond the 20 per cent mark and that this step had been decided on to ensure that the cuts did not get worse. The technical staff started up three 2000 MW stations: Cottam, Drax and Eggborough, and later three others, but 10 other stations were still shut down with 14 more on reduced load.

Also on 6 November the Secretary of State For Energy, Tony Benn, met both sides of the NJIC. He stated that the travel agreement could be applied, but to remote stations only. Clarification was sought and the next day, 7 November, while a further meeting was going on, news was received indirectly from the shop stewards' committee that they would recommend a return to normal working on Wednesday 9 November:

1 if pay was restored;
2 if their three claims would be discussed in March 1978;
3 if they, the shop stewards, were involved in these discussions.

A statement was issued by Tony Benn to the effect that these conditions 'presented no problems to the government'. Next day, 8 November, the two sides of the NJIC met him again. The boards' side told him that they were not prepared to pay those who, after due warning, had refused to work normally. The unions told him that whether the unofficial shop stewards were involved in negotiations was a matter for them, not the government. The EPEA also had strong objections. John Lyons made it clear to the Secretary of State that if the demands of the unofficial shop stewards' committee were met, EPEA members would close down the stations themselves.[14]

Things were now rapidly coming to a head. There were signs that the unofficial shop stewards were weakening, having realised that their three proposals for ending the dispute were unacceptable. Their leader resigned. *The*

Times, on 9 November, said that it appeared that the shop stewards were only talking about getting involved in the local negotiating machines. That day shop stewards in South Yorkshire stations claimed to have detected victimisation of two West Burton Power Station workers (never identified) and stated that they would request the shop stewards' committee to call for a national strike in their support. On the same day, however, the industrial staff at West Burton were voting to work normally. The next morning four South Yorkshire stations at the heart of the dispute – Thorpe Marsh, Ferrybridge C, Drax and Skelton Grange – also voted to work normally. Soon there were only three stations out of action.

Also on 10 November the new leader of the shop stewards said, 'We have lost the battle and we should accept the fact. The public, the government and the TUC are all against us.' On the next day the unofficial committee, meeting in Doncaster, voted to reject a strike call and to recommend a return to normal working as soon as possible. Except at one station, the men had by then anticipated that advice.

By Monday 14 November all stations had returned to normal working and so ended a dispute in which, at one time or another, 72 stations, with about 80 per cent of total capacity, had had some form of industrial action. The highest number of stations simultaneously recording a loss of output was 30, although a total of 50 recorded a loss of one day or more.[15]

AREA BOARDS AND CONSUMERS FEEL THE EFFECTS

In tackling the industrial action CEGB had not acted on their own. The Electricity Council were involved in major decision-making and, with CEGB, in co-ordinating the emergency operations of the area electricity boards. Once again these boards worked to the operational plans devised in the early 1970s. They rationed electricity supplies as fairly as they could through the rota system, consumers being kept informed of intended disconnections through the media and the boards' own points of contact. Some consumers, such as hospitals, sewage and water works, got priority treatment, although this was difficult to guarantee when the effects of the action were so unpredictable.

Consumers in all area boards suffered, first to a limited degree through voltage reductions, and then through rota disconnections. The extent of the cuts varied from day to day. On 31 October, one of the worst days, most parts of the country had power cuts between 4.30pm and 7.30pm. For example, 15 per cent of London consumers were without power for periods of up to 2 hours. The following day was worse and 2 November perhaps worst of all, with offices, industry, homes and hospitals throughout the country being cut off in the morning as well as in the evening peak. Many of these rota cuts were for up to three hours.

It is difficult to strike a balance in describing the extent to which homes, hospitals and other social services, factories and commercial centres suffered. It is true that some hospitals and businesses had their own electrical generators, but these often gave only limited supplies and were not always reliable. Commuters suffered inordinately from the failure of road traffic lights and railway signals. Some people were trapped in tower block lifts and had to be freed by the fire brigade. Some kidney patients experienced serious problems with supplies for their dialysis equipment. *The Times*, in a leading article on 5 November, referred to the ability of a group of workers to inflict on the public at large hardship, inconvenience, even danger, wholly out of proportion to the magnitude of the grievance.

LESSONS OF THE DISPUTE

Many power station industrial staff were deeply shocked and aggrieved over the CEGB refusing to pay staff who were not working normally, even though they had been warned well in advance that this policy was to be applied. Up until then, although it was common in British industry for strikers not to be paid while they were not working, it was not normally the practice to withhold all pay from staff who were turning up for work but going slow, working to rule or adopting other forms of industrial action short of a strike. Many thought that managers would give in and prove to be a soft touch. But that was not to be. Hundreds of men took their grievances first to local managers and, when they failed to get satisfaction, into the formal industrial relations machinery at district level. Many cases ended up at the NJIC where a joint sub-committee dealt with them at a succession of meetings in the year or more following the dispute. But the management of the industry stuck to their position and few individual claims were substantiated. A few cases were taken to the courts. Indeed the most publicised case, Henthorn and Taylor v CEGB, got as far as the Court of Appeal.[16]

No concessionary electricity was given to staff and while the principle of not paying anything for travel to work was breached the differential payment turned out to be of marginal value only. Improved shift pay, agreed from March 1978, would have been agreed anyway.

The firm application of the 'no work no pay' principle galvanised many managers and technical staff. They felt that they were being supported from the top. The managers also learnt from practical experience of the terms on which the EPEA and their members were prepared to help in an industrial dispute, namely when the dispute was unofficial and threatened supply. This was the first time that the technical staff had run the plant on a large scale in the absence of the NJIC operators who did not think that they would be able to do it. In fact they operated to a higher standard than normal. They achieved higher and more consistent output and set standards which the industrial staff operators were, on return to work, going to have to equal. The experience gave confidence to the technical staff and raised their standing generally. This was a significant event.

Managers and technical staff also learnt much about how, in the heat of daily conflict, to manage a situation in which demand was exceeding supply in a fluctuating, unpredictable way. They, and colleagues throughout the Board, also saw demonstrated once again that the National Grid, properly managed and operated, was an extremely efficient and flexible means of moving large quantities of electricity around the country in directions not envisaged.

The unofficial shop stewards must have learnt how difficult it is to organise and sustain industrial action in the power stations when managers, the EPEA, the technical staff, their own unions and the public were against them. The industrial staff must have seen that they gained nothing; indeed many of them lost money. The NJIC unions put a further effort into improving their links with their members.

Down to the time of the great miners' strike there was no further experience of large-scale industrial action in the stations, whether official or unofficial. The period – 1978–84 – was one of considerable change in the negotiated agreements for all groups of staff, with the 1980 reconstruction of the NJIC agreement a culmination of sixteen years of effort to achieve the terms of employment for industrial staff needed for full staff status.

Part II

The miners' strike 1984–5

This part tells the compelling story of the miners' strike of 1984–5, doing so for the first time from the standpoint of the CEGB whose strength and resourcefulness were strained almost to their limits. Keeping the lights on was a statutory duty of the Board, not a weapon in a political battle, a distinction which the board strove to maintain at every stage of this bitter conflict. Yet nobody could doubt that failure to maintain supplies would have changed the course of history. The story concludes with the return of the miners to work with nothing to show for their struggles, with the CEGB returning to normal, and the industry and the nation beginning to count the cost.

Note: In parts II and III the word 'we' is used frequently in the account of the 1984–5 miners' strike. It can refer either to the CEGB senior management team of which one of the joint authors was a member or the broader CEGB organisation, depending on the context. In many cases it is not possible to name a single individual who carried out an action since most events involved a wide range of people at all levels and it is convenient to refer to the group as 'we'.

Chapter 8

Conflict in context

This chapter is not intended to deal with the immediate causes of the 1984–5 miners' strike. Rather, it is concerned with the political, economic and industrial relations background which, indirectly rather than directly, helped to determine the attitudes of the NCB, CEGB, NUM and others who were either involved face-to-face or were drawn, in spite of themselves, into the conflict. The account starts towards the end of 1977 where it was left at the end of Chapter 7.

LABOUR'S LAST TWO YEARS IN OFFICE

The Labour government is still widely associated in people's minds with the 1978–9 winter of discontent,[1] which contributed to the Conservative party's victory in the May 1979 General Election and reinforced their intention to change the law governing trade unions and industrial relations.

This winter episode should not, however, entirely obscure the fact that some of the economic indicators were improving rapidly in Labour's last two years. Indeed in the last 12 months the GDP increased by 2.9 per cent, the balance of payments on current account was in credit by £707 million and the unemployment total (seasonally adjusted, GB) was down to 1 161 000, from its August 1977 high of 1 472 000. Weekly earnings of adult male manual workers were up by about 15 per cent and the RPI figure by 9.1 per cent, which though high was lower than in most years between 1974 and 1984. Days lost in disputes were, however, a different story.

In September 1977 the TUC had decided to support the return of the unions to free collective bargaining, although retaining the twelve months minimum interval between pay negotiations with a given employer. Days lost from strikes in both 1977 and 1978 were two to three times what they had been in 1976[2] and worse was to come. The government intervened in mid-1978 with a further phase of incomes policy, not supported by the unions, which provided that increases in earnings for any group, with certain exceptions,[3] should not be more than 5 per cent.

Earlier the Conservative party had established a policy group on the nationalised industries under Nicholas Ridley aimed, as he himself said,[4] at establishing tighter discipline in running these industries before they were privatised.

According to *The Economist* of 27 May 1978,[5] the group proposed that each of these industries should achieve a set rate of return on capital employed and this was included in the Party's election manifesto. The greatest deterrent to any strike, the group thought, would be 'to cut off the money supply to the strikers and make the union finance them'. These words were reinforced by the group's stated belief that the coal industry was the most likely battlefield. They wanted a Conservative government to build up maximum coal stocks, make contingency plans for the import of coal, encourage the recruitment of non-union lorry drivers by haulage companies to help move coal where required, and introduce coal/oil-firing in all power stations as soon as possible. The words were prophetic, although it has to be added that they did not affect CEGB contingency planning.

At the TUC in September 1978, in spite of the Prime Minister's personal appeal, the members endorsed a further call for 'responsible' free collective bargaining with no constraints other than twelve month intervals between claims. Then came a succession of strikes, mostly about pay and conditions. The big ones before Christmas 1978 included a nine-week stoppage at Ford's with 2 529 000 working days lost, in November/December a six-week stoppage by 20 000 bakery workers and from December 1978 to October 1979 the closure of *The Times*. In January 1979 2000 petrol tanker drivers stopped work, followed by many lorry drivers. A succession of one-day stoppages by 20 000 train drivers followed and from February to April one-day stoppages and other forms of industrial action by clerical and executive civil servants.

The worst industrial action, in early 1979, involved the 1 250 000 workers in local authorities and the health service, involving the loss of 3 000 000 working days,[6] and industrial action by water and sewage workers.[7] The resulting settlements were costly; they also led to widespread inconvenience and much distress.

The government and the TUC met several times in early 1979, the main practical item being comparability in determining pay in the public sector. On 7 March the government established a standing Commission on Pay Comparability under Hugh Clegg's chairmanship. Their work helped to keep immediate increases of a number of groups down to about 10 per cent while giving a number of hostages to fortune. Between August 1978 and May 1979, 13 500 000 days' work were lost in disputes.[8]

STATE OF THE ECONOMY, MAY 1979 TO MARCH 1984

The Conservatives came to office on 3 May 1979 with Margaret Thatcher as Prime Minister.[9] The basic economic aim of the new government was to reduce inflation by reducing the money supply, public expenditure and public borrowing. The government turned its back on the incomes policies of Labour, relying instead on ability to pay in the private sector, legislation to curb trade union power and, in the public sector, stronger financial controls.

The government's first two-and-a-half years in office were associated with serious problems for business and the wider community, particularly in manufacturing, a doubling of unemployment, increases in the minimum lending rate and an increase in taxation and public expenditure as a proportion of GDP.[10] According to MacInnes[11] the collapse in output and employment was the worst ever, outstripping that of 1920–22, and worse than that of the 1930s.

In 1982 the economy slowly started to improve and this improvement continued through 1983 (when the Conservatives won a huge victory at the June General Election)[12] and into 1984.[13] Unfortunately unemployment increased until, in March 1984, there were 3 000 000 people unemployed.

INDUSTRIAL RELATIONS AND EMPLOYMENT LAW, 1979–1984

The new government inherited industrial relations difficulties and could not be directly blamed for most early strikes. In its first 12 months 32 203 000 days were lost in disputes, most of this enormous loss being in steel in early 1980 (8 800 000 days) and from August to November 1979 a series of stoppages in engineering (16 000 000 days). The other strike that hit the headlines was that at British Leyland, which started in November 1979 and cost 190 000 days. It was associated with the sacking of a senior shop steward who, in the end, failed to gain the support of the shop floor even though his union, following an internal enquiry, concluded that he had been unfairly dismissed.

The government removed public bodies established by Labour, particularly the Royal Commission on the Redistribution of Incomes and Wealth, the National Enterprise Board and the Comparability Commission. The National Economic Development Council and ACAS remained, although the latter was shorn of its statutory powers of trade union recognition.

In August 1980 the government's first Employment Bill reached the Statute Book. It amended parts of the 1974 Trade Union and Industrial Relations Act and the 1975 and 1978 Employment Protection Acts. It also gave added protection to trade union members where a closed shop operated and to individuals dismissed for refusing to join a union on various grounds.[14] There were two provisions which bore closely on events before and during the miners' strike. One made picketing lawful only if carried out by an employee or trade union official from the employee's place of work (which outlawed flying pickets). The other was that the Secretary of State for Employment was empowered to issue a code of practice on picketing. The Act also provided for payments by the government to cover the cost of secret ballots relating to specified matters, including strikes.

The TUC and industrial unions organised further protests against this planned legislation, against unemployment and against cuts in public expenditure,[15] but the government stuck to its policies and, as the recession got worse, more employers were forced by their circumstances to take a harder line on industrial relations. The size of pay settlements started to come down and in 1980 and 1981 single-figure agreements were made in local government, the health service, engineering and elsewhere. Agreements remained relatively high, however, in coal, electricity supply, gas and water.

In January 1981 came an alliance of the Iron and Steel Trades Confederation (ISTC), the NUM and NUR against government attempts to push through closures and redundancies in coal, rail and steel, but collectively it did not achieve much, and in the miners' strike the NUM and ISTC were soon at loggerheads.

Unemployment rose to 2 300 000 by December 1981 (seasonably adjusted, GB) and industrial action was much less than in earlier years. The worst two cases in that year were five weeks of sporadic action by seamen and running strike action by over 500 000 civil servants protesting against the winding up of the Pay Research Unit and a pay offer about half that justified by the Unit's findings.

Probably the government's most anguished decision in 1981 was to give way to the miners' threat of strike action over pit closures in February, dealt with in Chapter 9. But even in this generally troubled year the number of strikes and days lost in disputes fell remarkably, the reduction being all but maintained in 1982.[16]

On 28 October 1982 the second Employment Bill became law, a measure which further amended Labour's legislation and strengthened the 1980 Act. Again it had a bearing on the course of the miners' strike. It introduced a new definition of a trade dispute to exclude all matters other than those between employees and their employer. It gave further protection to an employee dismissed for not joining a union, required that a closed shop should be approved in secret ballots, made union-labour-only contracts void, removed the trade unions' general immunity from actions in tort, replacing this by the same limited immunity afforded to individuals in the amended 1974 Act. It also provided that the maximum amount of damages that could be awarded against a trade union in proceedings in tort should be determined by the number of its members, ranging from £10 000 if the union had less than 5000 members to £250 000 if it had 100 000 or more.

The industrial relations scene in the year up to November 1983, the start of the NUM's ban on overtime, improved with the improvement in the economy and perhaps as a result of the mandate that the government received in the 1983 election. How the 1980 and 1982 Employment Acts influenced events we do not know, particularly whether they were more or less influential than heavy unemployment. Certainly the government had not yet had enough of trade union reform. In January and July 1983 came consultative papers on 'Democracy in Trade Unions' followed by a Trade Union bill which was enacted in July 1984, three months into the miners' strike. The provision having most bearing on the miners' strike was that which, in effect, gave unions immunity from legal action for organising industrial action conditional on the holding of secret ballots.[17]

CEGB 1979–1984

The last two years of the Labour government were a period of slow growth in the Board's business, although it continued to make operational profits. There was further plant commissioning, continuous improvement in thermal efficiency, a reduction in the number of power stations (although the average size increased), a reduction in the declared net capability of the stations, an increase in coal consumption even though coal (and oil) prices substantially increased. The number of staff fell.

The period between the election of the Conservative government in 1979 and the start of the miners' strike was one in which electricity supplied by the Board fell by 3 per cent. In the year to March 1981 the reduction was an unprecedented 4.1 per cent and it was not until 1983–4 that there was a substantial yearly increase of 3.4 per cent. System operation plans for the management of plant capacity led, over these 5 years, to the closure of over 10 000 MW of older, small generating units, 1000 MW of this plant being held in reserve. The fall in sales coupled with capacity increases from commissioning new plant had resulted in over capacity. The new plant programme had been agreed with the government and was consistent with their adopted economic growth assumptions – it did not envisage a loss of sales from recession. The plant closure programme closed the uneconomic surplus capacity and brought plant margins back to normal. Over 8000 jobs were lost through this process. The closure of uneconomic surplus capacity was accepted by the trade unions in the industry. It contrasted with the attitude of the NUM.

In this same five-year period the number of power stations fell from 131 to 90 and the net effect of the closures and new plant commissioning was that the generating capacity fell by 9 per cent. The change of plant mix resulted in an improved thermal efficiency. Coal consumed increased by 2.3 per cent, but with the heavy fall in (costly) oil consumption the total coal and coal equivalent consumed was down by about 8 per cent. There was an 18 per cent fall in the number of employees, including a 20.6 per cent fall in the number of industrial staff.[18]

The Labour government, in its last two years, had attempted to exercise greater control over public sector industries by introducing financial targets and cash limits, the latter becoming known as external financing limits (EFLs). The Conservative government, with its monetarist commitment, modified and intensified the use of these measures, which were a useful stimulus to the efficiency of the industry. The same measures were applied in coal and undoubtedly added to the pressure on the Coal Board to close uneconomic pits.[19]

Other developments in the Board during this period had a bearing on events in coal. Some directly or indirectly helped that industry. Thus in 1979–80 the Board decided to extend the lives of its most efficient coal-fired stations to forty years. More immediately, excellent progress was being made in building three 660 MW units to complete Drax, the biggest coal-fired power station in Europe. In the same year the CEGB and NCB reached an understanding under which the CEGB would 'use its best endeavours' to take up to 75 000 000 tonnes of coal a year from NCB, provided that the price did not exceed inflation. A further joint understanding, operating from November 1983, provided for a reduction in real terms in the price of coal over a four-year period, at the same time giving NCB a guaranteed market for a large part of its output.

There were, however, other developments, which could not have pleased the NUM. Thus following investigations of the Board's nuclear strategy the Secretary of State, David Howell, in 1979–80 gave his consent to the construction of a pressurised water reactor (PWR) at Sizewell, subject to support from a court of inquiry. The main plant was also ordered for a new gas-cooled reactor (AGR) at Heysham. The Board committed itself to increase the share of nuclear in its plant capacity. In July 1980 the government gave final investment approval for the Board's share of the 2000 MW cross-Channel power link with France. In early 1984 the first units were commissioned at the Dinorwig pumped storage scheme, which facilitated large economies in burning coal. The last of 3 660 MW oil-fired units at Littlebrook power station was commissioned in February 1984 by which time 3 out of 4 660 MW oil-fired units were operating at the Isle of Grain Power Station. Figures 8.1 and 8.2 (pp. 93 and 94) show the location of the power stations and the layout of the transmission network in March 1984.

In 1983–4 the Board increased its research into the causes of acid rain and committed itself to take action if it was demonstrated that power station emissions were causing damage to the environment. The Board also increased its commitment to explore the economic possibilities of renewable energy sources such as wind, tidal, hydro, wave and geothermal. In November 1982 it formally commissioned its first wind turbine at Carmarthen Bay. This was broadly the political, economic, industrial relations and CEGB background against which decisive events in coal were taking place.

Figure 8.1 Location of power stations 1984–5

Source: CEGB

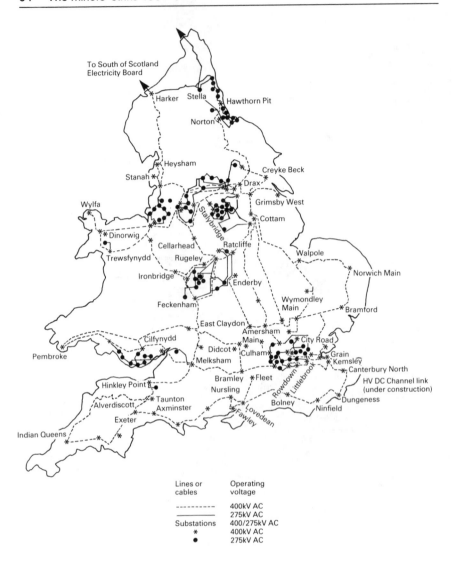

Figure 8.2 Transmission network 1984–5

Source: CEGB

Chapter 9

Preparations for the inevitable?

The general political, economic and industrial relations background to the 1984–5 miners' strike given in Chapter 8 included little or nothing that was new. However, there has been almost no public documentation concerning the role of the electricity supply industry in that strike and, in particular, its preparations for what was regarded as an almost inevitable challenge to its job of keeping the lights on. These preparations started well before 1984.

THE NEW-STYLE GOVERNMENT

We have seen that during Margaret Thatcher's period as Prime Minister from 1979 she and her colleagues put through three major acts of Parliament to curb the power and influence of trade unions and to curtail the immunity of pickets. The Employment Act of 1980 banned secondary picketing and left trade unions more vulnerable to legal action by those disadvantaged. There was an unanswered question in the minds of those who were involved with contingency planning in the CEGB and who had experienced the effects of the secondary picketing described in Chapter 5. Would any trade unions or their members, in pursuit of an industrial dispute, be influenced by the law or would they attempt and even succeed in operating outside the law? The assumption we made was that the National Union of Mineworkers and their members could be successful in defying the law and that it was wise to assume that secondary picketing would continue to be an important and potentially successful tactic if there was to be a future NUM strike. The important question in the early 1980s was how likely was another national coal strike.

Humiliation[1]

Derek Ezra, Chairman of the NCB, and Joe Gormley, President of the NUM, who had both been prominent in the events of the 1970s and the early 1980s, were approaching retirement. They were nevertheless to play an important role in some of the events that led to the strike. In 1981 David Howell, Secretary of State for Energy, looked to the NCB to implement the 1980 Coal Industry Act, which required the NCB to break even by 1984–5 without any subsidy. This implied a significant pit closure programme and it was apparent that there would be a strong reaction in the coalfields. The 66 000 miners in Yorkshire had already voted overwhelmingly to give Arthur Scargill, their President, and his executive freedom to call a strike or other industrial action if a policy of pit closures was implemented.[2] At a meeting between the NCB and the NUM on 10 February 1981 Derek Ezra outlined the proposed NCB response to the government's requirement. In answer to a question he predicted that between twenty and fifty pits would have to close over the next five years. There was a strong NUM reaction to this statement and Joe Gormley later told the press that he was seeking discussions with the government and that 'if they won't help we will ballot the lads and ask if they'll support us in national strike action'.[3] This was a clear ultimatum to the government that, unless financial support was given to avoid the expected closures, the industry would be shut down by a ballot-backed strike. Two interesting statements by Arthur Scargill were reported in *The Times*[4] during these events. One was that 'Mrs Thatcher has been out to get the miners since 1972 and 1974. If she throws down the gauntlet I can assure her of one thing. We will pick it up'. The other was that a strike could 'bring about conditions for an early election and get rid of this Tory government once and for all'. Within a few days the Durham, Yorkshire and South Wales coalfields were on strike. The country's strategic industries including electricity supply were not well prepared to withstand such a strike. The government had little option but to back down and were seen to have suffered a defeat.

It is regrettable that the understanding reached in February 1981 between the NUM, the NCB and the government, which led to the threat of a strike being removed, included not only a withdrawal of the pit closure programme and more compensation for miners retiring early but also that the CEGB's coal imports were to be constrained to what was described as 'the minimum level'. It was difficult to find a logical reason for defining any level as the minimum. However, the CEGB agreed with the government that this should be taken as 750 000 tonnes a year – the level of imports that had been received up to that time in the calendar year 1981. This was later to be a disadvantage when the extra coal from imports would have helped in building up coal stocks in preparation for the NUM industrial action and in maintaining stocks during the overtime ban that preceded the strike. In addition, following the decision, contracted import cargoes had to be sold at a loss. The CEGB were to receive compensation of £18 million to cover the extra costs resulting from that government decision.

Reference is made to these events in the books by Margaret Thatcher and Nigel Lawson.[5] Margaret Thatcher says that she was appalled that the government had entered into a battle that they could not win. She believed that the Department of Energy had not considered what would happen if there were to be a strike. Although there were substantial stocks at the pit heads the power station stocks were insufficient and they were the relevant ones in withstanding a miners' strike. She resolved to ensure that the government would not be put in such a situation again – power station coal stocks would have to be increased. Nigel Lawson said of Margaret Thatcher 'at the forefront of her mind was the half truth, that it was the miners who had brought down the last Conservative government in 1974; and the débâcle of the previous February had scarred her quite badly. It was indeed a humiliating episode'.

Joe Gormley delayed his retirement. It has been assumed that this was to ensure that Mick McGahey was not eligible as his successor on age grounds. In December 1981 Arthur Scargill was elected President of the NUM and in April 1982 took office. In the meantime, in September 1981, Nigel Lawson had become Secretary of State for Energy. There continued to be a need to contract the coal industry. Coupled with the obvious militancy of the new NUM President and his executive, this made a strike at some stage seem very likely.

Contingency planning

Following the events of early 1981 and before the election of Arthur Scargill, the government, through the Department of Energy, had started discussions with the coal, rail and electricity industries on preparations to withstand a coal strike. The contingency planning and the other preparations were to continue for several years under the close monitoring, co-ordination and prompting of the Department of Energy.[6] The plans remained however the responsibility of the individual industries. Gil Blackman, then the CEGB Member for Production, led for the Board. The meetings were chaired by Ivor Manley, a Deputy Secretary at the Department of Energy, who was to have the main co-ordinating role for government until the end of the strike.

This contingency planning was a usual part of the relationship between a sponsoring department and a nationalised industry. It was the duty of the government and the industries concerned to do what was possible to protect the public against threats to essential supplies and services. The difference on this occasion was that the scale of the preparations necessarily had to be large. The last two national coal strikes, in 1971–2 and 1973–4, had led to extensive interruptions of electricity supply.

Contingency planning on matters associated with electricity supply has a long history and a special significance. Since electricity cannot be stored and society is so dependent on it, failure to meet demand can result in the loss of many of the essentials of everyday life such as water supply, sewage services, refrigeration (and therefore many foods), heating and lighting. If failure results from a lack of fuel the transition from full electricity supplies to a very low level can occur over a relatively short time as fuel stocks run out. It can take several days to recover when fuel deliveries are restored. That period could produce calamitous conditions in the country. Such conditions were only narrowly avoided in 1972.

It was the clear responsibility of the government and the electricity supply industry to be able to deal with such a threat and to reduce the risk to society of such an emergency. Any other attitude would have been grossly irresponsible.

Given the vulnerability of electricity supply, there was a resentment among some in senior positions in the CEGB that the NUM had used this factor in earlier coal strikes. This resentment seemed to be shared by the electricity supply industry's own trade unions who had rarely used their strength to serve their own ends.

The vulnerability of electricity supply was well understood by many in the industry. An internal comment was that the majority of candles held by the public, in case the lights went out, were in the homes of electricity supply workers!

CEGB PLANNING AND PREPARATIONS

At this time the CEGB were developing contingency plans which included the operating strategy to be applied in the event of a strike. The responsibility for this was with the Operations Department under its Director, Frank Ledger, and his team of Ed Wallis, the System Operations Engineer, John Wooley, the Fuel Supplies Officer, and Granville Camsey, the Operations Services Engineer. Their plans guided the preparations for the strike and enabled the Board and the Department of Energy to understand how long electricity supplies could be maintained with the projected levels of coal stocks and oil-fired generation.

CEGB coal stocks

The level of CEGB coal stocks up to 1981 had been largely determined by the seasonal pattern of high winter and lower summer coal consumption and the need to give a reasonably uniform work load to the NCB and British Rail. There had been typically a high coal stock in the autumn and a low one in the spring. The CEGB had a policy that fuel stocks should be more than a nominal sixty days of consumption at all times.[7] That policy, coupled with the annual variation of electricity demand, resulted in what was viewed as an annual cycle of commercial coal stock with a maximum of 17 000 000 tonnes at the end of October and 11 000 000 tonnes at the end of March. In practice, there were few years that followed this planned profile. It was normal for industrial action of some kind in the associated industries to occur in a typical year and it was not unusual for other events to disrupt the plan. The result was that the difference between maximum and minimum coal stock was usually less than the plan; hence security from the coal stock was normally less in the winter than in summer. It was obvious that securing electricity supplies over a future miners' strike of unknown length required much higher coal stocks than normal.

The Board of the CEGB did not unreservedly accept the need for high coal stocks. The problem for the CEGB was in deciding what level of coal stocks was appropriate to satisfy the responsibility described in the Electricity Act 1957 for a continuous and efficient system of electricity supply. The legal responsibility of the Board was seen as determined by that. There was a strong feeling within the Board that, although it clearly had a duty to 'keep the lights on', it also had an obligation to the electricity consumer to supply the area boards at minimum cost through the Bulk Supply Tariff. A high level of working capital in coal stocks was not seen as being consistent with that objective. If support could be made available to reduce the financial burden there would be no problem.

This was not entirely a real issue because of the continuing over-production of coal by the NCB, which resulted from the failure to implement the pit closure programme. Even without the needs of contingency planning it would have been necessary to stock this surplus coal somewhere. Why not stock some of it at the power stations where it would ultimately be consumed? A scheme was therefore devised which enabled much higher coal stocks to be carried at power stations, with compensation to the CEGB for the extra costs of the accelerated delivery programme and for payment to the NCB for the excess coal to be deferred until it became part of the commercial stock. This deferred payment scheme had been a feature of the past commercial arrangements with the NCB during periods of over-production. Additional coal handling was necessary to implement the plan and the CEGB were also compensated for this. Having agreed to the strategy, which met both commercial and contingency planning requirements, it was a short step to start other preparations for a future coal strike.

The strike seemed even more likely as time passed since coal over-production continued and the public statements of the NUM leadership made it obvious that the necessary closure programme was not acceptable to them. It is ironic that the NUM's success in prevailing on the government to keep pits open in 1981 made it inevitable that any future NUM industrial action would be disadvantaged by the high coal stockpiles that the continuing over-production made necessary.

Politics or maintaining supplies?

Although the solution to the financial problems enabled the CEGB to prepare for a future miners' strike within its interpretation of its legal responsibilities, there remained some anxiety. The question that worried some of the Board's managers was whether the preparations to withstand a miners' strike were in fact a plan to defeat the miners and as such a political act or were they justified by the Board's duty to maintain security of supply? The continuing public statements of the NUM leadership and their several attempts to gain a majority of their national membership in favour of strike action helped to clarify matters and to emphasise the importance of protecting electricity supplies. When the strike actually occurred the correctness of adopting the policy of 'keeping the lights on' had few critics either within or outside the industry and became a strong central theme with which the vast majority of CEGB employees readily identified. After all this is what those in the industry had been doing throughout the history of electricity supply in the face of blizzards, severe gales and many other emergencies. It was their normal way of thinking – continuity of supply came above all else.

There was a possible exception and that was where CEGB employees were living in communities with some of the most militant of the miners. South Yorkshire was the most important example.

Essential supplies

In the 1971–2 coal miners' strike, as described in Chapter 5, picketing had been so effective that many power stations were literally under siege. In some cases even vegetables and milk for the canteens were not getting through. In addition, and far more importantly, other commodities essential for operation and maintenance of the power stations were not being delivered. These were the lighting-up oil necessary to maintain combustion stability in coal-fired boilers, diesel oil for transport and mobile coal-handling machinery, carbon dioxide for nuclear reactor coolant systems, hydrogen for generator cooling, and other chemicals for the treatment of water before use in boilers, and other essential industrial gases and supplies. Unless the high coal stocks were supported by sufficient stocks of these materials, the coal stocks were potentially of little or no value since a power station could just as readily be shut down for lack of other essential commodities as for lack of coal.

After the experience of the NUM strikes in the 1970s, CEGB policy had been to increase stocks of these essential commodities to equal six weeks of normal consumption. The decision was now taken substantially to increase this amount. There was no problem in principle in accepting the need for this. The materials were not fuel and the supply of them could not be seen as legitimate targets for pickets supporting a dispute in the coal industry. There had been a feeling of concern among many in the industry that these supplies had been stopped in the earlier strikes and that electricity supply consumers had been selected as the means to resolve a dispute in another industry.

The expenditure on the means of stocking additional essential commodities and the additional supplies themselves was ultimately sanctioned by the full Board (much to the relief of Gil Blackman who, up to that time, had been spending significant sums of money without the formal support of the full CEGB Board, albeit that the individual schemes were within his formal delegated level of authority). The policy then became one of holding essential materials in sufficient quantities to equal the endurance of the coal stocks, which were then planned to allow electricity demand to be met in full for twenty weeks. This programme involved the construction of additional storage facilities on almost every power station at a capital sum of £35 million and up to £43 million of working capital for the additional stored material.

The additional storage facilities necessary for carbon dioxide at nuclear power stations were a difficulty. It was the coolant for the gas-cooled reactors and was required in large quantities. The storage facilities required to equal the siege endurance capacity for other essential commodities were physically large and prohibitively expensive. In addition there were complications with the nuclear site licence conditions. It was decided to do some enlargement of facilities but to remain largely dependent on deliveries. Discussions were held with ICI, the supplier, so that they understood the importance of the deliveries in the event of a strike.

These initiatives were vigorously developed by the CEGB regions and co-ordinated by Granville Camsey, leading the Operations Services Branch at CEGB Headquarters. They were part of a strategy providing (i) that suppliers should do their best to deliver; (ii) that, where possible, there were alternative sources of supply; (iii) that adequate additional storage was in place, and (iv) that there were fall-back arrangements if needed. These additional arrangements included the planned use of helicopters to overfly the pickets as well as the use of road oil tankers in CEGB livery to get lighting-up oil through the pickets in the event of the suppliers being unable to deliver. These preparations are described in Chapter 19.

Building up stocks

From early 1981, when government and CEGB contingency planning began, to the start of the NUM overtime ban in November 1983, the CEGB's endurance capability was being built up against a background of industrial strife. There were not only threats from the NUM. British Rail were having difficulties with the rail unions and the CEGB were likely to feel the consequences.

There was a strike in the water industry in February 1983 that was potentially serious. Several power stations had difficulties either from shortage of water or reductions in its quality. However the dispute was resolved and did not affect preparations for a possible coal strike. It was worrying, however, and led the CEGB to strengthen its water supplies. Many power stations developed their own boreholes and thus became independent of the public water supply arrangements, a step which in some cases was also cost-saving when compared with water supply prices.

In the contingency planning discussions the build-up of fuel stocks and of the CEGB's ability to withstand an NUM strike was described as improving 'endurance'. This was a word and a concept that was to become important in the coming months and years. The endurance of the CEGB was the length of time that electricity demand could be met in full without coal supplies. The challenge was to develop means by which it could be improved. In particular the ability to switch from coal burn to oil burn was seen to have greater potential than had earlier been thought. Yet this required a considerable oil supply programme, involving an increase from 30 000 to 350 000 tonnes a week to be arranged by the CEGB over a relatively short period when the strike eventually occurred. Preparations were made for this by each of the major oil companies being told the quantity of oil that would be required and the time scales for building up consumption and purchase. Although the oil companies were expected to behave fully commercially and in their own interests, it was seen by us as helpful for them to be able to anticipate what was to happen and to be prepared to change their crude flows and refinery programmes at short notice to meet the changed market requirements. The oil companies advised the Board that oil availability and prices could present serious problems. A judgement had to be made on whether it was necessary for the government to seek powers to direct oil supply when the strike occurred, or to release some of the national strategic oil stocks. The government were disinclined to take such actions; they believed that the oil industry would respond adequately to the changed market. We remained apprehensive about the feasibility of setting up the required oil flow in the time available.

The coal stock build-up required a much higher rate of coal deliveries than was normal and it was to be strongly influenced by British Rail's ability to transport the high tonnages required. The rail transport programme was monitored closely, as was the tonnage of coal made available by the NCB. The original target agreed with the Department of Energy in February 1982 was 24 000 000 tonnes in stock at power stations as quickly as possible and at the latest by the end of October 1982. This was expected to be the maximum capacity of the stockyards. As stocks built up it was obvious that more could be accommodated and the target became 26 000 000 tonnes. In the event that target was achieved and of that figure almost 3 000 000 tonnes were under the special terms agreed between the CEGB, government and the NCB. The higher level of coal deliveries was continued through the winter period and the following summer so that, by November 1983, 30 800 000 tonnes were in stock, of which over 6 000 000 tonnes were subject to the special commercial terms. (This is described in more detail in Chapter 16.) This required unprecedented stocks at the individual stations and it was a tribute to their coal plant staff that they were able to accommodate the coal safely and in a manner that enabled efficient handling.

Industrial action on the railways

During the period of stock build-up several strike threats were made by the rail trade unions. For each threat, contingency plans were made to minimise their effect on the preparations. Many of the threats did not materialise. However, two periods of industrial action by the railway unions did occur in 1982 and the CEGB was driven to protect its coal stocks by burning additional oil, starting from 10 February and tapering off by 3 April. It was understood that there would be compensation from the government to cover this action but that was only forthcoming for part of the oil burn and this had an adverse effect for a time on relations between the government and the CEGB.

Preparations intensify

Not long after these events, in May 1982, Glyn England retired as CEGB Chairman and after an interval was succeeded by Sir Walter Marshall. He was briefed by Fred Bonner, Deputy Chairman, and Gil Blackman on the preparations being made and he supported them. He was keen to ensure good relations with government and that the preparations to withstand the strike were co-ordinated with them. At an early Board meeting under his chairmanship he declared his strong belief that it was the duty of the CEGB to keep the lights on if there were to be a miners' strike and got the full support of the Board for this policy. This was the meeting that also endorsed Gil Blackman's expenditure on increased essential commodity storage referred to earlier.

During 1982 and 1983 many in the CEGB were involved in implementing the plan to increase the capacity for essential commodities storage. This gave profitable work constructing tanks and pressure vessels to a number of small companies. Helicopter pilots were being trained to handle heavy loads, proving trial lifts being carried out at a remote airfield and the air traffic control arrangements being made for journeys from loading points to the power stations. Road tankers were being acquired and painted in the CEGB livery and CEGB drivers were being qualified as HGV licensed drivers to enable them to drive in supplies wherever there was an urgent need to get them through the picket lines when supplies by the normal contractors had failed.

An interesting event took place during these preparations. Lawrence Daly, who was then the General Secretary of the NUM, wrote to the CEGB making enquiries on the quantities and route details for coal transport from the pits to the power stations. It was a clear indication that the NUM were planning their picketing campaign for the forthcoming strike. It is difficult to believe that the NUM believed the CEGB to be so naive as to answer such a question. In the event a polite non-answer was sent back to Mr Daly and nothing more was heard of the enquiry.

The culmination of all these preparations was that by October 1983, the eve of the NUM's overtime ban, the CEGB were in a strong position. Coal stock, oil burn, acquisition plans and an essential commodities supply strategy were all arranged to give the CEGB the best possible chance of keeping the lights on.

Margaret Thatcher in the section of her book dedicated to 'Mr Scargill's Insurrection' describes Nigel Lawson's role during this preparatory period as 'to build up – steadily and unprovocatively – the stocks of coal which would allow the country to endure a coal strike'.[8]

Chapter 10

Overtime ban

By the autumn of 1983 good progress had been made in building up coal stocks and in making other preparations to deal with the threat of a miners' strike. There were grounds for expecting that a strike could have started before then and although there had been two NUM ballots in the preceding twelve months, in addition to one before Arthur Scargill took over as President, the recommendation to strike had been rejected on each occasion.[1] In October 1983 tensions between the NCB and the NUM were increasing over pit closures and it continued to seem likely that there would be a coal strike.

On Thursday 23 June 1983, two weeks before the NUM annual conference, the Monopolies and Mergers Commission, who had been studying the coal industry, issued their report.[2] It confirmed the NCB's view that the surplus production from high cost, low productivity pits was a crucial problem which was preventing the coal industry becoming viable. On the same day the NUM executive met and decided on a campaign against closures.[3]

THE ANNUAL PAY NEGOTIATION

At the NUM's 1983 annual conference in Perth delegates had been concerned with the two main issues of jobs and pay. They voted unanimously on 6 July to authorise the national executive to ballot the membership, 'at a time deemed to be most appropriate', if the NCB continued a programme of closures and manpower reductions. The conference also called for a claim to be submitted to the NCB for a 'substantial' pay increase at the coming annual pay negotiation.[4]

Nigel Lawson, as Secretary of State for Energy, had announced the appointment of Ian MacGregor as the Chairman of the NCB back in March 1983. He had been the Chairman of British Steel since 1980 and over that time the manpower level had been almost halved. His appointment was seen by the unions generally as highly provocative and almost a declaration of war. MacGregor did not take up his appointment until 1 September, just before the annual pay negotiation was about to start.

At a meeting with the NUM, on 30 September, to discuss the annual pay round, the NCB gave their answer to the union's claim. They made what Ian

MacGregor described as 'the first and final offer' of a 5.2 per cent increase on national grade rates. At that time it was not an unreasonable offer. The government had placed an upper limit of 5 per cent on public sector awards. Scargill described the offer ranging from £2.80 to £3.00 a week in take-home pay as an insult. The NUM called a special delegate conference for 21 October, which decided unanimously:

> to reject the NCB's proposals on wages as being totally unsatisfactory; to instruct the NUM executive to continue negotiations to secure an improved offer; to re-affirm the union's opposition to all pit closures other than on grounds of exhaustion, and to fight any further reductions in manpower levels; to resist the NCB/government plans to close 70 pits over the coming five year period, and to impose a full overtime ban from October 31.[5]

OVERTIME BAN

So at least for the time being it was to be the effects of an overtime ban that the CEGB had to deal with, not the full strike that the contingency planning had focused on. The two NUM strikes in the early 1970s had been preceded by overtime bans (see Chapters 5 and 6). On each of those occasions station coal stocks had been depleted with the result that, when the strikes occurred, there had been a much more serious challenge to electricity supplies. Is that what the NUM were planning this time? We had to assume that it was.

The CEGB had to do what could be done to preserve endurance capability through this difficult time. An overtime ban is the kind of measure that puts matters into the hands of the trade union's members. Although rules and advice may be formulated by the trade union leadership, the degree of enthusiasm with which they are applied by the members determines their effectiveness. It was unlikely that the volume of coal that would be available to the CEGB would be known until there was experience of the ban operating. There could be a disproportionate effect. Overtime was required in the pits to enable vital maintenance work to be performed in preparation for production shifts. Its absence could lead to production not being possible for much of the normal working time available.

When the ban started the CEGB watched events in the coal industry closely. There were reports that showed that production losses were not only likely to come from the direct effects but also from internal tensions between mining unions. These internal tensions were intended by the coal unions to have been dealt with by an understanding reached at a joint meeting of the NUM, the National Association of Colliery Overmen, Deputies and Shotfirers (NACODS) and the British Association of Colliery Managers (BACM), but as the industrial action continued there were strong discordant voices. Extreme difficulties were experienced in the relations between the NUM and the two supervisory and management unions who were seen by NUM members as adopting belligerent attitudes. This was not surprising, bearing in mind the problems they were facing in dealing with the disruptive effects of the action. The problems were to increase as the ban continued.

The effect on the weekly deliveries to the CEGB in the period up to the Christmas break was not large. However, because the effect was persistent it was having a worrying cumulative effect. There was an average shortfall of 85 000 tonnes a week – about 6 per cent of the programmed quantity. To help compensate for that, about 13 000 tonnes extra were being taken from non-NCB sources. Since there was still a commitment to restrict imports, it was not seen as possible to make good the loss with an import programme. The constraint on imports had been viewed by the NUM as an important part of the 1981 tripartite agreement and to have broken that commitment would have been extremely provocative. Since it had to be assumed that there was still a chance of a settlement in the coal industry imports on a large scale were judged by the CEGB to be unwise.

The CEGB were in danger of losing much of the advantage that had been gained over the last two years and there was little that could be done about it. The Board decided on one helpful measure, which would marginally infringe the import restriction over the holiday period. There would be no NCB deliveries for between one and two weeks and, with the effects of the overtime ban, only a slow build-up after that. It was decided to import 200 000 tonnes of coal from the Board's continental stocks[6] to Thames-side power stations, even though that would take our imports over the 750 000 tonnes import limit. There would be some advantage to the stations that were able to receive them.

The stocks on 1 January were recorded as 28 000 000 tonnes. We had hoped, before the ban, that it would be possible to maintain the stock level at close to the end of October peak of 30 800 000 tonnes. We had lost ground and the high electricity consumption over the remainder of the winter period was still ahead of us. We were unsure about what the effects of the overtime ban would be in the New Year.

The effects of the overtime ban increase

After the holiday period the shortfall in coal supplies was becoming more marked, with an increasing number of men being laid off in the coal industry because of the effect of the overtime ban. In January 19 000 men were sent home on one single day and there were approaching that number on other days.[7] The weekly tonnage lost due to the dispute almost doubled between the beginning of the overtime ban and February 1984 and deep-mined production for the three months ending February was 25.6 per cent lower than in the previous year.[8]

The continuation of the ban was causing a worrying fall in coal stocks. Through its contingency planning the CEGB was clear about how it should deal with a coal strike; it was less obvious how it should respond to a prolonged overtime ban. The 'phoney war' period was sapping the Board's endurance capability without presenting it with a sufficiently deep emergency to justify starting the expensive oil burn necessary to conserve coal stocks. At that time the heavy fuel oil used in power station boilers, at US$180 a tonne, was nearly twice the heat cost of coal. The decision to burn fuel at this high cost could not easily be justified.

The NUM were monitoring with satisfaction the effects of the national overtime ban and on 10 January reported to their National Executive Committee that over the first 10 weeks of the action over 4 000 000 tonnes of production had been lost. They also estimated the loss of revenue to the NCB at £200 million. There had been problems from loss of overtime earnings but the support for the industrial action was solid.

As early as January the National Union of Railwaymen (NUR) were pledging their full support in preventing the import of coal and sought a meeting with the NUM on the means by which the fullest co-operation could be achieved. This was a sign of things to come. During the overtime ban Lawrence Daly, the General Secretary of the NUM, retired and there was an election for his successor. The results announced on 24 January showed that Peter Heathfield, the Derbyshire Area Secretary, was successful but with a small majority.[9] He defeated John Walsh, NUM agent in North Yorkshire, who had been campaigning on a policy far less strike-oriented than his opponent. Heathfield was seen as a strong supporter of the present industrial action. The message to the CEGB was clear: we should expect the NUM policy to remain unchanged.

Will there be a strike?

The CEGB continued to believe that the overtime ban was the forerunner of a strike. There seemed little prospect of the two sides of the coal industry finding common ground on pit closures. Arthur Scargill and the NUM were insisting that a pit should never be closed on economic grounds but only on the grounds that its reserves were becoming exhausted. Yet the NCB had significant excess production capacity. Something had to be done. In addition the media presentation of the ideological and personality clashes between Ian MacGregor and Arthur Scargill clearly suggested dispute rather than agreement.

The CEGB continued to watch closely the effect of the overtime ban on its endurance capability. From the end of January it became necessary to relax the coal quality standards to improve coal flow. It was necessary to take whatever coal was available from the NCB, provided its quality approximated to the required standard. Much of it would have been rejected in normal circumstances. The Board was not going to allow its endurance to be weakened when a strike was so likely.

Weakening endurance

The effect of the depleting coal stock was being monitored with care. This involved the use of a computer modelling method normally used for estimating future fuel requirements and for simulating the future economic operation of the power system. The suite of computer programs had been modified to enable them to be used to predict endurance. This was an important feature of future management of the emergency. More is said on this subject in later chapters. However that modelling during February 1984 was showing that the Board's endurance potential was becoming seriously weakened. Even more seriously it showed that, if the present trend was allowed to continue and a strike occurred in the autumn, it would not be possible to meet electricity demand through the following winter. It became necessary to warn the government that CEGB coal stocks had fallen significantly and that, if the overtime ban and the reduction in deliveries were to continue, stocks would fall to 14 000 000 tonnes by the end of October and endurance would then be only 12 weeks in a strike.

The future security of electricity supply could only be ensured if either there was an end to the overtime ban or there was a strike that the Board could ride through. The prospects of the former were so slim that they could be disregarded. To be able to ride through a strike it was necessary for it to start in the near future, while our endurance was still reasonably high.

The NCB were preparing their plans for the coming year, seeing increasing evidence of the NUM preparing for a strike.[10] One sign to the senior line managers and experienced industrial relations officers was that the number of disputes and walk-outs was increasing. The tension in the coalfields was building up or, as many of them thought, being fermented by activists.

James Cowan, the Deputy Chairman of the NCB, was deeply concerned at the likely consequences of a strike for the coal industry. He met Mick McGahey in December and suggested to him that there were other, less damaging, ways of dealing with the differences between the NUM and the NCB. The discussion did nothing to remove Cowan's concern that a well-organised strike was inevitable.

At this time the NUM leadership's proposed strategy for a national strike was described as the 'domino theory'.[11] This was a method of causing a national strike by starting with a lesser strike, probably in a limited number of areas. Those on strike would then picket the working pits, bringing them out on strike, since as good trade unionists they would not cross picket lines. Thus through this domino effect all pits would eventually stop work and the strike would have become national. This had been openly discussed and the rationalisation from Arthur Scargill had been that 'you cannot vote on other men's jobs'. Such an approach did not need a national ballot and could be implemented quickly.

The theory seems to have been given strength and credibility by a belief that if a national strike was achieved and was supported by the Triple Alliance unions in transport and steel, then the government would quickly give in. There would then follow tripartite discussions as in 1981 and the NUM would get what it wanted. The NCB were preparing their plans for 1984–5 with the various indications of coming industrial action as the background and with a clear understanding of the need to reduce over-capacity. The area directors had been asked to develop their business plans and had been given production capacity reduction and budget targets. These were discussed with the Chairman and Deputy Chairman together with the likely extent of each area's support if there were to be a strike.

The NCB saw no advantage in avoiding facing the problem of pit closures and dealing with it. The policy of the NUM was clear: they would not accept pit closures on economic grounds, but only on grounds of exhaustion. In March the NCB were due to present their budget for 1984–5 to the coal industry consultative council, of which the NUM was a member. They knew what the reaction to the closures would be.

In making an assessment of the risks from their intended course of action the NCB were influenced by one important factor. They had strong reasons for believing that there would not be a full strike. James Cowan had held discussions with many in the NCB areas. As a consequence he had formed the view that the coming strike could be contained and that Nottinghamshire and parts of the Midlands would not come out on strike. He advised the National Coal Board that their contingency planning should be based on the assumption of a partial strike and on the containment of the strike in certain areas and districts. He believed that the coal production that could be expected from the miners remaining at work would greatly reduce the problems of a strike to their consumers and that the risk to their supplies should not prevent the NCB from following their intended course of action. In addition, if a strike were to follow the March announcement, they had the whole of the summer period of lower coal consumption to deal with the situation. If the decision was to be put off, it could be more serious. MacGregor said: 'if the country were to face a prolonged coal strike starting in March, the impact on our consumers would be less than if it were to start in October'. He also said that Peter Walker, Secretary of State for Energy, had expressed some anxieties about the continuation of the overtime ban. That was not surprising, bearing in mind the advice that he had received on the consequences to electricity supply from the ban continuing.[12]

DECISIVE EVENTS

The outcome of the NCB planning process was a closure programme that included Cortonwood pit in South Yorkshire as part of the overall 1984–5 budget. This was an economic closure in an area that was sure to react strongly to such an intention. In early March, when the NCB made known their plans at industry and area levels, there was the expected response – a strike, but only the partial one that they had predicted.

The rapidity with which the NUM leadership responded can be seen as evidence of premeditation. Within two days there was NUM executive approval of a resolution to make official any strike action that followed. Within six days Scotland and Yorkshire were on full strike. On the seventh day the domino effect from mass picketing had already resulted in 109 000 out of 183 000 miners being on strike despite many of them not having had a chance to ballot.

A more detailed account of some of these events appears in Chapter 11. They are referred to here to make two points which were important to the electricity supply position. One was that the NCB's judgement in deciding to go ahead with the closure programme from the beginning of 1984–5 was consistent with the electricity supply industry's needs and was ultimately vindicated. The other was that the NUM's response, and presumably their plan, had two features that were to have a big influence on the management of the electricity supply emergency. They were the timing of the start of the strike and the decision to go ahead without a national ballot, depending on the domino effect of picketing out pits to get a national strike. The timing was difficult to understand and no one has satisfactorily explained it. The only conclusion that seems credible is that the NUM leadership just could not countenance economic closure even if to do so was strategically wise. The timing had a big effect on our ability to sustain electricity supplies through the year-long strike, as did the lack of a ballot. The latter caused a split in the NUM, lost the sympathy and support of many trade unionists and made it easier for the CEGB to argue the merits of the steps necessary to keep the lights on.

The die was cast. The calculated risk that the NCB had taken and the NUM response set the form of the dispute and of the emergency that the CEGB had to manage. Events were about to move from the overtime ban and its problems to the strike emergency that the CEGB had developed its contingency plans to manage. As is frequently the way with emergencies this one was to be very different from what we had expected.

Chapter 11

Strike

It was almost a relief when the early March events led to what seemed to be the start of the miners' strike for which the CEGB had so long prepared. Even then it was not initially clear that there would be a sustained major strike. However, it was clear that the skirmishing was over.

PIT CLOSURES

The course of events started with the announcement by the NCB to local coal industry trade union officers on 1 March 1984 of the proposed accelerated closure of Cortonwood pit in South Yorkshire from April on economic grounds.[1] The manner of the announcement was not in accordance with the coal industry's established procedure but this was not as significant to the NUM as that the grounds for closure were stated to be economic. This was sufficiently provocative in the industrial relations climate of the South Yorkshire coalfield to precipitate a fast response from the NUM. In Scotland a similar situation had arisen over the proposed closure of Polmaise pit.

A further, and probably equally important, influence on the events that were to come was a meeting on 6 March of the Coal Industry National Consultative Council between the NCB and the unions at which the budget for the coming year was presented. The planned coal production in that budget implied an increased number of pit closures. The Board put forward a reasoned and, from their point of view, justified plan.[2] It was not surprising that, coupled with the strong local reaction to the Cortonwood closure, it gave a further opportunity for those who wished to do so to precipitate a strike. Within days a Yorkshire NUM area council meeting was called which voted for a total stoppage from 12 March. Since there was no overtime working, this was effectively from the last shift on Friday 9 March. Most Yorkshire pits followed that decision. The remainder were quickly pressurised to do so with some aggressive mass picketing. Scotland was following a parallel path. The Scottish NUM area executive on 6 March called for a strike from 9 March; the Scottish coalfield was on strike from that date.

HERE WE GO

The NUM National Executive Committee (NEC), on 8 March, approved by twenty-one votes to three a resolution declaring as official 'the proposed strike action in Yorkshire and Scotland and in any other area which takes similar action'.[3] By doing this the National Executive were effectively rejecting an alternative motion calling for a national ballot of all members on the question of closures.

So from 9 March the domino theory strike was due to start. With the winter behind it and with a coal stock of about 24 000 000 tonnes the CEGB thought that it was in a fairly strong position, although it was certainly not complacent. From 12 March flying pickets from Yorkshire were picketing out pits in other coalfields. The individual NUM areas were to have ballots in the days that followed. Of the 9 areas balloted only Northumberland had more than 50 per cent of the vote in favour of a strike. Despite that, by 15 March, because of the effectiveness of the mass flying pickets, work had stopped at nearly 140 of the NCB's 170 pits.

The domino theory was working but there were problems. According to David Prendergast, the reluctance of the Nottinghamshire miners to come out on strike in response to the early picketing of their pits had already led to some animosity at the NUM National Executive meeting on 8 March. This caused a Nottinghamshire NUM conference of branch officials and committee members on 10 March to discuss the harassment of their two NEC members outside the NUM Headquarters in Sheffield prior to the meeting and to express their contempt.

The 8 March NUM National Executive Committee had sanctioned a Nottinghamshire Area ballot to be held on 15–16 March. All NUM areas were advised not to send pickets into the Nottinghamshire Area prior to the ballot and to avoid picketing and intimidation on the day of the ballot. This request did not influence the mass pickets who now seemed to be out of control. On 14 March a picket from Yorkshire died, apparently from being crushed in the crowd of pickets and working miners, at Ollerton pit in Nottinghamshire.

The following morning Arthur Scargill appeared at the Nottinghamshire Area NUM offices at Berry Hill and demanded that the Nottinghamshire Area should come out on strike to avoid further violent confrontations. According to David Prendergast he was asked to leave in direct terms. A strong antipathy was growing between the working miners, mainly in Nottinghamshire, and the pickets who were applying extreme pressure and intimidation to bring them out on strike. It was not surprising that, when the result of the Nottinghamshire Area ballot was announced on Sunday 18 March, there was a large majority against a strike.[4]

Although some other areas had voted against a strike and had ultimately succumbed to the pressure from the Yorkshire pickets, a much deeper resolve was provoked among the miners in Nottinghamshire. The domino theory had precipitated a split that was to be of growing importance as the dispute continued.

Although Nottinghamshire became the focus of attention, pits were also continuing to work in Leicestershire, South Derbyshire, and in parts of Midlands and Western areas of the NCB. It is interesting to note that Mick McGahey[5] also judged the split in the NUM that resulted in Nottinghamshire continuing to work to be a direct reaction to tactics based on the domino theory.

On 19 March it was reported in *The Times* that the police were being mobilised from 20 of the 43 regional police forces and that 8000 policemen had been deployed since Thursday 15 March. It was said that the police would match the pickets man for man. In addition the National Reporting Centre was set up at New Scotland Yard to enable the national police requirements and resources to be co-ordinated to serve the needs of the individual chief constables. From this time the police were to play a very important role, markedly different from that in the miners' strike in the 1970s. The law had of course changed on secondary picketing and the police were to give strong support to the maintenance of the flow of materials to power stations through the pickets. More is said about this in Chapter 22.

Arthur Scargill made an interesting pronouncement on power station coal stocks at this time.[6] He said that stocks had been severely affected by the long overtime ban by the miners. He estimated that power station stocks had been reduced from 34 000 000 tonnes to 22 500 000 tonnes. The NCB issued a correcting statement saying that they had in fact fallen from 33 to 28 000 000 tonnes.[7] The NCB added that the overtime ban had had a minimal effect on pithead stocks; they had fallen from 24 500 000 to 22 000 000 tonnes. These NCB figures were close to those ultimately published in the Department of Energy's Energy Trends statistical bulletin.

A further coal stocks report in March was made to the NUM National Executive Committee by its Emergency Committee. It said that, since the commencement of the national overtime ban, over 9 000 000 tonnes of production had been lost with approximately 3 000 000 to 4 000 000 tonnes lost a week during the last month. Stocks of coal had been depleted at both the NCB and the CEGB to about the same figure as in 1972. Since the CEGB stock figure was 12 300 000 tonnes at the beginning of the 1972 strike (see Chapter 5) and 23 900 000 tonnes at the start of the strike in 1984 this report was wildly inaccurate.

The CEGB was watching these events with some anxiety. It was important to judge the extent of the strike and the probable duration not only to decide how best to use the limited coal available but, far more importantly, to decide when the more costly measures to conserve coal stocks should be started. The longer those decisions were delayed the more vulnerable would those power stations be that might not receive further coal supplies.

WHEN SHALL WE START THE OIL BURN?

By far the most important decision was whether to start the build-up of the major oil-fired generation programme necessary to conserve coal stocks. It was difficult to be sure whether the dispute had become sufficiently serious to justify the expensive oil burn planned as the CEGB's response to a full strike. The CEGB were inclined to believe that for the strike to endure it had to be 'solid'. Doubts on the legitimacy of the strike, many areas voting not to strike, and the strong resistance of some pits to being picketed out, caused the achievement of a 'solid' strike to be open to question. Eventually what the ultimate pattern of the dispute was to be and how long it would last began to seem less important than the growing urgency to start the remedial measures to protect the longer term prospects for electricity supply.

A courageous decision was needed to start increasing oil burn and on 26 March the Chairman, Sir Walter Marshall, made it, with the support of his executive director colleagues and later the full Board. It was a difficult decision. He felt personally at risk since he believed that if the strike collapsed after a short time everyone would then rationalise why a short strike was inevitable. It would therefore be difficult to justify in retrospect the high cost of burning oil. The same day he told Sir Philip Jones, Chairman of the Electricity Council, and the Secretary of State, Peter Walker.

The urgency of the decision made it impracticable to consult formally with the Electricity Council and the area boards. The Prime Minister, Margaret Thatcher, was told almost immediately. No disagreement with the decision or advice to the contrary was communicated to Sir Walter Marshall and that was interpreted as endorsement of the action. Margaret Thatcher in her memoirs *The Downing Street Years*,[8] states that she made the decision to start oil burn. She actually did so by deciding not to intervene.

The increased oil burn started on 28 March increasing over 25 per cent weekly steps to the full potential. This enabled the logistics of the massive oil supply programme to be built up over a number of weeks and enabled each stage to be delayed or even abandoned if the strike did not continue on a large scale. The decision was a crucial one, which ultimately resulted in nearly £4 billion of oil being purchased. That and other measures to keep the lights on were to cost over £2 billion more than would have been the normal cost of operations.

Had the decision been delayed for several weeks, which legitimate caution could have justified, it would have had serious consequences because of the inevitable consumption of coal stocks at those power stations which were, as it turned out, to receive no coal for a year. As it was, the delay already incurred over the period of uncertainty, coupled with the damaging period of the overtime ban, was sufficient to have already weakened the CEGB endurance capability from the robust position of October 1983. However, the lower electricity demands normally experienced over the summer period would require less fuel burn and that enabled the estimated endurance of the CEGB to remain substantial. At the beginning of April we advised the government that electricity supplies could be met in full, with a total loss of coal supplies but with maximum oil burn, for the 26 weeks.

The Times reported a further pronouncement of the NUM President in mid-April.[9] He was reported as saying that 20 per cent of the coal in stock at power stations had degraded to a point where it was unusable. The NCB said that there was little damage to its 21 000 000 tonnes of stock and the CEGB said it still had 20 000 000 tonnes at its power stations and that there had only been 0.5 per cent deterioration in its heat content in the first six months in stock and then no more.

We needed to understand what the pattern of the limited coal availability was likely to be so that it could be allocated and transported to the stations that could make the best use of it. Yet that pattern was difficult to identify in the early stages. The responsibility for the transport of coal was with the CEGB, the NCB being responsible for loading at pits. The method of transport was, in normal circumstances, almost exclusively rail. The pits and the power stations' coal-handling facilities, and indeed the conditions under which formal planning approval had been given to allow the original development of the power stations, were all on the basis of the coal being transported by rail. A large power station, of which there were many in the coal strike areas, normally requires between 5 000 000 and 6 000 000 tonnes of coal a year. That is the equivalent of 100 trains or 6000 lorries a week. It can be readily understood that local road systems could be seriously overloaded and that local people, some of whom had only reluctantly accepted the need for the power station, were not likely to be tolerant of coal being supplied other than by rail. This was to be an important issue as the strike developed.

SUPPORT FOR THE MINERS FROM THE RAIL UNIONS

The railways were to play an important part in the strike almost from the start. As the early days passed and the attitudes of trade unions and their members were becoming clear we recognised that the NUM was not the only problem. Many railway workers were not prepared to co-operate with the transport of coal from working pits. Although the legitimacy of a strike in which there had been no national ballot support was open to question, the majority of railway workers regarded working miners as strike breakers. Any doubt was removed when the Associated Society of Locomotive Enginemen and Firemen (ASLEF) and the National Union of Railwaymen (NUR), on 29 March, following a meeting of coal, transport and steel unions, instructed their members not to cross picket lines and to black the movement of coal and coke throughout Britain. There followed a confused period when, for example, a coal train would stop at a bridge where an NUM picket notice was displayed. The majority of those railway workers whose normal job was to handle coal refused to do so. British Rail had the opportunity to take disciplinary action against the staff who refused to work normally. It became apparent, however, that staff, particularly in some key signal boxes in Yorkshire, Lancashire and the Midlands and in mixed passenger/freight depots would take sympathetic action if their colleagues were disciplined. This almost certainly would have disrupted much passenger traffic, particularly on the East and West Coast main lines, the premier Intercity routes, and could even have precipitated a national rail strike. This was a risk that the CEGB and British Rail judged unacceptable. A war of attrition resulted. Since some staff were prepared to co-operate and others refused, the obvious remedy was to adjust shift patterns to enable some trains to be moved. Those of us in the CEGB who were working closely with British Rail at this time became deeply involved in the battle to maintain coal flow; we planned with them the risks of escalating the dispute that could be taken and helped them determine the priorities.

The difficulties were considerable. At each British Rail depot involved with coal supplies in the area where miners were working a drama was being enacted. Staff involved in transporting coal were coming under conflicting pressure from the NUM and their own unions on the one hand and loyalty to the local working miners and the instructions of BR management on the other.

In the North West coal from Point of Ayr, Haigh and Maryport pits to Fiddlers Ferry Power Station near Warrington was stopped by BR in agreement with us. British Rail judged that persistence in forcing coal through the railway system was highly likely to result in strikes and in serious disruption to passenger services in the North West from staff at Warrington and Preston signal boxes sympathetic to their union's instructions.

Shirebrook rail depot on the Derbyshire-Nottinghamshire border became the focus in supporting the lead given by the national railway trade union leaders. Normally Shirebrook train crews took coal from twelve pits of which ten were in Nottinghamshire and were working. The most important were Bevercotes, Bilsthorpe, Creswell, Ollerton, Sherwood, Thoresby and Welbeck. Shirebrook train crews transported the coal from these pits to four large power stations at Ratcliffe, High Marnham, West Burton and Cottam. See Figure 11.1 for these locations. Sympathetic signalmen on the routes concerned and the crews from that depot meant that at best there was no flexibility and deliveries had to be concentrated on Ratcliffe and High Marnham Power Stations. Since Shirebrook was a freight-only depot, British Rail were able to send home non-co-operative crews without fear of jeopardising passenger traffic. Almost fifty men a day were being sent home for refusing to operate coal trains from the working pits.

There was a problem of criminal damage to the railways which was obviously intended to frustrate the remaining rail-borne coal flow. An example that was to occur later in the dispute was the burning down of a signal box at Boughton on the route to High Marnham Power Station. This had little effect on deliveries but as with other examples of criminal activity it emphasised how vulnerable were those who continued to move coal.

Signalmen in the Worksop area continued to stop rail supplies to West Burton and Cottam Power Stations and the coal involved had to be diverted to Ratcliffe and High Marnham Power Stations. The movement of Rufford pit coal stopped by NUR/ASLEF militants at Mansfield was resumed following shift rostering amendments. This was another minor success for those battling to maintain rail-borne coal flow.

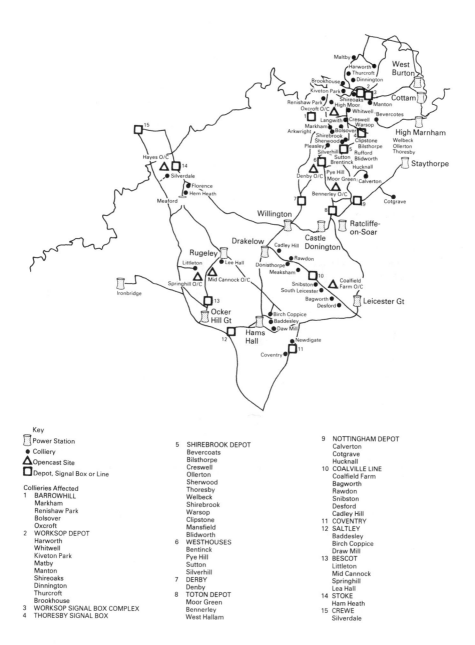

Key

🏭 Power Station
● Colliery
▲ Opencast Site
◻ Depot, Signal Box or Line

Collieries Affected
1 BARROWHILL
   Markham
   Renishaw Park
   Bolsover
   Oxcroft
2 WORKSOP DEPOT
   Harworth
   Whitwell
   Kiveton Park
   Matby
   Manton
   Shireoaks
   Dinnington
   Thurcroft
   Brookhouse
3 WORKSOP SIGNAL BOX COMPLEX
4 THORESBY SIGNAL BOX

5 SHIREBROOK DEPOT
   Bevercoats
   Bilsthorpe
   Creswell
   Ollerton
   Sherwood
   Thoresby
   Welbeck
   Shirebrook
   Warsop
   Clipstone
   Mansfield
   Blidworth
6 WESTHOUSES
   Bentinck
   Pye Hill
   Sutton
   Silverhill
7 DERBY
   Denby
8 TOTON DEPOT
   Moor Green
   Bennerley
   West Hallam

9 NOTTINGHAM DEPOT
   Calverton
   Cotgrave
   Hucknall
10 COALVILLE LINE
   Coalfield Farm
   Bagworth
   Rawdon
   Snibston
   Desford
   Cadley Hill
11 COVENTRY
12 SALTLEY
   Baddesley
   Birch Coppice
   Draw Mill
13 BESCOT
   Littleton
   Mid Cannock
   Springhill
   Lea Hall
14 STOKE
   Ham Heath
15 CREWE
   Silverdale

Figure 11.1 Colliery to power station railway connections

Source: CEGB Operations Department

Problems with oil deliveries by rail

The rail deliveries of lighting-up oil to the major coal-fired power stations were giving the CEGB similar problems. These supplies were dependent on the rail trade unions being prepared to work the oil supply trains. They interpreted the instructions from their trade unions as not allowing them to transport the oil. When asked to they either refused or, when pressed by British Rail management to accept, they were usually detered by even one picket on the route and stopped the train. At one time oil trains were stopped at many places in the northern part of the rail system.

It was the responsibility of the oil companies to deliver to the power stations. They were all cautious of replacing the failed rail flow with their own road tankers because they were concerned about the possibility of their depots being picketed and supplies to the rest of their customers being at risk. The CEGB decided that using small independent road tanker operators was the solution to the problem and more is said about this later.

This war of attrition in the early days of the strike was difficult for us to follow. The response to it was generally being co-ordinated by the local managers of the three industries concerned. However, the priorities and policies were being discussed and determined daily between the Directors of Operations for BR and the CEGB. Some tough decisions were made. They required judgement of the risks that could be accepted of escalating the dispute, and of the benefits from improved deliveries that might materialise.

ATTITUDES OF POWER STATION STAFF AND UNIONS

The attitudes of staff in power stations were critical, particularly those working in the striking coalfields. They were likely to be living in mining communities with close relatives on strike. Not surprisingly they were generally sympathetic to the miners' cause. In contrast, those staff in power stations in Nottinghamshire and parts of Derbyshire and Leicestershire, where miners were defying the attempt to picket out their pits, were strongly supportive of the local working miners.

On 19 March the electricity supply industry trade unions covering the technical and scientific staff, the clerical and administrative staff and two of the four covering the industrial staff gave advice to their CEGB members. Their statement said that members should continue to work normally. The unions emphasised the policy that the electricity supply industry should not be used to solve industrial disputes external to the industry. Despite that statement three of the industry's industrial trade unions had formal policies of support for the NUM and one of those was a party to the advice to work normally.

On 27 March the Transport and General Workers Union (TGWU) executive pledged its full support to the NUM and called on its members not to co-operate with the movement of coal. This was followed in April by more specific advice to TGWU members in power stations to black the handling of new stocks of coal and extraordinary transfers within station boundaries.

The attitude of the majority of CEGB staff was quite clear: they were unwilling to take industrial action in support of the striking miners. The fact that there had not been a national ballot and that many mines had been forced into the dispute through violent mass pickets were important factors. A further point that influenced them was that many CEGB power stations had been shut down for economic reasons over the past decade. That had been done with a high level of co-operation between management, trade unions and the staff in the closing power stations. It had been a difficult but well arranged operation. The reason for the closures had clearly been economic. It was difficult for those in the electricity industry to understand why the NUM regarded this as an unacceptable reason for pit closures. There was also continuing discomfort by many staff at the overt political objectives of some of those involved in the strike.

There was a mixture of trade union membership in most power stations. The problem was in those stations whose coal-handling plant was either entirely staffed with TGWU members or had a majority of them. Fortunately those TGWU power stations in the Midlands Region that were receiving coal from working mines elected to defy the official union advice and to continue handling coal. The problem was to be at the stations where miners were on strike.

So in the battle to retain rail-borne supplies it was important to gauge the ability of the power station management to get the coal handled by the coal plant staff following its delivery. In some power stations in certain areas it would have been so difficult to achieve this and the consequences of trying and failing were so disadvantageous that it was better not to try. By avoiding confrontation we were avoiding hardening attitudes and the creation of precedents that would be difficult to change later. However, where there was a probability of coal being handled it was worth high risks being taken by British Rail in forcing coal flows.

A good example of judging the power station and railway risks together occurred on the Coalville line in Leicestershire and at Drakelow Power Station to which it was the main source of supply. Some of the pits on that line were working and although there were many TGWU members on the station it was expected that the staff would handle the coal. Careful management of shift rotas enabled co-operative train crews and signal box staff to work at the same time and for some deliveries to be achieved. The success was assured when station staff did in fact handle the coal. This matching of co-operative railway staff became part of a continuing activity that was not always successful but helped our morale.

BRITISH RAIL'S APPROACH TO PROBLEMS

Maurice Holmes, the Director of Operations for British Rail at this time, remembers this phase well. In his view the strike had a great significance for the railways and more particularly for railwaymen. It followed a long period of run down in numbers and of modernising working methods. In many cases in the freight business the run down of numbers was related to pit closures. The railway and coal industries were closely related in the mining areas and coal was of great importance to railwaymen and their trade unions. There was also an established tradition of formal mutual support between the industries' trade unions. Maurice Holmes saw this loyalty as the background to the railway problems in maintaining coal flows at the start of the coal strike.

The railway management were prepared for the disruption. They carried out contingency planning with the main objective of protecting their commercial position. Since that essentially meant keeping running as much of their business as possible, it was close to the CEGB objectives at that time. Passenger traffic was protected as was the normal flow of oil and particularly traction fuel. It was important to transport sufficient traction oil to allow the diesel locomotives themselves to be supplied. Maurice Holmes confirmed the view that the unwise application of pressure at the militant depots and signal boxes could have resulted in major losses of trains on passenger services or even a national rail strike. The pressure that BR could apply to sustain the rail transport of coal was limited by this.

In managing the emergency Holmes visited British Rail's headquarters operating room each morning to review the availability of train crews reporting in, the number of wagons available to be deployed, and the number of routes and signal boxes available with sympathetic employees. He discussed these and other factors with the regional movements officers using teleconferencing facilities, deciding the actions to be taken. The sponsoring government department would be told of the position and also the Chairman and executive board members of British Rail. There were daily discussions with the CEGB's Director of Operations when the priorities, risks and potential benefits of the options available were discussed. Co-ordination was important at local level and was taking place with the CEGB regions.

As the strike continued the patterns of availability of coal and lighting-up oil became clearer and the attitudes of power station staff better understood. It was then possible to make better use of the supplies that were available. However, each time a new pattern of rail supply was set up the rail unions would seek to frustrate it. National officials would visit the working depots and harden the support for the strike. In mid-April, with rail-borne coal supplies down to only 200 000 tonnes a week from well over 1 000 000 tonnes, it was clear that alternative transport arrangements had to be made. It was vital that coal was moved in sufficient quantities from working pits to the power stations.

UNDERSTANDING THE CEGB'S ROLE

It was important to the CEGB that its staff fully understood the Board's position and the role it intended to play in the dispute. Staff living in the mining communities would be more difficult to influence than others. It was possible to convince the majority – indeed they needed no convincing – that it was the

CEGB's job to keep the lights on. This attitude, established in the early days of the dispute, was held by most staff throughout.

THE NOTTINGHAMSHIRE MINERS' POSITION

The position in the coalfields was still not entirely clear to the CEGB. One of the problems was that, although the Nottinghamshire miners had voted against a strike, their pits and some working pits in other areas were still being heavily picketed, despite police efforts. The determination of the miners to get to work was reassuring.

There was also some difficulty for us in understanding what was happening within the NUM in the areas where miners were working, especially in Nottinghamshire. The difficulty seemed to arise from the so-called hard left having a dominant position on the Nottinghamshire Area Executive. With a majority of members taking a clear no strike position it was necessary for the Executive to seek to resolve their problems by attempting to face both ways at once. A resolution adopted on 21 March said that those members who did not wish to cross picket lines should return home, but the area ballot decision gave members the right to go to work if they wished. The Area Executive at a later conference recommended that members should be instructed not to cross picket lines but the conference rejected this. There was a further attempt to get this through, following an NUM National Conference on 19 April, which called on all areas to join the 80 per cent already on strike. The Nottinghamshire Area Council meeting that followed had a minute stating that the conference resolution meant that anyone who was on strike was on strike officially and had the right to picket legally if he so wished. Together with an exchange by the Nottinghamshire NUM President with the NUM national leadership this resulted in a decree by the NUM that an 'official strike' existed in Nottinghamshire. The members ignored this, encouraged by the dissent of Roy Lynk[10] and David Prendergast, and continued working.[11]

ROAD HAULAGE BEGINS

The problems with the rail unions continued with the result that the disruption to rail transport was, surprisingly, of greater significance than the overall fuel supply shortage. Not only was it the major factor in determining the quantity of fuel supplied to the power stations but the transport inflexibility and uncertainty put at risk the sensible allocation of what coal was available. In particular it was difficult to determine what operating regimes were appropriate for the various power stations to help achieve the longest possible endurance. The policy intention was that stations with coal supplies should be used to the greatest extent so that those with no supplies could be used less to conserve stocks. But the question was which were the stations in each of these categories. They were later to be referred to as the haves and the have-nots.

It became increasingly obvious that to bring order out of chaos and to enable the coal being mined to be transported to power stations it was necessary to start a change from a rail-borne to a road-borne operation. This was started by the CEGB Midlands Region whose area covered that of most working pits. Apart from the obvious value of the additional supplies there were two considerations here. One was the Region's strong commitment to ensuring that miners who had gone through the picket lines at some personal risk and asserted their right to continue working should be supported by transporting their coal to power stations and the other by the Region's awareness of the effect of transporting this coal on those striking miners who would be considering their personal positions during the NCB's coming return-to-work campaign. A similar change-over to road-borne supplies was arranged for oil supplies for lighting-up and flame stabilisation at coal-fired stations.

Almost all of this road transport activity was taking place in the Midlands Region of the CEGB where, in the early stages of the strike, the Director General was Jim Porteous. Hugh Mathews was initially the Director of Production with responsibility for managing the power stations and fuel supplies. He later took over the responsibility for the general management of the Region as Executive Director.[12] He and Jack Evans, the Fuel Supplies Officer, were to bear the brunt of the road-borne coal supplies programme, together with their very competent staff.

PICKETING

Not only was there uncertainty about the pattern of the strike and the availability of coal; it was also not clear how much of a problem there would be from pickets. The early days of the dispute were dominated by internal differences within the NUM. The picketing out of working pits was the first priority for the striking miners. Other targets were to follow. By 28 March pickets began to be switched to power stations and the NUM called for a complete power stoppage. There was little response from the power workers whose trade unions had already given their advice to members.

Pickets were not a major problem. The general pattern was that the majority of power stations were picketed. At that stage the effect of the pickets varied. They were less resolute than in the 1970s strikes. Our large storage capacity of essential materials was well known and made the siege picketing of earlier disputes a tactic unlikely to yield success at least in the short term. The CEGB policy, developed in the early stages, was not to provoke mass pickets and not to seek to confront them. It generally resulted in the mass pickets dispersing. Then there were always opportunities to bring in deliveries when the picketing was at a more moderate level. With 90 power stations it was not possible for the NUM to keep a high level of effective picketing at all the stations all the time, particularly in the early days when they were being paid out of the NUM's funds.

Liaison with the police was important and maintaining this was the responsibility of the individual regions. Such liaison was particularly important in the Midlands Region where a road-borne coal flow from working pits to power stations was being built up. Liaison there was managed by John White, the Security Officer. The resolution of the police, particularly in Nottinghamshire, helped us to execute our planning and was a big improvement on the 1970s (see Chapter 22).

REVISING THE PLAN

During April the pattern of the dispute and of coal availability was getting clearer. It was likely that some miners would continue working, in Nottinghamshire in particular. It was obvious that there would be great difficulty in transporting their coal by rail. However a road-borne coal flow was being set up. Picketing was not as big a factor as had been expected and by skilful management it might have only a limited effect. Oil burn was being built up in accordance with the plan and coal burn being reduced. The large-scale oil purchasing operation was also under way.

However, it was still not clear how much of the coal from the working mines could in fact be delivered to the power stations. It was still not clear whether picketing would continue to fall short of the siege level that had been feared. We were not sure whether the oil purchasing operation would be successful. It involved a large quantity of oil and we had no previous experience of purchasing, delivering and discharging oil on that scale at our power station jetties. The emergency now being faced was different from the one for which we had prepared.

ENDURANCE STRATEGY

To understand what the new circumstances meant for the CEGB's endurance and to determine what its strategy should now be it was necessary to turn to the System Operations Branch and the CEGB's operational planning process, which it managed. It was the focal point of our operational management and System Operations Branch (under Ed Wallis, later to become the Chief Executive of Powergen plc) played the leading role in determining our endurance strategy.

Operational planning enabled the electricity supply system to be operated in the unusual power flow conditions. More importantly, it was used to devise plans for the best use of the generating units, given the fuel stocks and estimates of future supplies that were available. Operational planning also made it possible to predict accurately the length of time that electricity supplies could be maintained. This was an extension of the normal computer simulation studies used to plan operations. The ability to perform them to tight timescales was a skill built up in the CEGB over the years. It was of vital importance in managing the CEGB's response to the strike.

After the first few weeks of the strike these modelling methods enabled the CEGB to judge what endurance would result from a particular level of coal deliveries and of oil burn. In addition it could show what was necessary to be done to achieve a particular level of endurance. In other words it enabled the CEGB to manage the emergency by being able to predict the consequence of selecting particular options or of gaining or losing some advantage.

During April 1984 the conclusion from computer modelling was that if the planned oil burn could be achieved and the coal that was being mined could be transported to the power stations, then the CEGB could meet electricity demand in full through the summer and at least into the early part of the winter.

Chapter 12

Facing up to the long haul

It had been necessary to respond to the confusing early phases of the strike as events occurred. Compared with our expectations and the earlier contingency planning there was the unexpected benefit of some coal continuing to be mined. That benefit could of course only be realised if the coal could be transported to the power stations but we had set about achieving that. It was also necessary to implement the contingency plans as quickly as possible. This mainly required the building up of oil-fired generation supported by a sound oil procurement programme. We also had to gain full value from this change by giving the coal-fired stations, not receiving coal, reduced operating regimes in order to prolong the life of their coal stocks. There were also other steps that had to be taken in the first phase of the CEGB's response to the strike. These took most of the spring. They were to be followed by lesser measures that were devised to improve endurance further. These were managed and monitored carefully.

During the summer it began to appear that our response might not be sufficient to deal with a strike that was going on much longer than we had expected. In particular we could see that electricity supplies were at risk through the winter. In this chapter we give an account of the CEGB's early response.

INCREASING OIL-FIRED GENERATION

Increased oil-fired generation was the most important response. The vital steps to increase oil burn were taken between the 28 March and the 18 April. Each step was accompanied by a phased reduction in generation from the coal-fired stations whose coal stocks we were trying to conserve. By the time that the full oil burn was implemented, the new operating regimes designed to conserve coal stocks were in place at all the coal-fired stations not receiving supplies. Even the coal-fired power stations in the Midlands region that were still receiving coal were generating less because of the significant effect of the increased output from the oil-fired stations.

However, the oil-fired power stations were experiencing the biggest changes. They were normally used only to a limited extent because of the high cost of oil. They were now being called on to operate continuously at full load and had become the most important generating tranche on the electricity supply system. The CEGB had of course developed a plan to ensure that abnormal power flows on the transmission system could be accommodated. However, we now had to consider the power flows afresh because the generating role that could be given to the stations in the working coalfields meant that the power flows were different from those that we had expected. The overall effect was more generation in the Midlands and less in the North.

The South Eastern Region's oil-fired stations took most of the increased oil burn. These stations were the responsibility of Tom McInerney, the Director of Production for the Region, initially under Director-General Geoffrey Stone. Like Mathews in the Midlands, McInerney was, during the strike, to take over the general management of the Region as Executive Director.

The South Eastern Region had taken a large share of the CEGB's plant closure programme. The Board had reduced the number of its employees from over 70 000 to about 50 000 in the two decades to 1984–5. The number of generating stations in that time had reduced from 200 to 90 and many of the small power stations in urban areas supplying the local area board distribution system had been closed down. This was the case in the London area where many smaller stations had been replaced by a few large ones. The new stations were on the Thames and the Medway: at Grain, Littlebrook, Kingsnorth, Tilbury and West Thurrock.[1] They were all either oil-burning, dual-fired (oil and/or coal) or could burn some oil as a part replacement for coal.

In preparation for the increase in oil-fired generation the local trade union officials had been invited in for discussions with Tom McInerney. He reminded them that this was not an electricity supply dispute; our role as managers and that of the staff should be to work normally. It became obvious that many of the trade union officials were unsympathetic to Scargill's cause and so were many of their members in the south east. Yet there was still the strong possibility that a formal call for trade union solidarity could change this situation even though the strike and the picketing in the north were remote. All the power stations had burnt oil or, in the case of West Thurrock, gas in quantity. Therefore the pattern of fuel supply could, with at least some justification, be described as normal.

In March the advice given by electricity supply trade unions to their members was to work normally. Meetings were held by the management with local officials and the power station representatives to agree extensive changes to the working arrangements at Grain and Littlebrook D Power Stations. These changes stretched to the limit the advice to work normally. The stations had originally been manned to operate only part of their capacity and that for only two of the three daily eight-hour shifts Monday to Friday. They were now to operate all their generating units continuously. It is not surprising that the new arrangements resulted in high overtime. The staff concerned believed that they could interpret the advice from their trade unions liberally because there were many working miners and because the lack of a national ballot raised genuine doubts about the legitimacy of the strike.

Fred Kirkby, the Station Manager at Grain Power Station, remembers that although the staff elected to meet the requirements of the industry to keep the lights on, they had sympathy with some aspects of the miners' dispute. They found it difficult to resolve the conflict between being good trade unionists, having a rare opportunity to increase earnings, and proving how good a power station Grain really was. In fact the men at Grain Power Station worked the new shift arrangements. The overtime levels were, on average, over 30 per cent, bringing a considerable increase in pay. The staff were counselled about not entering into long-term commitments on the basis of their increased earnings. The expectation had to be that the present conditions would continue for only a short time.

The requirement at some of the Thames-side power stations was not only to change their operating regimes drastically but to change from coal-to oil-burning. It was also necessary to discharge oil tankers at rates much higher than they had experienced. This task was performed efficiently at Kingsnorth, which supplied both Grain and Kingsnorth.

Although generally there was not a strong feeling of support for the striking miners among the staff, there was some sensitivity about what could and should be done at Tilbury and West Thurrock Power Stations where the oil-based generation was later to become important.

The other major oil-fired stations were at Fawley and Pembroke in the South Western Region and at Ince in the North Western Region. They were all supplied from near-by refineries. At Ince there was an alternative tanker discharge source of supply. All were conventional oil-fired stations and although they were required greatly to increase their output compared with the recent past this did not produce major difficulties.

Oil procurement

The oil procurement programme to support the increased oil-fired generation went well. There was much concern about whether sufficient oil could be purchased without a large increase in price and a resulting high profile. Highlighting the scale of the supply arrangements would invite attempts to curtail them. Since the government had not been prepared to release some of their national strategic oil stock or play any other supportive role, we were on our own. The plan was to build up a purchasing and supply operation in stages and with a mixture of term contracts and spot purchases. Our objective, for many reasons, was to avoid a marked increase in oil prices. This was done with great skill by David Bridger and his team working under John Wooley, CEGB Fuel Supplies Officer. Despite purchases of heavy fuel oil, which at their peak were greater than the total crude production of the lesser OPEC members combined, the price only moved up slightly. It started at about US$180 a tonne and never went much over US$190 a tonne. The collapse to US$130 a tonne when the CEGB came out of the market at the end of the strike gave an indication of the effect of our volume of purchases. The CEGB purchased the oil for its own tanker-supplied stations and for Inverkip and Peterhead Power Stations in Scotland.

The stations that were fed by pipeline from nearby oil refineries received oil purchased under the normal supply contracts. There was a degree of market price relativity in those contracts so we had a further incentive to keep the spot price as low as possible. The whole of this operation was greatly aided by not becoming the subject of media attention and by the absence of the more determined efforts to stop the oil flow that a high profile would have induced. More detail is given in Chapter 17.

CONSERVING COAL STOCKS

The replacement of coal-fired generation by oil over 4 weeks in 25 per cent steps enabled the loading regimes of the coal-and oil-fired power station to be changed in stages. The purpose of the change was to preserve coal stocks generally, but more specifically the stocks at the stations not receiving coal supplies (the have-nots). In the early stages there were many power stations in that category.

In normal times the large coal-fired stations were used for continuous running at full load – called base load – and the smaller coal-fired plant and the oil-fired stations were used flexibly to meet the daily, weekly and seasonal variations in electricity demand. In general terms the daily peak electricity demand is twice that of the overnight minimum. Since electricity cannot be stored, generation output has to be controlled to meet consumer demand with some precision, minute by minute across each day. It is usual for about half of the generating plant in use on any day to be shut down overnight and started up in the early morning, a regime called two-shifting. Alternatively generators have to be run at low levels of output over the low demand period.

The cost is normally lower to two-shift than to continue running at low load. This was the preferred method of operation in this emergency since it was also more economic in the use of the limited coal stocks. Unfortunately it required the burning of oil for flame stabilisation at start-up and during the build-up of load. But would the oil be available for such a loading regime? There were doubts since the sympathetic action by the rail unions was preventing the supply of the necessary oil by rail, the normal method of supply.

This problem had several implications. One was that if coal-fired stations without coal supplies were to conserve their coal stocks they required a good supply of lighting-up oil. Yet many of these stations were in areas where oil deliveries were difficult to achieve. It was therefore necessary to determine what future loading regime for each station enabled both the limited quantities of coal and of lighting-up oil stock to be used in the best interests of overall endurance.

There were two distinct challenges: one was to make the best use of the coal that was available to the power stations; the other to restore coal supplies from the working pits to the highest possible level. The former was being handled by

Ed Wallis and his team who were determining the best operating regime for each generating unit. The latter was being tackled by the Midlands Region.

Road-borne coal

Having the unexpected good fortune that coalmining was continuing in parts of the Midlands, it was frustrating to be faced with the rail unions' refusal to transport the coal. It was vital to compensate for this by building up a road-borne transport programme as quickly as possible. Setting this up to the size needed was not easy. It was ultimately to require about 25 000 lorry movements a week, through rural and urban areas where the local population were generally unhappy about the new volume of road traffic carrying dirty coal. It required control of coal quantities, quality and payments for a form of supply that was completely different from that for which the weighing, sampling and other facilities at the stations were designed.

The road-borne deliveries, to compensate for the difficulties in rail-borne operations, had started during March. However these were not on the scale now required. The lorries had to pass through picket lines at both ends of their journeys. Some of the early road-borne movements ran into difficulties with large numbers of pickets at some stations. On these occasions the lorries were diverted to other power stations until picket numbers fell. The scale of the operations was gradually built up. During April road-borne deliveries were between 70 000 and 90 000 tonnes a week; by the end of May they were over 200 000 tonnes. How this was done is told in Chapter 16.

Imports from Scotland

The final stage in implementing the contingency plan involved Scotland. The arrangements made in the planning phase, before the strike, recognised the benefit of increased electricity imports from Scotland. These imports were possible because of the excess generating capacity of the South of Scotland Electricity Board. They had a generating pool with the North of Scotland Hydro-Electric Board. This pool had great diversity of fuel source with high nuclear capacity, substantial hydro-electric capacity and a significant oil-burning capacity, all of which made them less vulnerable to a coal strike. They were prepared to share the benefits of their more robust position by exporting electrical energy to England and Wales, providing that an appropriate price could be agreed. The price for the electricity transfer was originally based on a mixture of coal and oil generation costs but was later based on the oil-fired generation at Inverkip and Peterhead Power Stations. The transfer from Scotland was increased, in accordance with the plan, from the start of the CEGB's increased oil burn. In the early weeks of the strike the transfer was providing a weekly benefit over the normal level of exchange of 110 GWHs a week or the equivalent of about 50 000 tonnes of coal supply. Over the whole period of the strike they were to save us the equivalent of 3 000 000 tonnes of coal in support of the electricity consumers of England and Wales.

SPRING PROGRESS

All the planned steps to enable the electricity supply industry to keep the lights on were in place by late April. We were able to take stock. By the week ending 22 April heavy fuel oil burn had been increased from the normal level of about 30 000 tonnes a week to the maximum envisaged by the endurance plan of 360 000 tonnes a week. This reduced coal consumption by about 550 000 tonnes a week. Even with the effect of the rail unions' industrial action, coal deliveries from the working pits were over 300 000 tonnes a week. However in that same week power stations' coal stock reduced by 440 000 tonnes to 18 300 000 tonnes. Although the endurance measures were now in place and the future looked reasonably bright, the phased introduction of new regimes had seen the coal stock fall by over 6 000 000 tonnes since the strike started on the 12 March. We had paid a high price as a result of the time taken to build up the new operating pattern. The compensation was that it was all working well.

The endurance estimate was that electricity demand could be met in full for twenty-six weeks if all coal deliveries were to cease. If a coal flow of 500 000 tonnes a week could be achieved the endurance capability extended to February 1985. However we had not achieved such a flow. This was a clear and powerful motivation to those considering how to improve the coal flow from the working pits.

There was another problem, which made all this look unduly optimistic: that of the stations not receiving coal supplies. With an absence of lighting-up oil supplies they could not be used flexibly and we did not know how much this would weaken the general estimate of endurance. Our belief was that it could be significant.

DEVELOPMENTS IN THE STRIKE

At an NUM Special Delegate Conference on 19 April four separate motions, all calling for a ballot, were rejected and a motion was adopted by 69 votes to 54 for strike action throughout the British coalfields. This was one of the many attempts to make the strike official. However the NUM areas that were not on strike were not convinced. Although the left-dominated NUM Nottinghamshire Area Executive sought to exploit this opportunity it was not effective and did not change the minds of the working miners. The same conference agreed to change the rule requiring a 55 per cent majority for a national strike so as to make such action dependent only on a simple majority vote.[2]

Pickets

Although the striking miners were concentrating their major efforts on picketing out the working pits they were also applying variable numbers to the power stations. As the strike continued picketing was becoming more important. Some drivers who were members of the TGWU would not drive through the picket lines. In particular there were problems with the delivery of industrial gases. One way of dealing successfully with this was to reschedule the deliveries for night-time or weekends with different drivers. At night some pickets retreated to sit in their cars or left the site. Deliveries were ultimately being made successfully.

Carbon dioxide deliveries to nuclear power stations were important to the CEGB and picketing at a number of these stations was causing deliveries to fail, particularly where the pickets were disorderly. Arrangements were made for some of the more important deliveries, particularly to Hinkley Point Power Station, to be supported by the police.

NUM view of CEGB endurance

At the end of April *The Times* said that the strike had established a record as the longest stoppage in the coal industry since the General Strike of 1926.[3] The two strikes in the 1970s had been relatively short affairs. The vulnerability of electricity supply at those times had resulted in the need for an early settlement. Supplies were far less vulnerable this time and it was difficult therefore to judge how long the dispute would continue.

This question was obviously in the minds of many of those involved in the dramatic events of the late spring. Arthur Scargill, on 7 May, had been reported[4] as saying that coal supplies were down to eight weeks and that miners were clearly winning the dispute. As a response to that John Lyons, General Secretary of the EPEA, made sure through the media that the true, much stronger position, was known. In addition the Secretary of State and the Prime Minister each made statements within a few days,[5] one saying that stocks were 'exceedingly' high and the other that they would last for many months. Arthur Scargill had the last word in this exchange when he warned that the strike could go on for six months,[6] a comment which was hardly consistent with his earlier statement.

During May there was a belated and somewhat curious request by Peter Heathfield to the General Secretaries of all the trade unions involved with electricity supply asking them to accept that power stations should be 'deemed to be picketed' and that workers should not cross the picket lines. John Lyons of the EPEA replied as the Secretary of the Electricity Supply Trade Union Council on behalf of the unions. He said that such a proposal would be so far-reaching that it would seriously affect the whole country and therefore the whole trade union movement. He referred the matter to Len Murray with copies of the correspondence. Nothing more was ever heard about it.

Steel Industry

At the end of May the NUM turned their attention to the steel industry. The battle of Orgreave was in full swing as British Steel sought to move coke from the pit stock to their blast furnaces at Scunthorpe. Hundreds of pickets confronted police and tried unsuccessfully to prevent it. It was difficult for us to understand the NUM strategy. There had been a national steel strike a few years earlier that had had little effect on the economy. There was so much surplus world capacity and imports were so easy to obtain that the strike had failed. How were the NUM expecting to succeed in their strike by stopping the steel industry? We were pleased not to be the target, but could not understand why our industry was not the focus of their attention.

Peace talks

Also in May the first NUM/NCB peace talks of the strike took place.[7] The NCB had held discussions with NACODS and BACM at a routine consultative meeting on 17 April. The NUM would normally have been present but since the start of the strike they had decided not to attend such meetings. The NCB had said that they might be prepared to consider the phasing of the proposed pit closures if there were to be some movement on the other side. This had been relayed to the NUM and following further exchanges had resulted in the first peace talks of the strike taking place at Hobart House, the London headquarters of the NCB, on the 23 May. To enable the NUM delegation to enter the building without crossing a picket line the Kent miner pickets, normally at the entrance, had to vacate their posts.

The meeting had started with the NCB giving a general review of the coal industry and of the plan for coal.[8] Reference was also made to the effect of the NUM action on some critical pits. Eventually the direct question was posed to the NCB: were they prepared to withdraw the closure plan? The NCB were not prepared to say yes but suggested further discussions between representatives of the two sides. The NUM required agreement to that condition before further talks took place. There was no way forward and the discussion broke down after one hour.

Working miners

Meanwhile the working miners were still attending their pits despite the continuous war with the pickets; the support of an effective police operation was crucial to this. Nottinghamshire, Leicestershire, South Derbyshire and Western Area were all still producing coal. The response from the Midlands Region of the CEGB, in whose territory these pits were located, was to give a commitment that all the coal that was mined would be moved to the power stations. The thinking was that if miners could face the level of provocation being experienced to exercise their right to work, the CEGB should be committed to accepting the fruits of their labour.

ASSESSING THE SITUATION

Throughout this period we monitored developments closely. The System Operations Branch led in making weekly assessments of the trends in endurance and of the potential benefits from the options that were available. The monitoring and the modelling process that was related to it enabled managers to make regular reports to the CEGB Board and to the Department of Energy. These monitoring reports provided the factual basis for the weekly meetings between Sir Walter Marshall and Peter Walker, the Secretary of State. They were prepared by the operations department team of Frank Ledger, Ed Wallis, John Wooley and Granville Camsey. The weekly monitoring meetings reviewed coal supplies, oil purchase, deliveries and burn, operating regimes, transmission issues and essential commodities' deliveries and stock. They were also attended by Tim Beaumont from Public Relations and Neil Middleton from Personnel Department who advised in their areas of expertise and acted as co-ordinators with their departments.

In addition monthly review meetings took place between the operations team and the five regional directors of production. These meetings made detailed policies and determined actions necessary to maintain the CEGB's position. The best motivators at these meetings were the endurance predictions made by Ed Wallis's team. They made clear to all what needed to be done to maintain electricity supplies into the longer term.

The whole process was overseen by the regular policy-making weekly meetings of CEGB executive directors and in particular by Gil Blackman, the Board Member for Production, who chaired the Operations General Management meeting, which the regional directors general and the Director of Operations attended.

The electricity supply industry trade unions had been kept informed of what was happening throughout the dispute by Neil Middleton, enabling them to respond to questions from their members. We continued to explain that our responsibility was to meet our normal objective of keeping the lights on and that policy continued to receive their support. The government was also kept fully informed. Apart from the weekly meetings between the Chairman and the Secretary of State, Department of Energy officials were told about CEGB operations and assessments of future developments. The officials monitored, co-ordinated and influenced matters when necessary.

MAY PROGRESS

Progress had been made. Coal stocks were still reducing but at a lesser rate – by 300 000 tonnes in the week ending 30 May. Oil burn was well up to the target except for a problem at Pembroke Power Station. Oil supplies were adequate. Progress had been made in supplies from the working pits with road and rail deliveries having totalled about 450 000 tonnes a week in the second half of the month. Unfortunately the rail-borne deliveries were not going to some of the stations that needed them most since the flow had to be on the routes on which movement was possible. The result was that, in contrast to the general trend, coal stocks were increasing at Ratcliffe and High Marnham Power Stations.

At this stage the remedial measures were costing an additional £20 million a week, even though this was the period of lower electricity demand. Winter would see higher costs if the strike continued that long. The CEGB was predicting that it could keep the lights on well into next winter, but had no confidence that it could get through the high winter demands without power cuts if the strike continued that long.

The decisions needed had been taken and were generally being applied but in the late spring a number of additional actions were identified that would strengthen the security of electricity supply. Since we were still uncertain of the length of the strike they were well worth adopting.

Nuclear stations respond

Statutory requirements allowed nuclear power stations to run their reactors for two years following each inspection. The normal preferred shut-down time to carry out these statutory inspections was the summer period of low demand since the cost of generation to replace their output was lowest at that time. To avoid the shut-down periods falling in the winter, some of the reactors were normally shut down before the two-year period had elapsed. On occasions this could be after a run of only eighteen or twenty months. During this emergency the decision was taken to run for the maximum two-year period on all reactors, ensuring the greatest nuclear contribution to the endurance objective. This was capable of being wrongly interpreted as the taking of nuclear risks by the ill-informed or by those wishing to create mischief. One national newspaper printed such a story concerning the planned delayed start to a statutory inspection at Trawsfynydd nuclear Power Station.

Although the CEGB did not allow false information on nuclear safety matters to go uncorrected, the general public relations policy was to say as little as possible on endurance-related subjects. In particular no information was normally given on coal stocks. Almost anything that could be said was likely to be used by those who were challenging the security of electricity supplies to frustrate our efforts. This lack of information did not deter the press. Although they carried many accurate accounts they also printed some speculative stories, which in their gross inaccuracy were misleading to the opposition and therefore helpful to our purpose. Had the CEGB been deliberately managing a programme of false information it would have found it difficult to do a better job. The Board's public relations staff tried to avoid false information being printed but their influence was limited by not being free to give information that we regarded as confidential. This theme is developed further in Chapter 24.

Further oil-fired generation and problems

An opportunity arose at Grain Power Station to add to endurance. The large oil-fired stations had been planned when oil prices were much lower than now. They were completed at a time when the diversity of fuel source, to which they contributed, was to be of great importance. Grain, which had earlier been notorious as a construction site with major industrial relations problems, was now on course to complete its fourth 660 MW generating unit. In the event it was commissioned in record time by 30 April and, with other Grain units, was to play an important part in securing electricity supplies. So was the neighbouring Littlebrook D oil-fired Power Station where construction had also just been completed and three 660 MW units were available for full load generation. These two stations together had the potential to save the burn of 300 000 tonnes of coal per week.

To achieve the oil delivery programme it was vital to discharge oil tankers quickly. The most important unloading jetty was at Kingsnorth Power Station on the River Medway. It was the one source of oil supply for both Grain and Kingsnorth Power Stations, which had between them about 5000 MW of oil-fired capability. Kingsnorth Power Station, which was dual-fired, had in recent years been working towards achieving full output on coal. It had now returned to full oil-firing. The two stations together were to be a major part (about a third) of our oil-burning capability and it was difficult to discharge oil at a sufficient rate on the one jetty to keep them adequately supplied. They were to consume up to 160 000 tonnes of heavy fuel oil a week. It was gratifying that the purchasing, supply and discharge arrangements were working sufficiently well for this level to have been reached by a week in early May if not yet consistently.

However, not all the news was good. There was a failure of a steam chest on a turbine at Pembroke Power Station. A steam chest is the part which houses the governor valves that control steam supply to the turbine. A repair was made using a so-called cold welding technique,[9] which came from an exchange of technical visits with the Ministry of Power and Electrification of the USSR. We were indebted to them for a repair technology which helped us on a number of occasions. Unfortunately it was necessary to shut down the other three generating units at Pembroke for inspection to ensure that they were not at risk of similar failures and one of the steam chests had to be returned to the turbine manufacturer – NEI-Parsons – for repair. The safety of our operators had to be our priority. The generating units were all back in service within a few weeks. This setback to protecting scarce coal stocks was serious: it caused about 300 000 tonnes of additional coal to be burnt.

FURTHER PEACE TALKS

At the beginning of June there was pressure from several quarters for coal peace talks to be resumed. On the 8 June they did so with three on each side. Scargill,

Heathfield and McGahey for the NUM and MacGregor, Cowan and Smith for the NCB. Ned Smith was Director General of Industrial Relations for the NCB. At the 23 May discussion the full NUM National Executive had been present. A preparatory meeting for the June discussions had taken place at Monk Fryston Hall in Yorkshire between Cowan and the NUM top three. Cowan went through what was tradeable in the negotiation. This was to be used by Scargill in speeches he then made as evidence of the NCB being prepared to surrender, much to the consternation of the Secretary of State.[10]

The 8 June meeting took place in Edinburgh. The criteria for pit closures were discussed and the compromise means of dealing with closures for reasons other than exhaustion were reviewed. The meeting was inconclusive, but it was agreed to resume the following week on 13 June at Rotherham. Unfortunately this proved not to be a constructive meeting. Both sides blamed intrusive media attention. The meeting was adjourned.

MID-JUNE PERSPECTIVE

By mid-June the dispute had been going on for twelve weeks and it was over five weeks since full oil burn had been set up. Coal deliveries had reached a weekly level of about 450 000 tonnes to the Midlands and North Western Regions of the CEGB, but with only a small flow to the latter. The other three regions were receiving no coal and had received none since the dispute started. Hence the South Eastern, North Eastern and South Western Regions were running generating plant mixes comprising nuclear and oil-fired stations on full output and protected coal-fired stations that were operating on highly restricted regimes. Coal stocks had fallen to 16 000 000 tonnes and were at that time falling at the rate of about 250 000 tonnes a week. The estimate of endurance was that electricity demand could be met in full to the end of the calendar year if the present coal flow could be maintained.

The strike now looked set to continue for a long time and the question which caused the CEGB deep concern was whether it could do enough to keep the lights on through the coming winter? Regrettably the conclusion was that, unless it could improve coal flow or oil burn significantly, it would fail.

Summer overhauls

The summer period of lower electricity demand was the best time to overhaul plant. In the case of generating plant there was a legal requirement, under the regulations of the Factories Act, to shut down boilers and other pressure vessels after a defined interval for inspection by an independent authority. The same requirement existed for some equipment associated with the transmission system but this was less demanding and had a lesser effect on our strategy. So to preserve the power flows that were enabling us to save coal at the power stations not receiving coal supplies much of the transmission work was cancelled. In addition the Factories Inspectorate were about to agree that our boilers could operate for longer between statutory inspections. Through negotiation with the appropriate bodies the implementation of this change was accelerated and helped appreciably. More is said on this in Chapter 20.

At the beginning of the summer period advantage was taken of the normal pattern of the annual overhaul programme to do work at those stations that had generating units shut down to conserve coal. At Ferrybridge C Power Station this gave Derek Richardson, the Station Manager, an opportunity to remove the electrical rotors from two generators that were not needed for generation and to send them to Pembroke and to Ince B Power Stations via the works of NEI Parsons in Newcastle where they received some brief attention. The result was that Ince B, which had been without an electrical rotor for one of its generators because of decisions concerning an earlier repair and modification programme, was able to commission one of its large oil-burning units and make an additional contribution to coal conservation. Pembroke Power Station had an electrical rotor being repaired and on receiving and installing the ex-Ferrybridge rotor was able to return a generating unit to service.

Various events and a human tragedy

The oil flow was continuing to present interesting issues for the CEGB and one exercised the NUM and the popular press as well. This was the embarrassment to the NUM of Russian tankers supplying Kingsnorth Power Station. These were modern, efficient, fast-discharging vessels that were very useful to us. The story of how the media interest in mid-June resulted in the ships being withdrawn is told in Chapter 17. It was a pity as far as we were concerned that our veil of secrecy had been lifted as a result of persistent investigative reporting.

Life went on almost normally in some power stations. In particular the nuclear stations were only slightly affected by the strike-related events in the CEGB and the country generally. An electricity supply industry dispute concerning the grading of craftsmen came to a head in June at some of the nuclear stations. Two nuclear stations, Hinkley Point and Oldbury, experienced the novelty of not only having NUM pickets at the gate but also having their own maintenance staff as well. This lasted only a few days but surprised a number of lorry drivers making deliveries.

There was an industrial dispute at one of our most important suppliers during June. A series of negotiations had been continuing at ICI Billingham for some time. They related to the pay of the drivers who delivered much of the carbon dioxide to the nuclear power stations. The resulting overtime ban was disrupting supplies and had us anxiously watching supplies and storage levels. In fact stocks at Wylfa Nuclear Power Station were to become uncomfortably low. If this had been followed by more resolute NUM picketing it would have been necessary to shut down the power station. We were fortunate that the NUM did not seem to know of our local vulnerability.

On 15 June a picketing accident occurred. Joe Green, a miner from Kellingley pit, was killed by a lorry at the entrance to Ferrybridge Power Station. It was said that the driver was distracted by the other pickets. We fervently hoped that that would be the last such tragedy.

Towards the end of June and throughout July, there was evidence of an attempt by the NUM to ginger-up the picketing of power stations with several hundred of their members appearing at Cottam, Ratcliffe, Rugeley and then at West Burton Power Stations. No serious problems arose. An exception occurred on 17 June when *The Times* reported a claim by Arthur Scargill that secret plans were being drawn up by the government to seek parliamentary authority for power cuts to start at the end of August because of dwindling coal stocks at power stations. He said that his information had come from 'a high level' source inside the CEGB. The claims were denied by the CEGB and the Department of Energy. Our estimate of endurance with the then levels of oil burn and coal deliveries was twenty-five weeks.

Continuing stories of leaks from a mole in CEGB were to provide some further interesting misinformation later in the strike. The NUM were misleading their own members by these statements and giving them a confidence in success that the facts did not warrant.

Working miners

The NUM continued to apply heavy pressure to the working miners. They did this not only through intimidatory picketing but also through using every means to get the strike recognised as official. These attempts made no impact on the Nottinghamshire miners. The legal and political battle was intense; at one stage the Nottinghamshire NUM area offices were occupied by supporters of the strike.

Those who wished to continue working and their leaders – particularly Roy Lynk and David Prendergast – were not slow to turn to legal processes to maintain their position. This involved seeking to restrain the NUM leadership from treating the strike as official. More importantly for electricity supply it also involved starting legal action to force the NUM into agreeing that branch elections should take place in June, as usual. The elections were held, and resulted in the election of working miners in almost every case. This transformed the Area Executive into an anti-strike body, and gave some assurance to the CEGB that coal production would continue in the important Nottinghamshire coalfield.

JULY – STEADY PROGRESS BUT NEW ANXIETIES

July was a month of steady progress for the CEGB but also of growing anxiety about the coming winter. It was a month that saw the resumption of peace talks in the coal industry but also a national dock strike. The combination of the failure of the coal industry negotiations and the occurrence of the strike in the docks marked the low point of the emergency for the electricity industry. The prospects looked grim.

In July the coal delivery position in the CEGB's North Western Region was improved marginally by the establishment of a road-borne movement from Maryport in Cumberland, where open-cast coal was available, to Bold Power Station in Lancashire. The movement was suspended for a few days shortly after it was set up when the NUM President visited the adjacent pit. There was no point in being unnecessarily provocative. We did not wish to have an Orgreave on our hands.

In the meantime supplies were continuing to the Midlands Region with rail-borne supplies at about 200 000 tonnes a week. They were holding at that modest average level with variations reflecting the results of the continuing struggle between British Rail management and the rail unions. With road-borne deliveries the weekly flow of coal was now over 500 000 tonnes. The possibility of setting up an imported coal flow into the Thames-side stations was considered. Cumberland coal from Maryport was to be taken experimentally into Tilbury or West Thurrock Power Stations. After much discussion we decided not to try this change to the established pattern. The success of our endurance strategy was heavily dependent on the large-scale oil burn at the Thames-side stations: it was too vital to risk. The strong NUM and general trade union reaction that such a coalflow might have provoked would have put at risk the oil supplies necessary to support our tenfold increase in oil burn.

Dock strike

Precipitated by non-registered labour being used to unload iron ore at Immingham a national dock strike was called from 00.01 hours on 10 July.[11] The dispute related to the detailed working arrangements covered by the dock labour scheme and was therefore relevant to 'registered' ports.[12] The extent to which it could become a strike covering all TGWU members in all ports was not initially clear. At that time no imported or for that matter any other ship-borne coal supply was supporting CEGB operations. In fact Jim Slater, General Secretary of the National Union of Seamen, had said at the beginning of the dispute that there would be no coal flow into Britain transported by ships manned by his members. Our worry was the potential challenge to our massive oil burn. All of our supplies of heavy fuel oil were either directly or indirectly dependent on shipping and the port facilities necessary for discharging tankers, including tugs and berthing services.

All the registered ports came to a standstill and many of the unregistered ones. Traffic through the Channel ports was also rapidly brought to a standstill from 10 July, with large numbers of lorries stranded on both sides of the Channel. To avoid alienating the general public the holiday traffic was allowed on to the ferries; this greatly increased the tension between the port workers and the lorry drivers. In the meantime the immediate dispute at Immingham had been settled. Although British Steel had accepted a ruling by the National Dock Labour Board on 13 July, the national action was to continue until the agreement was ratified by the National Joint Council of the Port Transport Industry on 21 July.

During this period there was growing impatience and threats of violence from the lorry drivers waiting at the ports. There was pressure to open the port of Dover by the lorry drivers, many of whom were members of the TGWU. This became so difficult to contain that a local union official decided (on 19 July) to lift the ban on lorries. As a result the strike collapsed over the next few days and was more or less over when the national body ratified the local settlement. The main risk to the CEGB endurance strategy had been over the berthing of oil tankers because tugmen supported the strike. However tankers were berthed throughout the dispute either by berthing without assistance from tugs or by tugmen electing to assist.

A further problem arose over lighting-up oil supplies to the Midlands Region. The road-borne oil supply to the Midlands Region's power stations was dependent on road tankers loading at Avonmouth docks. During the dock strike lock gate operators were on strike and the seagoing tankers necessary to load the road vehicles were prevented from entering the docks. It was a great relief for us to see the end of this dock strike leaving us to deal with supply problems arising directly from the miners' strike. By now we felt that we understood most of the twists and turns of that, although we could never be sure.

Coal peace talks resume

During the dock strike peace talks resumed in the coal industry. These were held on the 5 and 6 July at the Rubens Hotel London, on the 9 July in Edinburgh and again on 18 July in London.[13] Towards the end of these long discussions the Coal Board's representatives thought that they were close to agreement. The controversial issue of economic closure had been dealt with by devising a third category of closure, the first two being exhaustion and severe geological difficulties. The third category was for pits whose reserves could not be 'beneficially developed'. Agreement to this was linked to the concession that the five pits which the NUM had made their main closure issue remained open. The overall deal was judged by some to offer to the union 80 per cent of what they wanted. The NUM President did not find it acceptable. The meetings were adjourned without an acceptable compromise being found.

These events occurred at a time when the NUM may have believed that the dock strike was giving them much support and that they were in a strong position. The offer they refused was seen by some trade union leaders, not directly involved, as sufficient for a settlement.

The railways

Although little is reported in this chapter, the battle between the rail trade unions and the management was continuing. As examples, in July there were problems with a hostile signalman at the Sherwood signal box in Nottinghamshire who was preventing rail-borne coal reaching the main line. Also on the Coalville line a militant signal man at Moira stopped the rail-borne coal movement from a pit on that line. Road-borne movements were substituted for the loss in each case. A further example was that four NUR branch officials had to attend a trade union disciplinary hearing over failure to persuade signalmen at Thoresby, Mansfield and Ollerton to take disruptive action. This type of problem was to continue and caused rail-borne deliveries to be less than 250 000 tonnes a week throughout the remainder of the strike and to fall as low as 96 000 tonnes during one week, despite about 600 000 tonnes of coal being available. These coal flows compare with up to 1 500 000 tonnes a week in normal times.

The docks again

Peace in the docks did not last. There was to be a repeat of some of the July events when a further dock dispute arose in mid-August.[14] A large bulk carrier sought to dock at Hunterston in Scotland with imported coal for the Ravenscraig Steelworks, although the unloading of such cargoes had been blocked by the TGWU registered dockers. The vessel docked on 23 August. The intention of the management of the steel plant was that it would be unloaded by members of the iron and steel trade unions in the absence of TGWU members. A national dock strike followed, which lasted at some ports until a special delegate conference on 18 September accepted a settlement formula and laid down a quota of coal for Ravenscraig.

HOW ARE WE DOING?

The summer was at its height and monitoring studies were concentrating on predicting the endurance capability of the CEGB through the winter. How long could the lights stay on if the strike continued? The original plans assumed that electricity supplies would have to be maintained for six months and we did not believe that the strike would last more than a few weeks. By late July it had lasted for eighteen weeks and there was no sign of an end. Although coal supplies had been available stocks had reduced more than the CEGB would have liked.

About this time, Sir Walter Marshall accompanied Peter Walker to a meeting with the Prime Minister, Margaret Thatcher. She had received a letter from Norman Tebbit, the Secretary of State for Trade and Industry and a member of the committee of ministers overlooking the strike. He said that he believed that power station coal stocks would run out in January and that the government should find a means of winning the strike during the autumn. This made the Prime Minister anxious and led her to ask for the meeting.[15] The implication for electricity supply was that if there was an expectation of the CEGB failing during the winter then that should be avoided by more extreme actions as soon as possible. The options included forcing coal flows, which at that time were not regarded as feasible, from the coal stocks of striking pits to the have-not power stations, and coal imports at a substantial level, both using military personnel if necessary. These measures would have been highly provocative not only to the miners but also to CEGB industrial staff, whose co-operation was essential to the continued successful management of the emergency. Sir Walter Marshall had carefully to consider the implications.

Although the CEGB's own endurance estimates were consistent with Norman Tebbit's letter, it was necessary for Sir Walter Marshall to make his judgement of the risk of the CEGB failing during the winter. He believed that it was possible for the Board to do even better than it was doing at that time and that the endurance estimates were pessimistic. He decided that he should reassure the Prime Minister by giving his personal promise of an endurance beyond those that the Board's modelling assessments were indicating. She accepted that reassurance and did not press for the more extreme actions to be taken.[16] The Board was therefore left free to manage with the sensitivity that was necessary to yield the best results. A more robust style at that time would have been counter-productive and would have run the risk of stimulating support for the striking miners among the uncommitted power station staff. Sir Walter Marshall did not discuss this meeting on his return. There was, in any case, a growing unease about the length of the strike and an increasing urgency to find a means of getting through the winter. We knew that we had to do better.

Chapter 13

Can we get through the winter?

Stock needed to be taken of what had been achieved during the summer. There were two main features to the CEGB response to the coal supply emergency. First the establishment of a road coal flow that, together with what was being forced through the railway system, gave total deliveries of about 500 000 tonnes of coal a week. Second, the establishment of oil-based generation, which had reached a burn of about 350 000 tonnes a week, well up to the optimistic forecasts of our earlier contingency planning and saving 600 000 tonnes of coal burn. The sum of coal deliveries and the coal equivalent of oil burn at 1 100 000 tonnes compared with a winter burn of two million tonnes a week. There was still a big shortfall. What else was it possible to do?

We decided that if we were to fail in our statutory duty to keep the lights on, we were at least going to do so after having tried everything in our power. A number of options were identified in a brainstorming session by the operations team. The System Operations Branch made many of the proposals and assessed the endurance benefits. The options were all intended to reduce the need for generation at the coal-fired stations, more particularly at the ones not receiving coal deliveries, the have-not stations. All were worth discussing with the regions.

OPTIONS

The following options were considered.

Kingsnorth Power Station

Tom McInerney thought that there was scope for increasing oil-based generation even further at Kingsnorth Power Station. This would yield benefits equivalent to 22 000 to 50 000 tonnes of coal a week.

Increased gas turbine use

There were gas turbine generators in most of the large power stations. They had been installed for two main roles. One was to provide fast-start generating capacity to supply the power stations' own electrical auxiliary plant in the event of emergencies on the transmission system. The other was to provide peak-lopping capacity over short peaks of consumer demand. There were also gas turbine generators in separate gas turbine stations intended to provide back-up generation to critical parts of the transmission system where it was not economical to build more conventional plant. They also provided peak capacity.

These gas turbines had not been used beyond their normal role up to that time because of the difficulty of supplying them with gas oil. In addition their design made it necessary to overhaul their gas generators after a relatively short period of use, normally about 1500 hours. This was consistent with their normal short duration peaking use but a disadvantage for prolonged generation. If they were to be used for that purpose the problems of oil supply and overhauling the large number of gas generators would have to be solved. If that could be done it would be possible to save up to 20 000 tonnes of coal a week.

Increased use of private generation

Although in 1984 the electricity supply arrangements could not be said to have encouraged the generation of electricity by private independent companies there were nevertheless some private generators connected to the system. They were generally associated with oil refineries, chemical companies and large manu-facturing complexes such as Shell, Esso, ICI and Ford. Would they be able and prepared to help? If they had secure fuel supplies and spare capacity it might be possible to purchase some electrical energy from them to supply the transmission network. The oil company generation at least could be expected to have secure oil supplies. Jim Allen, the Head of the Commercial Branch, estimated that if we could gain assistance from the private generators we could save between 21 000 and 42 000 tonnes of coal a week.

Voltage reductions

The daily demand for electricity through the winter was characterised by a sharp evening peak when industrial and commercial demand overlapped the lighting load at the onset of darkness. In addition preparation of the evening meal in many households coincided with this early evening period. The peak changed its precise timing through the winter months as the time of darkness changed but was generally between 4.30pm and 5.30pm. If two stages of voltage reduction, each of 3 per cent, were applied over this period there would be little inconvenience to consumers. Most would not even notice that it had happened. It would allow us to avoid running the generating plant that was short of coal and burning the essential lighting-up oil necessary to stabilise combustion. Although, at about 4000 tonnes a week, the saving in coal would be modest, it would be at power stations where we needed to make the most urgent savings.

Gas-fired generation

Hams Hall Power Station near Birmingham had in its early years been converted to gas-firing. Increases in the price of the gas supplied by the British Gas Corporation had made it uneconomic to continue and the power station had resorted to coal-burning but had preserved the capability to burn gas. In fact it used gas in the way that other power stations used lighting-up oil for flame stabilisation. If this power station could be put back to a full gas burn it would be helpful in further reducing coal burn. This could yield a coal burn saving of about 25 000 tonnes a week. However the attitude of the gas industry to assisting the electricity industry with which it was normally competing was not known at this stage.

System reserve

The successful operation of an electrical power system requires electricity demand to be precisely and continuously matched by generator output. If there is a failure to do this, frequency can fall and ultimately cause the power system to collapse with widespread loss of electricity supply – a risk to avoid. The price to be paid to avoid it is to operate with a number of partially loaded generators held in reserve so that they can increase output at short notice. These are able to make good losses of output caused by the breakdown of other plant or to compensate for errors in estimating consumer demand. This reserve plant, since it is only partly loaded, is inefficient and as a result burns more fuel for each unit of electricity than it generates. The Dinorwig Pump Storage Station in North Wales could be used for this purpose, but was better used mainly to reduce coal burn by generating over peak demands. If we could reduce the quantity of coal-fired system reserve plant we could save some coal.

Other actions

There were many other actions that the CEGB regions needed to examine further. When the review of endurance was discussed with the regional directors of production at one of the monthly meetings it was agreed that each of them would look urgently at what they could do to help. The main possibilities were further to increase oil burn and road-borne coal deliveries but there would be others. Work was begun to look for ways of improving endurance. It was to be some time before the results were seen. We continued to be concerned that they might not be sufficient.

PICKETS AND ESSENTIAL SUPPLIES

In the meantime there seemed to be a resurgence of picketing activity. Mass picketing, with sometimes hundreds at a power station's gates, was usually shortlived. However it was worrying when a number of incidents occurred together and seemed to constitute a new trend. In July for example there had been one occasion when there were 2000 at Cottam and 450 at Ratcliffe Power Stations. We were reassured when we learned that those at Cottam were only there because the police had diverted them from local pits.

A review of how picketing and the supply of essential commodities were being dealt with at this time showed that arrangements were working well. When there was an urgent need, suppliers timed deliveries for when there were few pickets; they certainly avoided periods of mass picketing. The police were helpful and when necessary escorted difficult deliveries. There was at most power stations some form of picketing for all or most of the time so that making deliveries involved drivers crossing a picket line. If the drivers of the normal supplier were not prepared to do so then the next step was to engage another company to make the delivery. If that failed then it was necessary to make several attempts before deciding that the delivery could not be made by the contracted supplier. There were further options and these are discussed further in Chapter 19.

Helicopters were retained as an option. A fee was being paid to the company involved to retain them as a contingency. We had not been close to using them up to now. British Steel and the working pits had received the brunt of resolute mass picketing. Picketing at power stations had not yet been a serious problem except for a few cases of mass pickets and some stone throwing when the windscreens of lorries and vans had been broken. Generally these incidents tended to be counter-productive with drivers and power station staff becoming more determined to work normally. Would picketing be a new factor for the winter or did the NUM know that we still had substantial stocks of all materials and regard us as being secure? We had no means of knowing.

TUC 1984 CONGRESS

As the CEGB was working hard to improve its ability to keep the lights on over the coming winter it was time for the TUC annual Congress. There was some anxiety about this. We thought that the outcome might present us with further problems. The September Congress was in Brighton. It had a full-scale debate on the strike. Indeed it was one of the most emotional occasions in the history of Congress. The retiring TUC General Secretary, Len Murray, had met Arthur Scargill to prepare a resolution that would give full support to the miners on condition that the NUM returned to the negotiating table and remained there under TUC influence. Murray and Scargill attempted to get the unanimous support of the unions in electricity supply but failed to sign up two of the most important unions. These were the EETPU, under their General Secretary, Eric Hammond, and the Engineers and Managers Association (incorporating the EPEA), under their General Secretary, John Lyons.

The vast conference hall was full. Outside and in the galleries there were hundreds of miners who had come to give loud, exuberant, support to the NUM delegation led by Arthur Scargill. Motion 25 and the supporting statement pledged full support for the miners in their struggle to save pits, jobs and communities and appealed to other workers to ban the movement of coal and oil substituted for coal. At the same time the motion provided that support would only follow detailed discussions with the General Council and agreement with the unions directly involved.

The motion was moved by Arthur Scargill and seconded by Jimmy Knapp of the NUR. Scargill was given a hero's welcome by most delegates, his call for support for the miners and the motion being repeatedly applauded. At the end he received a standing ovation. In contrast, when Hammond and Lyons spoke they were shouted down and slow-handclapped, receiving support from few delegations other than their own. Hammond described the motion as lacking credibility, adding that nothing would be achieved. It was dishonest and deficient. His union was not going to stop the power stations for this motion. However, if the NUM would abandon their political objective and also call a national ballot he (Hammond) would recommend to his Executive a ballot of his members to support the NUM. Hammond knew of course that this condition would never be fulfilled.

John Lyons stated that if Congress passed the motion it would be in the knowledge that 'one, you are pretending to the miners already on strike for six months that support is coming when it is not; two, you will do so, most of you, safe in the knowledge that you bear no responsibility whatsoever for the outcome of what you are deciding; and three, it will not work'. He added that 'the Electricity Supply Industry is not and never has been available to solve industrial disputes external to it, not even for the miners. This is the tradition of the whole workforce of the industry'. What the workers in electricity supply are now being asked to do, said Lyons 'is to stop using coal which the NUM has failed to stop being produced, and the transport unions have failed to stop being transported. It is because of these failures that the electricity supply industry workers are being asked to threaten the country with desolation'. Motion 25 and the accompanying statement were overwhelmingly supported.

All the unions in electricity supply subsequently met in their standing body, the Electricity Supply Trade Union Council (ESTUC).[1] They decided to meet the NUM under the auspices of the TUC. At their own next meeting ESTUC issued a statement that it was united in its desire for the earliest settlement of the NCB/NUM dispute and to maintain the good relationships between the ESTUC unions.

However, most of the unions (with most of their members employed in other industries) had supported the decision of Congress and this appeared to create a problem. The TGWU, the AUEW and GMBATU issued identical guidelines to their members in the industry, confirmed as advice and not instructions, against handling new supplies of coal or oil in substitution for coal but to continue to use normal oil deliveries. The unions nevertheless advised their members not to withdraw co-operation from management; they emphasised the terms of the TUC guidelines on picketing and the need to report for work normally.

The guidelines prompted stewards in some power stations to question the levels of oil deliveries while there were refusals in a few stations to burn new stocks of coal or to co-operate with oil overburn. The advice to co-operate over normal supplies of oil was helpful to the CEGB, particularly at some stations in Yorkshire, the South West and North West, which had received no lighting-up oil since the strike started. In some areas the sense of community between station staff and local miners on strike was strong and there was a general disposition to support the decision of Congress. These stations tended to be the ones that had not been receiving new coal or additional oil. Stations located where miners were at work such as Nottinghamshire certainly ignored the decision.

The fact is that, within the stations, the Congress decision made little difference. Many staff were co-operating with abnormal operating requirements such as oil overburn and plant modifications, two-shifting of base-load stations, continued generation by plant which had been formally closed, and road-borne fuel deliveries. Staff in the large, oil-fired stations and in the older ones came into their own and welcomed the more demanding operating regimes. The increased levels of overtime work also acted as an incentive. Within a month of the Brighton Congress those seemingly momentous events had, for all practical purposes, been forgotten.

FURTHER PEACE TALKS

The fourth series of peace talks took place just after the September Congress.[2] Between 9 and 14 September the NCB and NUM leaders met several times. The first meeting was in Edinburgh, which will be remembered as the one where MacGregor arrived covering his face with a plastic bag. The talks continued at Monk Fryston Hall in Yorkshire but moved to the offices of British Ropes in Doncaster to avoid media attention. When the talks resumed at the Rubens Hotel in London they again failed as they had done at the same location in July.

Following the breakdown both sides issued statements on their respective positions. The difference between the two sides was again the third category of pit closure, which the NCB described as being when the remaining reserves could not be 'beneficially developed'. The NUM preferred words that implied practicability rather than an economic criterion because they were still not prepared to accept closures on economic grounds. This latest failure made it almost certain that the dispute would continue into the winter. It also made it imperative to find ways of maintaining supplies through the coming winter peak electricity demands.

NUM IN CONTEMPT AND OTHER EVENTS

Through August and September there was renewed legal activity about the strike's official status and the NUM's vulnerability to action against secondary picketing (see Chapter 22). The South Wales NUM were fined on 30 July for contempt for defying an order made on 17 April to stop picketing Port Talbot steelworks. They immediately indicated that they would not pay the fine and on 1 August sequestrators were appointed to seize the union's assets.

Following parallel actions by some Yorkshire and some North Derbyshire miners Mr Justice Nicholls ruled, on 28 September, that the NUM must not describe the strike as official or dissuade members from going to work or from crossing picket lines unless and until there had been a national ballot showing a majority in favour of a strike. He also ordered that area branches should hold elections and that the NUM should not discipline working miners.

In October, following a statement by Arthur Scargill that he still regarded the strike as official, a fine of £200 000 was imposed on the union for contempt of court; Scargill was personally fined £1000. Both the union and Scargill indicated that they would not pay these fines. However, a payment was then made on behalf of the latter. On expiry of the time limit for payment of the union fine sequestrators were appointed. They froze the entire assets of the NUM held at national level until the court directed otherwise.

Novel initiatives

There had been a moment of light relief in August when it was drawn to our attention that the NUM had started a 'switch on at six' campaign. The idea was to cause all those who were sympathetic to the miners to switch on electrical appliances at 6pm each day. It was said that this would force the electricity board to employ more coal-fired power stations and thereby eat up stocks. We watched the trend of electricity demand but could not see any evidence of a sympathetic response.

About the same time, the CBI were trying to help keep the lights on. They asked their members to reduce electricity consumption by 10 per cent, which they estimated would enable electricity supplies to be maintained indefinitely rather than just 'well into 1985' as the government were then predicting. Sir Terence Beckett, the Director General, had written in these terms to all the chief executives of member companies. He had discussed this intention during a visit to the CEGB. Sir Walter Marshall had said that we did not wish it to sound as though we were in a weak position because we were not. The CEGB would have preferred this initiative not to have been taken. Nevertheless it went ahead. There was no evidence that the message was misunderstood and also no evidence of a response.

There was a worrying report at this time that the NUM or probably some of their members had obtained a CEGB Midlands Region identity card and were having replicas made which would enable them to gain access to some important and sensitive sites. The security guards at the power stations were alerted, but nothing came of it.

IMPROVING ENDURANCE

The work of improving endurance enabled some of the more difficult options to be further considered. The CEGB regions were making good general progress.

Oil-fired plant

In response to the challenge, major oil-fired plant was increasing its output. At Grain Power Station, Fred Kirkby, the Station Manager, was now operating all four of its commissioned units continuously on overload. He was achieving this despite the station being manned, at the start of the strike, to operate only three units for two of the three eight-hour shifts each day. Littlebrook D Power Station was also operating on overload. Pembroke and Ince Power Stations were now coming up to full load using the electrical rotors taken from Ferrybridge coal-fired Power Station.[3] Tilbury and Blyth Power Stations had recently started an oil overburn programme, the latter using heavy fuel oil delivered by large barges. This was shortly to be followed in a similar way by West Thurrock Power Station. These were important events for stations that were not receiving coal and were regarded as have-nots. These developments required engineering work and the active support of staff in stations that historically had experienced difficult industrial relations. The belief in the CEGB's duty to keep the lights on was proving helpful in achieving difficult things, although at West Thurrock Power Station there was frequently an industrial relations problem. However, John Lewis, the Station Manager, had at least been able to arrange for modifications to be completed to give an oil burn capability with the aid of some plant removed from the decommissioned power station at Brunswick Wharf.

At Kingsnorth Power Station, which had been designed as a dual-fired (coal/oil) power station, spare oil-burner equipment was re-installed. The station had been commissioned burning oil but had completed its conversion to coal burning. Brian Vickers, the Station Manager, had now arranged for it to be fully re-converted to oil. In addition to refitting spare oil-burning equipment new, larger, oil-burner tips were fitted to increase the oil-burning capability. The planned increase in output on oil from the station was achieved.

Gas turbines

It was planned that all gas turbines would be used to the extent to which they could be supplied with oil and their use was increasing. It would be necessary to set up a much bigger overhaul programme if this much higher level of use was to be sustained. There was an overhaul facility at Rolls Royce who were the suppliers of the gas generators but further facilities were needed. The gas generators were essentially aircraft jet engines, which were used not only for electricity generation but as the propelling engines in ships, particularly warships. The Ministry of Defence facilities were an obvious potential source of overhaul support. Granville Camsey and the CEGB Spares and Repairs Engineer, Roy West, made the approach. In addition Dennis Leason, the Director of Engineering in the South Eastern Region, set up an overhaul and repair facility in the Littlebrook Power Station regional workshop. It was also necessary to arrange with Rolls Royce for the supply of the spare parts.

We also had to set up the gas oil supplies. These were to be mainly road-borne, using the small, independent, oil companies that were serving the CEGB regions well in supplying lighting-up oil in spite of the pickets. As these arrangements were set up the load generated by the gas turbine fleet was gradually increased. An unexpected benefit was that this presented more picketing targets to the NUM who had to decide whether or not to spread themselves more thinly to cover the new generating locations.

The contribution from gas-turbine generators turned out to be much greater than expected, saving up to 80 000 tonnes a week of coal burn. By the end of the strike they were to save the burning of 1 330 000 tonnes of coal, mainly at the have-not stations. This highly successful campaign had required patient and meticulous execution.

Private generators

The CEGB commercial staff under Jim Allan were, with the assistance of the area boards, trying to increase the use of private generation. It was proving difficult since it was being interpreted as a sign of much greater weakness than was the case. It caused alarm to the boards and to their major consumers who were becoming aware of the campaign to sign contracts for the purchase of electricity. The CEGB decided not to continue since the disadvantages were seen as potentially greater than the benefits. It would have been disastrous if it had caused the NUM and their supporters to believe that the lights were about to go out.

Voltage reductions

Voltage reductions were seen in a similar light. Their contribution to improving endurance would be small but could be helpful. The disadvantage was that they would be seen as a sign of weakness and the forerunner of disconnections and a failure of electricity supply. It was decided that this disadvantage outweighed the benefits and the plan was discontinued.

System reserve

The proposal to reduce the quantity of partially loaded generators used as system reserve was believed to be a different matter. If we reduced the quantity of reserve, we had to take the risk that voltage reductions would be necessary. The probability of that occurring seemed acceptably low and, if it were to occur, it would only be for a short time and possibly only over part of the country. The option was discussed widely within the industry and in particular with the area boards and the Electricity Council. The outcome was that it was applied from the return to GMT at the end of October. This was a decision that we were later to regret. On 5 November there were problems from power stations experiencing wet coal and plant breakdown. The resulting loss of output made it necessary to apply a stage of voltage reduction to some areas. This was given much publicity and interpreted as evidence of electricity supplies being affected by low coal stocks. We changed the policy quickly back to the normal one for system reserve. Adeney and Lloyd state[4] that the Secretary of State was not amused at the time but the CEGB did not hear anything of his displeasure.

Gas-fired generation

Gas-fired generation looked promising and Jack Davis, the Station Manager at Hams Hall Power Station, was ready to receive gas supplies. It only required setting up with British Gas and it was hoped that this could be done quickly over the telephone, being supported by the paperwork as soon as that was possible. In fact it proved not to be as simple as that. Although the British Gas Director of Operations was prepared in mid-August to arrange matters in this urgent and informal way, the Board Member responsible was not and it proved necessary to negotiate a price and set up a formal contract. It took until 2 October to get the generators on full gas burn. The Board Member concerned had reasons for this caution. When he was a director of the West Midlands Gas Board he had been involved personally in the dramatic events during the picketing of the Saltley coke depot in 1972. He did not wish to do anything that could induce sympathetic industrial action in the gas industry, which at that time was supplying 46 per cent of the country's primary energy needs. The formal contract enabled British Gas to be able to argue to their employees and trade unions that the supply arrangements were the result of normal commercial arrangements between the two industries. They could even have given evidence of the several weeks that it had taken to negotiate the price.

HAVE WE DONE ENOUGH?

The direct effects of the campaign to improve endurance through the winter were that some improvement in oil-fired generation had been secured; that gas turbine output had been increased but could only be sustained if oil deliveries and overhaul facilities worked well; and that gas firing at one relatively small station was being started. However it had been decided not to continue with reductions in system reserve, the use of voltage reductions and purchase from private generators. It was not clear at this stage whether sufficient had been done to secure supplies. We were inclined to think not.

The System Operations Branch had continued to develop endurance monitoring and simulation techniques. The most important need at this time was to be able to assess the future use of coal and lighting-up oil at the have-not power stations, which had not received coal and in some cases oil since the beginning of the dispute. It was clear from this work that we would fail during the winter unless we could greatly reduce our need to use the have-not stations over the coming period of high electricity demand.

We must try harder

Those who could do anything to improve the CEGB's endurance did their utmost to do so. Nothing was too small. As the autumn progressed many new but individually minor developments were being undertaken. In the South Eastern Region, Tom McInerney arranged that oil-fired generating plant that had been taken out of service for closure and decommissioning, but not yet dismantled, should be brought back into service. South Denes Power Station near Yarmouth was brought back. Richborough Power Station in Kent had a chimney that had been reduced in height the previous year as a cheap alternative to repair on the assumption that it was unlikely to run much. It was being used more and more as its road-borne oil supplies were improved. There were environmental complaints. The Region had to settle a claim from car importers for the damage done by acid smuts, but the output was important. A gas turbine station at Hastings was brought back to life. Cliff Quay Power Station near Ipswich was restarted after its earlier closure and supplied the grid. Although it was coal-burning, a coal supply using lorries from the Nottinghamshire coalfield was arranged. Decommissioned generating units were brought back into service at Northfleet and Belvedere Power Stations on the Thames.

We observed that there were picketing benefits from these developments. The pickets were well informed and seemed to be aware of these new initiatives. They moved away from the major Thames stations to cover the growing number of these smaller power stations.

There was an increased sense of urgency in the Midlands Region. Hugh Mathews, Jack Evans, his Fuel Supplies Officer, and their staff put renewed effort into improving the volume of road-borne coal supplies. Up to that time road-borne coal movements had reached between 200 000 and 300 000 tonnes a week. Through July the volume had depended on the number of pits on holiday. In the peak of the holiday season the coal available in NCB coal stocks at the working pits had been used to compensate for the reduction in fresh-wrought coal supply. This coal flow became firmly established and remained as a supplement to the fresh-wrought coal flow as the pit holidays came to an end. The Midlands Region were able to find even more lorries and increased the weekly tonnage moved. Their effectiveness in setting up these arrangements was remarkable. It required arrangements with the local authorities and police in the areas through which the coal was to be moved. It was necessary to plan carefully the routes to be used, and to agree them with all the interested and responsible parties. Then it was necessary to exercise a relentless discipline on the haulage contractors. Although coal by road to the large Trentside power stations was not part of the terms on which planning consent for their construction had originally been given, the conditions now existing led to agreement being reluctantly given. It was necessary to keep faith with the local communities by seeing that the agreed routes were meticulously followed. The lorries were marked as suppliers of coal to CEGB power stations so that they could be distinguished from others.

There were attempts at sabotage and actual cases. For example a garage was burnt down that housed some of the lorries serving the power stations. To safeguard the fleet, defended corral-type parks for the lorries were set up. These arrangements were excellently carried out and made a growing and impressive contribution to improving our position for the winter. They were to result in road-borne supply movements being increased to about 500 000 tonnes a week (i.e. 25 000 lorry movements, with another 3000 oil tanker loads a week). Cottam Power Station reached a peak of 1286 coal lorries and 50 oil tankers in a twenty-four hour period – an average of one lorry every minute.

The autumn press

There was little in the press about electricity supply over the autumn but it was obvious from what did appear that reporters were having some difficulty in understanding why the lights were still on. There were many reports about how long it would be possible to maintain supplies. The official line was 'well into next year'. The NUM had claimed in July[5] that, according to two academic analysts, there would be problems from coal shortage starting in September. During August and September the press carried reports of the predictions by city stockbroker analysts. They generally believed the CEGB's position to be weaker than it was because they all under-estimated the scale of the oil burn.

The only accurate predictions were by Phillips and Drew[6] who estimated power station coal stocks at 16 000 000 tonnes in mid-October. At that time the CEGB stocks were 14 700 000 tonnes. With the addition of the Scottish stocks the estimate was about right.

Further increases in oil-fired generation

The recently established heavy fuel oil-based generation at Tilbury, Blyth and West Thurrock Power Stations was now becoming more important and making an even greater contribution to the security of supplies. The lack of oil storage facilities at the two Thames stations was a problem and it was necessary to carry out frequent tanker unloading operations. This required day-in-day-out discussion and persuasion of the industrial staff, particularly at West Thurrock, who were not always sure how to judge the conflicting pressures between loyalty to fellow trade unionists on strike and the duty to keep the lights on. The result was that at this station oil burn was limited.

The review of what had to be done if the Board was to get through the winter had led to a highly motivated drive to increase oil burn at coal-fired stations. This required additional oil pumps, heaters and pipework together with modifications to burners. For many stations these were major engineering projects. This was not the case for a few stations in the Midlands Region, which had in their earlier histories experienced difficulties with coal-milling plant and had installed higher oil overburn capability to compensate. All the stations that were able were increasing their contribution to winning the battle for winter security of supply.

The increase in gas turbine generation was given a boost in September with the return to service of Bulls Bridge Power Station just west of London. It was a relatively new power station but, because of the high price of gas oil, had been closed and its gas generators removed to be used as part of the fleet of spares for gas turbine generating units generally. In August we decided that it should be brought back into use and by the middle of September it was back to full production using oil through a pipeline from Esso's West London oil terminal. Esso were later to give us magnificent support by persisting in honouring the supply requirement in the face of a trade union threat to close down the depot if they continued supplying the station. This was a critical time when it was still not clear that we could get through the winter. We were telephoned by Esso to ask whether the supply was important and we explained in confidence how critical all supplies were at that time. Esso stuck to their guns and risked a loss of supplies to many other consumers including Heathrow. The supplies continued and Bulls Bridge was important during the winter period.

SEPTEMBER EVENTS

September 1984 continued as an eventful month. In addition to the TUC, a further stage in the saga of the NCB/NUM peace talks and much work by many in the CEGB to prepare for the coming winter, there were the continuing problems of pickets, supplies of essential commodities and a number of lesser but still important issues to deal with.

Carbon dioxide supplies to nuclear stations remained a worry. Since we had limited storage we were very dependent on timely deliveries. The industrial action by ICI tanker drivers was continuing. This resulted in the stock levels at some nuclear stations being much lower than we were comfortable with. Resolute picketing could have caused many of these stations to be closed down but this had not occurred so far. There had been problems however and some deliveries needed a police presence.

One amusing facet of the nuclear picketing story occurred at Oldbury Power Station. Here the NUM picket had a caravan parked in a lay-by next to the station entrance. It was parked over a manhole beneath which was the water meter and valve for the power station's water supply. Had the valve been closed the station would have been forced to shut down within hours.

In September there was another resurgence of picketing with large numbers appearing at individual power stations for short periods. For example between 6am and 8am on 17 September about 500 pickets, accompanied by many policemen, appeared at Eggborough Power Station in Yorkshire. After two hours they dispersed and left about thirty pickets at the station entrance. The strategy of the NUM towards the electricity supply industry and in particular to the picketing of power stations was difficult to understand. It seemed to be almost random and it certainly missed many opportunities to further the cause of those on strike.

North Western Region had been steadily contributing to the CEGB's efforts, not least through its nuclear power stations, which were doing well, and the new oil-fired Ince B Power Station, which was now coming up to full output. In September the Region was becoming more important in coal flow terms and in taking advantage of the back-to-work movement in the coal industry. Under Jim Craig, the Regional Director General, and Roy Houghton, the Director of Production, a road haulage programme had been operating effectively on a modest scale for some time. During September it was gratifying to see its position further strengthened by the first deliveries since the strike started from Parkside Colliery to Bold Power Station and from Bickershaw Colliery to Huncoat Power Station.

THE NACODS DISPUTE

By the end of September the CEGB was faced with the potential loss of supplies from all the working pits with the NACODS ballot.[7] The National Association of Colliery Overmen, Deputies and Shotfirers was the trade union covering the coal industry's supervisory grades, and continued production at the working pits depended on them. A vote in favour of strike action by them would be a serious blow to the CEGB's plans. The NCB were attempting to reach an accommodation with them but it was going to be touch and go. The dispute had been precipitated by the NCB withdrawing the ruling that enabled NACODS members to be paid for not attending work if by doing so they would have to cross picket lines. The discussions to resolve this problem were made more urgent by a ballot in favour of strike action.

Two other issues became caught up in the dispute. They were the proposed cutback in productive capacity and the NCB's attitude to conciliation procedures. NACODS had suggested a system of independent arbitration over pit closures. ACAS became involved in efforts to settle the dispute. The stoppage by NACODS was scheduled to start on 8 October, but was called off at the last moment. ACAS held discussions not only with the two disputing parties but also with the NUM and BACM. On 16 October the NACODS executive decided to take strike action with effect from 25 October over the closure issue. The proposed stoppage was ultimately called off by the union's executive on 24 October on the basis of an agreement reached with the NCB under ACAS auspices the previous day. NACODS had regained the right to payment when they did not cross picket lines, had obtained agreement to a new pit review procedure with an independent body to adjudicate on any pit the union wished to keep open, and the withdrawal of the closure decision for the five contentious pits until reviewed by the new procedure.

An attempt had been made to involve the NUM and to gain a settlement between them and the NCB but this had failed. We were greatly relieved by the removal of this threat to coal supplies. There is some doubt whether NACODS members would have stopped work at the working pits. But it was good that this was not going to be tested.

END OF SEPTEMBER REVIEW

By the end of September there were detectable improvements on a number of fronts. Each week electricity generation from oil-fired stations was higher than in the previous week, coal deliveries were increasing and coal stocks were slightly higher. The end of September coal stock level at 14 700 000 tonnes had only reduced by 600 000 tonnes since the beginning of July.

Coal deliveries had increased from the 400 000 – 500 000 tonnes level typical of the summer to 700 000 tonnes. The road-borne delivery rate had increased to a magnificent 500 000 tonnes. It was partly dependent upon heavy stock lifts by the NCB. It would not be possible to maintain that level from fresh-wrought coal and the NCB coal stocks that were accessible at working pits were limited. Some stocks had yet to be opened up for supply to the CEGB. There were problems in some cases in doing that since the local planning authorities had to give permission for the road-borne lorry movement in the absence of railway support. Some were very sensitive about doing so. However persistence, and in one case the possibility of the stocks suffering spontaneous combustion and causing a serious environmental problem, finally led to the freeing of the coal flow. Overall the longer term supply expectations from fresh-wrought coal were the most reliable guide and, with the production level for deep-mined coal at just over 2 000 000 tonnes a month at this time, the prospects were not so bright. One possible answer was to open up coal flows from the coal stocks at the striking pits but that would be difficult, and potentially disturbing to other parts of the operation. Oil burn had now reached 474 000 tonnes a week and with gas-fired generation was saving the consumption of about 800 000 tonnes of coal a week. Since the start of the strike the capacity of plant burning oil had increased by many initiatives from just under 8 GW to almost 15 GW.

Generation from gas turbine generators was increasing under the new policy and had reached the equivalent coal saving of 40 000 tonnes a week.[8] The effect of everything done to reduce the coal burn was a saving of 900 000 tonnes of coal a week. The additional weekly costs of these measures had increased as their effect had. They were now costing £34 million a week compared with £20 million earlier in the strike.

The important question was had the CEGB done enough? It has first to be understood that the recent desirable trend in coal stocks had come partly from the low levels of electricity demand over the autumn period. The requirement for fuel burn would increase markedly through the winter. The main problem was that the stocks at the have-not stations were still coming down. Would they hold out? Our general coal stock position could be reasonably healthy yet we could still fail if the have-not stations were to run out of coal. This can be illustrated by the position in the North Eastern Region. It was judged wise for Bob Weeks, the Director General, and John Banks, his Director of Production, to maintain a careful approach to the movement of fuel in Yorkshire, where most of the large stations were situated. An example was Drax Power Station, the largest have-not station. In early April it had a coal stock of about 1 250 000 tonnes, but by the beginning of September it had fallen to 722 000 tonnes. Yet the station would have to be used in the coming winter. The present coal stock represented only about 4 weeks' supply for the five 660 MW generators then commissioned on the station. It had received no coal or oil since the dispute started.

We were faced with the need to force coal supplies to the have-not stations or to find means by which we could use them less. The former approach would put at risk the stability that had served the CEGB well up to that time and could put at risk some of the fuel flows and abnormal methods of working for which we had gained acceptance and upon which we were dependent. If we pushed too hard we could provoke solidarity with the miners that could cause our initiatives to be counterproductive.

Avoiding the use of the have-not stations had been the CEGB's policy up to now but that would not be feasible during the winter's high electricity demands. We had to face the problem of forcing coal flow to at least some of these stations over the early part of the winter.

Chapter 14

Winter

Despite all that had been done, as the winter started the CEGB believed that it could not get through it without some power cuts. The general position was good but the problem of the power stations that had not been receiving coal, the have-nots, remained a serious threat to keeping the lights on. If we accepted that we were going to fail, and that was the implication of having any cuts at all, it was necessary to advise the government. The options were to have planned rota disconnections over high demand periods at an early date or to wait until some power stations ran out of coal, when larger scale and more disruptive cuts would become unavoidable. The CEGB decided that it was not prepared to live with this belief. We already felt that we had moved up a gear, with the success of the campaign to improve endurance. There was confidence that we could do more; certainly there was a resolve to try.

The main problems of the have-not power stations came from the industrial relations climate in which the CEGB was working: it felt that it had to be careful about how much pressure it put on its power station staff. Yet it was determined not to fail and to see electricity supply as the means of settling a coal dispute as it had been in the early 1970s. For the reader to understand the issues, it is important to refer briefly to the industrial relations background in the electricity supply industry at this phase of the coal strike.

THE INDUSTRIAL RELATIONS SITUATION

The industrial relations climate was highly variable across the Board's power stations with wide differences of attitude. There were a number of influencing factors. One was the location of the stations. Those stations built in the coalfields recruited staff as the coal industry was running down. It was not surprising that they recruited operatives and craftsmen who were ex-miners. It was common for the staff at those stations to live in mining communities and for many of them to have sons, brothers or fathers who were miners. As a direct consequence there was a sharp difference between the attitude of power station industrial staff in the working coalfields and those in the areas where miners were on strike.

The power stations remote from the coalfields were not affected by the split between the working and striking miners. They were influenced by other factors, an important one being official trade union advice. Relations between the trade unions and management were good, with senior trade union officials knowledgeable about and supportive of the industry. There was effective and well-used negotiating and consultative machinery. The union members were used to receiving advice from their officials and that advice normally had a big influence on their behaviour. Some of the industry's senior trade union officers themselves were in a difficult position with the conflict, on some occasions, between their union's official policy and their loyalty to the industry employing their members. Their informal advice had to take both into account.

There were differences between stations that came from the varying industrial relations climates that existed before the strike. Some were 'difficult' stations with a degree of antipathy between staff and managers. Others had more co-operative attitudes. These differences were sometimes related to regional factors, for example some Merseyside and Thames-side stations had long traditions of conflict and contrasted with many of the Midlands stations.

All these factors were to influence the preparedness of station staff to co-operate with actions that could, under some interpretations, be regarded as strike-breaking. The main argument used by CEGB managers was that their responsibility was to keep the lights on. This was what the industry normally sought to do. There was a strong public service ethic in the industry and this simple message had a big influence.

Through the strike managers had done what they could to set up oil and coal flows, to handle the fuel and to burn it. In some stations this was not too difficult, but in others some of the staff had shown themselves to be so difficult that to force issues would have resulted in industrial action. The policy had been to do what could be done to promote longer endurance short of provoking a hostile reaction. That reaction would certainly mean that the CEGB gained less and could result in stimulating an organised reaction to its endurance measures and greater unity with the striking miners. The Board had gained much by its policies and would have preferred to continue the subtle pressure to gain more and more support for what it was trying to achieve. However, the problem of the have-not power stations now presented such an urgent challenge to winter electricity supplies that the Board had to take bigger risks to force through fuel supplies and to use them for generation.

Trade union guidelines

The first important actions to improve the position were to arise from a chance benefit that came from the trade union guidelines for members following the TUC 1984 Congress. Part of the advice was that their members should co-operate in the delivery and use of normal oil supplies. This was too good to miss: the initiatives were to be used over a period to gain improvements in oil supply. The advice from the electricity supply industry's trade unions to their members gave an authoritative definition of what they should or should not do. Although the guidelines were written with the intention of limiting what their members should do, they presented the opportunity for management to expect or require the staff to do more where they were currently doing less than the advice. In late October and early November this was used to reintroduce lighting-up oil supplies at Drax, Fiddlers Ferry and Eggborough Power Stations where the staff's support for the strikers had been extreme. At Drax this was for six tanker loads per day – about 120 tonnes. It was started very tentatively with the expectation of mass pickets and great difficulties in sustaining deliveries; however these did not materialise.

The importance of this development cannot be overstated. It was the first change in the situation of the have-not stations and it was successful with less reaction than could have been expected. At the same time the oil enabled the three stations concerned to be used with far more flexibility than would otherwise have been the case. We were sure that this change would not have been possible without the new and more specific guidance from union officers to their members. Unfortunately it was also specific about not handling new coal supplies and it was necessary to live with that at these particular stations for the present.

COAL TO THE HAVE-NOT POWER STATIONS

We next had to face the problem of coal supplies to the have-not power stations. Ed Wallis's System Operation team assessed the coal that the have-not stations would need over the winter. Although the stations would be used as little as possible to preserve their stocks, it was inevitable that they would have to be used to a greater extent as the demand for electricity increased over the winter. The estimate was that they would need 3 500 000 tonnes of coal up to April 1985. The problem was that, despite all that had been done to improve the situation, they were more than 400 000 tonnes short of that quantity in October. The CEGB needed to keep in mind however that the estimates were for an average winter. A severe winter would require higher coal burn and could more than double the deficit. It would be possible to judge progress in the future by assessing the trend of that deficit.

If the Board could gain a coal flow and make use of it, even if at only some of the have-not stations, then we might be able to get through. The larger stations where there were problems were Eggborough, Ferrybridge C, Drax, Blyth and Thorpe Marsh in the Yorkshire part of the North Eastern Region, Fiddlers Ferry on Merseyside in the North Western Region, Aberthaw B in South Wales and Didcot in Oxfordshire, both South Western Region stations. There were also a number of smaller stations.

To explore the options separate meetings were arranged with the directors and managers of the North Eastern and South Western Regions, which were the main prospects. Gil Blackman chaired them. The North Eastern management confirmed that the risks to existing gains were far greater in their power stations, situated as they were in the most militant of the striking coalfields. It was decided that the Region would prepare a plan for forcing through coal flows but not take the risk of implementing it until it was essential. It might be possible to avoid it if progress was made in other regions.

The South Western Region was different. Roy Beatt, who had taken over on the recent retirement of the Director General, Douglas Pask, managed a region whose stations had played a major part in sustaining nuclear and oil-fired output up to that point. It was now to play an important part in changing the have-not situation. We decided that attempts would be made to re-establish oil and coal flows to Didcot, to the two power stations at Aberthaw, and to Uskmouth, a smaller station.

Didcot Power Station

Didcot was the first and most promising option. Norman Holland, the power station manager, with his team, and the Midlands Region fuel supplies team under Jack Evans, were to prepare the programme carefully. Not only were there problems to be overcome with the attitude of trade union members on the station, it was also necessary to persuade the local authority of the need for the road-borne coal flow and the choice of routes. Norman Holland and his colleagues started by greatly increasing the volume of road-borne oil supplies during October. The station had already increased the boiler oil-burning capability and could use the oil. During early November this reached a peak of approximately 4000 tonnes a day. The industrial relations preparations were then made to start a step-by-step process of reintroducing a coal flow. The Midlands Region arranged a road-borne flow of coal from Leicestershire. The staff at Didcot were under pressure from the trade unions and other external bodies supporting the NUM cause, and were therefore reluctant to use the coal. The receipt of coal supplies started on 20 November. It was first stocked separately and the station had the novelty of having a 'white' coal stock and a 'black' coal stock. Initially the coal-handling staff would not touch the black coal. They were then persuaded to handle it but would not put it to the reclaim hopper, which would have enabled it to be conveyed to the boiler bunkers for burning. Through a long and intense process of persuasion the coal was eventually burnt. It was not until 20 January that this regime was sufficiently secure for Didcot no longer to be defined as a have-not station. This process took effort, patience and time and the outcome was never sure. However, it did work and ultimately made a big difference to the Board's position.

Not only were the power station's internal industrial relations problems important to the outcome. The road-borne coal supply route through the Vale of the White Horse raised public relations difficulties; the arrangements were planned and managed with care and were successfully executed.

The South Wales power stations

Roy Beatt was also making progress in South Wales. On 11 November lighting-up oil supplies were resumed to Aberthaw Power Station, an important precedent in an area with a well-organised NUM. It had been seen as a difficult location in which to gain improvements. The oil burn potential was important.

Uskmouth, a smaller power station near Newport, was able to resume coal deliveries on 11 December using a private coal source from Cardiff docks. This was a further useful step.

South Eastern Region and Brighton Power Station

Tom McInerney also decided to make progress with coal, setting up a coal flow from Cumberland by ship to Brighton Power Station. It was only a small station but coal-based generation there would help. The National Union of Seamen, with Jim Slater their General Secretary, were solid supporters of the NUM. The ship owners who normally supplied the coal stations on the coast and estuaries explained to the CEGB that they had been told by the NUS that if they moved coal they would be 'blacked' for ever. Tom McInerney had been considering the reintroduction of coal deliveries into the Thames Estuary stations but this would put at risk the benefits of a large, stable oil burn. There was much to lose and only marginal benefit. This was not true of Brighton, which was a smaller station and of course geographically separate from the Thames. A shipping company offered a ship despite the NUS threat, the *Kinderance*, with a carrying capacity of 3000 tonnes. The ship was loaded in Cumberland, sailed and was successfully berthed at Brighton on 20 November, having passed through lock gates operated by TGWU members. The station staff required some persuasion and encouragement to unload since the coal was not from a 'normal' source for Brighton. Then hundreds of NUM pickets appeared at the station, obviously having been told of the impending arrival of the ship. They applied much pressure to the station staff. The police who were present in numbers were not at all happy. The pickets decided to take matters into their own hands and occupied a coal unloading crane during a meal break. The station staff strongly resented this and their attitude to the miners was changed by that event. Alan Stevens, the Station Manager, decided to respond quietly. All the electricity supplies to the crane were switched off for 'safety reasons'. The cab heaters were electric and the weather was cold and within twenty-four hours the miners came down and the pickets melted away. Coal unloading then continued without problems and the CEGB had another have-not station that was now receiving a coal flow.

Ship owners had a number of successes after this test cargo. They wished to move coal and were prepared to take it anywhere. However, it was not until close to the end of the strike that it was unloaded at the Thames stations.

North Western Region

Although the 2000 MW Fiddlers Ferry Power Station was a continuing problem as a large have-not station, the Region were making progress elsewhere. On 27 November a coal flow was established to Padiham Power Station near Burnley, so another have-not station had its status changed. However, it was a small one with only 112 MW capacity.

THE GENERAL SITUATION

In parallel with the work of establishing a fuel flow to such stations there was progress with other endurance-improving actions. There were two ways of judging the progress being made. One was the measure of the overall flow of coal, the other the level of oil burn and coal stocks. At the end of November the heavy fuel oil burn had climbed even higher. It was now at over 500 000 tonnes a week, reducing the coal burn by 900 000 tonnes a week. The gas turbine plant was now saving nearly 80 000 tonnes of coal burn a week. This was higher than we had expected. The Midlands road-borne coal flow had remained high, aided by some pits returning to production. Our position was strong with 14 500 000 tonnes of coal still in stock. We believed that we could keep the lights on into the summer if we could continue to make progress at the rate we were doing.

The monitoring of the have-not stations' coal had been continuing week by week over the early winter. By the end of November the assessment showed that those stations had used 147 000 tonnes of coal less than we had expected. This was because of the better than expected oil burn and other measures to reduce the stations' use. It was also because of the absence of cold weather. The result was that the have-not stations were estimated to require 3 748 000 tonnes of coal to April and now had coal stocks that were only 271 000 tonnes short of that. The deficit had been reduced from 418 000 tonnes since 1 October. This did not include the benefits of the coal flow to Didcot since we had no evidence at that time that the staff would co-operate with the use of the newly delivered coal. The Board had made progress but more, much more, was needed. We might yet have to take the high risk of forcing coal flows into the large Yorkshire stations.

NCB INDUCEMENTS FOR A RETURN TO WORK

While the CEGB had been improving its position and was now less pessimistic about getting through the winter, there had been important developments in the coal industry. Following the breakdown of peace talks on 31 October the NCB made an announcement on 2 November that those miners who returned to work by 19 November would qualify for holiday, bank holiday and rest day pay since the strike began and for a £70 Christmas bonus. The total inducement was over £500. For some underground workers the offer was prolonged beyond that date and a lesser sum was generally available for those who returned up to 23

November.[1] These developments were important to the course of the strike and were closely watched by the CEGB.

The NCB area directors had been working for a long time to persuade miners to return to work. Approaches had been made to individuals taking into account where they lived and the need to provide a secure means of getting them into work and back home through the picket lines.[2] Some progress had been made but the return to work before this new initiative could only be described as a trickle. But now, in the two middle weeks of November, over 10 000 men returned to work.[3] The number of pits without men regularly at work halved from 84 to 41. There was a strong reaction from the striking miners with increased violence on and around the picket lines and an upsurge of vandalism.

The culmination of the expression of anger and frustration was an incident in which a taxi driver taking a miner to work at Merthyr Vale colliery in South Wales was killed. A block of concrete was dropped from a bridge on to his car. During December and January the rate of return to work slowed but was still higher than the trickle before November and the evidence was that, once men returned to work, they stayed. NCB coal production increased marginally and had to be moved from an increasing number of pits.

PICKETS AND OTHER FACTORS

The pattern of the strike and the CEGB response continued more or less unchanged through December and into January 1985. Mass pickets appeared from time to time. The NUM's picketing policy and strategy remained difficult to understand and continued to seem random. Difficulties in getting essential commodities into stations occurred from time to time but were not serious. It looked as though the CEGB would not now need the helicopters. Oil burn continued and in December had reached its high point of over 500 000 tonnes a week. Oil purchase and delivery were continuing to keep pace with need, but there were to be difficulties in the new year.

One problem worth mentioning was the difficulty John Lewis, the Station Manager, had in persuading West Thurrock Power Station staff to handle oil. In early December the oil tanker *Sten* moored at the jetty and it took much discussion and ultimately a ballot of all station staff before it was decided that it could be discharged. This is cited as evidence of the sensitive industrial relations climate within which we still had to manage.

CONFIDENCE GROWS

Just before Christmas an important landmark was reached. Since 1 October the have-not power stations had consumed about 500 000 tonnes of coal less than expected. They were now in the much stronger position of requiring just under 3 000 000 tonnes of coal in the period up to April and actually having in stock 100 000 tonnes more than that. This was still not an entirely secure situation since a spell of severe weather or a problem with oil could lead the Board into a coal deficit again. However, the trend was strongly in the right direction; the CEGB were almost safe.

The surplus of coal at the have-not power stations could now be judged against their coal needs beyond April. The daily peak electricity demands and the effects of the power transfer limits of the transmission network were such that it would be necessary to run some of the have-not power stations into June to avoid power cuts. This would require 110 000 tonnes of coal over that necessary to run to April and they just about had that amount already in stock. If the favourable trend continued, and in particular if the developments at Didcot led to it becoming established as a have station, then the Board was secure not only to the beginning of the summer but into the coming winter. The have-not stations would not be required to run in the summer.

At this time the new 2000 MW cross-Channel cable link with Electricité de France (EDF) was in the final stages of construction. Sir Walter Marshall decided, with the support of his executive director colleagues, that there would be an attempt to accelerate the completion of the work and the commissioning of the cable so that the electricity imports would strengthen the Board's position over the early winter of 1985–6. Accordingly Gil Blackman took over the chairmanship of the project board, which was managing the British end of the link with the objective of meeting the tighter timescale. In addition EDF were asked to ensure that their work would enable the link to be commissioned early. The link was arranged in two parts and each had the capability of reducing coal burn at CEGB power stations by 78 000 tonnes a week.

The combination of the stronger position of the have-not power stations and confidence in the commissioning date for the new link with France led Sir Walter Marshall to be able to advise Peter Walker at one of the regular briefing meetings that the Board now believed that it could keep the lights on during the whole of 1985. It has to be said that there was a degree of optimism about this prediction. It would be a tough target to achieve, nevertheless it could be done. We were at that time improving weekly our endurance capability. It was a worthy objective and we would have to be successful.

The Secretary of State issued a statement over Christmas that electricity supplies could be maintained throughout 1985. The timing of the statement was excellent, just before the coldest part of the winter. It received wide coverage and had a big effect on the public and the strikers. Its impact was partly because Peter Walker was sparing in his public statements. He had successfully distanced the government from the dispute and when he spoke he therefore commanded attention. There was as a result more public confidence in our ability to keep the lights on.

Except for this important statement the Christmas and New Year holiday period was quiet. The NUM President attracted some publicity by appearing on the power station picket lines. On Christmas Day he appeared at Ferrybridge B Power Station and on New Year's Day at Thorpe Marsh Power Station gates with twenty of his NUM colleagues.

JANUARY EVENTS

Aberthaw Power Station oil deliveries in November had allowed John Fairclough, the Station Manager, to set up a programme of oil overburn generation in that station. This was helpful at a have-not station. Aberthaw had been recognised as being vulnerable to the efforts of pickets since the access road was between embankments. Mass picketing could be difficult for the police to control. Such an event occurred on 9 January with about 160 pickets attempting to stop oil deliveries. Despite the difficult situation the police were able to control them and we were encouraged by oil supplies continuing. The station oil-based generation now looked more secure.

WINTER PEAK DEMAND

As January progressed the drift back to work in the coal industry became more marked with the NCB telling the Board that they expected production to be restarted at Kellingley and Selby collieries in Yorkshire and Whittle colliery in Northumberland. If the CEGB wanted that trend to continue it had to keep meeting electricity demand in full and show no sign of weakness. The winter peak demand had not yet been reached and we were still not entirely sure that we would be able to meet it in full. If we failed, even because of a technicality unconnected with the crisis, the situation could change dramatically. Much political capital would be made out of any problem in meeting peak demand in full. The main risk came from having to reclaim stock coal. When the peak demand occurred it would be during freezing weather and difficulty in handling the frozen coal could reduce generation output.

The peak demand normally occurs during a period of cold weather in December, January or February. There was a potential for a high peak in any of these months if low temperatures produced a high heating load. On 16 and 17 January cold weather was experienced with temperatures below freezing all day and moderate to heavy snow falls in the south. This was sufficient to cause high peak electricity demands on both evenings and on 17 January the highest ever electricity demand of 46 215 MW was met in full over the half hour ending 5.30pm.

Although we had not yet got through the winter this was for the CEGB an excellent event that we thought must demonstrate its strength. The Board gave it maximum publicity, the announcement being made the same evening. It coincided with press coverage of an NUM Executive meeting and seemed to have a chilling effect on that meeting. This was probably the signal to the NUM and the striking miners that they were at the beginning of the end.

END OF JANUARY

By the end of January the coal flow to Didcot and the pattern of its use had become so well established that it was no longer regarded as a have-not station.

That change was sufficient for the monitoring predictions to show that the have-not stations now had sufficient coal stock to allow the Board to meet consumer electricity demand into the autumn. In addition Gil Blackman was driving for early completion of the cross-Channel link. The effect of this additional benefit was that we were growing in confidence that we could avoid power cuts in 1985.

It was noted in our routine internal monitoring report at the end of January that the additional cost of operations up to that time was £1490 million and that the weekly additional cost was just under £50 million. This high cost was worrying, but if we were to keep the lights on it could not be avoided. Wise oil purchase was all that was available to us as a measure within our control and we continued to do what we could to keep prices down.

On 23 January a tanker was arrested on Kingsnorth jetty by the Admiralty Marshal. The vessel was the subject of a dispute over the payment of a repair bill. The arrest was to make inoperative the oil unloading facility for Grain and Kingsnorth Power Stations, which together were about a third of our oil burn. It took until 28 January for the matter to be cleared up and some reduction in oil burn at the two stations was necessary.

In January HM Customs and Excise judged that certain Caribbean oils were being received with unsound certificates of origin. They believed that they should be subject to EEC duty when their certificates claimed that they were tax exempt. This was to constrain oil availability for some time since suppliers did not know what their tax position would be. It became necessary for the CEGB to agree to take the risk to free up oil deliveries.

There was a marked lack of urgency by the public authorities who were dealing with these issues. Neither seemed to understand how much depended upon a speedy resolution of the problems. Perhaps the Board was experiencing one of the consequences of its own low profile public relations policy. Both the above incidents, described in detail in Chapter 17, could have had serious effects on the last stages of the dispute.

THE NUM AND THE RETURN TO WORK[4]

During January the return to work in the coal industry continued. In mid-January 2000 or more NUM members were returning to work each week and nine pits started producing coal for the first time since the strike started. As this was taking place informal meetings between the NCB and the NUM had been set up. They led to further meetings between the NCB, NUM and NACODS.

This was the sixth series of talks since the strike started. They led to the preparation by the NCB of a further document to provide the basis for a settlement. The events led to a meeting between the Prime Minister, the Secretary of State for Energy and the TUC on 19 February. This was followed by discussions between the General Secretary and Deputy General Secretary of the TUC and the NCB, which arrived at new review proposals. These were presented to the NUM on 20 February in a document that they understood to be the NCB's final position. The proposal was essentially to implement the agreement reached with NACODS. The document was rejected by the NUM National Executive Committee.

The dispute between the striking miners and those who continued to work was taken further in January. The proposed disciplinary procedure, known as NUM Rule 51, had been an important point of contention since the summer of 1984. Nottinghamshire NUM feared that it would be used to try to discipline those who had continued to work. In January the NUM National Executive Committee took the first steps towards suspending or expelling the Nottinghamshire NUM. In the event the special delegate conference necessary to follow up the action was not held. Nottinghamshire NUM made certain that they could control their own affairs on this and other matters by changing their rules to give the local area rules precedence over the national rules in the Nottinghamshire area.

END OF FEBRUARY – THE END APPROACHES

By the end of February there were increasing signs that the strike would end shortly. Production had resumed in parts of the Yorkshire coalfield. In the CEGB the position was improving rapidly. A coal flow had been started to Aberthaw Power Station on 15 February and ship-borne supplies from the North East to Thames power stations were about to resume. The CEGB endurance position had become extremely strong and it was now sure that its higher risk plans would not have to be implemented. In any case in the changed environment they would now not be difficult to achieve.

In February there had been growing support among the striking miners for a proposal to return to work without a settlement and with the dispute continuing. This did not seem initially to be acceptable to the NUM leadership. However, by the end of February the number of miners who had returned to work, according to the NCB, had passed 50 per cent and in the week ending 1 March nearly 9500 miners returned to work. An NUM delegate conference held on 3 March ordered a return to work on 5 March without a settlement. This was not obeyed by all the areas but by 11 March all had returned.

THE CEGB HAD KEPT THE LIGHTS ON

Although the dominant feeling was relief that the strike was over, it would be false not to admit that there was a feeling of achievement among the CEGB's management team that the Board and its staff had maintained electricity supplies. This was tempered by an awareness of the suffering of striking miners and their families and by concern about the high cost of the strike.

Chapter 15

Back to normal and counting the cost

The return to work in the coal industry marked the end of a long and exhausting period for many in the CEGB. It had been a time of continuing anxiety over whether electricity supplies could be maintained but the CEGB had been successful and it was now time to return to normal operations.

The strike was of course seen as a major event. It had involved all the energy industries in one way or another, the steel industry, the rail and road transport industries and also shipping and docks. Unlike the coal disputes of 1971–2 and 1973–4 it had had only a small impact on manufacturing industry. The explanation was obvious: this time the CEGB kept the lights on and there had been no three-day weeks. Because the Board kept its head down, what it had done seemed not to be fully appreciated; indeed it was hardly known to industry, the media or the general public.

The significance of what was seen by some as Margaret Thatcher's victory over Arthur Scargill has been referred to by three ex-cabinet ministers in their autobiographies.[1] Their general theme was that the strike was a revolutionary challenge that had to be resisted. Margaret Thatcher's view of the challenge is conveyed by the title of the chapter in her book that she dedicated to the strike, 'Mr. Scargill's Insurrection'. The outcome, according to them, enabled industrial change, started by the Thatcher government, to continue to the end of the decade.

In economic terms it involved the loss of 25 000 000 working days[2] and the addition of £2.75 billion to the Public Sector Borrowing Requirement. According to Nigel Lawson, Chancellor of the Exchequer at the time, it reduced output, worsened the balance of payments, exacerbated unemployment, increased public borrowing and undermined the pound, as well as being partly responsible for sharp increases in interest rates in the summer of 1984 and the early days of 1985.[3]

The strike came at a time when the power of the trade unions was in decline. A number of factors, including legislative and economic, were tending to reduce their influence. If the strike had been successful it might have restored some of the lost ground. It would certainly have demonstrated the power of combined trade union action. The strike was a direct challenge to the NCB's ability to close down uneconomic surplus capacity and as such was seen to challenge management's right and ability to manage. If the NCB had lost, many other managements would have been weakened including, probably, the CEGB's.

Adeney and Lloyd[4] make a general judgement, quoted by Lawson[5] and worth repeating here: 'Few episodes in the Thatcher government's life went so well as its handling of the miners' strike. It won its main objective: it faced down the weightiest constitutional challenge it was likely to face on the UK mainland'.

THE CEGB'S LOW PROFILE

The miners returned to work with the dispute not settled. Judged by any rational criteria the strike had failed and the main reason for its failure was that it had not caused an emergency in electricity supply. Statements by the NUM leadership and the government during the strike showed that it was the view of both sides that success or failure would depend upon whether or not the lights stayed on. However, the manner of the return to work left the basic reasons for the result less than clear, certainly to the general public and even to many commentators.

This was partly, if not largely, the result of the deliberate policy of the CEGB to eschew publicity. There was the potential for recriminations in trade union circles and many of the Board's staff had elected to adopt the public service objective rather than the advice of their union. The Board did not wish to expose them to criticism by drawing attention to the role that the Board had played. In addition the Board did not wish to give information about the means by which it had been able to maintain supplies. If there was to be another strike it did not want to have gratuitously provided the unions with the information they needed to succeed. These considerations led to a decision by the Board to keep its head down. No publicity was to be sought and no information would be given. This would continue the successful public relations policy of the strike.

The policy was to have a marked effect. While the ex-cabinet ministers' autobiographies played down the role of the CEGB, this contrasts with less public indications of the government's view of the importance of the CEGB's work. Lord Marshall tells the story of a potential embarrassment that he had to deal with. About three months into the strike the Prime Minister wished to say publicly that the CEGB had been doing extremely well. Peter Walker was well aware of the CEGB's policy of saying little and also that the Board's public service responsibility was the clear reason for what was being done. He discussed Margaret Thatcher's intention with Sir Walter Marshall, as he then was, and they advised her not to make the statement in the House of Commons that she had been planning. The CEGB's concern was that praise from the Prime Minister could have made our actions look as though they were politically motivated, which was the last thing we wanted.

After the strike the government's view of the CEGB's contribution was clearly marked by the peerage received by the Chairman. In addition there were to be two OBEs, one awarded to one of the authors and one to Hugh Mathews, which also were taken as recognition of the role the CEGB had played. Gil Blackman, who had carried much of the responsibility, was already the holder of a CBE and that made it difficult for his contribution to be recognised in the Honours List.

GETTING BACK TO NORMAL

When, in early March, the strike could be seen to be coming to an end all the elements of the endurance strategy were operating at their peak. The most important commitment was oil purchase. No further purchases would now be made and the objective was to reduce the supply in an orderly way with the cargoes already purchased. On 5 March, the date of the main return to work, some 800 000 tonnes of heavy fuel had been purchased and were in transit to the CEGB. The burning of this oil enabled oil-fired generation to be reduced in phases, which fitted in with the resumption of coal deliveries and the general return to normal operations. Because of this policy it was not necessary to sell cargoes on the open market.

We were interested to see what would happen to the market price for heavy fuel oil when we stopped our purchases. By careful purchases and by coming out of the market from time to time we knew that we had prevented prices from rising above the US$200 per tonne level. This had required a steady nerve from time to time but over the year-long strike the price had been generally held steady at US$180 to US$190, about the level at which we entered the market. When we stopped our purchases, the price of heavy fuel oil in north west Europe dropped from US$190 per tonne to US$130 over a few days. This was a clear guide to the effect that our purchases had had on what would otherwise have been a falling price.

The resumption of coal production and of normal rail services took far less time than might have been expected. Within two months the coal supplies available to the CEGB were well up to normal levels and coal stocks were again increasing. In 1985–6 the NCB reached record levels of productivity, earnings were the highest yet paid in the industry as a result of the productivity incentive scheme, and 27 pits which could no longer produce profitably were closed – 25 of them having been agreed at local level. Sales to the CEGB rose to a record 80 000 000 tonnes and CEGB coal stocks rose to just under 20 000 000 tonnes. To mark the transformation in the coal industry's performance and the new start that was now being made, the NCB decided that they would in future trade under the name of British Coal.[6]

WHY DID THE LIGHTS STAY ON?

A number of factors unintentionally helping the Board to keep the lights on are of particular interest.

NUM strategic and tactical failings

The first was that the NUM leadership decided to achieve a national strike through the application of the domino theory. It was a policy that did not include a national ballot but which depended on the use of mass pickets to bring pits and coalfields out on strike, even though they had ballot majorities against such action. The British miners have always had the respect of the general public and the instinctive support of many in their fight for proper pay and conditions, but the violence and intimidation associated with these tactics were to lose the striking miners many friends. The declared political objectives of Arthur Scargill lost the good will of many more.[7] The loss of support extended to many trade union members, particularly in electricity supply. When faced with having to decide whether to support the NUM or to perform tasks necessary to maintain electricity supplies most chose the latter. As good trade unionists they might not have taken that view had the proper democratic processes been successfully followed by the NUM.

The NUM's split

The application by the NUM of the domino theory was also the direct cause of the split in the NUM itself. The continued production of coal in Nottinghamshire and other parts of the Midlands that came from that obviously helped the Board.

The split in the NUM led to a prolonged and diverting dispute between the working miners and the NUM leadership over whether the strike was official or not. That and the legal proceedings connected with picketing, contempt and sequestration occupied the NUM leadership when they should have been directing the dispute. The overall effects of the domino theory turned out to be a split union, continued coal production, doubts about whether the strike was official and a marked loss of sympathy for the NUM's cause. It was an outcome that even the advocates of the theory must have found disquieting.

The NUM's preoccupation with internal affairs and the continuing battle in the courts may have been one of the reasons for the lack of a co-ordinated attack on power stations. The CEGB expected better organised and more determined picketing than occurred. If, as we believed, the success of the strike was likely to come from a stranglehold on the electricity supply industry, it was difficult to see this reflected in the NUM strategy. The attention to power stations could be described as no more than haphazard compared with 1971–2.

A further failure of the NUM leadership was in the timing of the strike. When faced with the issue of principle over economic closures the leadership would have lost credibility if there had not been a robust response, but to call for a strike at that time was strategically wrong. The summer period of the strike yielded little benefit to them compared with what would have come from continuing the overtime ban to the start of the winter.

A redeeming factor for the NUM was the support from the rail unions, which came close to sterilising the coal produced by the working miners. Together with the support from the Transport and General Workers Union through the two dock strikes and their advice to members in the power stations, these were the most helpful commitments to the NUM that any union could offer. But all this support was not sufficient to compensate for the inherent weaknesses in the form and timing of the strike.

An unexpected factor for the CEGB was the length of the strike. All its contingency planning before the dispute had assumed a strike of six months. It was surprising that it continued for a whole year. Operational planning, managed by Ed Wallis and his team, enabled the CEGB to plan well ahead during the strike and to deal with the consequences of its extended duration. Without that the length of the dispute could have played into the hands of the NUM in spite of their strategic ineptitude.

CEGB STRATEGY

The CEGB's strategy was basically to replace coal by oil-fired generation and to transport the coal that was available to as many power stations as possible. This was to be done without forcing issues with staff to the point of stimulating a strong reaction favourable to the striking miners.

There were two levels of strategy. One dealt with the general problems of oil burn and coal availability and the other with the specific problems of the have-not stations. The first strategy was successful and ensured, early in the winter, that a large-scale failure of electricity supply was not going to occur. The second took most of the winter to resolve.

The CEGB's major strategic decisions and their effects were as follows.

Imports from Scotland

The electricity demand that had to be met by CEGB power stations was reduced by the purchases from the South of Scotland Electricity Board. These amounted to 6.7 TWHs compared with 2.9 TWHs in the year before, the equivalent coal burn savings being 3 000 000 tonnes and 1 300 000 tonnes respectively. This was well up to the assumptions in our contingency planning before the strike.

Nuclear generation

The output from nuclear stations was the highest achieved up to that time. The troubled AGR stations were beginning to improve, a trend that unfortunately did not continue over the following three years. The output from nuclear plant was 36.9 TWHs compared with 31.3 TWHs the year before. That improvement saved about 2 500 000 tonnes of coal burn.

Oil-based generation

The total electricity output from oil-and gas-fired generation[8] was 88.0 TWHs which saved a total of 39 600 000 tonnes of coal burn compared with a normal 4 000 000 tonnes of coal equivalent from oil. The 35 600 000 tonnes of coal burn saved by this increase was by far the most important factor in maintaining electricity supplies. It had almost twice the effect of the contribution from the working miners. Oil burn peaked at over 600 000 tonnes through the winter. Had it remained at the 360 000 tonnes envisaged in the pre-strike contingency planning it would have saved 10 000 000 tonnes of coal less. The coal stock at the end of the strike was only 11 100 000 tonnes so it can readily be seen that the additional oil burn was crucial to our success. This additional oil burn mainly came from the late summer campaign to improve endurance to get through the winter. That can now be seen to have been essential.

Coal supply

After oil-fired generation the next most important factor was the coal supplied during the strike. About 24 000 000 tonnes of deep-mined coal was produced by the working miners. In addition open-cast coal continued to be produced normally and some coal was available from NCB stocks. The rail unions' support for the striking miners was so effective that only 11 900 000 tonnes could be transported to power stations by rail. This would have been insufficient to have kept the lights on over the winter period. It was the large-scale road-borne coal movement organised by the CEGB Midlands Region that enabled advantage to be gained from the working miners' output. That operation was to supply 16 900 000 tonnes of coal and was crucial.

The influence of the working miners was of course much more than the coal they produced. The political, legal and other consequences of the split in the NUM were important factors influencing strongly the eventual outcome.

Coal stocks

The pre-strike contingency planning had oil-fired generation and high coal stocks as the main components of the endurance strategy. When the strike started the CEGB's coal stocks had fallen from the October 1983 peak of 30 800 000 to 23 900 000 tonnes, this being the effect of the NUM overtime ban. In the period from the start of the strike on 12 March 1984 to the full endurance measures being implemented on 22 April the coal stocks had fallen to 18 300 000 tonnes. They were to fall by a further 7 200 000 tonnes to 11 100 000 tonnes by the end of the strike.

Of the total fossil fuel burn over the strike of 81 000 000 tonnes of coal or coal equivalent, 12 800 000 tonnes came from coal stocks. This compares with the quantities already quoted for oil burn and coal deliveries of 39 600 000 and 28 800 000 tonnes respectively.

WERE ALL OUR ACTIONS NECESSARY?

The general assessment must be that all the steps taken were necessary. Without any one of them electricity supplies could not have been maintained over the winter. Even with the measures taken the margins were narrow in the late winter. These judgements are particularly true for the have-not power stations. Had the endurance-improving actions not been taken we would have been forced to take higher risks. It is difficult to judge what would have happened if coal flows had been forced into the difficult stations. It would probably have led to strong opposition and to a greater unity with and support for the striking miners. It would certainly have led to deeply divisive industrial relations which could have put at risk the whole endurance strategy. That risk would only have been taken if the CEGB would otherwise have failed to keep the lights on. The energy, skill and inventiveness of many people enabled that to be avoided; the fortunate result was that CEGB industrial relations were not adversely affected.

WHAT DID IT COST?[9]

The additional costs of fuel and electricity purchases resulting from the strike had been carefully monitored weekly through the period. The costs had resulted from: higher than economic levels of oil burn; operating uneconomic plant brought back into service from reserve or after decommissioning; and purchasing more electricity than usual from the South of Scotland Electricity Board and other external sources. They had been assessed by comparing the costs of what normally would have been incurred had there not been a strike with the actual costs. The comparison for the full period of the strike is shown in Table 15.1.

Other costs were: staff costs £4 million, depreciation £2 million; materials and service £13 million and interest charges £41 million. The total extra costs including those in Table 15.1, were £2020 million. That considerable cost should be considered in the context of the CEGB's turnover in 1984–5 (excluding the strike costs) of £7454 million and that for the industry as a whole shown in the Electricity Council's accounts as £9442 million.

WHO FOOTED THE BILL?

The issue of who should pay for the extra costs of keeping the lights on came up at an early stage of the strike. Most of the costs arose from the additional fuel costs and the normal way for the CEGB to recover this excess was through the fuel price adjustment in the bulk supply tariff.[10] If that had operated through the strike it would have led to adjustments to the prices of bulk supplies to area boards, which reflected the fact that the average price of fossil fuels had increased by nearly 50 per cent because of the high volume of oil burnt. The increase in electricity price would have been about 0.9 pence per unit on the then average

Plate 1 An entrance to the shafts of a disused London tube station converted to bomb-proof wartime accommodation for national control of the grid system.

Source: National Grid Company

Plate 2 Stray barrage balloons dragging their cables caused more wartime grid faults than enemy attacks.

Source: National Power

Plate 3 Warmly clad in coats and mufflers, members of the Central Electricity Board meet by candlelight during a power cut in the 1947 fuel crisis.

Source: Associated Press

Plate 4 December 1970. A darkened Piccadilly Circus during the fourth day of the work-to-rule and overtime ban by power station industrial staff.

Source: Hulton Picture Library

Plate 5 Winter 1962-3. Transmission teams called out to repair damage to overhead lines are exposed to snow driven by gale force winds in the Pennines in efforts to keep power flowing.

Source: National Grid Company

Plate 6 Miners' pickets on the Thames at Battersea Power Station in January 1972.

Source: Hulton Picture Library

Plate 7 Rail coal deliveries to build up stock in preparation for a miners' strike. This is a so-called 'merry-go-round' train normally used to supply the large stations.

Source: Powergen

Plate 8 Helicopter trials to enable supplies of essential materials to be delivered to power stations over pickets.

Source: National Power

Plate 9 Grain Power Station achieved record output during the 1984-5 miners' strike and saved 9 million tonnes of coal burn.

Source: Powergen

Plate 10 Trawsfynydd Nuclear Power Station in North Wales like other nuclear power stations saved coal burn in the 1984-5 miners' strike.

Source: Nuclear Electric

Plate 11   The Kingsnorth oil jetty was the single point of supply for oil to Kingsnorth and Grain Power Stations which were the greatest concentration of oil-fired generation in the CEGB.

Source: Powergen

Plate 12 Publicity photograph for the BBC television programme based on the book - broadcast on 23 April 1994.

Those pictured (as listed below) were all members or staff at the CEGB during the 1984-5 miners' strike, excepting Howard Sallis, co-author (back row, extreme right) who was at the Electricity Council.

From left to right, front row:
Ed Wallis - Systems Operation Engineer; Lord Marshall - Chairman; Frank Ledger - Director of Operations (co-author); Gil Blackman, Board Member for Production.

From left to right, back row:
Hugh Mathews - Executive Director, Midlands Region; Tom McInerney - Executive Director, South Eastern Region; Derek Parry - Station Manager, Cottam Power Station; Des Healey - Shop Steward, Didcot Power Station; Fred Kirkby - Station Manager, Grain Power Station; Peter Vey - Director of Information and Public Affairs; Roger Jump - Station Manager, Drax Power Station; Norman Holland - Station Manager, Didcot Power Station; Ken Fort - Coal and Ash Plant Foreman, Didcot Power Station; Roy Allan - Shop Steward, Didcot Power Station; John Wooley - Fuel Supplies Officer.

Source: National Power

Table 15.1 Fuel consumption and costs

	Consumption (in MTCE*) % of total		Costs £ million		
	Actual	Without Strike	Actual	Without Strike	Difference
Coal	40	79	1757	3491	−1734
Oil	39	4	3753	381	3372
Gas	1	0	57	0	57
Nuclear Fuel	16	16	532	532	0
Purchases of Electricity	4	1	338	73	265
Total	100	100	6437	4477	1960

* MTCE means millions of tonnes of coal equivalent
Source: CEGB Annual Report and Accounts, 1984–5

price to consumers of 4.5 pence. Such a change would have fully met the additional costs of the measures taken.

In the early months of the emergency it was decided not to allow the fuel price adjustment formula to operate in this way, at least while discussions took place on who should pay. Later, following consultation with the Electricity Council and area boards, the CEGB resolved to limit the operation of the fuel price adjustment so that the additional costs were not passed on to its consumers.

The view of the industry was recorded in the Electricity Council's Annual Report for 1984–5 in the foreword and review of the year by the Chairman, Sir Philip Jones. He said that maintaining supplies through increased oil burn and other measures had imposed costs amounting to some £2020 million. The industry's strongly held view was that these costs should not be passed on to the electricity consumers through higher electricity prices on the grounds that the issues at stake in the miners' strike were essentially national ones. He added that, at the end of the strike, the government had accepted this view.

The result was that the industry in general and CEGB in particular made losses for the year 1984-5 of £1723 million and £1945 million respectively.[11] Had it not been for the strike the financial out-turn would have been profits of £297 million and £75 million respectively. The industry shared the burden by area boards accepting exceptional charges from the CEGB in aggregation up to half of the additional costs attributable to the strike and subject to a maximum in the case of each area board of half of that board's area reserve. This led to an exceptional charge of £934 million to them, and to the CEGB carrying the remaining £1086 million. As a result the reserves of the industry were substantially reduced and the financial targets earlier set by government were not met. In fact, instead of making a net payment to government of £746 million under the external financing limit (EFL) for 1984–5 it was necessary to increase external financing by £523 million.[12]

The answer to the question who footed the bill is, therefore, that since the direct result of the measures taken was to impact on the EFL, thereby increasing the public sector borrowing requirement, it was the tax-payer who paid.

CONCLUSIONS

The costs were substantial but they have to be set against the responsibility of the industry and the CEGB for continuity of electricity supply. There was no ambiguity about the Electricity Act and its interpretation by the government and the industry. It required a 'continuous' supply and unless the industry was relieved of that responsibility that is what it had to make available to its consumers.

What was done was necessary to maintain supplies and, in contrast with the great coal strikes of 1971–2 and 1973–4, the country's electricity consumers did not suffer a three-day week or any disconnections. For this outcome those who were managing the CEGB's operations felt a deep sense of gratitude to a whole range of people and institutions from the Department of Energy, the Electricity Council and the electricity boards to the working miners, the police and the road transport drivers of hundreds of coal lorries. Above all, however, the CEGB was grateful to its own staff in power stations, transmission districts, system operation and at regional and Board headquarters. They overcame a succession of difficulties, lived up to the best traditions of public service and enabled the CEGB, in keeping with its best traditions and its statutory duty, to keep the lights on.

Part III

Resource management in the 1984–5 miners' strike

The CEGB succeeded in maintaining power supplies during the strike by careful use, within its strategy, of a number of key resources. These included system operations, plant, oil, transport, manpower, chemicals and information. Each chapter in Part III tells the story in some detail of how their use was planned, put into effect and constantly adapted to changing needs. These are the elements of crisis management in one of the nation's basic industries.

Chapter 16

Coal on the move

A general account of coal supplies and their relevance to the CEGB's endurance objective was given in Part II. Some of the events briefly described there are expanded here and new material added. The story is one of collective achievement by many people against considerable odds.

A CEGB VIEW OF THE NCB

The attitude of the NCB to the CEGB influenced how we viewed the arrangements to withstand a coal strike. The political climate since the two nationalised industries were established and the privileged position of the NCB made us feel over-dependent on the coal industry. Although there were other, and often cheaper, sources of primary fuel supply, it was in practice inevitable that nearly all of our fuel needs were met by the NCB. The other options of coal imports, independent indigenous coal supplies and oil-fired generation, were limited and at best marginal, which led to the relationship not being that of normal supplier and customer. Although there was collaboration on many issues, it was not uncommon to be told by NCB managers that it was the duty of the CEGB to take and burn the coal that NCB had mined. What made matters worse was that we considered the coal industry's management to be greatly influenced by the NUM. Indeed it was only a slight exaggeration to say that we felt ourselves the captives of an industry largely controlled by the NUM.

We were well aware of the hardship endured by mining communities in the past and of the dirty and hazardous coalmining environment and had much sympathy for the miners. Despite that, it was in the clear interest of our own customers that there should be a more commercial coal industry, which closed down its high cost surplus production and took full management control of its affairs. If it was to remain a monopoly, we at least wanted to see it become a lower cost monopolist.

In Chapter 9 reference was made to the agreement of the CEGB to accept additional supplies of coal in order to build up power station stocks. This led us into a strong commitment to prepare for the likely NUM strike and to solve many problems in managing higher coal flows and larger coal stocks than ever before.

We had no intention of being the weak link if the NUM took industrial action that interfered with how we ran our business.

ACCELERATED COAL DELIVERY SCHEME

The commercial arrangement with the NCB for the stock build-up programme was the accelerated coal delivery scheme. This was agreed with the Department of Energy and the National Coal Board in February 1982. In response to the CEGB's concern that the additional costs should not be borne by electricity consumers, the agreement applied to all deliveries not commercially required. The crux of the scheme was that the cost of these extra supplies would be withheld from the monthly payments to the NCB at an agreed figure of £40.30 a tonne, comprising £37.50 a tonne pit head price and a notional transport cost of £2.80 a tonne. In addition, a further £2.00 a tonne would be withheld to cover stocking and handling costs and, whereas the monies withheld to cover coal and transport would be recovered by the NCB when the coal was eventually burnt, the stocking and handling charge would not.

This scheme continued, with modified prices following the NCB's November 1982 coal price increase, right up to our achieving the peak coal stock in October 1983 at the start of the NUM overtime ban. By that time 6 000 000 tonnes had been supplied under the scheme. Arrangements were made to pay for this tonnage when it was used during the strike.

IMPORTS

Chapter 9 referred to the events of early 1981, which led the government to agree with the NCB and the NUM to limit CEGB imports to the minimum practical level. This was defined as 750 000 tonnes a year. Through the early months of the accelerated delivery arrangements there were frequent debates with government about this limitation but we could not budge them; the minimum was not increased.

Although some cargoes were sold, by October 1982 there were 2 250 000 tonnes of CEGB coal in stock at continental ports with over 2 250 000 tonnes to be delivered from Australian contracts over the following twelve months.[1] With only 750 000 tonnes being allowed as imports to power stations this led to an expectation of 3 750 000 tonnes being in stock on the continent by October 1983. There was a big contrast between dealing with the surplus of imported coal, which could have been delivered relatively easily to the Thames power stations, and the problems that we encountered in achieving the extra coal flows for stocking.[2]

BUILDING COAL STOCKS

The coal stock targets at the power stations were successively 24 000 000,

26 000 000 and 28 000 000 tonnes. Each target was set for a date which seemed at the time a likely one for the start of the coal strike. Ultimately 30 800 000 tonnes were in stock by October 1983. This greatly exceeded earlier predictions of coal stockyard capacity at our stations. Earlier we had thought that it would be necessary to purchase additional land to accommodate the extra stocks. Had we done so it would have been necessary to install extensions to the coal-handling facilities to allow the more distant stocks to be worked.

To avoid spontaneous combustion coal stocks have to be consolidated by being run over by the heavy earth-moving equipment used for stocking out and recovering the coal. The problem was to stock coal to a greatly increased height and yet to have inclines that the earth moving equipment could cope with. Spontaneous combustion could cause the whole stock to be lost or require costly and embarrassing corrective action. The shape of the stock was of a ridge with a flat top and steeply sloping sides. It was common for the ridge to be curved and even in some cases horseshoe shaped. Later, when the NUM had aerial photographs taken, this led them wrongly to conclude that we had great holes in our stocks and much less coal than we claimed.

The coal stock story is shown graphically in Figure 16.1 and the distribution of the coal between stations in Table 16.1. The coal stock increase can be seen in the context of the past levels of stocks. The challenges of the stock build and of the high weekly coal transport programmes were severe.

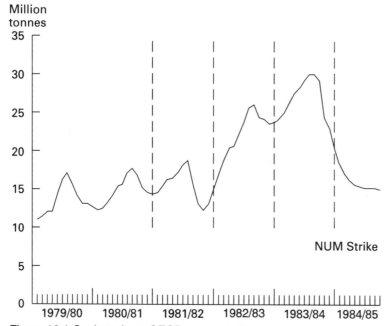

Figure 16.1 Coal stocks at CEGB power stations

Source: CEGB Operations Department

Table 16.1 Coal stock distribution

	Start of Stock Build April 1982	Peak of Stock Build October 1983	Start of Miners' Strike March 1984
South Eastern Region			
Acton Lane	17	16	–
Battersea B	39	21	–
Brighton B	126	172	124
Cliff Quay	96	96	40
Deptford	42	13	–
Goldington	70	4	–
Kingsnorth	458	901	614
Little Barford B	70	30	–
Rye House	46	2	–
Tilbury B	356	1109	1014
West Ham	22	17	–
West Thurrock	355	1079	984
Central Stock	2	10	–
Total	**1698**	**3393**	**2776**
South Western Region			
Aberthaw A & B	553	892	560
Carmarthen Bay	53	20	–
Didcot	440	1359	811
East Yelland	32	9	2
Rogerstone	46	5	–
Uskmouth A	2	–	–
Uskmouth B	116	182	158
Total	**1244**	**2453**	**1531**
Midlands			
Castle Donington	277	520	357
Cottam	1064	2281	1777
Drakelow A & B	206	1414	355
Drakelow C	405	–	711
Hams Hall	146	194	166
High Marnham	511	687	434
Ironbridge B	344	1104	806
Meaford	89	84	43
Nechells	4	–	–
Ratcliffe	825	1645	1147
Rugeley A	217	450	281
Rugeley B	398	1085	900
Staythorpe A & B	196	404	315
Stourport B	57	30	2
West Burton	982	2320	1801
Willington A & B	385	901	607
Total	6123	**13118**	**9702**

Table 16.1 Continued

	Start of Stock Build April 1982	Peak of Stock Build October 1983	Start of Miners' Strike March 1984
North Eastern Region			
Blyth	405	1089	832
Doncaster	25	–	–
Drax	1449	1791	1649
Eggborough	824	1650	1259
Elland	80	100	97
Ferrybridge B & C	1307	2422	1737
Keadby	56	7	–
North Tees	49	–	–
Skelton Grange A & B	235	452	332
Stella North	83	137	157
Stella South	147	174	160
Thorpe Marsh	453	1198	1175
Wakefield	115	158	166
Total	5228	**9179**	**7564**
North Western Region			
Agecroft	70	251	187
Bold	79	120	96
Carrington	104	152	135
Chadderton	15	–	–
Connahs Quay	48	–	–
Fiddlers Ferry	842	1867	1722
Huncoat	31	49	35
Padiham	77	138	116
Roosecote	37	44	31
Westwood	33	41	25
Total	1336	**2664**	**2348**
CEGB TOTAL	15629	**30807**	**23921**

Note: Due to rounding, totals and sub-totals may not equate to the summation of individual station values.

Source: CEGB Operations Department

In the 1982 and 1983 period of stock build-up the availability of suitable NCB coal was surprisingly one of the problems. Although the NCB production level exceeded its sales, the surplus coal was not all of appropriate quality. There were some differences of opinion between the CEGB and NCB over how much of their available production could meet CEGB quality standards. We required coal that could be handled by the power station coal-handling plant and burnt with sufficient effectiveness to allow the power stations to maintain full load. The quality requirements were well understood and were applied. The NCB had substantial quantities of coal in stock. Some of it was suitable, some could be made suitable by further treatment, but some was entirely unsuitable because of a high chlorine content (which caused corrosion of boiler furnace tubes). One view of events during this stock build-up period was that the NCB saw the increased supply programme as an opportunity to sell coal that would normally have been rejected on quality grounds. The CEGB had to do the best it could in balancing the need for volume against the disadvantage of lower quality. One of the NCB area marketing managers made a comment to his CEGB equivalent that 'Arthur Scargill is the NCB's best salesman by far'.

The transport of the increased coal supply also presented problems. It was necessary to transport typically 1 850 000 tonnes a working week compared with a normal CEGB weekly programme of 1 650 000. The additional quantity may not seem much but, since the British Rail investment in rolling stock and the manning arrangements were based on both being fully utilised at the normal weekly tonnage, to achieve greater flows required additional hours to be worked. We were not sure what the attitude of the railway workers would be to that opportunity. In the event, apart from two periods of industrial action, it was possible to achieve the target.

The period of the ASLEF strike in January and February 1982 is referred to in Chapter 9. The gross effect of that strike was the loss of about 4 000 000 tonnes of coal. However an increased oil burn and a later increased coal flow restored the position. Periods of disruption to coal and oil flow from industrial action in the supplying of associated industries were not unusual in the 1970s and early 1980s. From 1976 to 1983 there were five years in which there was some form of industrial action on the railways, two in which there were disputes affecting road-borne oil and coal supplies and two in which there were area level NUM strikes. Only one year was free of fuel supply disruptions. They all gave us problems.

During cold weather in early 1982 there were problems loading and moving coal by rail. There were, however, some compensating improvements when the NCB made an agreement with the NUM to increase the weekend loading of trains at pits. The railway system was always hard-pressed to supply the normal requirements of the large, highly-loaded power stations in the Aire Valley of South Yorkshire. The increased supply requirement could only be met with everything operating to its full potential. It was to remain a critical part of the stock build operation right up to the strike. We were helped to some extent by the eagerness of train crews to work overtime when needed. These issues were generally dealt with successfully at the long-standing tripartite meetings between BR, NCB and CEGB regional officers.

THE STRIKE AND THE ROAD-BORNE COAL MOVEMENT

Coal supply problems from the NUM overtime ban and the start of the strike are described in Chapters 9 and 10. The main difficulty was how to transport the available coal to the power stations, given the unparalleled support for the striking miners from the railway unions. The massive road-borne coal movement was so important that it is worth adding to what was said earlier. From a normal low level the road-borne coal movement was to peak at over half a million tonnes a week, involving about 25 000 vehicle movements, some of only 5 miles and others of over 150 miles. With parallel oil deliveries and the need to move ash by lorry many power stations resembled Trafalgar Square at peak time.

At the beginning of the strike NCB coal production seemed to cease. The industry appeared to be in shock. Coal supplies in general, including imports, had ended. As the position cleared and the Nottinghamshire miners resumed work, some coal again became available to us. In addition, in the words of Jack Evans, the Midlands Region's Fuel Supplies Officer, we looked hungrily at the untouched NCB stocks. He had a complete record of all stocks held within his regional boundaries and started immediate negotiations with the NCB who wished to help and were interested in turning their wasting assets into cash.

Although some railway coal movements continued after the start of the strike, the long and hard struggle to maintain and improve them was to continue throughout and was to yield little improvement.[3] Meanwhile the main means of delivering fresh-wrought and stock coal to power stations would have to be by lorry. Since the available coal was in the area of the Midlands Region of the CEGB it became their role to organise its transport. Much of the remainder of this chapter comes from Jack Evans' recollections of how the road-borne movement was managed.

Managing the road-borne movement of coal

The most urgent requirement was to clear all new production. Some of this was poor quality, but we had to demonstrate that if miners were prepared to defy the intimidation of the mass pickets and continue working, we would purchase, move and burn the coal they produced. In fact the CEGB Midlands Region management made a commitment to the NCB area directors that they would take all new production and this they did with the full involvement of the power station managers and staff.

The build-up of the fleet of road haulier contractors occurred in phases as the need for greater coal flow increased. The first phase involved clearing the fresh-wrought production. The queues of lorries at the working pits at this time were embarrassing to the NCB and we tried hard to avoid them. Further phases were associated with increases in coal production, the working of stocks and also with the need to improve endurance through greater coal flow and supplies to the have-not power stations. The volumes of road-borne coal were to increase from 100 000 tonnes a week in May to 300 000 in August and to over 500 000 in November. The progress is shown in Table 16.2. The fact that many of the lorry drivers were members of the TGWU and that that union had formally advised their members not to move coal made little or no difference.

At each phase there was a search for vehicle fleets that were available for one reason or another. Since the strike was national there were lorries laid up in some areas. These were identified and all owners who were willing to relocate were

Table 16.2 Weekly coal deliveries in thousands of tonnes

Week ending	Rail	Road	Canal/ conveyor	Total	Remarks
11 Mar 84	1021	167	66	1367	Inc. 113kt. seaborne
18 Mar 84	461	97	16	670	Inc. 96kt. seaborne
25 Mar 84	455	82	12	574	" 25kt. "
1 Apr 84	426	83	10	519	
8 Apr 84	239	68	16	323	First significant attempt by rail unions to stop coal flows
15 Apr 84	207	80	17	304	
22 Apr 84	259	69	14	342	
29 Apr 84	154	48	8	210	Easter Holiday
6 May 84	295	84	20	399	
13 May 84	209	106	16	331	May Day Holiday
20 May 84	275	165	19	459	
27 May 84	259	200	17	476	
5 Jun 84	121	98	6	425	Whit/Spring Bank Holiday. Start of Colliery Holiday Period.
12 Jun 84	243	221	19	483	
17 Jun 84	210	258	18	486	
24 Jun 84	176	272	18	466	
1 Jul 84	172	265	19	456	
8 Jul 84	199	239	13	451	
15 Jul 84	166	291	14	471	
22 Jul 84	190	318	18	526	
29 Jul 84	107	309	10	426	} Peak Colliery Holiday Period
5 Aug 84	96	321	12	429	
12 Aug 84	116	319	16	451	
19 Aug 84	130	331	20	481	
26 Aug 84	154	334	19	507	
2 Sep 84	128	265	15	408	Late Summer Bank Holiday
9 Sep 84	198	376	15	589	
16 Sep 84	200	435	17	652	
23 Sep 84	203	461	21	685	
30 Sep 84	197	483	22	702	
7 Oct 84	210	468	24	702	
14 Oct 84	171	484	23	678	
21 Oct 84	187	519	25	731	
28 Oct 84	180	494	21	695	
4 Nov 84	188	522	23	733	
11 Nov 84	158	525	26	709	
18 Nov 84	156	513	25	694	Flow to Didcot established
25 Nov 84	153	500	29	685	Inc. 3kt. seaborne
2 Dec 84	182	509	25	719	" " "

Table 16.2 Continued

Week ending	Rail	Road	Canal/ conveyor	Total	Remarks		
9 Dec 84	156	514	28	701	Inc.	3kt. seaborne	
16 Dec 84	182	510	27	722	"	"	"
23 Dec 84	165	474	20	662	"	"	"
30 Dec 84	5	52	–	60	"	"	" Christmas Holiday
6 Jan 85	100	257	12	372	"	"	"
13 Jan 85	177	477	24	689	"	11kt	"
20 Jan 85	147	429	28	615	"	"	"
27 Jan 85	192	434	28	668	"	14kt	"
3 Feb 85	196	422	26	654	"	10kt	"
10 Feb 85	231	390	29	661	"	11kt	"
17 Feb 85	180	410	25	622	"	7kt	"
24 Feb 85	209	475	28	725	"	13kt	"
3 Mar 85	219	454	28	727	"	26kt	"
10 Mar 85	358	454	31	963	"	120kt	"

Total 30 055kt

Source: CEGB Operations Department

signed up. All this involved continuing negotiations with haulage companies to take account of the rapidly changing circumstances. It was demanding in time and effort and involved at least two members of staff in every discussion to witness agreements and to ensure probity. When smaller, more distant companies were available they were introduced to the existing main hauliers to work as subcontractors to facilitate sound administration.

The Midlands Region fuel supplies staff who were running the operation had their own yardstick on prices and were ready at all times with rates, routes and conditions before negotiations began. Road movements were generally cheaper than those in the British Rail price agreement, and it is interesting to note that the cost of the whole road operation turned out to be cheaper than if British Rail had undertaken this task. It must be conceded, of course, that long distance bulk movement by rail is cheaper and any profit from transport at this time was at least partly offset by the many payments made towards road repairs.

The facilities for sampling and weighing rail-borne coal at pits and power stations were important to managing the normal cash flow between the CEGB and the NCB. Over £3000 million a year normally flowed as a result of the figures that were agreed. These facilities were not usable when loading lorries. The problem was how to ensure the overall integrity of the purchases and deliveries.

Getting the fuel inside our own stockyards was our main interest. At the outset, the NCB's ability to produce acceptable and accurate statements of loading was poor. The power stations were also ill-prepared and under-staffed to document deliveries. The hauliers, with many of their drivers new to the area, to the pits, to the power stations, and to procedures, were totally confused; documentation was considered a luxury. To keep hauliers financed and on the road provisional payments were made while we caught up with the administration as best we could. At a later stage it was pleasing to report that the hauliers, without exception, opened their books to CEGB fuel supplies personnel for assessment and confirmation.

Pickets

All the road-borne deliveries had to go through the picket lines. On many occasions these were at both pits and power stations. There were occasions when the picketing was so intense and threatening that the drivers were reluctant to run the gauntlet. At those times we either redirected the movement to other stations or, in some instances, arranged a special team of drivers, known in the Region as the 'A Team' or the 'Bridgehead Drivers', the name which they themselves had adopted.

While one might consider financial necessity as the reason for the attitude of the drivers, we had the impression that they had little sympathy for the miners' actions and, if anything, judged that the miners already had many advantages over most other industrial groups in remuneration and job security. CEGB did not get involved in that debate.

Life in the lorry fleet

Although passing through the picket lines at each end of the journey could be exciting, the lorries and their drivers were always at some risk. To protect lorries overnight they were placed in a series of defended corral-type parks. Many of the lorry drivers who were from outside the area – and many of them were – elected to park overnight at the working pits. Security was good there and washing and canteen facilities were made available. Many of these lorries had large modern cabins with a bunk that allowed the driver a degree of self-support.

Despite the security arrangements drivers were attacked and lorries were set on fire. One large haulage company had a windscreen contractor virtually in permanent residence. It was normal for drivers to have a pick-axe handle in their cabs and many elected to take German shepherd dogs with them as added protection. Fear of reprisals after the strike led many small hauliers to paint over their livery in an effort to conceal their identity.

There was a wide range of vehicles and companies. There were 5 major contractors, each with about 50 vehicles of their own and up to another 100 sub-contracted. Many businesses were one-man affairs. There were about 5 000 lorries operating to CEGB instructions through these arrangements under 300 contracts. The lorries ranged from 38 tonne articulated modern vehicles to standard flat-topped vehicles adapted to carry coal. With 25 000 lorry movements a week and with a daily peak of 1286 coal lorries to one station (Cottam), we had reached the point where it was not possible to be selective. Provided that the lorries were legal by being roadworthy and licensed and were being offered at a reasonable price they were accepted.

ORGANISING ADDITIONAL COAL MOVEMENTS

The Midlands Region fuel supplies staff became the organisers of transport for widening the fuel supply operation. Coal movements were successfully arranged to Aberthaw and Uskmouth Power Stations in South Wales. Those stations' coal quality requirement meant that they drew off some of the best coal available to the Midlands stations. There was an added concern in setting up this operation: the vehicle fleets of the Welsh operators were withdrawn at the last moment, which put some strain on the other supply arrangements. Similar road transport arrangements were set up to supply power stations in other parts of the country, some of these coal flows being crucial to improving the CEGB endurance position and enabling us to maintain electricity supplies over the winter. A link to South Denes Power Station (East Anglia) was established, but after consideration of its strategic value, the route being long and tenuous with its drain on vehicle resources, the deliveries were discontinued.

Considerable tonnage was delivered to Brighton Power Station, but some local people were not impressed. Their attitude seemed to be 'Keep our lights on, but please, dirty coal-carrying juggernauts are not in keeping with Brighton'. If the lights had not been kept on their attitude would probably have been different.

As the coal industry gradually returned to life the pledge that we had given to the NCB to move all production became a burden. We did, however, stand by it, hence the long distance movements from Scotland, the Lake District and Durham. The Midlands Region, because they managed the early phases of the coal movement successfully, continued as the road transport organisers for coal that became available in other regions. They also honoured the pledge by moving stock and fresh production from Bold Colliery on Merseyside, where the adjacent power station staff for a time refused to operate the connecting conveyor. Once again a multi-haulier operation moved the coal, this time to West Midlands stations.

Our drive to improve endurance led to stations being transformed from those not receiving coal and therefore being operated on a coal stock conservation regime to becoming stations receiving coal and operating normally. Didcot Power Station was the most significant example, as described in Chapter 14. Its change from have-not to have status was one of the turning points in the winter. The first deliveries to Didcot were planned to arrive one Monday morning in November at 9.15am, after the staff had arrived having minimum knowledge of our intentions. Articulated vehicles were loaded in the Midlands on Saturday morning, all drivers being instructed to deliver to Ratcliffe Power Station. The trailers were then stabled all over the Midlands with drivers unsure of the reason for failing to complete their journey. Drivers had no true knowledge of their destination until early Monday morning when setting out to re-engage the trailers and deliver to Didcot. It was necessary to exercise tight discipline on the subsequent deliveries through the Vale of the White Horse, as explained in Chapter 14. First deliveries took place as planned.

Opening up Yorkshire

As production resumed at some Yorkshire pits there was the question of where the coal should be sent. The answer was to East Midlands power stations. When the Kellingley and Selby collieries started up in early February 1985 we were aware that they were indeed located in hostile territory. As the ferocity of the pickets from Yorkshire had been experienced elsewhere, we knew that our drivers would be at risk.

After close consultations with Yorkshire NCB management on reception facilities, local routes and, in particular, loading arrangements, we decided that each of the four different haulage companies to be used would be identified by different coloured discs, squares, triangles or oblongs with each destined for one of four different East Midlands stations. We were ready but very apprehensive. In the event the operation went without a hitch.

FRAUD

It would have been surprising, with the scale of the programme and the hurried arrangements that were frequently necessary, if there had not been some sharp practice. As protection against this the internal auditors were closely involved in giving advice and overseeing the commercial arrangements. In addition a full checking and reconciliation process was set up. Nevertheless one contractor contrived to take advantage of a long-haul journey to deliver coal that was certainly of much lower quality than he was picking up from a high quality NCB stock pile. The results of sampling and analysis at the station alerted us to this. The overnight break in the journey was under suspicion as providing the opportunity to mix in other material and to allow some of the high quality coal to become available for separate sale. It was difficult to get the evidence and after consulting the police we decided that all we could do was to cancel the contract, having lost in the process. Bearing in mind the scale and circumstances of the operation, it is remarkable that there were few examples of this kind.

ENVIRONMENTAL FACTORS

Damage to the roads and the environment were uppermost in everyone's mind. All vehicle drivers were under strict instruction. Every vehicle had to be kept clean, every load had to be sheeted, every route carefully planned and negotiated.

It was unfortunate for us that virtually all pits were set up to dispatch all of their production by rail. With the failure of British Rail to fulfil their commitment because of their trade unions, many problems surfaced. Sometimes our failures to meet the highest standards were only too apparent. After careful and explicit instruction to move Cortonwood stock, a new Yorkshire-based haulier was commissioned to get on with it. In spite of every effort to do this quietly BBC cameras just happened to be in position on a motorway bridge on the route to the power station and filmed the movement. It was incredible that the cameras had filmed probably the only unsheeted vehicles in our entire operation. Apparently the new sheets on order had not arrived on time, owing to the unexpected demand on vehicle sheeting. The mistake was not repeated, at least not on television!

Before any coal movements were set up between a pit and a power station the route was carefully planned. The county and local authorities were consulted. This was important since the planning consents did not allow the use of road-borne coal deliveries in normal circumstances for some power stations. In addition discussions normally took place with the police. There were two problems for the local authorities: the environmental effect and the possible damage to roads from the greatly increased volume of heavy traffic. Both were carefully monitored by us and by them. There is no doubt that by the end of the strike the volume of road traffic had caused damage. Under the provisions of the appropriate transport act local authorities were allowed to claim the cost of repair from users for abnormal traffic. Our stance was not to accept any claims on A-class roads but to negotiate on B roads and others.

The attitude of the local authorities varied and we got the strong impression that some of them were strongly pro-NUM and wanted to use the claims process to punish the CEGB and the NCB for supporting the working miners. Negotiations were sometimes protracted, with a number of interesting twists. At Ironbridge Power Station the council had asked us not to use the A4169 (Jiggers Bank) but the B4380 from the west, which was subsequently badly damaged. They then charged us £300 000 for the damage. In the case of Nottinghamshire County Council the discussions went on for a long time before ultimately being settled out of court at the level of our original offer of two or three years earlier. During this time the minor roads around Cottam and West Burton Power Stations were not properly repaired. In total we paid out well over £1 million but even so our transport costs were still lower than if we had used rail.

THE RESULTS

It is interesting to note that 17 000 000 tonnes of coal were moved by road during the strike. The public, other than those actually on the routes, were hardly aware of this. Certainly there was little press coverage. The road-borne coal movement was an extremely important part of the CEGB's response to the miners' strike and to the railway unions' support for that strike. If the Midlands Region of the CEGB had not been so successful, the CEGB would not have been able to use most of the coal from the working mines and would not have been successful in keeping the lights on through the winter of 1984–5.

Postscript

After the strike, the CEGB retained some road-borne deliveries to every possible station. One reason was that we wished to be able to claim, in any future dispute, that road-borne supplies were normal. At many stations there were problems in doing this for more than a marginal tonnage, but we went as far as we could. This was strictly outside the terms of our contract with British Rail but bearing in mind the performance of the railways during the strike they chose not to press the point.

Chapter 17

Oil: the £4 billion story

Our endurance strategy was heavily dependent upon building up and then sustaining a high oil burn. To do this we needed an oil procurement programme and preparations for that started about a year before the strike. The first steps were discussions with the government and the oil companies on how the large flow of oil would be established. The lack of government help, the pessimistic predictions of the oil companies and our knowledge of the sheer size of the exercise worried us. The procurement task was ultimately to be even larger than we had expected and to involve the purchase of over 24 000 000 tonnes of oil costing almost £4 billion.

PREPARATIONS

During the first half of 1984 discussions with government made it clear that they would not become directly involved. The oil companies had advised us that the heavy fuel oil quantity envisaged could not be readily met from the North West European market and that in any case we should expect high prices. The government questioned this advice and indicated that they were not prepared to consider reviving the Oil Industry Emergency Committee,[1] which could have produced a co-ordinated response to our requirements by the oil companies. In addition they were not able to release oil, even temporarily, from the national strategic stock because of their obligations through the International Energy Agency (IEA).

It was important to do what we could to reduce uncertainty in advance of the emergency. We were planning for the heavy fuel oil burn to be increased from 30 000 to 350 000 tonnes a week (in the event the maximum weekly burn was some 560 000 tonnes with a further 100 000 tonnes a week purchased by the CEGB for the Scottish stations). The oil companies' reactions during the discussions in early 1984 were as follows:

1 They displayed near incredulity at what was then the CEGB endurance objective of six months, with most companies doubting the wisdom of raising oil burn at all since they believed that oil supply could not be sustained at the necessary level.

2 The rapid rate and size of the increase in oil purchases would cause heavy fuel oil prices to explode from the then US$180 a tonne to around US$250 a tonne initially, possibly levelling off at about US$230 a tonne. They believed that some of the postulated rise in heavy fuel oil prices would help to compensate for an expected collapse in the prices of lighter oil products, which would be in surplus as additional crude oil was processed.

There was a wide range of views among the oil companies on how the additional heavy fuel oil should be made available and purchased. One company believed that the necessary quantities simply could not be achieved. The views of the remainder included the following strategies:

1 We would have to relax the oil quality specification and be prepared to take oils with 4 per cent sulphur content (normal limit 3 per cent) and high asphaltenes[2] (normal limit 10 per cent). Both these would have environmental disadvantages.
2 We would have to buy crude oil, set up special refining deals and compensate oil companies for losses when the price of light oil products fell, since they would be an inevitable byproduct and would be surplus to market requirements.
3 Additional storage would have to be secured for crude oil and heavy fuel oil in North West Europe, probably including VLCCs (very large crude-carrying tankers) moored in Norwegian fjords.
4 We should not set up any unusual deals or other special arrangements.

In the event the CEGB decided, after much consideration and some trepidation, to leave it to the market to provide. This decision was mainly influenced by the lack of any credible alternative that the government was prepared to support.

The discussions with the oil companies had served a useful purpose. They were all now aware of the scale of our intended purchases and the pattern of build-up. This would assist them in reviewing their crude and product trading arrangements and refining programmes when the strike occurred. It would enable them to be more responsive by having a better understanding of what was likely to happen. The oil companies would normally be expected to operate to their own commercial objectives, but we hoped that we could persuade them to take account of the national interest. We believed that, if they understood our intentions, we might achieve this.

OIL BURN STARTS – SUPPLIES BY PIPELINE

When the decision to increase oil consumption was taken at the start of the miners' strike the Board decided to increase oil-fired generation in four equal steps at weekly intervals, consistent with the estimates of oil availability made by the major oil companies which were supplying the pipeline-fed stations.

Pipeline supplies to three of the major oil-fired power stations were from oil refineries. Esso were suppliers to Fawley Power Station on Southampton Water, Gulf and Texaco to Pembroke Power Station in South Wales and Shell to Ince Power Station on Merseyside. The rate at which oil-fired generation could be increased at these stations was entirely dependent on the availability of oil from the refineries. Following the decision to start the high oil burn the build-up of oil supplied by pipelines from refineries was in accordance with the plan. The oil supply continued throughout the long strike as a reliable flow.

NUM attempts to stop the oil and other problems

There were attempts by the NUM to stop the oil. These included 'picketing' the oil supply pipeline between the Esso Fawley refinery and Fawley Power Station. This was intended to pose to the trade union members at the refinery this question: should they supply oil by pipeline across a picket line. Since the oil supply was entirely normal and part of the long term operations at the refinery there were no real grounds for interruption and none occurred.

There were problems in burning the Fawley oil over quite a long period because catalytic fines carried over in the oil caused the boiler combustion chambers to become coated with a thick slag. This threatened to shut down the power station. However, a technique was developed for water-lancing the slag with the boiler on-load. The sudden quenching of the deposit in the hot furnace caused it to shatter and break away from the boiler tubes to which it had been adhering. This technique enabled the station to continue operating until Esso were able to reduce the problem of fines carryover.

The other main attempt by the NUM to stop oil flow was at the Shell Stanlow refinery where there was pressure from the NUM on the oil industry trade union members to stop the pipeline supply of oil to Ince B Power Station. This culminated in the workers at Stanlow taking a vote on 8 May on whether to continue supplying the power station. Fortunately the vote was in favour of continuing.

There was also an attempt by the NUM to persuade the oil industry trade unions to stop the pipeline flow of oil to Bulls Bridge Gas Turbine Power Station during the winter. Reference is made in an earlier chapter to how Esso resisted that pressure.

The other challenge to the pipeline supply of oil was from the dock strikes, which were also described in Chapter 12. They did not last long enough and were not sufficiently effective to disrupt the refineries supplying us. They had the potential to cause much damage to our endurance strategy and it was a great relief when there was a return to normal working. It has to be said in praise of our oil company suppliers that they were generally prepared to dock very large crude tankers without tugs to ensure that their business remained normal. In Southampton Water the threat of doing that was sufficient to gain the co-operation of the tug crews.

SPOT OIL PURCHASES

The other oil-fired power stations were supplied by CEGB fuel purchasers buying oil on the international spot market. This procurement programme was a major and demanding job. It required deliveries to be kept closely in line with burn because there was relatively little storage at the power stations. For example, the usable storage capacity for Kingsnorth and Grain Power Stations on the River Medway was only about ten days of full load consumption. This demanded careful scheduling of tankers, many of which were bringing oil from thousands of miles away. The jetty serving both power stations was at Kingsnorth. The staff there, who were responsible over the strike for the reception and discharge of over 6 500 000 tonnes of heavy fuel oil, won unstinting praise from the oil industry for the manner in which they handled the inevitable queues of vessels throughout the strike without serious mishap and nearly all of it over a single jetty. Later in the dispute the jetty of the old BP Kent refinery next to Grain Power Station was brought back into service and gave some relief to the traffic on the Kingsnorth jetty.

The CEGB oil purchasing team was under the leadership of John Wooley, the CEGB Fuel Supplies Officer, who was later to hold a similar post with Powergen and to receive an OBE. His team consisted of David Bridger, Jim Wharton and Mike Blake. It was their role to purchase and arrange delivery of the oil to support a burn of 350 000 tonnes a week initially, but which later increased to over 600 000 tonnes a week, including Scotland. There was much sensitivity about whether, when the scale and cost of the increased oil burn was widely understood, there would be a reaction to it in some quarters or even a concerted effort by the NUM to attempt to frustrate it. Either way, the less it grabbed the headlines the better. The big escalation in heavy fuel oil prices that some of the oil companies had predicted would certainly have been noticed. It was also in the interests of the Board, the whole electricity supply industry and the public sector purse that we kept prices as low as possible.

The CEGB's oil situation was totally different from that for coal in that it had not been possible to prepare an oil stockpile. In addition the purchasing operation could not be got under way until the strike and the increased oil burn had actually started. Just before the strike the spot price for heavy fuel oil in North West Europe was about US$180 a tonne. The object was to purchase the oil in such a way that the price would be affected as little as possible.

When purchasing actually started there were many offers based on the assumption that prices would rapidly increase, that we would have difficulty in buying the oil quantity needed and that we would be forced into panic buying. As a policy we refused to purchase any oil that was offered above US$190 a tonne. In an effort to control prices and to remove as much panic as possible from the market-place, the oil purchasing team stuck to this policy for as long as possible. With increasing consumption, stocks were allowed to run down as a tense battle of wills developed with the potential sellers.

In the end our limit of US$190 a tonne was generally maintained. Thereafter, despite increasing requirements, a combination of careful purchasing and increasing oil availability resulted in prices falling to US$180 a tonne for some months and only returning to US$190 a tonne during the extreme winter conditions in early 1985 when oil consumption for electricity generation exceeded 600 000 tonnes per week. The spot fuel oil price trends are shown in Figure 17.1, page 209.

The control of the purchase price required strong nerves. As prices drifted up from time to time, or when there was a shortage of cargoes at acceptable prices, it was necessary to stop purchases. This usually brought prices back to a more acceptable level, but they were anxious times until purchases were resumed.

In contrast to the assumptions made in the contingency planning only a small proportion of the additional heavy fuel oil supplies were refined in the UK. Despite fears of competitive bidding for the same supplies by us and the major oil companies, spot prices for heavy fuel oil were limited because there was a world-wide oil industry response. This was largely the result of a general recession and relatively low oil demand elsewhere.

As the strike developed, the transfer of electric power from Scotland became linked with the oil burn in the two large Scottish oil burning power stations at Inverkip and Peterhead. It was agreed that, to avoid competition in purchasing heavy fuel oil, we should purchase for them as well. This increased the requirement for oil purchase by up to 100 000 tonnes a week. The overall oil burn increased substantially through the strike and reference to that and how it was achieved is made in Chapter 20. The result was that the oil purchase requirement peaked at over 600 000 tonnes a week. Information taken from CEGB archives shows that total oil burn for electricity generation increased as shown in Table 17.1.

Table 17.1 Oil Burn increase

Week of oil burn	Oil burn thousands of tonnes a week		
	CEGB	Scottish	Total
Wk 1: March	#62	*0	62
Wk 3:	230	12	242
Mid-April			
Wk 4:	313	10	323
Wk 19: Early August	383	30	413
Wk 25: Mid-September	462	49	511
Wk 34: Mid-November	532	84	616

Typical oil burn would have been 30 000 tonnes.
* SSEB oil-fired plant not being used for energy transfers to CEGB.
Source: CEGB Operations Department

It is interesting to recall that, in the exploratory discussions with the oil companies during 1983, doubts had been expressed about the ability of the oil industry to meet the CEGB's estimate of maximum oil requirements, then put at some 350 kt per week. In the event, as a result of the tremendous efforts made, oil-fired generation was at no time limited by oil purchasing problems.

Maximum oil burn, which was ultimately limited by power station plant capacity, was achieved at both CEGB and Scottish power stations in January 1985: CEGB 561, Scotland 100: total 661 kt a week. This meant that over 50 per cent of electricity demand was being met from oil generation. The oil burn consumption for the full period of the strike is shown in Table 17.2, page 201.

With this scale of oil requirement there was continuing concern that purchases in the spot market would send prices out of control. Early in the strike we considered limiting direct purchases from the spot market by letting contracts to major oil companies and refiners. In the event this proved to be more expensive. At power stations next to refineries the CEGB had no choice but to pay the commercial price to the suppliers. Similar prices (significantly higher than directly purchased spot cargoes) were asked and refused for supplies to Littlebrook Power Station. A contract for one cargo a week with Amerada Hess (a Virgin Island refinery introduced to the CEGB by the Department of Energy) was shortlived because of the imposition of EEC duty (around US$6 a tonne) which appeared to make this source uncompetitive. Thus the CEGB took the higher risk but cheaper route of buying oil directly on the spot market. Figure 17.1, page 209 shows the way that spot prices moved during the crisis. At the peak, the breakdown in supplies was approximately:

directly purchased by the CEGB: 400 kt a week
acquired by major oil companies: 250 kt a week

Because of oil company predictions of a significant deterioration in oil quality (e.g. higher sulphur, vanadium and asphaltenes),[2] which could have created serious emission problems at power stations, quality as well as price had to be controlled as far as possible. Although quality standards had to be relaxed to some extent continued pressure from the CEGB and co-operation from the oil industry resulted in qualities far better than predicted.

When purchasing on the spot market the CEGB made use of traders and brokers who scoured the world for suitable oil at an acceptable price. Fairly quickly, a broad pattern of supply was established with a proportion of oil in large tankers (40 000 to 50 000 tonnes) for Kingsnorth and Grain Power Stations and the Scottish stations normally coming from the Caribbean area, and supplies for Littlebrook (also serving the smaller stations) in smaller tankers (20 000 to 25 000 tonnes), usually coming from North West Europe. When this pattern was established things began to run well. There were a few occasions when oil from the US Gulf/Caribbean was limited because storms delayed shipping and a few other cases where oil burn had to be marginally reduced because of supply difficulties. Three incidents that affected supplies are worth recounting.

Table 17.2 Oil burn–consumption 1984–5 (thousands of tonnes)

Power station	Grain/Kingsnorth	Littlebrook D	Fawley	Pembroke	Ince	Small oil-fired Stations	Other stations and oil overburn	CEGB Total	Inverkip	Peterhead	Scottish Total	Grand Total
Week * −1 oil burn	11	11	16	19	0	3	2	62				
1	34	42	22	22	6	3	2	131				131
2	65	44	22	18	15	4	2	170	7		7	177
3	100	47	31	29	19	2	2	230	12		12	242
4	105	66	62	43	19	16	2	313	10		10	323
5	117	68	56	50	19	29	2	341	9		9	350
6	106	79	63	54	19	31	2	354	17		17	371
7	111	78	63	42	19	27	2	342	16		16	358
8	110	77	72	35	18	26	2	340	16	6	22	362
9	102	75	73	9	19	25	2	305	17	6	23	328
10	103	71	66	1	18	22	2	283	12	–	12	295
11	107	71	69	17	10	21	3	298	16	1	17	315
12	106	74	61	28	19	27	3	318	16	2	18	336
13	110	74	66	32	19	25	3	329	18	4	22	351
14	108	70	66	38	18	27	3	330	17	18	35	365
15	99	72	63	29	18	30	12	323	17	6	23	346
16	98	79	66	35	19	31	14	342	17	15	32	374
17	103	73	63	45	17	31	15	347	16	4	20	367
18	134	74	65	51	18	23	14	379	17	10	27	406
19	134	82	61	50	9	33	14	383	17	13	30	413
20	143	79	61	49	18	33	24	407	19	20	39	446
21	145	71	62	49	19	40	36	422	23	22	45	467
22	137	82	64	33	19	41	35	411	29	23	52	463
23	121	56	51	50	19	43	36	376	34	17	51	427
24	155	61	68	48	32	40	40	444	37	11	48	492

Week												
25	157	69	66	53	35	41	41	462	37	12	49	511
26	143	84	63	50	38	40	47	465	27	15	42	507
27	159	60	60	62	35	38	60	474	16	37	53	527
28	162	60	59	62	25	39	72	479	35	25	60	539
29	107	50	69	54	32	44	61	417	36	29	65	482
30	98	64	62	69	37	46	91	467	37	35	72	539
31	117	60	67	73	38	39	84	478	39	30	69	547
32	128	79	58	70	38	46	93	512	38	33	71	583
33	135	80	48	52	38	46	83	482	42	43	85	567
34	147	76	61	62	39	53	94	532	41	43	84	616
35	139	78	52	67	33	57	88	514	50	42	92	606
36	154	67	55	64	36	57	101	534	38	43	81	615
37	149	72	49	68	38	55	87	518	40	46	86	604
38	119	80	52	69	35	49	82	486	44	36	80	566
39	123	71	60	62	38	52	89	495	50	46	96	591
40	128	59	49	55	38	37	87	453	37	39	76	529
41	128	57	52	67	36	49	87	476	42	40	82	558
42	144	70	56	61	37	58	89	515	51	45	96	611
43	155	89	61	64	37	61	94	561	51	49	100	661
44	143	51	57	55	37	59	105	507	51	49	100	607
45	154	76	62	61	38	54	108	553	50	47	97	650
46	127	76	63	68	38	53	80	505	46	43	89	594
47	151	58	66	69	38	52	92	526	52	47	99	625
48	167	78	61	64	38	46	82	536	51	45	96	632
49	153	81	60	56	39	50	63	502	42	43	85	587
50	174	46	54	72	39	31	64	480	13	22	35	515
51	144	34	51	65	32	20	34	380	10	23	33	413
52	66	36	51	61	19	23	22	278	26	–	26	304
53	34	30	52	28	1	12	9	166	38	–	38	204
Total for 53 weeks kt	6558	3556	3092	2640	1427	1937	2461	21 671	1539	1185	2724	24 395
%	30	17	14	12	7	9	11	100				

*Number of weeks after decision to enhance oil burn

Source: CEGB Operations Department

Table 17.3 Coal-fired stations with oil burn capability

	Power station	Oil burn output capacity at end of strike MW
NE Region:	Blyth B	300
Mid Region:	Cottam	240
	Ironbridge	150
	Rugeley A	60
	Rugeley B	200
	West Burton	200
	Other Midlands Plant	140
SE Region:	Tilbury B	1000
	West Thurrock	210
SW Region:	Didcot	400
	Aberthaw	200
	Total	3100

Source: CEGB Operations Department

The Soviet tankers

At one stage USSR tankers were being used to bring heavy fuel oil from the Caribbean to Kingsnorth Power Station. These were modern, efficient vessels of 50 000 tonnes that carried USSR crude oil to Cuba and picked up fuel oil for the return journey to Europe. This suited the USSR vessel owners, it suited the CEGB, and it helped to keep transport costs down. Unfortunately for the CEGB, the UK press picked up or were alerted to this traffic. Much publicity was given on the lines of 'Reds helping to defeat miners' and this soon resulted in the ships being withdrawn from serving the CEGB. This was an embarrassment. The availability of ships was reduced and shipping rates increased. Oil supplies to Kingsnorth were slowed until older, less efficient vessels could be brought into service.

The arrested tanker

On Wednesday 23 January 1985, a Liberian tanker was arrested on the Kingsnorth jetty by the Admiralty Marshal. The vessel was the subject of a dispute between the owners and a foreign shipyard over alleged non-payment for work done many months previously. Although the CEGB was not involved directly in the dispute, it was informed that the vessel must remain on the jetty until the legal process had been satisfied – which could take many weeks or even months. This was potentially disastrous for the CEGB. The Kingsnorth jetty was completely blocked. No oil could be delivered there, a queue of oil tankers was forming in the Medway and demurrage charges were increasing rapidly. Most important of all, Kingsnorth (2000 MW) and Grain (2640 MW) Power Stations (about one third of the CEGB's oil-fired generation) would run out of oil within a very few days at a time of high demand for electricity and at a critical period in the strike. Any failure to meet the demand for electricity in full would have been interpreted by the NUM membership as a sign that they were winning the battle.

The arrest by the Admiralty Marshal had been made during Wednesday night, but the full implications were not known at the CEGB's operational HQ until early on Friday morning. A QC was briefed immediately and a hearing arranged before the Admiralty Registrar for Friday afternoon. Unfortunately for the CEGB the legal establishment was not persuaded of the need for an urgent decision: the law was the law. There were no other safe berths to which the arrested vessel could be transferred and it was unreasonable to expect the Registrar's staff to work over the weekend in an attempt to find a solution! Accordingly, the CEGB would have to return to the court on the following Monday morning. This was discussed with the Department of Energy to obtain their support and also with the CEGB Chairman, Sir Walter Marshall. We considered boarding the ship and getting it moved but were advised that we could be in contempt of court. More careful reflection led us to decide to stay clear of further complications, which we were advised could include personal penalties. It was no time to go to prison.

On the following Monday, after much argument over costs, the Registrar ordered the tanker to be moved from the Kingsnorth jetty that afternoon. A precautionary reduction in generation had been made over the weekend, but the tanker was moved just in time to allow oil deliveries to be resumed to Kingsnorth/Grain Power Stations and avoid a shut down. The Registrar ruled that the CEGB should pay the costs of the court action: 'They are a large organisation and have a lot of money to spend'. Thus ended one of the major crises in the oil supply story.

HM Customs and Excise stop the oil flow

In January 1985, HM Customs and Excise (HMCE) became increasingly worried about the import into the UK of heavy fuel oil from non-EEC sources. Oil products from the USA, Gulf and some Caribbean islands are subject to an EEC duty of 3.5 per cent of the value of the oil as delivered. Oil products originating in the ex-colonies, or processed there, were not. HMCE investigations in the Caribbean had concluded that certain local customs inspectors there were issuing unsound certificates of origin. Accordingly, HMCE warned traders selling cargoes of such oils to Europe (mainly the CEGB at the time) that UK HMCE would levy the 3.5 per cent duty despite the certificate of origin provided by customs authorities in the Caribbean. A minor panic ensued. Traders initially refused to supply the CEGB. Later they required written guarantees that the CEGB would pay the duty in the event that HMCE so required.

The CEGB held long meetings with HMCE and with the Department of Trade and Industry, pointing out that no other European customs service interpreted the rules as HMCE did; the oil products were flowing from the Caribbean to other European destinations without problems. The net result of HMCE activities, apart from disrupting the flow of fuel oil to the CEGB, was that the UK would pay about US$7 a tonne more than other European consumers for the same oil and that such monies would go to the EEC since they stemmed from an EEC duty. Ironically this happened at a time when the Prime Minister was conducting difficult negotiations with the EEC aimed at reducing the UK's net contribution to the EEC budget.

Throughout this period HMCE were adamant that they were right and their European counterparts wrong. The matter was raised at Ministerial level by the CEGB and eventually HMCE became less draconian and oil started to flow again, albeit at a higher cost to the CEGB. Indeed, HMCE investigations and negotiations went on for several years after the strike ended. Although the CEGB managed to recover some of the money paid wrongly to suppliers in the most blatant cases, the whole affair cost the CEGB a great deal of money. A story circulating within the CEGB, which could be apocryphal, was that Peter Walker sent a memo to Nigel Lawson saying that his staff were about to succeed where Arthur Scargill had failed.

HMCE continued to pursue the letter of the law against the CEGB for some time after the strike. Although Kingsnorth Power Station staff, under great pressure during the strike, worked closely with local customs officials, errors were made in recording the value of some oil deliveries. For example, where oil and freight charges were invoiced separately, the EEC duty was not always levied on the freight component, as it should have been. HMCE centrally insisted that the responsibility for such 'technical' errors lay with the CEGB. A big investigation was set up involving many hours of work by the station, CEGB Fuel Supplies Department and Legal Division staff. At the end, the errors were corrected and HMCE magnanimously agreed not to prosecute the CEGB, subject to the CEGB agreeing to pay a fine of several thousand pounds. The CEGB refused and invited HMCE to prosecute. After much spluttering HMCE conceded. It was difficult not to conclude that, although we knew how to deal with the emergency caused by a year-long miners' strike, dealing with the bureaucratic machinery of HMCE was well beyond us.

SUPPLYING THE SMALL OIL STATIONS, OIL OVERBURN AND LIGHTING OIL

Chapter 20 describes how our oil-burning capacity was increased through the strike. Part of that increase was from recommissioning or increasing the output of some of the old and generally small oil-fired stations. They were mainly in the South Eastern Region. They were supplied by small vessels ranging from 1200 to 9000 tonnes, which were loaded at Littlebrook Power Station from the oil storage facilities replenished by the main spot oil purchasing arrangements. About 1400 MW of generating capacity, with an oil burn capability of about 50 000 tonnes a week, was supported by these arrangements.

In addition a number of coal-fired power stations were capable of burning appreciable quantities of oil as a supplement to coal-burning. This was called oil overburn. All of them had some capability from the equipment normally installed for starting up and for flame stabilisation. However, many of them had their oil burning capability greatly increased by new engineering work carried out during the strike. The stations that were in this category are shown in Table 17.3.

The total oil burn requirement for this category of plant grew considerably through the strike as the ingenuity of power station engineers found new ways of replacing coal-fired generation by oil. The supply arrangements varied. Blyth B Power Station in Northumberland was supplied by barge deliveries from the Tynemouth oil terminal. Deliveries were increased from three a week to forty a week and were maintained at that. This required careful management of the station industrial relations and commendable efforts by Whitakers, the suppliers, to sustain volume. If there had been a repeat of the aggressive picketing experienced early in the strike at Blyth it might have been necessary to end the supply. However it was difficult for the NUM to mount an effective picket because of the position of the barge unloading point.

MAINTAINING OIL SUPPLIES BY ROAD AND RAIL

The power stations mentioned from the Midlands and South Western Regions normally received their oil supplies by rail. The story of the battle to maintain rail-borne supplies and the reversion to road was told in Chapters 11 and 12. It is worth describing some aspects of that from the perspective of Les Jonathan who, under David Bridger's leadership, co-ordinated these supplies.

The CEGB coal-fired power stations used oil fuels for lighting-up and flame stabilisation in their boilers and also for the mobile coal-handling equipment. Gas turbine stations also burnt light gas oils. This range of oil fuels was designated 'miscellaneous oils' to distinguish them from the heavy fuel oils burnt for main generation at the large oil-fired power stations. Before the strike, the CEGB bought these miscellaneous oils under exclusive contracts with big international oil companies with UK refineries, and from large national oil distribution companies.

Almost from the first day of the strike the CEGB was left largely to its own devices to ensure the delivery of miscellaneous oils to power stations. The major oil companies had given assurances that they would do all they could to help, but although they did make oil available at their refineries and major depots, few made any significant effort to deliver to the power stations.

The support given to the NUM by members of ASLEF and the NUR in frustrating the transport of oils by rail caused a shift in emphasis by the CEGB to road-borne oil at all the big coal-burning stations. It would have been possible for the big oil companies to supply by road, but they were reluctant for their drivers, tankers and depots to become involved with picket lines or 'blacking' of deliveries in case supplies to the rest of their consumers were affected. When we had to use alternative methods the miscellaneous oils that were delivered by independent distribution companies were mostly bought from UK refiners, so the refiners continued to profit from the high oil prices engendered by the strike despite their reluctance to deliver.

An attempt was made to avoid the rail and road problems at Drax by the use of a pipeline from barges operating on the River Ouse. This failed when the pipeline contractor's workforce blacked the project in a show of unity with the NUM cause. Loss of the rail supplies made necessary a switch to road-borne oil, not only to supply the oil needed for lighting up the coal-fired boilers but also to cater for the overburn capability that was introduced to eke out the coal stocks at power stations in the Midlands and South Wales. To replace one trainload of oil required some thirty-five road tankers. Also the off-loading equipment for road-borne oil had to be quickly modified and extended to cope with the convoys of road tankers.

Although road deliveries started from a low level (5700 tonnes) they soon became adequate everywhere except at Fiddlers Ferry and Ferrybridge Power Stations. Even at Fiddlers Ferry, which had difficult industrial relations, the deliveries were eventually introduced after helpful trade union advice and protracted negotiations with the power station shop stewards and those at Texaco's Eastham oil terminal.

The number of road tankers used to supply power stations during the strike ran into many thousands, some of which had not been on the road for many years. Where they all came from was something of a mystery. But that episode provided a good illustration of the power of market forces: there was a need for road transport, freight rates rose and the vehicles were made available. Among the few winners from the strike were the road hauliers and oil distribution companies. The losers included members of ASLEF since, after the strike, all oil deliveries to Drax and Ferrybridge 'C' Power Stations were switched to pipeline. In addition, about 10 per cent of all previous rail-borne supplies to other stations were switched permanently to road to demonstrate that road-borne oil from a second supplier was a normal feature at each station. Oil supplies to other critical stations also presented some interesting problems.

Didcot Power Station

The station was fed, during the strike, with about 150 loads a day from Avonmouth and Thames terminals. When, in addition, oil deliveries for the gas turbines were established, it was not uncommon for traffic jams to stretch back to the M4 motorway, a distance of about thirteen miles.

Aberthaw Power Station

Potentially this was a difficult site to supply because of some sympathy within the station for the South Wales NUM. The first tentative step was to arrange one road tanker a day. The rate was gradually stepped up, but never to the point where it would provoke a confrontation with the station workforce. Some flying pickets attempted to interfere with these deliveries. In an attempt to confuse the pickets, who sometimes followed empty tankers back to their depots, oil for Aberthaw was drawn from Thames-side terminals rather than from the nearer terminals at Barry or Avonmouth. This arrangement achieved its purpose but did add to the already heavy traffic on the M4 heading for Didcot.

Aire Valley and Thorpe Marsh Power Stations

The Ferrybridge site was the only one that failed to take any oil during the strike. There were difficulties at the other three South Yorkshire stations at first, but in the autumn, again following the trade unions' advice and careful management of local industrial relations, deliveries of ten loads a week to each station were set up. This rate was gradually raised and eventually deliveries went in at will. One concession made to the local shop stewards was that all lorries entering the stations had to display the company's registered office address plus a logo. This was to ensure that non-union drivers were excluded. This was considered by the CEGB to be a small price to pay for getting oil into stations in the heartland of the dispute.

Main gas turbine stations

Even before the strike, gas oil was dearer than other fuels, so the gas turbines were seldom run and then only for peak lopping. Bulls Bridge was supplied by pipeline; the others were normally supplied by rail. During the strike no rail deliveries were possible; road transport was used instead. When intensive running of the gas turbines started in the autumn it meant that some 20 kt of gas oil had to be delivered each week to each station. This equated to six tankers an hour, twenty-four hours a day, seven days a week throughout the winter.

It came as no surprise that there were no objections to the increased traffic to Taylors Lane (Willesden), Leicester and Ocker Hill (West Midlands) Power Stations since the transport routes were mainly through industrial areas. However, it was gratifying that few objections came from the residents of the leafy lanes of outer suburbia in Letchworth and Watford. Presumably the people living there judged it was best not to impair the efforts being made to keep the lights on.

OIL SUPPLY – OBSERVATIONS

During the year of the strike more than 24 000 000 tonnes of oil were purchased, at a cost of nearly £4 billion. It was a massive job managed by the CEGB's oil purchasing team. It supported a ten-fold increase in oil consumption and saved about 42 000 000 tonnes of coal consumption. It played the most important part in maintaining electricity supplies.

The oil supply programme was more successful than could have been envisaged during the contingency planning phase. It proved possible to meet the requirements of a much larger oil burn than earlier planned (600 000 tonnes a week compared with 350 000 tonnes) without the need for government intervention and without heavy increases in oil price. The oil companies' concerns proved unfounded. The Department of Energy's judgement that there was no need for the government to intervene was sound or was made so by the skill and enterprise of the CEGB oil purchasers and the traders and brokers supporting them. The ability of the oil trade to respond to market needs was convincingly illustrated. Although escalating oil prices were avoided during the major oil burn, when the CEGB withdrew from the heavy fuel oil market the price level fell almost immediately to US$130 a tonne from the level of about US$190 that it held for a full year. This is shown in Figure 17.1.

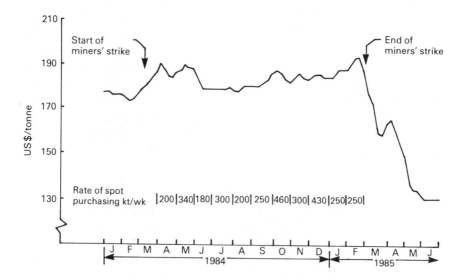

Figure 17.1 Spot fuel oil prices (weekly average of Platts mean CIF NW Europe, 3 ½% sulphur)

Source: CEGB Operations Department

Chapter 18

The power system: innovation and flexibility

The CEGB had a unique advantage in managing the electricity supply emergency caused by the 1984–5 miners' strike. It came from the development of the techniques normally used for planning the operation of the power system, namely the ability to predict the longer term effects of the changing circumstances with which we were faced. It is difficult to overstate the value of this facility and innovations that improved it as the dispute went on.

The operational management of any electricity supply industry is highly dependent on the control of the power system that is its core. This control and the management processes that support it strongly influence the cost of operations and the security of supply. The techniques and skill developed to perform that task not only made it possible accurately to predict how long electricity demand could be met in full for given levels of coal stock, coal deliveries and oil-fired generation, but also enabled us to determine how we should operate the power stations and transmission system to maintain supplies for the longest possible time.

Although the basic systems had been developed over many years their adaptation to strike conditions and our management of the emergency were dependent upon Ed Wallis and his system operation team. Their reports provided guidance and a strong stimulus to us all. They showed clearly what had to be done to survive and monitored the success or failure of initiatives.

THE POWER SYSTEM

The power system, made up of the generators, transmission network and the points of supply to the distribution systems, is an entity since its parts are highly interactive: any part can affect the others or even the integrity of the whole. If that fact is not fully understood and fully taken into account, there can be serious consequences. New York State, France, Southern Germany and Tokyo have all experienced power system collapses in the last few decades. They are traumatic events and can leave the population without any electricity supplies for long periods. In New York supplies to 30 000 000 people were lost for 14 hours in 1965 and for 25 hours in 1977. Events of this kind occur more often in developing countries. We have never had such an incident in this country but have been close to it on a few occasions.

OPERATIONAL PLANNING

To avoid this risk and others, computer modelling techniques are used to simulate the operation of the power system, as part of the operational planning process. This includes the assessment of overall fuel burn to enable the economic allocation of fuel. It also includes the co-ordination of generator and transmission overhaul plans for each week up to three years ahead. With about four hundred generators and an equal number of transmission lines it was essential to assess system security with the planned plant out of service. The National Grid Control Centre was then able to sanction the release of plant for overhaul with some confidence. Thus the integrity of the system was tested both well ahead and day-to-day to ensure that events such as lightning strikes or the failure of an overhead line or generator could be dealt with. Not only has a system collapse to be avoided but also any loss of supplies or unacceptable swings in voltage or the frequency of the AC supply. Operational planning and a review and monitoring process make it possible to respond with whatever is necessary to ensure an acceptably low risk of failure from events outside the control of the operator.

All this is a long-established, well understood, and well developed technology. The CEGB arrangements were advanced and well used and encompassed not only system security but also economic operation. They guided the operation of the system, including generators, to meet consumer demand at minimum cost throughout the year. They also enabled the primary fuel requirements to be estimated, which is described as 'energy modelling'.

System operations prepared for the strike

There had been a number of threats of an NUM dispute, particularly during the spring and summer of 1983. We judged that there was a strong likelihood of a dispute starting in November 1983, coinciding with the annual pay round negotiations. The method of operation, to be adopted if the strike materialised, was as follows:

1 maximum output from nuclear power stations, through indefinite continuous operation;
2 maximum output from oil-fired plant, assuming continuity of oil supply, and only limited reductions in output at times of low system demand;
3 maximum imports from Scotland, subject to not weakening its own position unduly and being able to agree the price of our energy purchases;
4 minimum use of coal-fired plant, with the rank order of stations based primarily on stocks of coal related to station output capacity;
5 maintenance of normal standards of system security, as far as possible;
6 continued normal system control room practices.

The transmission network's development had been guided by planning standards that included the capacity to accommodate large-scale power transfers.[1] Despite this it was likely to limit full use of the power station endurance strategy because of the exceptional power transfers that were required. Previous abnormal operations had shown how flexible the network could be in dealing with unusual patterns of power flow, but we had to be sure. Simulation studies in 1983 had suggested that the system would be able to deal with the new operating strategy which would require a total reversal of the normal north-to-south power flows. We knew our operating margins would be small, but we believed that we could manage. We therefore planned the operating regimes for the generating plant and intended that coal-fired power stations would be loaded in an order that would allow coal stocks at the individual power stations to be run down equitably in a planned way, stations with high stocks being used more than those with lower stocks. Operational planning studies were mounted monthly through the summer of 1983 so that, for any possible strike start-date, an appropriate operating plan would be available for immediate use.

Where should we stock the coal and how much oil do we need?

As the coal stocks were being increased the allocations of coal to individual power stations were being determined. They had to be based partly on the practical considerations of where coal was available, the capacity of the stockyards and the time scales over which the preparations could be made. It was also important that the coal should be stocked where it could best contribute to system endurance, taking into account power station output capacity and conversion efficiency. Lighting-up oil was stocked in sufficient quantities to support the burn of the stocked coal with the regime which would give maximum endurance.

Guided by this policy, by the end of October 1983 we had a well distributed coal stock amounting to 30 800 000 tonnes and a complementary stock capability of some 400 000 tonnes of lighting-up/stabilising oil. We calculated that the combined stocks of the fuel at coal-fired power stations would enable electricity demand to be met in full, without further supplies, for a period of six months.

Further energy modelling

We believed that, once a dispute got under way, energy modelling would be the cornerstone of the CEGB's operational planning and that it was important to continue developing it. Improvements were made over the period of the strike.

There were two kinds of model. One was aimed at showing the consequence of a set of input assumptions. It enabled the results of applying a proposed policy or set of decisions to be predicted, thus facilitating a 'what if' type of dialogue. The other type of model was to aid the short-term decisions on the detailed operation of the power system.

Operational planning during the strike

The early weeks of the strike saw a rapid decline in the deliveries of coal to the CEGB power stations. Not until mid-April was it possible to regard the continued working of a major section of the coal industry as a serious prospect. By early May 1984, all the evidence pointed to some coal continuing to be available, amounting to some 400 000 tonnes a week. This pattern of delivery, coupled with the maximum oil-burn strategy which had just been established, led us to believe that a system endurance significantly in excess of the earlier six-month commitment could be attained. Maximum effort was therefore devoted to adapting the contingency plans to a different, yet more favourable, set of circumstances.

The first requirement was to recognise the distinction between stations that were still receiving deliveries of coal (the haves) and those that were not (the have-nots). This distinction had a big effect on the operating regimes decided upon for the individual power stations. With the onset of seasonally lower electricity demands, operational planning showed that it was possible to shut down many of the have-not stations, which were in greatest need of coal-stock protection. This process had to be reversed progressively with the return of higher demands in the autumn. The requirement for plant flexibility, to reduce the use of coal, at stations where we were protecting coal stocks led to a greater requirement for lighting-up oil. Yet supplies of this oil were not getting through to the most vulnerable stations. However, early recognition of the problem enabled energy modelling to determine the best overall regime for each station, given its limited coal and oil stocks.

The second effect of the continued availability of some coal was, of course, to improve our endurance beyond the original estimate of six months. The extent of that improvement depended on the actual levels of oil burn and of coal supply. It was necessary to find a way of showing the effect on endurance of these fuel inputs so that it was possible to see the effect of improving them or of losing ground. Such a display could provide the motivation to regional managers to extend endurance beyond the 1984-5 winter.

The 'Knee' curve monitor

Based on the energy modelling programmes referred to it was possible to carry out studies that identified endurance end-dates for a variety of weekly rates of coal delivery and heavy fuel oil burn. A variant on this theme was a graphical representation of the endurance end-date, plotted against the weekly rate of coal delivery and assuming continuation of maximum oil burn (see Figure 18.1). This graph became known as the 'Knee' curve.

By comparing the graph of actual coal deliveries to date with the level necessary to secure supplies of electricity throughout winter 1984–5, it was possible to form a judgement of the necessary improvement. This form of presentation was highly influential, in the summer/autumn of 1984, in making us

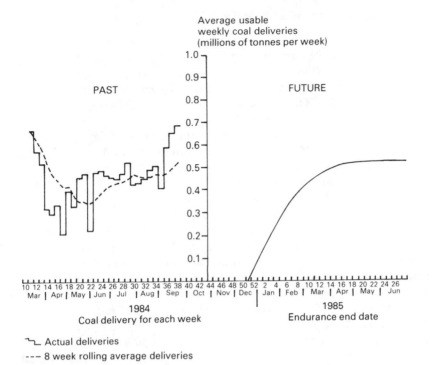

Figure 18.1 System endurance assessment
Source: CEGB Operations Department

realise that with only a limited improvement in nuclear and oil-fired generation or of coal flow the winter demand could be met.

The curve displayed is for the end of September. An improvement in nuclear or oil-fired generation would cause the curve to move downward, and for the coal flow necessary to get through the winter to be lower than the level of about 500 000 tonnes shown. Consistent achievement of coal deliveries above that critical level would ensure survival over the winter even without improvement in nuclear or oil-fired generation. In the months before December that comparison showed that we were unlikely to get through the winter. By December the general position was good but we still had the problem of the have-not stations which this curve does not display.

The have-not coal monitor

Once it became apparent that the dispute was likely to extend beyond our original assumption of 26 weeks, the distinction between the have and have-not stations would assume even greater significance. See Figure 18.2.

At first it appeared that this problem would cause a failure to meet demand at

| | | Week 47 and cumulative from week 40 (thousands of tonnes) | | |
		1 October 1984 ESTIMATE	ACTUAL	DIFFERENCE
Coal Burn	Last Week	224	144	−80
	Cumulative from 1 October	1085	938	−147
Stock Level		3330	3477	+147
			ESTIMATE	
Remaining Winter Coal Requirement		3748	3748	
Coal Shortfall		418	271	−147

The estimate of coal stock shortfall, over the 1984/85 winter period, is now 271 kt.

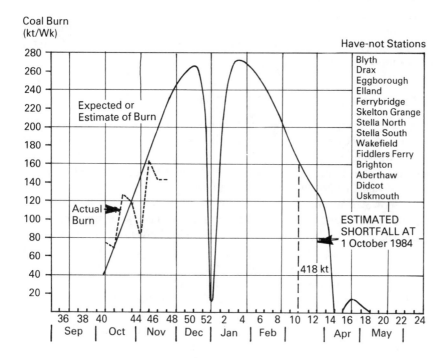

Figure 18.2 Have-not stations coal burn: example for week 47 (end November)
Source: CEGB Operations Department

some time during the mid-winter of 1984–5, deliveries of coal could be made to some of those stations which had not been receiving any. To understand the scale of the problem and to measure progress in overcoming it, it was necessary to devise a monitoring method. This was done by plotting week-by-week coal burn at those stations against that forecast and showing how this affected the coal stock shortfall for their expected use through the winter period. At the start of the winter the have-not stations had 418 000 tonnes of coal less than we required to get through the winter. The monitoring showed that shortfall to be consistently reduced week-by-week through the winter period.

Bearing in mind that these have-not power stations were always at the margin, the coal stock deficit was the balancing term between two large quantities (coal burn and coal availability). The result was that the monitor also served to illustrate, more starkly than ever, just how finely balanced the situation was. It was this monitoring display that clearly illustrated both the need to introduce coal deliveries to Didcot, Brighton and Uskmouth Power Stations and the benefit from these successes. It was another powerful tool.

The example shown in Figure 18.2 is for the week ending 25 November 1984. It shows the list of stations that were the have-nots. It also shows that they were estimated to be required to burn 3 748 000 tonnes to meet their share of consumer demand to the end of the winter but that they had only 3 477 000 tonnes in stock. Hence, there was at that time a coal stock deficit of 271 000 tonnes. However, that was a big improvement on the estimated shortfall or deficit of 418 000 tonnes on 1 October.

OPERATION OF THE POWER SYSTEM

The power stations' operating regimes for maximum endurance had to be tested to ensure that they enabled the power system to be operated securely with the unusual transmission power flows. It was vital that a single-minded pursuit of the endurance objective did not result in risks of a widespread disruption of electricity supplies from a transmission failure.

The power flows on the transmission network were different from those normally experienced. Assessment of the effect of this started well before the strike. The normal pattern was for flow from the relatively low cost coal-fired power stations in the north and Midlands to the high electricity demand areas in the south and south east. The oil-fired stations with high production costs in the south were normally used as little as possible. There were limits to the power that could be transmitted through the grid. These are normally referred to as transmission constraints and a number of such pinch-points were normal and well understood in the everyday operation of the power system. The pinch-points were to be different with the power stations operating to their changed regimes during the strike. The major power flows were then from the south to the midlands and north, with some heavy flows, particularly overnight when

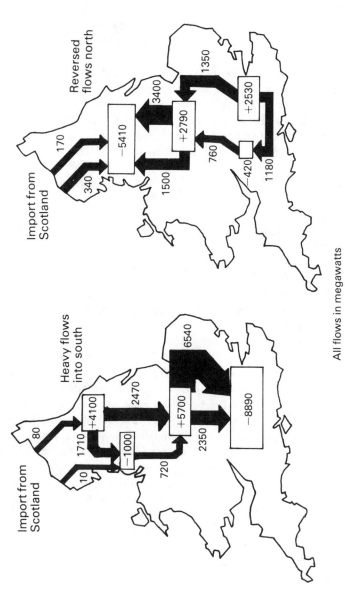

BEFORE NUM STRIKE 1983/84

Import from Scotland

Heavy flows into south

80
1710
10
+4100
−1000
720
2470
+5700
2350
6540
−8890

DURING NUM STRIKE 1984/85

Import from Scotland

Reversed flows north

170
340
−5410
3400
1500
1350
+2790
+2530
760
−420
1180

All flows in megawatts

− Importing area
+ exporting area

Figure 18.3 Winter power flow pattern (daytime)
Source: CEGB Operations Department

it was possible to shut down northern coal-fired power stations. Figure 18.3 illustrates this change.

In the contingency planning exercises carried out in 1983 some of the transmission constraints on these flows had been identified and some plant modifications made to relieve them. However, not much was possible or indeed could be justified since some modifications were expensive and would have taken years to complete.

Operational planning enabled the role of the pumped storage power station at Dinorwig in North Wales to be used to good effect.[2] Because of technical factors there were some constraints on its use under normal operating conditions. However, remedies were applied during the strike that enabled the plant to perform its normal task of pumping overnight, using power generated by oil-fired plant, and generating by day, thereby reducing the need for the have-not coal-fired stations to operate.

There are many other examples of how the operational planning and the system operation skills of the system operation team enabled the endurance objective to be successfully met. Unfortunately, however, they generally involved complex technical issues out of place here.

OPERATION OF THE TRANSMISSION SYSTEM

To cope with the large power transfers it was necessary to keep overhead lines and other transmission equipment in service as long as possible. Fortunately there were few breakdowns but it was a time for avoiding maintenance and living off our fat. It was normal to take transmission lines and the associated substation equipment out of service at one- or two-yearly intervals to inspect and to carry out any necessary remedial work. During the strike that work was not done on any equipment if system operation predicted that its withdrawal from service could cause constraints on oil-fired generation or any other difficulty for our endurance. It was obviously necessary to deal urgently with plant breakdowns and other problems that caused transmission constraints on oil plant output. One such problem occurred at Easter. Power system oscillations became a difficulty over two periods of light consumer demand overnight. Such a phenomenon was not unknown and generally arose with large power transfers from Scotland. They are generally indications of inherent instability and if not dealt with promptly can have serious consequences, even including power system collapse with major losses of supply. On these occasions the right corrective actions were taken. Unfortunately the solutions to the problem included reductions in the energy transfers to the CEGB power system from Scotland.

A number of transmission problems arose from maintaining security of supplies to the area boards in parts of the power system where generating plant, in order to save coal stocks, was not running. One such difficult area covered West Yorkshire and East Lancashire. To deal with this it was necessary to run a generating unit at Ferrybridge Power Station that we would have preferred to shut down to conserve coal at this have-not station. However, if the unit had to shut down for any reason the security of supply standard would not have been met for eight hours while another generating unit was being started from cold. During that time the area was vulnerable and any further adverse event would have caused a loss of supply. It was necessary to shut down the generator in June; fortunately there was no loss of supply. It was obviously the right policy to take bigger risks than normal to save coal. However, there was always a worry that if losses of electricity supplies resulted, this could be interpreted wrongly to mean that we were running out of coal.

A similar situation existed in the north east. In the absence of sufficient generating plant running at the power stations in Northumberland and Durham there were local security of supply problems in those areas. Hartlepool Nuclear Power Station could have solved the problem by running at continuous high output. However, the station was at its early commissioning stage and experiencing problems. Without Hartlepool, if the coal-fired power stations in the north east were to be operated to secure supplies, their coal stocks would run out in three months. It was decided to arrange automatic switching so that in the event of a transmission line tripping, 300 MW of non-essential electricity consumer demand would be automatically disconnected. This was a controlled step, which limited the interruptions of supply until it was possible to start up plant or the transmission line could be returned to service. It avoided the running of generating plant all the time as protection against an event that might never happen. No losses of supply did in fact occur and coal stocks were maintained at a number of stations not receiving supplies.

A number of local difficulties occurred because of transmission plant failures. One arose because of the need to repair the cooling system for a 275 KV cable in London, another because of a fault on a cable across the River Mersey between Lister Drive and Birkenhead. Neither resulted in losses of supplies but the latter meant that Fiddlers Ferry – a have-not station – had to run and use some of its non-replaceable coal stocks.

A transformer failure at High Marnham Power Station resulted in reduced levels of power transfer into the critical West Yorkshire area where there were a number of have-not stations. Fortunately this did not occur until mid-February when the strike was nearly over.

CONCLUSION

The ability of the System Operations Branch under Ed Wallis to predict the effects of the changing situation during the miners' strike provided the basis for managing the emergency and gave a strong incentive to taking the necessary actions. It was not always possible to act on the endurance-extending advice that was given because of the fine balance that had to be struck between what was necessary for maximum endurance and what was possible in the difficult industrial relations climate. Nevertheless the clear knowledge of what could be done to keep the lights on and the consequences of not implementing it was invaluable.

The transmission system proved to be flexible. Its power transfer capability was effective and invaluable. The CEGB transmission planning standards, which had resulted in such a flexible system, enabled us to use the full potential of the Board's generation capacity. That success was a fitting tribute to those who had planned and built the supergrid.

Chapter 19

Essential supplies: from helicopters to CO_2

The strategy for ensuring that power stations had adequate supplies of all the materials essential for normal operation was an important part of the CEGB's preparations for the miners' strike. As described in Chapter 5, the NUM strike in 1971–2 had demonstrated the vulnerability of power stations to the stoppage of supplies. It was not surprising that fuel deliveries were targets for NUM pickets. It was not so obvious that supplies of industrial gases, water treatment plant chemicals and engineering materials could be legitimately linked to a dispute in the coal industry. Yet these had been targets for the pickets in 1971–2 who eventually stopped all our supplies. Each power station had effectively been under siege. Even food for the canteen was being stopped by the zealous picketing miners. Trade union traditions were so deeply entrenched in the minds of the suppliers' delivery drivers that, whatever the logic of the situation, most would not cross a picket line.

With this knowledge, and despite the provisions of the 1980 and 1982 Employment Acts, the CEGB in 1983–4 arranged its affairs so that the power stations could continue to run for a long time even with siege-level picketing. Although secondary picketing left the NUM vulnerable to legal action we thought it prudent to assume that the NUM would again picket our stations and that all material going to the power stations would be at risk.

WHAT WERE THE ESSENTIAL COMMODITIES?

The commodities that are essential for the normal safe operation of a power station are these:

Lighting-up oil

This is necessary in coal-fired boilers because coal combustion is not stable at low load and during start up. Oil combustion provides greater control of heat input into the combustion chamber and helps to stabilise the coal flame. The flexible operation of power stations is dependent on the availability of lighting-up oil. In addition, propane is used in some boilers to ignite the oil burners so propane is also essential.

Generator cooling

The main electricity generators are cooled by water and hydrogen under pressure. The properties of hydrogen make it an excellent coolant. It is vital for a hydrogen-cooled generator to have a plentiful supply. It is possible to operate with air cooling but only at greatly reduced output and with risk of damage. To carry out maintenance or repairs it is necessary to remove the hydrogen from the generator. Work is then carried out in a normal air environment. To avoid an explosive hydrogen/air mixture during filling and emptying, carbon dioxide is used as an intermediate gas. Both hydrogen and carbon dioxide are therefore essential.

Water treatment plant chemicals

Electricity is normally produced by generators driven by turbines using steam from a boiler. To achieve the highest thermal efficiencies it is necessary to operate with steam at high pressures. One hundred and sixty times barometric (atmospheric) pressure is typical. To avoid corrosion of the boiler and damage to the turbine blading at these pressures and the associated high temperatures it is necessary to use pure water. The normal public water supply has to be purified by being passed through water treatment plant.

The water treatment plant used in power stations is normally of an ion-exchange type using resin similar in operating principle to a domestic water softener. The plant requires regeneration from time to time. The regeneration chemicals used are sulphuric acid and sodium hydroxide. These are also essential to continued operation.

Other essential commodities

It is also necessary to use other chemicals for water treatment, condensate polishing, boiler water dosing and feedwater dosing. Without going into the technicalities, these chemicals are also essential to avoid long-term damage to plant which, depending on the detailed local arrangements, are likely to require supplies of aluminium sulphate, ferric sulphate, lime, hydrazine and ammonia. They are generally required in smaller quantities than the regeneration chemicals referred to earlier.

It is also necessary to have sodium hypochlorite for dosing of the sea or river cooling water to avoid algae growth, but it is possible to manage without this for a time. Lubricating oil, transformer and switch oil, greases and diesel oil for mobile equipment are also necessary, as are spares and plant items for the normal maintenance of the plant.

Nuclear power stations

The coolant for the reactors at all British nuclear power stations before Sizewell B is nuclear grade carbon dioxide. It is the medium that removes heat from the reactor core and transmits it to the boilers, which generate steam to drive the turbines. Carbon dioxide is therefore of great importance to a nuclear power station. It is normally stored as a liquid at low temperatures in pressure vessels. The storage vessels are expensive and supplies of this gas, which has to have high purity, are essential to continued operation.

Consumption

The average weekly consumption of these commodities is shown in Table 19.1.

Table 19.1 Weekly consumption of essential commodities at power stations

Commodity	Typical large, coal-fired station	Typical large, oil-fired station	Typical nuclear station advanced gas cooled reactor
Lighting-up oil and stabilisation Oil	600 tonnes		
Propane	1 tonne	1–2 tonnes	–
Hydrogen	2500 cu. metres	2500 cu. metres	100 cu. metres
Water treatment Chemicals:			
Ferric sulphate	4 tonnes	4 tonnes	2 tonnes
Sulphuric acid	12–30 tonnes	12–30 tonnes	6–15 tonnes
Sodium hydroxide	12–30 tonnes	12–30 tonnes	6–15 tonnes

Source: CEGB Operations Department

ENDURANCE STRATEGY

The CEGB endurance strategy for its main fuels was aimed at keeping the lights on for twenty-six weeks following a total loss of coal supplies. It was necessary to have a parallel strategy, which would ensure that essential commodities were available in sufficient quantities to enable the potential of the fuel strategy to be realised. It was decided that this should be dealt with by three main means. First, arrangements should be made with those suppliers who gave us the best possible chance of maintaining deliveries even in the face of resolute picketing. Second, adequate storage capacity was necessary so that the stations could operate normally for a prolonged time even without new deliveries. Third, fall-back arrangements had to be made that would enable alternative 'last ditch' delivery facilities to be used if the other plans failed. It was also necessary to have monitoring arrangements to help manage the preparation phase and to provide management feedback on essential commodities stocks and deliveries in the strike when it occurred.

The issues of supplies, fall-back arrangements and monitoring were all managed by Granville Camsey as Headquarters Operations Services Engineer with his team of Roy West, Alan Bradshaw and Phil Willet. The regions were to do all the work necessary to provide the increased physical storage arrangements at the power stations.

Maintaining deliveries

We normally contracted with various suppliers for these materials under contracts that were arranged centrally. They were the responsibility of Phil Willet. In the preparatory phase much thought was given to who should be our suppliers. Contracts were awarded only after assessing the company's industrial relations record and their willingness to supply 'at all costs'. It was clearly pointed out to the contractor that they were about to be committed to supplying our power stations. It was their responsibility to do so, pickets or no pickets. We would not accept less. Where there were doubts, arrangements were made, in the jargon of the time, to 'dual source'. This provided greater flexibility and reduced the possibility of failure of supply should the drivers of any one company not cross picket lines.

Special arrangements had to be made for carbon dioxide supplies to nuclear power stations. The supplier to all but one power station was ICI. Planning meetings were held with them before the strike to develop and agree the strategy and to consider how to help their drivers through the pickets. The main theme was to ensure an excellent communications system that would enable CO_2 supply requirements and the extent of picketing to be known by both the parties and for decisions on deliveries to be made in consultation. As a result a computer terminal from the ICI management information system was placed in the CEGB emergency information room and a high level of co-ordination was achieved.[1]

Before the autumn of 1983 we had the most secure set of supply contracts that we could arrange. They had yet to be tested, of course, and we felt that they might need reinforcement.

Storage capacity

Until the NUM strikes in the 1970s it was normal for the storage capacity for these commodities to be what commercial judgement dictated. It was necessary to limit the level of working capital but to have sufficient storage to deal with the uncertainty of deliveries, in bad weather for example. After the two coal strikes in the 1970s it became Board policy to stock six weeks' supplies of all commodities essential to normal operations. In 1981, when we were carrying out contingency planning in preparation for a future miners' strike, it became apparent that the stocking facilities for essential commodities had to be greatly increased. We made successive revisions to our estimate of how long our coal stocks would enable us to maintain electricity supplies. The requirement for storage of essential commodities had to be increased at each stage. By August 1982 it had been decided that the storage of these commodities should equal the primary fuel endurance target of six months. This would require capital works of £35 million and, when fully charged, an increase in working capital of £43 million.

This decision required a four-fold increase in storage capacity and necessitated the provision of several hundred additional storage vessels. The scale of this increase can be illustrated by reference to the main chemicals used for regeneration of the water treatment plant. Typical weekly usage rates of sulphuric acid and sodium hydroxide for a major coal-fired station are up to 30 tonnes a week; thus increasing storage capacity from 6 weeks to 26 weeks required a typical increase in station storage capacity from 70–180 tonnes to 300–800 tonnes for each chemical. For all the Board's stations we required a total stock capacity of over 16 000 tonnes of sodium hydroxide and over 14 000 tonnes of sulphuric acid. This is the equivalent of approximately 900 road tankers of sodium hydroxide and 800 road tankers of sulphuric acid.

Exceptions to increased storage

There were two exceptions to the general policy of increasing endurance by increased storage. They were hydrogen and nuclear-grade carbon dioxide.

Hydrogen supplies

A new approach was adopted for hydrogen. Hydrogen is normally stored as a pressurised gas and increasing storage in this form would have necessitated the use of vast numbers of hydrogen cylinders. Instead of this, plant was installed in which hydrogen was produced on site by a process using a 2:1 methanol/water mixture. This was introduced at all stations except those few in which hydrogen gas was already manufactured on site by electrolysis or at small stations where the hydrogen requirements were so small that a bottle supply sufficed.

Nuclear grade carbon dioxide

For a number of reasons we decided to depend on nuclear grade carbon dioxide supplies continuing during an NUM strike. For one thing, the quantity of additional carbon dioxide required to provide 26 weeks' endurance at all nuclear stations was calculated to be 24 272 tonnes, at an estimated cost of £57 million. In addition to the high cost there were difficulties in finding a suitable storage space on the relatively small nuclear sites that would satisfy the Nuclear Installations Inspectorate.[2]

If it came to the worst the nuclear safety requirement armed us with compelling arguments that could be deployed with the pickets and we were planning fallback arrangements including helicopter deliveries (described later), which would enable the Board to fly in small quantities of liquid CO_2 as a stopgap.

THE CONSTRUCTION PROGRAMME

The construction programme for these additional supplies was covered by many contracts that were managed by the engineering departments of the five regions. As the increased storage capacity was being installed at the stations, progress was being monitored weekly. We were pleased and relieved that by the programme date of 1 November 1983, with the few exceptions described later, all the necessary additional storage had been installed and was ready for use. Close liaison with the manufacturers was maintained throughout the construction of the additional storage and also with the commodity suppliers who were given advance warning of the requirements for filling the new storage facilities as they became available. They did well in meeting this large additional requirement.

There were a few unfortunate experiences. One was with a company that manufactured methanol storage vessels and the associated hydrogen storage vessels for several stations and also water treatment plant chemical storage vessels for a few. Despite weekly monitoring it was not discovered until a late stage that this supplier had overstretched his capability and as a result of that pressure had provided storage vessels with defective welds. While some were repairable others had to be scrapped and replaced, an exercise which was not completed until 1985. It was necessary for the stations involved to hire tankers to provide the necessary chemical storage and cylinders to provide the hydrogen storage.

'LAST DITCH' SUPPLY ARRANGEMENTS

We considered it necessary to develop contingency plans to deal with the emergency that would arise if there was effective siege-level picketing and normal methods of delivery failed. Work was done on three options.

Helicopters

During 1983 a study was carried out of the arrangements necessary for helicopters to be used in an emergency. One possibility was to supply power stations with essential commodities by flying them in over the pickets. The study considered what the pick-up sites would be: safe routes; landing site locations; safe approaches to landing sites and the possible use of these arrangements in daytime or at night. It was necessary to study air traffic control factors and to decide the most suitable helicopters and contractors.

Included in the survey were the requirements for the transport of dangerous goods (for example sulphuric acid), the operational guidelines that should be adopted and all the other actions necessary to set up a large airborne transport of supplies. We acquired special storage vessels for the transport of nuclear grade CO_2 and carrying frames for sulphuric acid and solid sodium hydroxide, together with equipment to enable these to be transferred into the normal station storage facilities.

Lifting and flying trials were set up with British Airways Helicopters Ltd. Since we did not wish to publicise what we were doing, the trials were carried out at Beccles in Suffolk over two weekends. The first trial was to give the helicopter pilot experience of operating the BV 234 Chinook (a large double rotor helicopter) at its maximum all-up weight, and for the CEGB team to learn how to operate with helicopter crews to position loads accurately at power stations and loading sites. The second trial was to prove the specialist equipment that had been designed to carry gas and chemicals.

The first weekend was initially not successful because, as a result of a faulty weigher, the helicopter was being asked to lift beyond its capability. When this was corrected all worked satisfactorily. The second weekend attracted many observers who wanted to know what was happening. They were told that it was an exercise to practise lifting heavy loads – which was true and accepted as a reasonable explanation. A photograph of these trials appears in the plate section.

The specialist equipment was proven and all ended satisfactorily. The initial view of the large double-rotor helicopter failing to lift the load with its blades forming a double Vee-sign remained as a vivid picture with the CEGB team. Eventually we gave a contract to Bristows to provide helicopter services and, although it was never used, we were indebted to them for all the help they gave us in maintaining this option through the strike. It provided much needed confidence in our ability to supply.

CEGB road tankers

It was possible that contract road-borne supplies of sulphuric acid and sodium hydroxide might fail to get through the pickets when our own vehicles might be successful. This had been the case at some power stations in the 1971–2 coal strike. It was worth renting our own tanker fleet as a fallback between normal delivery by contract vehicles and the more extreme measure of helicopter delivery. We rented a tanker fleet for this purpose. We approached a number of organisations but only Transport Development Group offered help. Others refused as they were concerned that potential adverse reaction from their own drivers would prejudice their operations. The tankers were collected on a piece-meal basis from a number of depots in order not to alert each company's own drivers. They were painted in CEGB orange and delivered to our central stores at Didcot. In addition CEGB drivers were trained and qualified as heavy goods vehicle licence holders. The arrangements were maintained in a state of readiness throughout the strike.

During the strike this situation did provoke some picketing by striking miners at our central stores when it was leaked that some of the tankers were located there.

Seaborne deliveries

A study was done on the possibility of delivering nuclear grade CO_2 by sea as a parallel to the helicopter study. This was carried out for us by BP Shipping. A workable plan could not be successfully developed, mainly because security fencing at the coastal nuclear sites prevented the ready use of amphibious craft. The conclusion was that, while it was possible to supply some stations by sea, it required heavy expenditure. We decided not to go ahead.

THE PREPARATIONS ARE PUT TO THE TEST

Comments on essential commodities deliveries and the effects of picketing have already been covered, but it is worthwhile making a few additional observations here. Our preparations meant that we were in a strong situation when the strike occurred. The level of picketing fell short of the siege level that we had prepared for. It was however a continuous factor and there were many failures to deliver across picket lines by our suppliers. These were followed up and pressure brought to bear on suppliers who usually responded by more resolute attempts at delivery. BOC deliveries worried us for some time before this was drawn to the attention of their Chief Executive who was a non-executive director of the CEGB at the time. We had heavy stocks and the picketing was usually sufficiently variable ultimately to allow delivery. We were never really threatened at fossil-fired power stations. There is a view, shared by some of those who knew the situation, that the lack of effective pickets came partly from a general awareness by the NUM of the extent of our stocks and that, because of our preparations, the battle was never really joined. There are other factors, which are discussed in Chapter 22.

The position at nuclear stations was far more critical. There were some serious problems from the effect of picketing on deliveries. Early on in the strike an informal agreement was reached with pickets to allow 'routine' delivery of CO_2 to South Western Region nuclear stations where picketing was causing difficulties. Later this arrangement was rescinded by the NUM. Positive management resulted in ICI drivers continuing to cross picket lines. From time to time it was necessary to arrange police protection. The close links with the suppliers were invaluable during this period.

At Trawsfynydd Nuclear Power Station CO_2 deliveries continued in the face of resolute picketing, thanks to the firm line and persuasiveness of the ICI drivers' supervisor. The scaled delivery level he agreed with the pickets was more than adequate to meet the station's needs.

During the strike there was also a prolonged pay dispute between the carbon dioxide tanker drivers and ICI. It is a tribute to all concerned that this dispute and the NUM strike were always seen as being separate and that nuclear carbon dioxide deliveries were maintained throughout the year-long NUM dispute. Delivery of nuclear carbon dioxide, we repeat, was critical and nuclear output was marginally affected by some shortages.

CONCLUSIONS

The lack of essential supplies could just as easily have shut down our power stations as the shortage of fuel supplies. However, the lack of well-organised and determined picketing on a wide scale meant that, although there were local problems, there was no real challenge to the general situation. This was partly a result of the form of the strike: the split in the NUM, the preoccupation with legal wrangles, and the lack of funds all resulted in the picketing not approaching the intensity of 1971–2.

The Board's preparations may in retrospect look as though they were too expensive and too elaborate. However, it should be remembered that, if we had faced a strike supported by a majority from a full NUM ballot, it could all have been different. NUM solidarity with the full availability of funds could have resulted in a much more resolute challenge; then all our preparations might have been needed. In the event it is likely that our preparations, which were certainly understood by the NUM at local level, were themselves responsible for causing the NUM to realise that their actions could only have a limited effect.

Chapter 20

Generating plant: problems and opportunities

In addition to the main strategy it was possible for endurance to be extended by a series of additional actions many, although not all of them, small. Together they made the difference between failure and success. Once the strike had started we concentrated on developing any means by which we could increase endurance. The need to do so became more urgent in late summer. The possibilities included increasing the output of oil-fired generating units, changing coal-fired units over to oil-firing, and recommissioning closed oil-fired power stations. Much activity and ingenuity was involved.

MAJOR OIL-FIRED POWER STATIONS

A main question was how could we increase oil-fired generation. Four weeks into the strike there was just under 8000 MW of oil-fired plant capacity available. The oil burn was increased from 30 000 to 350 000 tonnes per week from which 1.45 TWHs of electricity were generated and that met 36 per cent of the total springtime electricity requirement. By November we were burning 600 000 tonnes a week of oil and gas from which 2.3 TWHs were generated, which met 50 per cent of the higher winter electricity requirement. The generation from oil had increased from being 80 per cent of that from coal to being 145 per cent. The build-up of oil-and gas-fired plant capacity in that time is shown in Figure 20.1. It had a big effect on our endurance position. How did that transformation occur?

The level of oil burn that we had expected in our contingency planning was achieved after the first few weeks of the strike. It was based on thirteen of the sixteen large oil-fired units being available for full load generation. We set about improving that. Two of the generating units, one at Ince Power Station and one at Pembroke Power Station, were not available because each of the generators was without an electrical rotor.[1] These had been used as spares to enable a works modification programme to take place to the family of seventeen NEI-Parsons generators of similar design. When the strike started the oil plant became important to us. In contrast, Ferrybridge C Power Station, in the middle of the Yorkshire coalfield, was not receiving coal and was unlikely to do so during the strike. It would be sensible for the electrical rotors, which were similar, to be

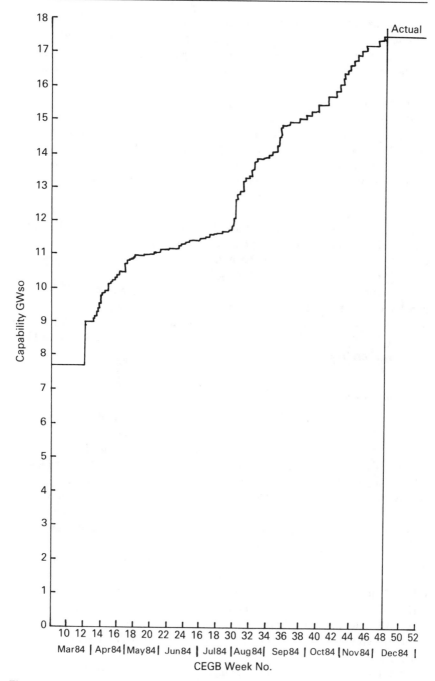

Figure 20.1 Oil and gas generation capability over 1984–5 miners' strike

Source: CEGB Operations Department

removed from that station and installed at Pembroke and Ince – the oil stations without rotors. This had to be managed with much sensitivity by Derek Richardson, the station manager at Ferrybridge C, as it was close to several militant pits and many of the power station workers had close relatives who were striking miners. Yet we needed them to do some of the work necessary to allow the rotors to be released and transported to the oil-fired stations. In recognising that the station was unlikely to run over the summer lower electricity demand period the opportunity was taken to do a full overhaul on two turbine-generator units. The electrical rotors were sent to Parson's works for inspection before being despatched to the two oil-fired power stations, one in Cheshire and one in Pembrokeshire. This all took some time, more than we could really afford. However, by September two more oil-fired generating units were helping to conserve our coal stocks. This was to be important at Pembroke Power Station because in May there had been a steam chest failure on one of the turbines. With the completion of the repair programme and the installation of the ex-Ferrybridge C electrical rotor Pembroke was ready to play a full part in our coal-conserving strategy, which it did to the end of the strike.

Unit two of Ince Power Station had not been commissioned following construction since its electrical rotor had become part of the programme referred to earlier. On the electrical rotor becoming available rapid progress was made in carrying out all the commissioning tests and the unit was worked up to full load in a very short time.

Oil plant history

Most of the CEGB's oil-fired plant had been ordered and built when oil prices were much lower in the 1960s. In the 1960s and early 1970s the heavy fuel oil being purchased for power station consumption was lower priced than coal on a comparable heat basis and was expected to continue to be so. This enabled the CEGB, through building oil-fired power stations, to gain some diversity of fuel supply and to present the NCB with competition which otherwise was not available.

The CEGB built sufficient oil-fired capacity to become at one time the largest oil purchaser in the Western world. Several oil price hikes during the 1970s and early 1980s made oil for power generation much more expensive than indigenous coal. Oil-fired stations had their operating regimes reduced. Many of the smaller oil-fired stations had been closed down and were in various stages of decommissioning. The larger, newer and more efficient power stations that had survived had partly done so by greatly reducing their costs. It was normal for them to have less than half the staff level that they had when operating at full output on cheap oil.

The coal strike brought a large change in their affairs. From being marginal generating plant used to the least extent possible and with some of the stations approaching closure, they had become the most important stations. There were a number of implications for this change: one was that the staffing arranged for low levels of output now had to be able to cope with continuous full-load generation. Another was that the needs of this plant were now of first importance, in contrast to their low priority in the past. The electrical rotor story described earlier was an example.

Increasing oil-fired generation output

The last of the Grain Power Station generating units was nearing the end of its construction period and commissioning had started in the early weeks of the strike. It was obviously desirable to carry out this work in the shortest possible time to gain the benefit of the additional oil-based generation. In fact it was commissioned in record time – from first connecting it to the grid system to working up to full output with all its systems working correctly was five days. This was the fastest time ever achieved by the CEGB and was described as a world record.

Not long afterwards it was decided that we should use the overload capability that was available at Grain and Littlebrook Power Stations. At Grain the units were designed to allow certain operational adjustments that could give an overload output of 705 MW against a normal output of 660 MW. Testing the plant revealed that 740 MW and 690 MW were available. Experience of the use of these levels of output was sparse. However, it was decided to increase output permanently to the higher overload figure but to monitor critical parameters to enable the station to reduce output if plant damage was encountered. Conditions were satisfactory and the plant was run on continuous overload to the end of the strike. Some problems were encountered and in October, before the higher winter levels of electricity demand, it became necessary to shut some of the Grain and Littlebrook units to do urgent repairs. However, the problems were not serious and the plant was returned to service fairly quickly. Over the financial year 1984–5, which closely corresponded with the duration of the strike, Grain supplied 17.99 TWH to the power system and Littlebrook 14.92 TWH, both of which were higher levels than the CEGB record power station output up to that time. Between them they provided more than 15 per cent of the supplies to the grid system and reduced coal burn by some 15 000 000 tonnes.

Ince B, Fawley and Pembroke oil-fired Power Stations were all at full output. Ince B had to await the arrival and installation of the electrical rotor from Ferrybridge C Power Station but then had a reliable high-load run to the end of the strike. Fawley and Pembroke Power Stations had their problems. Fawley had boiler fouling problems (described in Chapter 17). Pembroke had steam chest problems and at the beginning of the strike was without one of its four generating units (referred to in Chapter 12). Despite these problems Fawley supplied 12.98 TWH and Pembroke 11.25 TWH, both representing a fine performance and together saving the consumption of 10 000 000 tonnes of coal.

Table 20.1 Oil and gas generation capability at peak demand period during January 1985

Power Station	Capability Mwso
Ince	960
Grain	2524
Littlebrook D	1893
Kingsnorth*	1940
Fawley	1932
Pembroke	1900
Belvedere	345
Northfleet	456
Richborough	342
South Denes	248
Hams Hall*	360
Blyth B*	300
Cottam	240
Ironbridge	150
Rugeley A	60
Rugeley B	200
West Burton	200
Other Midland Plant	140
Tilbury B*	1000
West Thurrock*	210
Didcot*	400
Aberthaw*	200
GTs	1600
TOTAL	17 600

* Stations engineered for additional generation from oil or gas burn during the miners' action

Source: CEGB Operations Department

COAL-FIRED POWER STATIONS

It is normal for coal-fired stations to have a limited oil burn capability for start up and for periods of flame stabilisation; during steady running this oil burn is not normally used. During the strike a number of stations carried out equipment conversions to achieve oil-fired output beyond that normally available. Table 20.1 shows the oil burn capability of the CEGB achieved during the strike, with those stations asterisked which further extended their oil burn. Their activity is described as follows.

Kingsnorth Power Station

Designed as a dual-fired (coal and oil) station, Kingsnorth Power Station was a prime candidate for conversion to oil burning. Spare oil-burner equipment was reinstalled, which increased by one third the number of oil burners. Additionally, the existing burners were fitted with new over-size tips to give one-and-a-half times normal oil flow. Air distribution in the boiler then proved to be the limiting factor, although full load on oil alone was all but achieved on every unit. Since the station was originally designed on a dual-fired basis, no additional equipment had to be purchased.

Tilbury B Power Station

Before the strike Tilbury B Power Station only had a modest capability to burn oil for lighting up and flame stabilisation. During the strike, the station went through a succession of engineering modifications, starting by replacing the entire set of oil burners with a larger size. To supply sufficient oil to these burners, eight pumps were added to the pumping system (removed from the closed A station) and the standby set of pumps was also used continuously.

Beyond these provisions the station found that careful readjustment to oil system valves and layout gave such an increase in oil pressure at the burner tips that sufficient oil could be burnt to generate 1000 MW at the peak. It was also necessary to control chimney emissions and the coal systems were modified to recirculate fine ash from the precipitator flue-gas cleaning equipment to the coal mills. The fine ash behaved as a coal substitute and enabled the precipitators to clean up the emissions from the oil burn.

West Thurrock Power Station

At the start of the dispute West Thurrock Power Station was being converted to burn heavy fuel oil for lighting-up purposes. This was to contain costs, since the original design was for low viscosity lighting-up oil which is more expensive. The higher viscosity of the heavy fuel oil necessitated the installation of additional heaters and the existing oil burners were given larger burner tips. With these initial modifications, West Thurrock could generate up to 210 MW on oil.

The greatest limitation to extending oil burn, however, proved to be the pumping system from the delivery jetty to the station buildings (built for lighting-up oil deliveries only). Consequently additional oil pumps were purchased and others taken from the closed Brunswick Wharf Power Station. The piping systems were adapted appropriately. Thus the generation output of West Thurrock Power Station on oil only was raised from 50 MW to an ultimate potential of 1100 MW, although due to industrial relations problems at the station this potential was not fully realised during the dispute. As described in Chapter 14, the station industrial staff's sensitivity over what was correct action led to protracted discussions and even, on some occasions, ballots before the decision was taken to discharge a tanker. The delays caused by these negotiations reduced the oil-fired generation from the station.

Blyth B Power Station

This station, north of Newcastle in the North Eastern Region, normally used fuel oil only for lighting up the coal-fired boilers. Bob Klotz, the station manager, set out to increase the station's oil-fired generation capability to the maximum. This involved engineering changes to pumps, pipes, burners and control systems and modifications to the old marine terminal, which was designed to handle only limited deliveries of oil. Three ships were chartered and modified to operate a shuttle service of about five trips a day from the Esso oil depot on the River Tyne.

Local industrial and public relations problems had to be overcome as a result of an accumulation of vanadium pentoxide in the precipitators (a normal consequence of burning some oils) and increases in local pollution. Oil burn capability was increased to 300 MW initially and to 450 MW by February 1985. The station was able to burn extra oil equivalent to about 700 000 tonnes of coal over the 12-month period.

Didcot Power Station

At the beginning of the miners' action, Didcot Power Station had a contract under way to increase the capacity of its oil handling system by a factor of three. This comprised new oil pumping, heating and pipework. The new system was pressed into early service and the old system was also retained. In addition the station switched from a heavy to a medium fuel oil (lower viscosity) to maximise oil throughput. Burner tips were changed for a larger size at selected positions where this was feasible, to make use of the increased oil flow.

To sustain the increased burn, in common with some other coal-fired stations, it was found necessary to adapt the rail delivery installations for road tankers. A concrete apron was built up to the trackside and a multipoint reception system for the road tankers was installed. It was also found prudent to make changes to the delivery pumping configuration to increase fuel flow rates.

Aberthaw B Power Station

Equipment was installed by Aberthaw B Power Station to accept road deliveries of fuel oil, where previously all supplies had been by rail. One third of the oil burners were entirely replaced by an improved type of equipment. Oil burner tips on the remainder were also changed, to give three times the oil flow. A further gain in oil burn was achieved by the station changing from heavy fuel oil to a medium (lower viscosity) oil. The resulting oil burn enabled the site to offer 200 MW peak output from oil burning.

Hams Hall Power Station

Equipment was held by CEGB to convert Hams Hall to firing gas. This dated from an earlier period where the station played a role in the development of the gas grid[2] (which was under construction at the time). The station reinstated this equipment by removing and substituting the appropriate burners and connecting specialist gas supply equipment. The station was then able to generate 360 MW at full load on gas alone.

Midlands Region

In addition to the stations already described there were a number of Midlands Region power stations that had the capability to burn more oil than was normal for a coal-fired unit. This capability had been introduced to supplement coal burn at times of difficulties with coal handling and milling plant. All told it gave an oil burn capability of 1150 MW.

Small oil-fired stations

A number of smaller oil-fired generating units had ceased generation in the years before the strike and others were under notice of closure. As many units as possible were returned to service during the strike. This was mainly in the South Eastern Region, where a good degree of success was achieved. Belvedere, Northfleet, Richborough and South Denes Power Stations together gave over 1700 MW of oil-fired capacity to reduce coal burn.

OIL PLANT CAPACITY INCREASE

The overall effect of all these initiatives is shown in the increase in gas and oil-fired capacity of 8000 MW to 17 600 MW achieved in January 1985 and shown in Table 20.1.

STATUTORY INSPECTIONS

The law required that all boilers and other pressure vessels that were part of the nuclear, coal and oil-fired generating units had periodic inspections. Under the Factories Act periods were prescribed for the operation of boilers and other pressure vessels, after which they had to be inspected by authorised surveyors. The object of the inspections was to ensure safety and the integrity of the plant until its next statutory inspection.

The CEGB was the largest operator of water tube boilers in the country and had become the leading authority on their technology. Extensive research and development successfully applied over the years had given high levels of reliability and efficiency. The independent inspecting authorities worked for insurance companies and they and their organisations were well informed on the Board's technical advances. They had supported us in successful negotiations with HM Factories Inspectorate to gain their agreement to longer prescribed periods between inspections. In the early 1980s the inspection interval was being changed from 30 to 38 months for the large 500 MW and 660 MW generating units.

Although the logic of the situation was that, since the concession had now been made it should be immediately applied; there were, however, complications caused by the terms of the Act. They said that, once an inspection certificate had been issued, the date for the next inspection quoted in that certificate must be adhered to. The Act then strictly required the new arrangements to apply after the first inspection following the extension of the interval between inspections. At the time of the strike we had a number of oil-fired boilers and coal-fired boilers at stations receiving coal, important to endurance, which were going to have to be shut down because of the small print and without any logical reason.

Fortunately there was a means of keeping a boiler in operation beyond the certificate date. This required the formal application for a period of extension for a particular boiler to the Technical Branch of HM Factories Inspectorate. This was a substantial task but we were supported by confidence based on firm knowledge of the integrity of the plant. The Technical Branch, if satisfied with the application, made a recommendation to the local district inspector to the effect that no action should be taken against the operator if the boiler stayed in service beyond the certificate date.

This was done successfully for sixteen important generating units. Some district inspectors expressed disquiet and complained to CEGB officers that they were being used for what they regarded as political strike breaking. All this made a substantial contribution to conserving coal stocks at the stations not receiving coal supplies. It was managed for us by Alan Bradshaw, working for Granville Camsey.

GAS TURBINES

The decision to increase the output from gas turbine generators to help us get through the winter had a number of plant consequences (Chapter 13 refers to some of them). They resulted mainly from the need to overhaul the gas generators at 1500-hour intervals. The gas generators are aircraft-type jet engines and usually require combustion chamber and gas diffuser repairs together with other work as part of the 1500-hour service. The service can be done on a production line basis and has to be supported by the appropriate spares.

As referred to in Chapter 13, the large number of gas generators to be overhauled made it necessary to use three repair and overhaul facilities. They were at Rolls Royce, the Littlebrook workshops of the CEGB South Eastern Region, and the Ministry of Defence establishment at Fleetlands. All of the repair and maintenance work was normally done by Rolls Royce at either their Ansty or East Kilbride works. In an attempt to gain a degree of self-sufficiency and to provide a price negotiating edge, we had been developing a limited gas engine repair capability at the Littlebrook workshops. Here unserviceable engines were dismantled, some components replaced and others such as combustion chambers repaired in-house or contracted out. All of the repair and maintenance activity was supported by the CEGB's own centrally held pool of spare engines and spare parts located at Didcot.

The dramatic increase in use of the gas turbine generating plant meant that the normal servicing arrangements would be overwhelmed. Other repair facilities had to be sought. The most promising of those available were the Royal Naval establishment at Fleetlands near Portsmouth. Overtures were made to the Admiralty and ultimately to the Ministry of Defence and a visit to Fleetlands was arranged. Roy West from Granville Camsey's branch was impressed with the repair facilities not only for their capability and the quality of the work but (as an ex-Portsmouth dockyard apprentice) by being entertained by a Commander RN who suggested that he should pay his own 85p lunch bill.

The repair programme based on the three facilities became important to the overall strategy. As the repair workload intensified it became necessary to ask the Admiralty to increase its support and to seek the loan of Olympus gas engines from spares held in support of the propulsion units in a number of its large vessels. The Royal Navy was unable to make such a gesture unilaterally. Within the NATO alliance it was necessary to gain the agreement of the NATO partners with whom the spare engines were pooled.

The arrangements for loaning engines and spares were ultimately agreed with the Royal Navy, but after a tough negotiation and a formal commercial agreement. Part of the agreement was to move the engines and spares around in unmarked vehicles. This was a particularly sensitive issue for two reasons. One was that a military repair facility helping the CEGB to keep the lights on might be seen as the military helping to defeat the miners. The other was that a big staff reduction was taking place; the trade unions and the local community were very unhappy and looking for grounds to attack the management of the establishment.

Despite strenuous efforts to keep the MOD support under wraps, a zealous reporter on the *Portsmouth Evening News* lighted upon the upsurge in work at Fleetlands and published an article about a possible reprieve for the many whose jobs were to be lost. Luckily this was not picked up by the national media, so a possible embarrassment to us and the government stemming from this direct support for the CEGB was averted. Overall the repair arrangements worked well and the gas turbine fleet helped us get through the winter.

CONCLUSIONS

The period of the 1984–5 miners' strike was an active one for CEGB engineers and engineering generally. It was a time of much innovation and effort to improve oil-fired plant output. The improvement over the early part of the winter was the most important factor in maintaining electricity supplies over the winter peak demands. Without it we would have failed. The aggregation of many individually small contributions had certainly made the difference between failure and success.

Chapter 21

The managers, the unions and the staff

Much has been written in earlier chapters about the Board and its managers' relations with the trade unions and staff. This chapter attempts to show these relationships at the time of the 1984–5 miners' strike as a coherent whole.

THE UNIONS AND THE STAFF

Eight trade unions were recognised in the industry, all of them with some representation within CEGB. Within the Board the EPEA had the largest membership, the GMBATU being the largest industrial staff union and NALGO the largest clerical and administrative staff union. Over 85 per cent of the CEGB's staff were members of one or other of these unions.

The structure of the industrial relations machinery and the unions' role in this are referred to in Chapter 1 and Appendix I. The Electricity Supply Trade Union Council (ESTUC), representing all eight unions, met regularly and worked closely. The staff were well paid, co-operative and productive. Staff surveys showed that most subscribed to public service standards and were proud of the Board's achievements. They also had, in general, a strong commitment to their unions as they operated within the Board.

However, it would be wrong to suggest that staff attitudes were uniform or that staff and their unions simply went along with management plans, methods, and decisions. As we have shown, there were occasional clashes of interest and moments when militant groups seemed to hold sway. Nevertheless the contending parties, in difficult situations, mostly seemed to be looking for sensible solutions. The price of breakdown was alarmingly high and everyone knew it.

UNION POLICIES AND PRACTICES

All of the trade unions except the EPEA[1] had a majority of their members outside the industry and the decisions of the unions during the strike should be seen in that light. Throughout the dispute the NUM had the formal support of the executives of most of the unions, the EPEA and the EETPU[2] being the clear-cut exceptions.

In March 1984 the GMBATU, EPEA, EETPU and NALGO issued advice to their electricity supply memberships to work normally. In the same month the TGWU Executive had pledged its full support to the NUM and had called on its members not to handle the movement of coal and extraordinary transfers within station boundaries.

In May the NUM met the transport unions, including the TGWU, and undertakings were given to call for sympathetic action, particularly at power stations. The EETPU Executive, at its national ESI conference, rejected this call unless the consent of all trade unionists was demonstrated through a ballot, in which its recommendation would be to vote no. At about this time the NUM decided to make a greater picketing effort at the power stations and an NUM circular, originating from the meeting with the transport unions, urged power workers to regard all power stations as deemed to be picketed and not to cross the picket lines. This was condemned by ESTUC, including the TGWU representative. It was ignored by nearly all CEGB staff.

In August, some regional conferences of the GMBATU shop stewards in the industry reinforced the significance of the NUM ballot issue by deciding that no support would be given to the miners unless the NUM itself held a ballot.

In Chapter 13 an account was given of the debate on the strike at the TUC Annual Congress on 3 September. The ESTUC subsequently decided to meet the NUM under the auspices of the TUC, following which there was a further ESTUC meeting. The statement made after that meeting said that ESTUC was united in its desire for the earliest settlement of the NCB/NUM dispute and to maintain the good relationships between the ESI unions. The statement added: 'Working relationships between the Trade Unions on the Council are very good and, indeed, have got steadily better over the years. All the Unions on the Council will therefore keep in touch with each other'. However ESTUC could not maintain a united front on support for the NUM, with six unions supporting the TUC decision and the EPEA and EETPU rejecting the call. The EETPU canvassed the idea of a national ballot of all ESI union members but this did not find general favour. The EETPU proceeded with its own postal ballot, which included 43 000 members in all electricity boards (not just the CEGB). The decision was to reject the TUC policy, by 20 042 votes to 3864. The EPEA decided not to hold a ballot but reaffirmed its earlier policy of opposition to calls from the NUM for sympathetic action. While advising members to work normally and not undertake the work of other staff, the EPEA stated that the position would be kept under review.

The TGWU, AUEW and GMBATU issued identical guidelines to their members in the industry, confirmed as advice and not instructions, against handling new supplies of coal or oil in substitution for coal. They nevertheless advised members not to withdraw co-operation from management and emphasised the TUC guidelines on picketing and the need to report to work normally. The guidelines prompted stewards in some stations to question the levels of oil deliveries, particularly in relation to pre-strike levels, and some men in a few locations refused to burn new stocks of coal or to co-operate with oil overburn.

STAFF ATTITUDES

Quite clearly the overwhelming majority of CEGB staff were unwilling to take industrial action in support of the striking miners, despite these guidelines. Many co-operated with abnormal operating requirements, such as oil overburn and plant modifications, two-shifting of base-load stations, continued generation by decommissioned plant, and road-borne fuel deliveries. The increased level of overtime work acted as an incentive, while staff at large oil-fired stations and older stations in particular welcomed the increased load on their stations.

We have seen that where local mining communities were made up of striking miners, staff in the power stations tended to follow the advice of some unions to limit co-operation with management but where the local pits were working, as in the East Midlands and to a limited extent elsewhere, co-operation was wholehearted.

The reasons that most trade union members in the CEGB, particularly industrial staff, were not prepared to support the miners differed from one region to another. As some of the trade unions had said, the traditional view was that the ESI should not be used to resolve disputes in the mining or any other industry. This would explain, for example, the limited industrial action taken by CEGB staff during the 1974 miners' strike. Equally significant was the fact that, unlike 1974, the miners themselves, in the absence of a national ballot, were not united in support of the dispute and a substantial and gradually increasing proportion of miners continued to work or returned to work. Again unlike 1974, the NJIC trade unions did not as a body support the NUM. CEGB staff and the trade unions had co-operated with major reductions in manpower, both as a result of power station closures and productivity schemes, and might therefore have had little sympathy with the NUM attitude to the closure of high-cost pits. Finally, a view developed that the NUM leadership wished to prolong the strike for its own political objectives.

THE MANAGERS' RELATIONS WITH STAFF

The approach of the Board and its managers throughout the dispute was to encourage staff to continue to assist the Board to meet its statutory responsibility to supply electricity. Industrial relations managers supported and facilitated operational requirements. This involved regular and detailed contact with production managers at national, regional and local levels. Resulting actions were often complex and inter-related.

Board policy meant, at its best, retaining the goodwill of staff and, at its least, not alienating them either by a specific dispute or by giving undue public prominence to their efforts. The unofficial shop stewards' movement had reacted in a hostile way to the resolution of the 1984 NJIC pay claim and this illustrated the potential for militant staff to exploit an issue if managers had not reacted with the utmost care. Initially staff were not asked to undertake duties that, based upon local knowledge, managers judged they would not do; the staff were redeployed to other duties. This gave local managers the opportunity to convince staff of the need to work normally and generally led to the isolation of the few individuals who had advocated industrial action. Part of this process was to clarify to staff that their actions would constitute a breach of their contracts of employment.

In many cases this approach led staff to accept the need to handle new deliveries of fuel. In other circumstances actions were taken to bring the issue to a head, again without provoking a dispute. For example, more co-operative staff on different shifts might be asked to perform the duties, thereby isolating unco-operative individuals. Managers retained the right either to redeploy staff to alternative duties or, where generation was at risk, to require them to perform duties which they might have refused. At no stage was there negotiation with staff or their representatives about what work should be done.

BOARD AND MANAGERS' RELATIONS WITH TRADE UNIONS

The Board sought to consult national trade union officers fully about local difficulties, or potential difficulties, particularly where questions of interpretation of their own guidance arose. This enabled the Board and the unions to maintain the traditionally good working relationships as far as possible and to avoid a legacy of mistrust once the dispute ended. On both sides there was a wish to avoid the actions of each side resulting in a formal dispute; mutual respect and understanding of each other's positions helped with this. For management's part this did not conflict with operational objectives: it was judged that that was the best way to keep the lights on.

The national officers of the industry's unions had a great desire not to prejudice either the good relationships with the Board or the close relationships between themselves, which they had worked so hard to establish over the years. For example, lobbying of the industry's national officers by NUM delegates on the eve of the TUC Congress debate disclosed a solid ESTUC front of opposition to the involvement of the ESI membership. Following Congress all the ESTUC officers supported the view that there should be no individual union statements to members pending an ESTUC meeting. Even when it became clear that the unions would be taking different views on sympathetic industrial action, the ESTUC statement urged officials and members to do 'their utmost to avoid any inter-Union conflict or recrimination that might arise from the differing policies of the ESI Unions in this matter'. In fact this principle was adhered to by the ESTUC unions and their officers throughout the dispute, despite the strains created by their unions' national policies.

In such a confused situation the Board and their managers had to make careful judgements about which officers should be approached on which issues and at what stage. For example, it might be known that an officer would be bound to react formally and unhelpfully to a particular question, which would therefore not be put. The relationship between the Board and the unions remained such that the Board's ability to meet an all-time record demand in January, ten months after the beginning of the miners' strike, was not impaired.

THE OUTCOME

In dealing with industrial relations during the dispute the Board unquestionably had two great advantages: first, the traditionally good relations between the Board, the unions and staff and the strong public service commitment to keeping the lights on; and second that the unions collectively were ambivalent in their attitude to the NUM under the leadership of Arthur Scargill. In those turbulent twelve months there was no occasion when management, through their own actions, were faced with their own staff taking strike action that interfered with supplies – which, after all, was overwhelmingly the point.

Chapter 22

Who is my brother?

The CEGB's experience of picketing by striking miners in 1972 had been severe and had left its mark.[1] The Board did not forget the statement made by Arthur Scargill in June 1975[2] and quoted in Chapter 4 on the importance in a major strike of attacking the power stations. It was against this sort of background that the CEGB prepared for the 1984–5 strike for nothing had happened in the intervening nine years to make us think that Scargill had changed his approach.

PICKETING AND THE LAW

There was one major difference this time, namely a change in the law on picketing. The 1980 Employment Act, Sections 16 and 17, limited lawful picketing to that which takes place at or near the pickets' work place. Other forms of picketing, and particularly picketing which was not peaceful, meant that the trade unions responsible lost their immunity and left themselves open to action by employers, suppliers, consumers and anyone else affected by picketing, including those who wanted to pass through pickets to get to work. Section 15 of the 1982 Act tightened up on the 1980 Act by depriving unions of immunity where unlawful acts had been authorised or supported by senior officials or where, once committed, they were not repudiated by a responsible official.

Legal judgements during the strike

During the strike the law relating to picketing was clarified in the courts. In November and December 1984 a few South Wales working miners sought interlocutory injunctions[3] against the South Wales branch union, its executive officers and trustees and against the NUM and its co-ordinating committee. The injunction restrained the branch union and its servants, agents and officers (including the officers of the lodges of the five pits concerned) from, *inter alia*, assisting, encouraging or organising members of the branch union to congregate or assemble at or near the pit gates in numbers greater than six or for any purpose other than peacefully obtaining or communicating information or peacefully persuading any person to work or abstain from working.

This judgement clearly constrained the union in organising demonstrations and large intimidating pickets and gave further authority to the Code of Practice on picketing issued with the 1980 Employment Act, which had recommended that, primarily since excessive numbers tended to produce violence and disorder, pickets at the entrance to any place of work where a strike was taking place should be limited to six.

During the strike there were other important cases in which aggrieved parties sought protection in the courts against excessive picketing. Arising from Taylor (RH) v NUM (Yorkshire Area),[4] the High Court imposed a fine of £200 000 and when the union refused to pay a sequestration order was issued against all the union's property. Fines imposed on the NUM were taken out of sequestrated funds and later, despite the absence of any apology, the contempt was cleared.[5]

The earliest case of an aggrieved party going to the courts was in mid-March 1984 when the NCB applied for and was granted an injunction restraining picketing at their pits, but it was never followed up. A month later the High Court granted an interim injunction[6] restraining the NUM (South Wales Area) by its agents or servants from continuing to instruct or otherwise encourage its members from stopping, approaching or in any other way interfering with the free passage of the plaintiffs who were the Read Brothers, Forest of Dean hauliers, working their lorries in and out of South Wales steelworks. After the injunctions were issued some of their lorries were stoned by pickets and their drivers abused. The High Court regarded this as contempt and at the end of July fined the South Wales Area of the NUM £25 000 for each of two cases of contempt.

Other court actions also went against the NUM and while these cases were not directly concerned with picketing they influenced workers in road transport and in the Generating Board in their attitudes to NUM picketing. These cases all concerned balloting. In May 1984 three working miners in Nottinghamshire (to which were added over 630 other named or identified plaintiffs) sought injunctions[7] that the strike called by the NUM and the Nottingham area was unlawful on the grounds that it was in breach of the rules of both the national and area unions. The defendants (Chadburn and others) were members of the Area Executive Committee of the NUM (Nottingham Area) and were instructed, together with the NUM at National level, to lift the instruction given by an area official that the strike in Nottinghamshire was legal. This decision was later reinforced by similar court declarations relating to two other areas culminating in September when the High Court declared that the strike in the Derbyshire area was in contravention of the rules of the NUM nationally and in the area and was unlawful.[8]

The Generating Board's attitude to use of the courts

The Board's policy, endorsed by its Executive Committee in November 1982, was that it would not be appropriate to pursue legal action during a strike unless very serious operational difficulties were otherwise likely to arise and there was some chance that the situation could be improved by resorting to legal remedies. The Board's policy in deciding whether or not to initiate civil actions, for example against secondary picketing, has therefore been consistent with the government's approach to employment legislation, which has been to facilitate civil actions at the discretion of the parties concerned and not to impose a duty upon the parties to invoke the law.

The Board's view after the strike was that at no stage in the dispute would legal action by the Board against either the NUM or the ESI unions have been helpful. On the contrary, legal action by the Board against the NUM would have led to confrontation, while action against a section of its own staff would have risked reducing endurance.

PICKETING AT PITS, STEELWORKS AND COKE PLANTS

In the first three months of the strike, the national and area organisations of the NUM concentrated most of their manpower on picketing working pits, steelworks and coking depots. The greatest concentration of picketing in March, April and May was on the working pits in Nottinghamshire where large numbers of striking miners, many from Yorkshire, confronted working miners and police and where violence and intimidation were commonplace. One of the largest concentrations was at Harworth Colliery where, on 2 May, there were estimated to be 8000 people. There were many concentrations at single pits running into four figures.

The most dramatic of the picketing scenes was probably that played out at the Orgreave Coke plant outside Sheffield. For a month or so large numbers of striking miners, their allies and the police confronted each other outside the gates in what was in some ways a replay of the Saltley Depot battle of the 1972 strike. In one of the sporadic outbursts of violence and confrontation at Orgreave, on 30 May, Scargill was arrested and charged with obstruction. Action at the coke depot culminated on 18 June when an estimated 10 000 men confronted thousands of police in a battle that did not, on this occasion, end in victory for the miners. Indeed, as Kim Howells said: Orgreave 'never succeeded in stopping a single lorry'.[9] It led many strikers and sympathisers to realise that the police would probably always be able to muster a force that was more than capable of standing up to the largest concentrations of strikers and their supporters that could be mustered.[10]

PICKETING AT THE POWER STATIONS – THE EARLY MONTHS

In the early months of the strike there were pickets at most of the large power stations throughout the country, but mostly they were few in number with peaceful picketing.[11] At the end of March the TGWU, the three rail unions and the NUM met and produced a recommendation 'to black all movements of coal in Britain and request all members of our unions not to cross picket lines'. Unions in electricity supply had instructed members to work normally, but in early April the TGWU told their members not to 'replenish coal stocks'. This instruction was, however, only effective in the North Eastern Region of the Generating Board.

Fairly typical figures at the big power stations in these early months were of from five or six to up to twenty pickets with most of them drifting away in the evenings. The numbers were higher for the odd day at a number of stations such as Blyth (North Eastern Region), 100 at the end of March, and Drakelow (Mids), 50 in early April. In May the nuclear power station at Hartlepool (NE) experienced several days with 30 to 50 strikers, while on one day there were 80 to 90 at the oil-fired station at Fawley on Southampton Water (South Western). An unusual event occurred on 13 May when there was heavy picketing at Ramsgate Harbour aimed at stopping delivery of 950 tonnes of heavy fuel oil to Richborough Power Station nearby. The police made thirty-two arrests and the oil got through.

In May the NUM secretary wrote to 'all unions representing the fuel and power industries' stating, among other things, that 'all power stations are picketed or deemed to be picketed and I am calling on trade unionists not to cross those picket lines'. This clearly was conveying that the union realised the importance of power station picketing but that their members on strike were fully stretched elsewhere. The Electricity Supply Trade Union Council addressed their reply to the TUC stating that the NUM's letter ought to be considered 'by the whole trade union movement'; nothing more was heard of it.

Pickets at the stations, even when small in numbers, nevertheless often had a serious impact on events. Sometimes transport drivers delivering various supplies to the stations were persuaded to turn back at picket lines, even those manned by only two or three strikers, while some train drivers refused to go further on seeing messages draped over bridges above railway lines stating that this was an official NUM picket line.

Here are a few occurrences from those early months, although they recurred sporadically throughout the strike. Some ICI drivers refused to deliver caustic soda to Tilbury Power Station (South Eastern), and a British Oxygen Company driver refused to cross a Littlebrook Power Station (SE) picket line with industrial gas cylinders. Pickets away from the station boundaries at Ferrybridge C (NE) and Drax (NE) stopped oil lorries; coal, oil and propane deliveries could not get through at Fiddler's Ferry Power Station (North Western); water treatment chemicals at West Thurrock Power Station (SE) and turbine oil deliveries at Didcot (SW) and Fawley Power Stations (SW) were interrupted, while tanker drivers with lubricating oil were turned back at Sizewell Nuclear Power Station (SE). In one case supplies for the station canteen were turned back, but not apparently at the second time of asking.

Most CEGB power station employees, both early on and throughout the strike, moved through the picket lines to work without encountering problems. No doubt some felt varying degrees of sympathy for the men on the picket lines and the cause they stood for, but many certainly felt that the strike was none of their own making, that secondary picketing was against the law, and that the NUM had failed to gain the support of their membership for strike action in a national ballot. In stations in locations where pits were working, many power station staff felt a loyalty to the working miners. We know that many drivers in big companies such as ICI, BOC, Shell and BP had mixed feelings. Many were members of the TGWU and in some cases their union loyalty or pressure temporarily at least overrode loyalty to their employers.

There was much that the CEGB could do to meet these situations. Sometimes the same driver or a different driver with the same load came back next day and moved through a picket line without being stopped or perhaps found that the picket had disappeared. Sometimes supplies were transferred, at local garages and elsewhere, from vehicles in their company liveries into CEGB vehicles, which moved readily into the stations. Small 'anonymous' oil delivery company drivers were more ready than drivers from the big companies to move through picket lines. In several stations pickets went away at night and deliveries were brought in then. In other cases pickets only manned one entrance to a station and, unknown to them, supplies were flowing in through another.

The police also had their role. Where there was a handful of pickets at a station, the same pickets turning up every day to stand peacefully in front of their braziers, there was usually no policeman present. But the police were on call and turned up rapidly, and usually in sensible numbers, if something was brewing.

Some deliveries were, of course, more urgent than others. For example, carbon dioxide is important in nuclear generation and could not realistically be stored in great volume. In such cases a police escort was sometimes needed and provided. Sometimes police got wind of a planned demonstration and as numbers built up and pickets began to block the station entrance the police might explain to them that they were not a legal picket but a secondary picket and that, if they did not move on, they would be arrested. On a few occasions, even in these early days, there were flurries of activity with stones being thrown at the windscreens of cars and lorries and a certain amount of pushing and shoving (not necessarily ill-humoured) between police and pickets. The only death at a power station picket throughout the strike occurred at Ferrybridge C Power Station in South Yorkshire in mid-June when a picket was knocked down by a lorry. Certainly it was one death too many.

POWER STATION PICKETING IN THE SUMMER

In the months of June, July, August and September picketing of working pits continued to preoccupy the NUM, although there was some increase in picketing in a few of the CEGB's big stations. It was clear by now that the NUM had no industry-wide control of picketing. Whatever the union's intentions, the area or coalfield NUMs ran the picketing programme or attempted to do so. It must have been extremely difficult for them because local strikers often had their own priorities and anyway the amount of money that the area NUMs could hand out to defray travel expenses became pitifully small, if not non-existent. South Wales seemed to be the most disciplined and purposeful area, but at no time was the CEGB able to discern a picketing pattern and purpose at its stations. Sometimes we knew that we were vulnerable at particular stations because of a critical supply shortage, but although pickets sometimes responded to rumours, they rarely got hard facts to work on from inside the stations.

In early June Hartlepool Nuclear Power Station (NE) had from 30–40 to 70–80 pickets present for a week or so and we detected a hardening of their attitudes. Sixty Kent miners, on 6 June, once again gathered pickets at Ramsgate to try to stop the unloading of oil for Richborough Power Station and several demonstrators were taken to court by the police and charged with assaulting police, destruction of property and threatening behaviour. Three hundred demonstators turned up at Cottam and West Burton Power Stations (Mids) but they were peaceful and there were no pickets present next day. Numbers certainly grew at some of the big Midlands stations, including the 2000 MW Ratcliffe Power Station, just outside the city of Nottingham.

At Cottam Power Station (Mids) on 12 July there were 2000 demonstrators present, but within a short time they had been reduced to 6. The demonstrators had apparently been on their way to a working pit and had turned up at Cottam after the police had turned them away. The demonstration was peaceful and, to avoid aggravation, some supplies for the station were diverted elsewhere for a short while. On 16 July there were forms of behaviour in the Midlands that seemed to be quite random: 700 demonstrators at Cottam Power Station reduced to 8, 400–500 at High Marnham Power Station (Mids) reduced to 20 and 450 at Ratcliffe reduced to 50. Police kept an eye on things but nothing much happened. In August picketing fell to a low level, although the National Union of Seamen refused to allow bargeloads of oil to be delivered to Blyth Power Station (NE).

The Board thought that after the TUC in Brighton in early September, with the passing of the resolution giving support to the NUM and the striking miners, there would be increased pressure through picketing and other means at the power stations. In general this was not the case, although there were 200 and 300 demonstrators at Hartlepool Power Station on different days, 150 and 500 at Eggborough Power Station (NE) and 200 at Thorpe Marsh Power Station (NE). These demonstrators were rowdy with some stone throwing, but the police were in full control. Supplies were interrupted but were restored next day when the demonstrators had gone home.

THE FINAL PHASE

Between October and mid-February the pattern of power station picketing was much as before, with low levels of picketing generally at the big stations, plus a number of local demonstrations, often very large indeed and sometimes accompanied by minor damage to property, stone throwing and the like. But situations never got completely out of hand, if only because the speedy arrival of police reinforcements could be relied on. Two occasional features, not referred to before, were the issuing of leaflets making the miners' case and the organisation of demonstrations by the South Eastern Regional TUC. Intended mass pickets at some London stations were sometimes advertised in the Communist newspaper, *The Morning Star*. Since times and places of bus departures and destinations were also advertised it was not difficult for station managers to make their preparations and put off deliveries for the short periods involved.

Hartlepool Power Station was visited by 300 demonstrators in early October and 200 returned in early November. Oldbury (SW), another nuclear power station, received 300 pickets on 5 October plus a large number of policemen, some mounted, some with riot shields. A demonstration at Didcot Power Station (SW) on 24 October, organised by the South Eastern Regional TUC, attracted 300–500 people with a more or less equal police presence to ensure order. In early November a similarly organised demonstration took place at Taylor's Lane, a gas turbine station in Willesden (SE), no longer the old coal-fired station (see Chapter 3).

Leaflets were distributed at a demonstration at Didcot Power Station attended by 30–50 people on 9 November, mainly it seemed made up of students from Oxford. On 12 November, a day when about 2000 miners returned to work and on which there was a good deal of violence on pit picket lines, there was a peaceful demonstration by 600 at West Thurrock Power Station (SE). A peaceful demonstration of 200–250 at Littlebrook Power Station (SE) was addressed by 5 Members of Parliament. At a number of demonstrations at this time leaflets were being issued appealing for support 'at this critical stage of the dispute, with the sequestration of NUM funds'. Pickets at Blyth Power Station (NE) were issuing a bulletin 'The Northumberland Miners' Strike Bulletin'. It stated, among other things, that 'the key to the victory is now the power stations. Stocks at many power stations are extremely low. . . . If workers in the power stations abide by the TUC guidelines then power cuts are inevitable. Victory will be ours'. An unusual demonstration at the end of the month was at Brighton Power Station (SE) when hundreds of demonstrators took matters into their own hands in an effort to stop a coal ship unloading. Some actually occupied the coal handling cranes but they came down within twenty-four hours. As so often, the demonstrators rapidly melted away.

In spite of Christmas, the cold, the dark days of winter and the steady return to work of many striking miners, the pattern of picketing and demonstrations at the power stations continued much as before. In early December, a leaflet emanating from West Thurrock Power Station stated that it was 'the first power station to be taken off the National Grid due to solidarity action being taken by seamen and power workers. For six weeks output has been nil or a maximum of 20 per cent of its normal capacity'. On 10 December 400 demonstrators and 150 police assembled at nearby Tilbury Power Station but after a few speeches they dispersed peacefully. On 16 January 300 demonstrators were at Didcot Power

Station, with banners not only from South Wales and Nottinghamshire lodges but also from Brent. Once again, at Tilbury 600–800 turned up at 7.30am on 21 January to hear Tony Benn MP and Jimmy Knapp. On 28 January 250 pickets were at Dungeness Power Station (SE) and 200 at Thorpe Marsh where more leaflets were handed out.

Throughout the strike there had been occasional sizeable pickets and demonstrations at stations in the North West such as Westwood, Bold, Agecroft and Padiham and on 11 February 300 turned up at Carrington Power Station outside Manchester where pickets managed for a while to close the main gates stopping coal deliveries. One policeman was injured by a coal lorry and was taken to hospital. This day – 11 February – was indeed the last day on which there were large demonstrations at power stations. The South Eastern Region TUC and the Kent NUM combined in a day of action, with 450 demonstrators at Tilbury Power Station, 450 at Taylor's Lane Power Station and 200–300 at Richborough Power Station. Thereafter the daily numbers at CEGB power stations as a whole fell to something like 100 a day all told and the leaflets being given out here and there referred no longer to victory but to ensuring that the miners were 'not defeated'.

On 1 March, when the strike was disintegrating and the drift back to work had become a rush, there was still a total of 83 pickets at 25 power stations. On 5 March, when the strike was over, three stalwarts remained at the gates of one power station.

THE POLICE AND THE POWER STATION PICKETS

The police played an important part in controlling power station picketing. Station managers had always maintained good relations with the local police and they sought to reinforce these when the strike was imminent. Senior regional managers similarly maintained contacts with chief constables. At an early stage the police established a National Police Reporting Centre at New Scotland Yard which marshalled resources nationwide and board members and head office senior officers maintained contact. Later a National Police Intelligence Unit was set up at Enderby in Leicestershire to gather and co-ordinate intelligence on picketing activity. With the movement of vast quantities of coal by road, especially in the Midlands, the value of detailed and constant liaison between the CEGB and the police could hardly be exaggerated.

The tactics of pickets varied and the police responded variously. The identification of flying pickets and the collation of information on their targets by the police became sophisticated, giving power station managers some time, at least, to prepare for what was to come.

A few of those who wished to disrupt electricity supplies resorted to methods other than picketing. These included hoax bomb threats, attacks on vehicles and the disruption of traffic flows to the stations. The police coped with this, as they did in warning station managers about unusual interest shown in remote station installations like cooling-water pumphouses. Having said this it must be added that the attitude of many, if not all, chief constables to the Board and to the pickets was very different in the 1984–5 strike from their attitudes to the miners' strikes of the early 1970s. As we said in Chapter 5 on the 1972 strike, the basic objective of the police then was to protect people and property and to preserve law and order. We added that the objectives of some chief constables were served by the CEGB stopping deliveries and thus avoiding provoking the pickets. Indeed this request was made on a number of occasions. The explanation of the change in police attitudes in 1984–5 was, of course, the change in the law. As stated at the beginning of this chapter, in the 1970s secondary picketing was not illegal, but the 1980 Employment Act changed all that in ways that we defined.

This was the law that the police now had to enforce and since (illegal) secondary picketing was directed, among various places, at the power stations, it was inevitable that the police appeared to side with the Board against the pickets. Particularly in the early days of the strike, in order to reduce the impact of the flying pickets on Nottinghamshire pits which were working (as well as, on some occasions, East Midlands power stations), the police established themselves in large numbers not only at the pits but at the main road intersections in South Yorkshire and North Nottinghamshire in order to divert the flying pickets.

In the Board we were of course aware that such activities were raising issues concerning civil liberties in the minds of a number of people, but we would be dishonest to pretend that the CEGB did not welcome the easement of its problems brought by the police.

CONCLUSION

While we state that picketing of power stations was, in general, not so severe as in 1972, this does not mean that life was easy for the station managers and their staff. At its minimum, passing a few pickets at the gate when going to work was, for many, an uneasy experience. The unpredictable variations in the numbers and behaviour of pickets made it extremely difficult for managers and staff to plan deliveries of supplies and to optimise generation and nobody knew if or when the picketing might become much worse.

Picketing is essentially a siege condition and when it happens to be light and ineffective the only difference in the state of mind engendered, compared with days of heavy picketing, is one of degree. The miners' strike was a severe experience for the strikers; it was also an experience that the men and women in the stations were only too eager to put behind them.

The fact that power station picketing was, in general, comparatively light and ineffective can be attributed to many causes. The CEGB had made extensive preparations to go on generating electricity for long periods without new supplies and this tended to wear pickets down. The number of striking miners was far fewer than in the early 1970s and they had too many targets apart from the stations – working pits, coking plants and depots and steelworks. The NUM and the striking miners had inadequate funds to finance the picketing, especially after sequestration of union funds. The evidence was that there was no nationally co-ordinated picketing strategy and the NUM's organisation of picketing, both nationally and in most areas, was poor. Support from the general body of unions was patchy, partly at least because there was no national ballot for strike action.

Certainly there were periods when the rail unions and the transport drivers of the major suppliers gave substantial support by not passing through picket lines, but it was only in Yorkshire that the CEGB's management advised against the movement of coal over a lengthy period because of fear of large-scale and possibly violent picketing. In general the efforts of rail and road drivers to support the miners were not sufficiently sustained.

As the strike went on many factors conspired against the pickets. They were sometimes stopped by the police even before they reached a power station or were dispersed on arrival as being illegal secondary pickets or causing obstruction. Many of the strike's most active participants found themselves in court where they were given their release on condition that they did not rejoin illegal picket lines.

Finally there was the actual experience of picketing, which became insufferable to some, standing hour after hour at power station gates with nothing to do but scavenge wood for the brazier, chat to a single policeman, and watch the normal flow of traffic going in and out of the station.[12]

Chapter 23

Partners: the distribution boards

We gave accounts (in Chapters 4 to 7) of the duties and responsibilities of the 12 area electricity boards in England and Wales in managing relationships with their 20 000 000 customers during the strikes of the 1970s. In those strikes the result of the industrial action either of some power station staff or of the miners was to reduce electricity generation and supply to a point at which, from time to time, it had to be rationed. The boards' rota disconnection plans were explained in Chapter 5.

In the 1984–5 strike electricity rationing was not necessary; this was the fortunate outcome that had been achieved. Before the strike, it was necessary to prepare contingency plans, which were worked out by the industry with both determination and the expectation that they would prove more refined than previous arrangements. In the 1970s curtailment of customers' supplies had, in general, to be done by staff manually operating switches in sub-stations spread around the boards' areas. The general improvement in system control arrangements by the area boards had included heavy investment in telecontrol equipment, which enabled switching to be done from the boards' control centres and with much more selectivity.

The area boards were nevertheless involved during the 1984–5 strike in local supply issues in two respects. First, where board equipment had faults or needed to be serviced on the sites of picketed property, normally pits, the pickets were sometimes unwilling to allow board staff to pass through to do the job, or at any rate made a great deal of fuss about it. Staff understood that they were not to make a challenge when there was opposition but mostly in the end some sort of accommodation was found. Secondly, local supplies were at risk where a local power station that normally supplied the local distribution networks had to be shut down to conserve coal stocks. This problem existed, for example, at Skelton Grange Power Station in Leeds and meant that area board engineers had to devise and operate new network configurations, sometimes providing supply at reduced security standards.

The other involvement over supplies or at any rate potential supplies occurred at the stage at which it appeared that the CEGB would not be able to get through the 1984–5 winter without power cuts. The area boards were asked to investigate actual and potential purchases from local independent sources of generation. These were usually industries that generated electricity for their own use or had substantial standby sets. A good example was British Steel who generated electricity from steam produced by burning gas made from coking plants. The investigations were dropped when area board chairmen advised the CEGB that they might be construed to mean that the supply position was desperate. However, by that time some contracts had been agreed and these continued to the end of the strike.

Boards received many calls from customers asking what was likely to happen to their supplies if the 1984 strike materialised. Anxiety was more widespread than previously in the business community because of the extension of continuous process working and the increase in highly sensitive computer processes. There were limits to the assurances that area boards could give. Area boards had responsibility for collecting payments for electricity and appliance sales from customers who, because they were on strike, were less able to meet their obligations. Those four or five area boards with large numbers of striking miners had this experience and in the remainder of this chapter we deal briefly with the experience of the two area boards, Yorkshire and East Midlands, which had the most difficult problems.

YORKSHIRE ELECTRICITY BOARD

Energy sales

The business of Yorkshire Electricity Board, below head office, was managed by four managers, one for each of the Board's geographical areas. Two of these contained most of the pits: West Yorkshire (including Leeds, Wakefield and Castleford) and South Yorkshire (including Sheffield, Barnsley, Doncaster and Rotherham).

The effect of the strike was that total energy sales decreased by 3.3 per cent compared with the previous year. Sales of energy to the coal industry in Yorkshire fell from 1509 GWH in 1983-4 to 714 GWH in 1984-5, a drop of about 53 per cent (this incidentally saved the CEGB about half a million tonnes of coal). Sales to customers suffering directly from the strike also fell sharply.

Debts and the code of practice

In December 1984, when the strike had been going for nine months, the South Yorkshire management reported on the position. About 10 000-12 000 area customers were employed by the NCB. Of these, 7000-9000 were paying their bills, 750 of them through prepayment meters. Special arrangements had been made to help 3000 customers, but 20 per cent of them had failed to meet the revised terms and further adjustments had been made. Since about half of all special payment arrangements failed in normal circumstances this was regarded as quite an achievement. By December thirty-five miners' homes had been disconnected in South Yorkshire, but only three remained so at the end of the month. At that time the average debt of those with special arrangements was £60 per household, which should be read against an average YEB mining household's normal bill of £44 a quarter. There had been a general reduction in the use of electricity by striking miners and there was evidence that this was continuing.

In the West Yorkshire area, where there were about 30 000–35 000 miners, about 10 000 were paying by special arrangement, the average debt being only £25–£30. Up to December 1984, 110 households had been disconnected and 30-50 homes remained so.[1] In the Board as a whole the outstanding debt attributable to the strike was £1 250 000 by December.

Long before the strike YEB, with all other boards, had a published code of practice for the payment of debts and this continued to be applied during the strike. Boards did not discriminate between striking miners in debt and other debtors. All were expected to pay for current consumption and contribute something to reducing their debts. Debtors with a good record remained valued customers and most striking miners lived up to this reputation.

Where all the money came from was not known to YEB. No doubt friends, relatives and well-wishers helped and a number of striking miners had wives in paid employment. Some sold their cars and other property to raise money. Banks, building societies and insurance companies eased up on payments due to them. The NUM received money from other unions and supporters. YEB knew that the Yorkshire NUM had an order of priorities for paying bills, with electricity second on that list. They kept local links with NUM officials and warned them when a member was at risk of being cut off. When at the last moment the member produced the necessary cash staff did not ask intrusive questions. Some money arrived anonymously from the local pit.

Community problems and staff roles

In addition to problems caused directly by the strike, YEB, in common with others in the local community, suffered from a general increase in lawlessness. There was damage to a number of YEB shops, sub-stations and vehicles, and goods, equipment and materials were stolen. The rise in such crimes reflected the absence of the normal police presence on the beat as officers were called to the picket lines and other social factors.

Life was not easy for YEB employees. Many lived in mining villages and had striking miners among their families and friends. Daily contact in these circumstances was bound to involve provocation and conflict from time to time. Nevertheless staff behaved with great restraint and propriety, carrying out their work calmly and competently, concentrating on the objective of maintaining supplies and customer services in a dispute which was none of their making.

EAST MIDLANDS ELECTRICITY BOARD

Union divisions

EMEB experience was mostly similar to that of YEB, but there were some differences at least of emphasis. In Yorkshire all the pits were on strike and there was no challenge to the NUM hegemony; in the area of EMEB this was not so. In what is now called the Nottinghamshire coalfield all pits (more than twenty) worked throughout the strike; neighbouring Derbyshire and Leicester had a mixture of pits working and on strike.

It might be thought that in Nottinghamshire EMEB had no problem with their coal industry customers, but the working pits were picketed, sometimes by so-called flying pickets from Yorkshire. Board employees had their share of problems in getting into Coal Board premises to work on EMEB equipment. Further, a proportion of Nottinghamshire miners remained committed NUM members and up to 3500 were on strike, creating payment problems for the Board.[2]

One of the most complex situations was located at the village of Shirebrook on the Derbyshire-Nottinghamshire border, dominated economically by the pit and the railway freight depot. While the pit was on strike many miners who lived there were carried in specially protected buses to work at nearby pits like Thorsby, Welbeck and Clipstone, and transported back at the end of work. Shirebrook pit was heavily picketed. There was a strong police presence and much social division between striking and working miners and their families. EMEB employees had to deal with these different groups as they read and emptied meters and this perhaps unique situation had to be handled for a period of twelve months with great sensitivity and forbearance.

Payment arrangements

Where pits were on strike EMEB had much the same experience as YEB over payment arrangements. At the time of the strike EMEB were moving away from the installation of prepayment meters, but in the mining areas this had to go into reverse. In the Mansfield district alone over 2000 prepayment meters were installed. Various community groups gave considerable help to striking miners in the payment of their bills. Often these groups were run by the churches and chapels and by miners' wives with funds collected from far and wide, including supportive trade unions. The Citizens' Advice Bureaux were also a stabilising and constructive local influence. EMEB staff do not appear to have been attacked or intimidated; nor was any significant damage to Board property reported.

GETTING BACK TO NORMAL

The area boards in mining areas had in normal times enjoyed an excellent relationship with miners as customers: they had a good record of paying their bills and using the boards' shops. During the stressful time of the strike it was remarkable how that good will was sustained, a credit to the mining communities and the boards' staff. As soon as the strike was over mining families started to clear their bills. It took some time, but help was forthcoming with the release of disputed social security payments in 1985.

Throughout the 12 turbulent months of the strike there was, between the CEGB and the area boards, as well as with the Electricity Council, a spirit of goodwill and co-operation which showed the industry at its best. CEGB expressed its gratitude on every suitable occasion.

Chapter 24

Information: handle with care

At the start of the dispute the CEGB Executive decided on a public relations policy that was to have far-reaching consequences: the best way to achieve success in maintaining electricity supplies was to do it but not talk about it.

A POLICY OF KEEPING COMPARATIVELY QUIET

There were two main reasons behind this policy. First, there was the need to maintain secrecy about the Board's policies and operations to maintain normal electricity supplies. The CEGB was to turn the electricity supply system on its head. There is no doubt that if the NUM and its supporters in the rail unions had information about the strategy and in particular the detail of these plans they would do their upmost to frustrate them. Secondly, at all times during the year-long strike the Board had to be sensitive to the attitude and reactions of its own staff and their trade unions.

Support for miners at some power stations, because of close communal links, meant that the Board could not risk sending in supplies of coal once deliveries by rail were stopped by the rail unions. This included Drax, the largest power station on the supply network. The Board learnt early in the strike what a minefield public relations were going to be during this year-long, highly publicised dispute. During the early days, in April 1984, the then Chairman, Sir Walter Marshall, visited Didcot Power Station. The local media heard about the visit and turned up at the gates asking to see him. He gave an impromptu press briefing on the steps of the administration block. The questions were about the Board's ability to maintain supplies and Sir Walter gave strong reassurances about the security of the nation's electricity. At that point a train bringing coal supplies to the power station arrived and the attention of the small group of journalists was drawn to this as evidence that coal was still flowing to the power station.

That train was the last to deliver coal to Didcot Power Station during the dispute. Whether this was due to publicity in the media on its arrival, or the posting of NUM pickets on a railway bridge leading to the station, may never be known. The then Station Manager at Didcot is convinced, to this day, that it was media attention. There was no doubt about media impact in a situation three weeks later. *The Observer*'s Science Correspondent, Robert McKie, asked to interview Sir Walter on nuclear issues at the time that the massive public inquiry into the construction of Britain's first pressurised water reactor nuclear power station (PWR) at Sizewell, Suffolk, was taking place. He came to the interview with a list of questions on the miners' strike. At the end of the interview he put these to Sir Walter and, following his inclination to be as open and helpful as possible, the Chairman answered them. Most of the questions were about coal supplies and were innocuous, but one turned out to be a bombshell.

The question related to the cost of the strike and its impact on electricity prices. Sir Walter thought for a moment and then responded by saying that the additional costs of the strike were currently running at about £20 million a week, mostly the cost of running the oil-fired stations flat out and burning more oil, which was much more expensive than coal. He speculated that these additional costs would have to be met by the electricity consumer, but was unable to say when they might be reflected in higher electricity prices. *The Observer* interpreted the Chairman's comments as indicating that electricity prices might have to go up by 1.5 per cent for every five weeks the strike continued, and ran the story prominently with the headline 'Electricity Prices to Rise'. *The Observer*'s story was a good scoop as the first comment from an authoritative source of the costs of the strike. *The Sunday Times* also carried the story and it was followed up by other papers.

The Secretary of State for Energy, Peter Walker, was regarded by the CEGB as a most skilful politician and a master in handling the media. On being told of the stories in *The Observer* and *The Sunday Times* on Saturday evening, when the first editions became available, he telephoned Sir Walter at home and vented his irritation. The Chairman in turn telephoned Peter Vey, his Director of Information, then settling down to a quiet Saturday evening. 'The Secretary of State has just ruined my weekend so I am passing on the agony to you'. Not much could be done that evening, but on Sunday the CEGB and Department of Energy's press offices worked hard and with some success to play down the forecast costs of the strike and the possibilities of electricity price increases.

This episode, which turned out to be a storm in a tea cup, brought recriminatory letters to the CEGB from Department of Energy and electricity industry officials (prices were the responsibility of the area boards and were co-ordinated by the Electricity Council). The incident emphasised how tightly media relations had to be controlled and showed the government's nervousness about the strike and its outcome.

In contrast a much later media leak giving chapter and verse on the costs of the strike hardly caused a stir in government circles although it embarrassed the Board. The leak occurred in the early part of 1985. The CEGB was introducing a computerised management information system, known as ViewData, which was being cascaded down through the organisation. Sensitive information was confined to Board members. One such item fed into the system was the draft balance sheet for the 1984-5 financial year. This showed the CEGB having made a huge loss, close on £2 billion, due to the cost of the miners' strike. How many Board members accessed this 'secret' information on their display screens in their offices is not certain, but by that evening they were sharing it with millions of television viewers! The balance sheet details had been leaked to a freelance journalist who had passed it on to Channel 4 News. Despite a thorough investigation, the mole was never found.

While this leak was embarrassing for the Board, which was naturally concerned about how such sensitive financial information could get out, unlike the earlier publicity on costs it did not raise government blood pressure – perhaps because the battle was won by then. It did however rekindle the debate on how dealing with the strike should be paid for.

Other than these two incidents, the CEGB Executive's view was that public relations were well handled and ran smoothly during the strike, unlike those at the National Coal Board where débâcle followed débâcle. The Coal Board, of course, faced much greater difficulties and pressures, but a significant difference between the two organisations was that the CEGB's Director of Public Affairs and Information had the full confidence of the CEGB Chairman and Executive and was thus able to exercise control without interference. At the Coal Board, the NCB's able and experienced Director of Public Relations, the late Geoff Kirk, did not agree with the way Ian MacGregor was handling the media and was also being second-guessed by several outside advisers in whom the NCB Chairman appeared to have greater confidence. In the end Geoff Kirk considered his position to be untenable and took early retirement. He had built up enormous good will and support among the media for the NCB and with his departure it was felt within the CEGB that much of this was lost.

It is also surprising, given the political nature of the strike, that there was not more whistle-blowing from the CEGB. Where this did occur, it tended to concern the operation of the Board's nuclear power stations, a traditional source of information leaks because of the fierce controversies nuclear power created, not least in some parts of the CEGB itself. During the miners' strike the Sizewell inquiry added to the controversy. There were also leaks about the running and maintenance of the existing nuclear stations that led to false claims, which had to be answered, that in order to get the maximum contribution to power supplies, the CEGB was putting output before safety. An example at Trawsfynydd Nuclear Power Station was referred to in Chapter 12.

LIMITS TO KEEPING COMPARATIVELY QUIET

The CEGB's policy of severely restricting information on how it was going about maintaining electricity supplies meant that there was the danger of a vacuum of authoritative information, which could be filled, mischievously or not, with false rumours. It was certainly in the interests of those who actively supported the strike that the country should be progressively plunged into darkness, playing on the memories of the blackouts experienced in the 1970s disputes. Clearly if the impression could be created that blackouts were about to happen this would give heart to the strikers and their supporters and put pressure on the government to settle the dispute and end the strike.

There was therefore a battle for public confidence. This meant that the CEGB could not remain silent. It had to find ways to scotch rumours and maintain public confidence on the key issue of how long normal electricity supplies could be maintained, without giving away how this was being done. Judgements about endurance, as it was called, changed with changing circumstances. The importance of this aspect was fully taken into account in all the Board's operations during the strike. Peter Vey attended the weekly meetings of the CEGB Executive and had access to all policy and operational matters. He was able to report on media and public relations aspects. Public attitudes during the strike were monitored through attitude surveys, which showed tremendous support for the Board's policies and operations to maintain normal supplies. A senior member in the Board's public relations staff also attended the weekly meetings of the operations team who were responsible for running the system and maintaining normal supplies.

In addition, there were twice-daily meetings of key public affairs and information staff to assess the media situation and decide what actions and responses might be needed. Close liaison was maintained with the press offices of the National Coal Board, the Department of Energy and the Electricity Council. Although rumours proliferated, many of these were on peripheral matters, particularly on the operation of the CEGB's nuclear stations.

KEY QUESTIONS ON COAL STOCKS

The key questions asked by the media were on coal stocks and coal supplies: which power stations were getting what supplies, how and when? This was information that the Board was unwilling to provide because it would have been useful intelligence to the NUM and the union's supporters. Arthur Scargill, in the absence of authoritative information from the CEGB, claimed from time to time that coal supplies were about to run out and on one occasion quoted a CEGB mole as the source of that information. To counter this story the CEGB press office suggested to the television news networks that they hired helicopters and went to look for themselves – the coal mounds at the major power stations were visible from the air. Television News did precisely this and very reassuring pictures of immense coal stocks at power stations appeared on the television screens, convincing evidence that the strikers' claims were wrong.

ENDURANCE

This was just one aspect of the campaign to win and maintain public confidence, which intensified as the long strike continued and as summer and the battles of the picket lines receded. With the lengthening evenings of autumn, electricity demand shot up, particularly after the clocks went back in October. The focus once again was on endurance. During the early months of the strike the CEGB, as we have seen, had been working secretly on all kinds of ingenious plans to eke out the limited coal supplies and stretch endurance beyond the limits of the strikers' resolve. The first measure was designed to by-pass the rail unions' ban on transporting coal from the working pits to the power stations. This involved a massive operation to transport the coal by road.

Convoys of lorries working round the clock moved nearly 17 000 000 tonnes of coal during the strike. This was obviously a very visible operation and was a nuisance to people living on or near the routes. While the routes were planned to try to reduce inconvenience to a minimum, there were a few cowboy operators who ignored the agreed routes until threatened with loss of the business. The road transport operation brought many local public relations problems, which had to be dealt with promptly, but in general the public found the operation reassuring.

The other measures which gave the Board increasing confidence that endurance could be greatly extended beyond what had originally been expected were largely out of the public limelight. As winter tightened its grip, efforts to sway public opinion intensified. The strikers played on memories of the blackouts of the 1970s, exploiting the CEGB's reluctance to provide chapter and verse on how they were going to continue to maintain supplies. The government was anxious to reassure the public on the Board's ability to continue to maintain normal supplies.

Two significant events were to occur around the turn of the year. First, in December, following a complex review of endurance capabilities, the Board concluded that, in the prevailing circumstances, the CEGB could keep the lights on during the whole of 1985. The Chairman gave this encouraging and significant news to Peter Walker at the regular briefing meeting at the Department of Energy. The government decided to make this public, appreciating how reassuring the public would find it and what a blow it would be to the NUM and those on strike.

The Secretary of State therefore issued a statement on endurance over Christmas, normally a quiet time for news. It received wide coverage. The statement did much to reassure the public and was seen as a blow to the strikers. It was also attacked as a statement from a government whose reputation rested on beating the miners. Although the statement was based on information and reassurances provided by the Board, as the government acknowledged, it provided no details about how the CEGB expected to maintain supplies during 1985. The statement did, however, strongly refute claims that blackouts were imminent and calmed public concerns fuelled by rumours and by speculation from, among others, stockbroking firms, about coal stocks and the security of electricity supplies. One negative consequence of the government's statement was criticism from the industry's trade unions that the Board were getting involved politically in the strike.

What was really needed to convince the sceptics, and scotch for good the doubters, was not words but a demonstration that electricity supplies were as secure as the government claimed. The opportunity came on 16 January in a most dramatic way. During that day temperatures fell and electricity demand rose steadily. It became clear during the afternoon that, at the peak time for demand between 5pm and 5.30pm, when factories and offices were still working and domestic demand was also high, there would be a record demand for England and Wales. Once National Control were satisfied that the demand would be a record – and that it would be met without difficulty – it was decided to alert the media, issue a statement, and invite the broadcast media to come to National Control to see for themselves.

This was done with the most dramatic coverage, particularly on the main evening TV bulletins. It was followed on 17 January by an even higher electricity demand that was also met in full. The media were now convinced that the CEGB could keep the lights on during 1985 as the government's Christmas statement claimed. It was also interpreted as a body blow to the strikers and clearly did much to undermine their morale. Indeed the strike started to collapse progressively and finally finished in early March, twelve months after it had started.

PROBLEMS IN RETURNING TO NORMAL

The CEGB put in hand the process of returning to normal operations. The media were anxious to find out just how the Board had managed to keep the lights on for such a long time; they were aware of some of the main elements like the transport of coal by road, but wanted more detail and the inside story. The government, aware of the size of the victory won over trade union militancy and the electoral bonus that this would bring, wanted to pay public tribute to the CEGB.

The Board, however, wanted none of this. During the strike, the Board's position had been that, in the extraordinary measures it took to maintain normal supplies, it was not acting politically either to defeat the miners or to support the government. It was carrying out its statutory duty to maintain normal supplies. On this basis it had received the full co-operation of most of its staff and trade unions during the strike. It had no wish to put at risk good employee relations through boasting or public endorsement by the government of its role.

The Chairman therefore urged the Prime Minister, Margaret Thatcher, not to thank the CEGB publicly for its efforts, as she wished to do. The Board continued to maintain a low profile in the media; inside stories of how the CEGB helped to beat the miners were discouraged and the CEGB gave virtually no briefings or interviews on this. Acknowledgement of the importance of the CEGB's role came in the Birthday and New Year Honours lists following the strike. However, the strike was becoming history, no longer the centre of public and media attention.

PRICE PAID BY CEGB FOR DISCRETION

The public's lack of knowledge about the extraordinary lengths that the CEGB went to to keep the lights on and about the strength of a unified production system in England and Wales had implications for the debate over the structure of the industry in the lead up to privatisation two years later. Because of its policy of keeping its head down the Board, a comparatively unknown organisation despite its importance, lost an opportunity to make itself better known in favourable circumstances. Where the Board was known it was often for aspects of its operations that were unpopular, such as nuclear power or the siting of new power stations. In the debate on privatisation the Board found it had few allies or friends. To what extent better public knowledge about the Board's crucial role in the miners' strike would have helped in its case for less radical structural changes under privatisation will never be known.

For the most part the CEGB's comparative silence during the strike and afterwards on how it was keeping the lights on did not arouse media hostility. Most journalists appreciated the reasons for this. However, it did help to further the myth among the media that the CEGB was a secretive organisation.

Of course the politicians, particularly government ministers, did appreciate what the Board had achieved and for a time the Board bathed in political approval from the ruling party. Nevertheless, political memories are notoriously short. The Board's efforts in keeping the lights on and thus saving the government's bacon counted for little during discussions on the structure of the privatised electricity supply industry. Lord Marshall and the CEGB Board welcomed and supported privatisation but opposed the break-up of the integrated generation and transmission system. The government chose not to be influenced by that view.

Part IV

The future

In 1990 the industry was radically reorganised. The Generating Board was divided into three generating companies and the National Grid Company. All but Nuclear Electric plc are now in private ownership.

The questions that irresistibly arise at this point in the book are whether supplies could be threatened in the future; what forms the threat might take; and whether the 'new' industry is equipped to deal with them. It is not only the ownership and organisation of the industry that affect the answers but also such aspects as fuel diversification, the operation of the electricity market and the strength of trade unions.

Part IV thoroughly explores these questions. There are grounds for giving reassuring answers, but highly relevant political and economic factors could change. Confidence needs to be tempered with caution. The issues are of great importance and are central to this book.

Chapter 25

Keeping the lights on in the 1990s and beyond

Since the events described here the electricity industry has been restructured and privatised. The questions that naturally arise are whether this 'new' industry might have to face challenges to its ability to keep the lights on in the future and, if so, whether it would be able to meet them.

The new arrangements for dealing with emergencies are inevitably compared with those in the nationalised industry era when the CEGB was responsible for generation and transmission. As a single organisation it had central planning for generation and transmission development and for the operation of the power system. Contingency planning for emergencies was carried out within this organisation and in consultation with the rest of the industry. It was not necessary to set up any new or special arrangements: the command structure was already there.

The structures of the energy and associated industries and the industrial relations climate in which they operated increased the probability of disruptions to supplies. Monopoly electricity, railway and coal industries, with virtually no diversity, left electricity supplies vulnerable to a dispute in any of them. In addition, being government-owned, they were seen by the government of the day as instruments of their policies and occasionally, by some trade unions, as a means through which government policies might be challenged.

Industrial relations in the nationalised electricity supply industry were generally thought to be good by the standards of the time. There were constructive and supportive trade union officers who understood the industry and, when necessary, spoke out in its defence. There were, however, divergent interests from time to time and over the forty-two years of nationalisation there were, as we have seen, five occasions when there was industrial action on a substantial scale. Three incidents were official overtime bans with some form of work-to-rule and two were unofficial and involved some strike action. These occurred at a time when the industrial relations environment generally tended to accept industrial action much more readily than in the early 1990s.

During this time there were three national miners' strikes, each preceded by an overtime ban, two in the 1970s and one in 1984–5. In the first strike the government were slow to understand the electricity supply risks and the country came close to a catastrophic collapse of electricity supply. The second strike coincided with an oil supply crisis from OPEC actions following a Middle East war. The combination of oil and coal supply difficulties added greatly to the emergency. It led the government to call a general election, in which it was defeated. The third strike, because of successful emergency management, did not cause any curtailment of electricity supplies.

There were also periods when power cuts, sometimes severe, were necessary because of plant shortages. The most serious power cuts followed World War II and were the result of inadequate plant construction over the war years. The shortage took until the mid-1950s to overcome. There was a similar period in the 1960s arising from unprecedented demand growth but the power cuts were much less disruptive than the earlier ones.

There were also numerous lesser threats to electricity supplies from area-level miners' strikes and periods of industrial action in railways, road transport, docks, shipping and water supply. All were disruptive but not sufficiently so to make substantial power cuts necessary. In the late 1970s and early 1980s, over a seven-year period (as described in Chapter 16), there was only one year when there was no industrial action influencing fuel supplies.

It is not surprising that contingency planning and the management of emergencies became highly developed skills in the CEGB. There were many opportunities to learn from experience. At the same time the Electricity Council and the area boards developed rota-disconnection plans and facilities which, together with the plans for curtailment of electricity use by orders developed with the sponsoring government departments, led to the industry being capable of managing all likely emergencies.

The period of public ownership was mostly one of fairly steady, though not spectacular, growth with a good record for continuity of supply by world standards. This is illustrated by the fifteen years to March 1985, the end of the year-long miners' strike. Apart from the effects of the two strikes in the 1970s there were, for all reasons, load disconnections over three periods totalling only 123 hours. The overall loss of supplies from emergencies was less than 0.01 per cent. This is the nationalised industry record with which the 'new' industry will be compared. Briefly, the old structure was one where emergencies were likely to occur but where the means of managing them were readily available.

THE NEW STRUCTURE

The structure of the industry was changed by the 1989 Electricity Act and by the vesting of the new companies on 31 March 1990. In England and Wales the main structural change was to split the CEGB into two fossil-fired generating companies (National Power (NP) and Powergen (PG)), a nuclear generating company (Nuclear Electric (NE)), and the National Grid Company (NGC), the last being responsible for managing the transmission assets, system operation and pumped storage. Nuclear Electric was the only company remaining within the public sector.

A further major change was the introduction of competition in generation. This was achieved both through the setting up of a market for electricity – the pool – and the progressive opening up of the market for direct sales to customers with choice. The pool is operated within rules agreed by a Pool Executive Committee and, in some aspects, approved by the Director-General of Electricity Supply and the Secretary of State. The Pool Executive Committee is structured to be representative of the generating companies, the regional electricity companies (RECs), interconnected countries and large users. The National Grid Company is represented on the Pool Executive Committee and on its sub-committees but has no voting rights. The pool operation, together with the administration of the settlement system which manages the money flow, is undertaken by the National Grid Company on behalf of the pool members.

In the period following privatisation there have been many changes. The RECs commonly carry out their traditional functions through separate businesses for distribution, supply, and trading. Some are developing overseas interests and most have diversified into electricity generation.

The two major generating companies in the private sector, National Power and Powergen, plus the National Grid Company, have set themselves to become international energy companies, while at home they have diversified. The National Grid Company are developing a major telecommunications business. National Power have acquired a US power generation company and have significant interests in power plants in Portugal, Spain and Pakistan. Powergen have, with a US partner, formed the largest independent gas company in the UK and are involved in a joint coal and power generation venture in the former East Germany.

In addition, there are an increasing number of independent generating companies building generating plant and already several GWs of their plant are connected to the transmission system. They will take an increasing share of the market and at the same time increase generation and fuel diversity. The main generating companies are likely to continue to diversify and may even reach the point where their British generating activity is not their main business. Ultimately companies will be free to take part in mergers and takeovers, which are likely in time to change the structure of the industry almost out of recognition.

SECURITY OF SUPPLY

Although some aspects of security of supply are left to the market, in the new competitive arrangements there are some defined responsibilities. The Secretary of State and the Director-General of Electricity Supplies (DGES) each has a duty to exercise the functions available to him to protect the interests of electricity consumers 'in respect of continuity of supply'[1] and 'to secure that all reasonable demands for electricity are satisfied'[2].

The Transmission Licence requires the NGC to plan and develop the transmission system in accordance with the planning standards of the CEGB. It also requires the transmission system to be operated in accordance with the operational security standards of the CEGB.[3] The RECs, through the Public Electricity Supply Licence, must make arrangements sufficient to meet the generation security standard of the CEGB.[4] There are further requirements for dealing with fuel security issues; these are described later.

The effect of these requirements is that, if they see that a plant shortage is likely to arise, the Secretary of State and the DGES have a responsibility to oversee the market and to take whatever steps may be available to them. For example, the DGES could, in these circumstances, increase the value of lost load and this would increase pool price at peak times and give a financial incentive for generators to build generating plant. The RECs and NGC must maintain security standards in the decisions they make that could influence the security of supply. In the case of the RECs the generation security standard (i.e. the one covering plant capacity) will only be capable of being met to the extent that the generators have plant available.

CONTINGENCIES AND EMERGENCIES

The new structure has made it necessary to define the arrangements for emergencies that will enable the government and the industry to manage electricity supply in the national interest.

Electricity supply emergencies

Provisions in Section 96 of the Electricity Act 1989 dovetail with provisions in Section 3 of the Energy Act 1976. Together they cover any 'civil emergency' which, in the opinion of the Secretary of State, 'is or may be likely to disrupt electricity supplies'. Under them the Secretary of State may (after consultation) issue directions to network operators and licensed generators to prepare and maintain contingency plans and to participate in the Contingency Planning Review Panel (CPRP). The scope of this participation is set out in the Electricity Supply Emergency Code, which specifies that the CPRP must be chaired by the National Grid Company and must include the chief executives of National Power and Powergen, together with senior officers of three regional electricity companies and one Scottish supplier; it may also co-opt others. The CPRP's job is to give advice to the Secretary of State on threats and options; it must endeavour to seek agreement, and all licensed parties must give it all the information it may reasonably need. Information provided may not be used for any other purpose. The CPRP must also report to the Secretary of State on the effectiveness of any measures taken, and issue statements during actual emergencies.

The main options envisaged are orders restricting consumption by industry and commerce, and directions requiring rota disconnections, where such orders alone are expected to be ineffective. Network operators are accordingly required to plan for rota disconnections over a wide range of severity, capable of being implemented at 48 hours' notice. The pattern to be used is set out in some detail in the Electricity Supply Emergency Code.

Fuel security

Further provisions of the 1989 Act[5] enable the Secretary of State to issue directions to power station operators and transmission companies on stocks of fuel and other materials and how these should be used during security periods declared by a direction of the Secretary of State.[6] There is a requirement through their individual licence conditions for all parties to comply with the Fuel Security Code. This requires that each takes part in contingency planning in which the National Grid Company will play a pivotal role. The National Grid Company may be directed to consult the generators to provide information and advice to the Secretary of State and also to operate the transmission system in any specified manner or with any specific objective. Unlimited fines may be imposed for non-compliance with directions.

The effect of these measures is to provide a means by which contingency planning can be carried out for the industry as a whole and by which central decision-making and direction can take place. It follows closely the arrangements that were successful in 1984–5, and which were inherent in the nationalised industry. There would, of course, now have to be a radical departure from the normal management of operations should these arrangements have to be applied.

FUTURE EMERGENCIES

The threatened or actual serious loss of electricity supplies is a reasonable definition of an emergency. An emergency might arise for a number of reasons.

Transmission

There are two possible reasons why the transmission network might cause a failure to meet consumer demand. One would be insufficient installed power transfer capability and the other insufficient of that capability in service to enable consumer demand to be met. The first could arise from insufficient investment in transmission or from generation and transmission plant developments not being adequately co-ordinated. The second could arise from loss of transmission circuits because of extreme weather, plant breakdowns or industrial action. Distribution circuits could be similarly affected.

Generation

This is a parallel to the transmission causes of failure. There could be a failure to meet consumer demand in full because there was insufficient installed generation capacity. This might arise from insufficient investment in new plant either because consumer demand and the potential for sales had grown at an unexpected rate, or because generators had not built plant despite potential sales from it. A further reason could be that too much plant had been closed down and decommissioned. As with transmission, failure could also occur because, although there was sufficient generating plant capacity installed, there was not enough in service to meet consumer demand. This could arise if technical problems caused a greater than expected level of breakdown or because of industrial action. It is also possible for this type of failure to arise from adverse weather but this is less likely than for transmission.

Fuel Supply

Failure could be caused by insufficient primary fuel supplies to maintain electricity generation at the required level. This occurred in the two miners' strikes of the 1970s. The characteristic of a fuel supply emergency is that electricity demand can be met in full until individual power stations use up their fuel stocks. Plant output then depends on deliveries of fuel. Curtailment of electricity supplies may be significant, highly disruptive and protracted. Vulnerability to this last type of emergency is thus dependent on the level of fuel stocks, the diversity of fuel sources, the diversity of transport and the reliability of the individual suppliers.

MANAGING FUTURE EMERGENCIES

The new structure has changed the probability of some of these events occurring and their possible severity.

Transmission

Transmission system development in England and Wales remains centrally planned and managed by the National Grid Company who should be able to oversee generating capacity and consumer demand trends. The planned development of transmission should not be hampered by lack of a strategic perspective, but for the following reasons it is not possible to have a power system development strategy. Although the National Grid Company can guide generating companies, it cannot refuse to connect a generator to the grid system, provided that the generator meets a number of requirements of which compliance with grid code standards is the most important.[7] The National Grid Company cannot compel a generator to remain in service. This can lead to problems from short notice of generation closures or from generation developments being difficult to support with the necessary new transmission lines. The latter is most likely to occur in environmentally difficult areas and there are many such areas. The public's perception of the need for new lines may be even more difficult to influence in the private sector era than it was when the public interest could more readily be argued.

Other causes of insufficient transmission capability could be a reduction in the transmission planning standards or the National Grid Company not strictly complying with the standards because of tight financial constraints causing them to delay capital expenditure. The latter is unlikely since one of the most important assets of the National Grid Company is its transmission licence and it would not wish to put that at risk. In any case resulting problems would not be on an emergency scale.

A transmission capability emergency is unlikely to arise. If it did occur it could cause some load shedding in the regions deficient in generation over limited periods of the day. It might be necessary for the Secretary of State to activate the Contingency Planning Review Panel, but this is unlikely since the load shedding arrangements need only be those which should normally be in place.

The remaining class of potential transmission emergency – insufficient installed power transfer capability in service – is different. This is most likely to arise from extreme weather. Blizzard conditions or gales coupled with iced conductors are two obvious winter conditions that have caused serious problems in the past. High ambient temperatures coupled with highly loaded transmission lines have also been the cause of serious failures but should not happen with a well-run power system. Extensive physical damage from high winds is another possibility.

The main needs in dealing with these emergencies are first to be able to control and to recover from the immediate problems caused by the transmission line faults. This is the role of the grid control centres and their staff. Their control aids are geared to deal with such events. The further phase is to restore the lines to service and this requires work in the field. This would be done by the National Grid Company, although the potential scale of the work and its difficulties should not be underestimated. Similar problems could affect the distribution networks and would be dealt with by the RECs. Control of consumer demand during these difficulties would come from the normal load shedding arrangements.

Generation

The short-term effect of setting up a market and of the growth of independent generation has been that a plant capacity surplus has been created. This is likely to persist for a few years until plant closures restore a balance. Looking to the longer term a substantial or persistent shortage of generating capacity would be evidence of a failure of the new market arrangements. The financial incentives of the pool with a plant deficit should offer an opportunity for profitable investment and mean that plant shortage was remedied. This process is aided by the National Grid Company Seven Year Statement, which is revised and published annually. Among other things, it provides information on estimates of future electricity demand, plant capacity and margins. In addition the Secretary of State and DGES have responsibility under the Act, referred to earlier, which means that they have to keep a close watch on plant margins. A difficulty could arise from the time interval between the perception of a deficit and new generating plant being commissioned. During that time, which could be several years, it might not be possible to meet electricity demand in full. With the present rules that would mean high pool prices over the daily periods of shortage and would in one way or another be reflected in prices to consumers. The likely result would be that consumers would try to avoid the high price peak periods and the deficit would be reduced to some extent – an interesting feedback advantage not available in the nationalised industry era through the bulk supply tariff except in a blunted way over longer periods.

The failure to meet demand would have to be dealt with by the normal arrangements for demand control, namely voltage reductions and disconnections over peak periods.

Managing loss of generating capacity in an emergency

The possibility of industrial action leading to significant loss of generating capacity is discussed later. Here we consider the emergency management requirements in such an eventuality. An emergency would require management at the company or station level where the industrial action was occurring. It would require the co-ordination of the other generators to make good the capacity loss as far as possible and would require management of load reduction by orders and/or by disconnections.

The extent of the emergency would depend on the actions of the company, the trade unions and employees involved in the dispute, who would be trying to make judgements on the degree of confrontation and the revenue and capacity loss that they would be prepared to see. In the case of the trade unions there might be a phase in the dispute when the leaders lost control to activists within the power stations. Indeed they might have lost their control long before the dispute. This could add to the seriousness of the dispute. The remaining emergency management issues would be for the Secretary of State, advised by the Contingency Planning Review Panel, to decide. Depending on the depth and length of the dispute, it would be necessary to consider whether the Secretary of State's emergency powers should be exercised. All the necessary powers and means of managing the emergency are available to him.

The effect on the pool of a plant shortage from industrial action could be high prices, from which other generators could benefit. However the Pool Executive Committee have agreed rules that would apply in these circumstances aimed at keeping pool prices at about their normal level, allowing additional costs to be recovered through other means. Technical problems or adverse weather are unlikely to be the cause of other than marginal or short duration problems; they could be dealt with by normal methods.

FUEL SUPPLY

The risk of a fuel supply emergency under the new structure has fortuitously been greatly reduced, at any rate into the medium term. The quantity of gas-fired generation, the increase in imported coal, and the increase in nuclear generation all contribute to much greater diversity of fuel supply and greatly reduce the probability of a serious supply problem. This position contrasts with that in the 1980s when 75 per cent of electricity generation was from NCB coal. The diversity of energy type and source of supply now means that the loss of any one type or source would have a much reduced effect. In addition most of the oil-fired capacity which was so important in the 1984–5 miners' strike is still available. The diversity is made more marked since the imported coal is likely to be from countries that are politically and geographically different both among themselves and from oil exporting countries.

In the longer term, the degree of diversity will be in the hands of those in the market. In the absence of an energy policy or framework, diversity may be lost, particularly if gas turbine plant continues to gain market share and nuclear and the old oil plant capacity is shut down. It is, however, difficult to see one primary energy supply source ever approaching the dominance that British Coal once had.

The powers available to the Secretary of State under the 1976 and 1989 Acts, coupled with the requirements placed on the companies under their individual licence conditions, should be sufficient to allow all the necessary elements for managing an emergency to be available. The National Grid Company would undoubtedly have to play the pivotal role. As a private company it would be inappropriate for it to act in the same role as the CEGB. Its role would be to advise the Secretary of State by providing energy analyses to aid his determination of appropriate stock holdings in preparation for an emergency and to aid his decision-making if an emergency arose.

There are other differences from the past. One is that the generating companies as PLCs are managed by executive directors who are required by company law to serve the interests of their shareholders. They would have to be directed to take any actions in the national interest that were against those interests but, subject to that, would no doubt wish to be as responsive to their customers' needs as they could be. The other difference is that it is now inappropriate for the government to accept any responsibility for additional costs and there is no means by which that could happen. The provisions of the Fuel Security Code and of the various licences cover the audit and recovery of additional costs incurred in fuel emergencies. Further, the DGES has said that, for civil emergencies, he would consider favourably requests for the recovery of costs necessarily incurred.[8] The result is that electricity consumers would bear the costs. This would certainly make public relations in an emergency more difficult. The government and the regulator could expect analysis and criticism of their handling of the crisis and they would have to consider the level of public disclosure of what was being done and why. The difficulty of explaining energy supply and power system issues should not be underestimated.

Supplies of CO_2, hydrogen and other non-fuel resources

Shortages of non-fuel essential supplies were a critical factor in the 1971–2 miners' strike. The question may arise again whether, notwithstanding the reassuring comments made here on fuel supplies, the industry could still be vulnerable to interference with supplies of other materials.

Industrial action within the industry is discussed in the next section. The dominant factor in such a situation would be the loss of capacity from the direct effects of the action rather than the shortage of essential supplies. The possible interference with supplies as a result of an industrial dispute in the supplying or transport companies is very different. The independent generators and the combined cycle gas-turbine stations of National Power and Powergen would be just as vulnerable to the loss of essential supplies as the CEGB were in 1971–2 unless they had the appropriate level of storage. The Fuel Security Code provisions enable the Secretary of State to require particular levels of stocks for strategic materials.

One factor that has changed is that, notwithstanding an emergency, the culture of supplying companies is now one which has a much stronger driving force to meet the needs of customers. Suppliers could be expected to be more resolute in the face of pickets. In addition, if there was interference from secondary pickets the generators would probably have recourse to law; they could also expect police assistance to force deliveries, if necessary.

Dealing with such a threat would initially be a problem for the company or companies involved. Any resulting loss of capacity would however have to be dealt with through the emergency management arrangements and might need action by the Secretary of State, advised by the Contingency Planning Review Panel. With the formal powers available, the provisions of trade union legislation, increased storage capacity and various sources of supply and means of delivery, such a threat would be unlikely to be a critical one.

INDUSTRIAL RELATIONS

As described earlier most nationwide electricity supply emergencies have occurred because of industrial action in the industry or the industries supplying it, mostly the latter. Both the general economic environment and the detailed industrial relations arrangements have changed since the events described in this book. To understand the risk of emergencies from industrial relations problems it is necessary to consider briefly the nature of these changes.

Electricity supply industrial relations

Relations between management and the unions and staff have greatly changed and will continue to do so. Most staff continue to be covered by collective agreements on terms and conditions of employment, but these agreements cover single companies only, while all managers and many senior professional staff are now on individual contracts of service. These are radical departures. The significance of the changes affecting the latter grouping cannot be over-emphasised: those involved are now fully committed to their company and its objectives, whereas previously there was inherently an element of equivocation. The National Grid Company, Powergen and Nuclear Electric plc have each negotiated with their unions a single agreement covering all of their staff (other than those just referred to), while National Power have three agreements, one covering clerical and administrative, one technical and scientific, and one industrial staff. All the companies have decentralised their industrial relations decision-making and one if not more seems to be heading for local (e.g. single power station) agreements negotiated by staff representatives supported by their unions.

These agreements are far more flexible than the old ones and have reduced the constraints on managers in managing their workforces. They were introduced with the support of majorities in ballots, encouraged by attractive initial terms. Since privatisation staff numbers (and therefore union numbers) have fallen drastically with no shortage of volunteers for the selective severance terms on offer. Annual pay settlements for the private companies have been above the cost of living level in exchange for increased productivity. The companies have also offered an element of performance-related pay, although not as part of the collective agreements; by this means the staff, with the shareholders, share in the rewards of improved profitability.

The possibility of major disruptions of supply

Could relations between the generators and/or National Grid Company and their unions deteriorate to the extent that the unions would ballot their members on strike action intended seriously to disrupt supplies? It cannot be assumed that relations will remain as peaceful and co-operative as in the first years of privatisation. The competition in the electricity supply market and the need to show a continuing trend of improving profitability are likely to bring pressures to reduce manning costs further, especially if companies diversifying abroad are not as successful as they expect. Before too long there may not be scope for further labour productivity improvements justifying annual pay deals above inflation, although in the short term there may be further pressure on numbers at the long-established coal-and oil-fired stations and the nuclear power stations. One or more of the companies may have to reduce severance terms and/or resort to compulsory redundancy, which would obviously not improve relationships.

It cannot be ruled out that a world economic recession could have such a serious impact on the British economy that there could be a further large increase in unemployment and a further increase in public borrowing. The government could be forced to take measures that could have the effect of reducing the real incomes of those in employment, including electricity supply. Such measures could lead to resistance from unions and staff in the industry as they experienced a fall in living standards.

The options that presumably would be considered by one or a group of electricity supply trade unions and staff representatives are strike action or a form of action short of a strike in part of a company, a whole company or throughout the industry. The unions might come under pressure from militant groups who, in trying to muster support, would no doubt point out the low manpower levels and flexible working arrangements that had been conceded. The influence of these groups would be weighed against the need expressed by the unions and the general body of their members to survive. The effect of competition between the major generating companies, but more particularly between them and the independent power producers, would mean that the survival of a company or a power station could not be taken for granted. The desire to preserve jobs would be a powerful influence on the majority and a deterrent to industrial action.

The unions and staff representatives would find difficulty in organising a major stoppage across the generating sector under the present employment laws, especially those provisions relating to balloting and secondary and discontinuous action.[9] The potential role of the courts would also cause the unions anxiety.

If a strike were confined to one company the generation of electricity would continue elsewhere with those companies protected by law against secondary action and with trade unions anxious to avoid the risk of the courts sequestrating their funds. If the staff were covered by a single agreement for industrial, technical and administrative grades many of those staff would be unlikely, on past showing, to vote for a stoppage. If the strike call related to union members in a company, such as National Power, with three collective agreements, the unions would not only have to take account of continued generation in the other companies but that those covered by the other agreements or personal contracts in the same company might operate plant with others brought in to augment their numbers.

To legalise the equivalent of a national strike across the generating sector would require six separate ballots, each with a majority in favour. It would involve the unions co-ordinating action between discrete groups of staff, probably with differing priorities and degrees of commitment, and with the employment laws stacked against them. There would also be an increasing amount of plant operated by independent generators and probably a need to pay members on strike either partly or in full. Organising such a strike would simply be impractical and the unions, with all their experience, would know it.

Strike action of a potentially less far-reaching nature might be of three different kinds. One to persuade the managers and staff of the national grid to take strike action or to operate the grid in a less than optimum way. But the effect of a strike by industrial staff would take a long time to have any effect; further, the senior staff managing the grid are not parties to the collective agreements and would be unlikely to respond to such a call. Coercion would be illegal.

Secondly, the unions might seek to call out selected major power stations in the different companies but again, to remain within the law, there would be major problems to overcome relating to balloting, secondary and discontinuous action and the availability of other staff to assist in plant operations. The companies would not simply sit idly by but would act to influence the attitudes and behaviour of staff on strike or, more to the point, before they had embarked on such a course.

Thirdly, would remain the possibility of industrial action less than a strike, specifically a ban on overtime and work-to-rule in power stations. In 1970 and 1977, in the one case officially and in the other unofficially, and at a time when there were no effective legislative restraints, the actions produced mixed results. Now the terms of the new collective agreements, current custom and practice, personal contracts and performance-related pay agreements would mean that such actions would be extremely difficult for the unions and/or staff represent-atives to organise while remaining within the law. The unions would also know that in the wake of serious industrial action the companies, like those following the 1926 strike, would not be content simply to restore the *status quo ante*.

These scenarios are not only hypothetical, they are also fanciful. The unions and those they represent are much too sensible to throw away agreements and relationships that are better than those generally prevailing in British industry. Over many years management and unions have learnt to do business with one another, even in the most unpropitious circumstances, and the unions would not, like praying mantises, be inclined to throw all that away in one great gesture of virility.

What would happen with a change of government and legislation more favourable to trade unions it is impossible to say. It would be unwise to conclude that the trade unions in the industry could never threaten supplies. The industry and the government clearly hold the same view or they would not have established the contingency planning and emergency management arrangements. The companies and unions could normally be expected to build on the best of the industry's industrial relations traditions and eschew, in this complex and vital industry, thoughts of confrontation.

Industrial relations in associated and supplying companies

We find it difficult to believe that any union or group of unions now operating in associated industries would attempt to achieve their objectives on pay and conditions by putting pressure on electricity supply. With the present structure of the industry, the present workforce, employment legislation, diversity of supplies and other factors, the chances of success would be negligible and be seen by the unions to be so.

There may, however, be some commentators and radical industrial groupings who see decisive strike action being called for by the TUC in the face of a serious deterioration in the economic and political situation, a further heavy increase in unemployment, a sharp fall in living standards and a government whose anti-union legislation was thought to be so severe as to threaten the survival of the trade unions themselves.

The TUC, this scenario might assert, would call for strike action aimed at bringing down the government. It would seek 'a quick solution' by instructing relevant unions to call out workers in key industries including electricity supply, gas pipelines, water, sewage, transport and new technology. A number of industries and services, including those in the City of London, are now increasingly dependent on such technology. We consider that such scenarios are also fanciful. We believe that, in a national economic crisis brought on largely because of the collapse of international markets, the government would itself be seeking the co-operation of opposition parties, the unions and the people of this country to tackle the issues together. It would be a time of reconciliation and co-operative action rather than the opposite.

In such a crisis, even if the government did not act in this way, we do not think that the TUC or the major unions would call for strike action. Not only are they not structured and motivated as they were in 1926, they are not very much like they were even in 1972 and 1974, when the miners, supported by the union movement generally, were the strikers. Then unemployment was around the one million mark and trade union membership was about 12 000 000. Now unemployment is around 2 600 000 and TUC-affiliated union membership is down to 8 000 000 or so, with a serious weakening of the unions' position as a consequence. Further, the social composition of the membership is radically different, with the white-collar unions predominating where twenty years ago it was the manual workers. Many of the white-collar members are women, many of whom are in part-time employment. Most white-collar workers are employed in much smaller groupings than the factory groupings of twenty years ago. Many members are middle class, or aspiring, many have heavy financial commitments, and the thought of solid strike action is simply not part of their union consciousness. Even if some of the vulnerable industries remain strongholds of manual worker trade unionism the TUC would not get the necessary authority, even if it were inclined to seek it, to trigger sustainable action in such strongholds.

The scenario is a nightmare, whereas the trade union leaders are wide awake. Not only do they know that, with their current memberships, they would not get the necessary support. They would also be aware that two thirds of the workforce are not in unions anyway. Above all they would see that, in the circumstances envisaged, strike action would do nothing to help their members or the government get out of their difficulties. On the contrary it would manifestly make things worse. Unions, just like other pressure groups, have no appetite for presiding over their own demise, or are any less responsive to genuine calls to help the country in its difficulties.

EMERGENCIES IN A COMPETITIVE ELECTRICITY SUPPLY INDUSTRY

Dealing with emergencies in the competitive electricity supply industry would be very different from doing so in the days of the CEGB. The disaggregation of generation, transmission and distribution, together with the introduction of competition, means that the industry now operates according to different concepts. Although each company has some responsibility within the Act and its licence to consider security of electricity supply, no single company has a clear overall responsibility similar to that of the CEGB. The change from the public service-based industry to competition, and electricity being treated as a traded commodity, has a number of implications for the management of emergencies.

The transition to full competition and consumer choice is to be completed by 1998. If that is achieved then security of supply could, at least to some extent, be that for which the consumer is prepared to pay. Additional security can come from accepting additional costs. The trade-off between risk and cost could be reflected by choice in the supply contracts, which could be available to consumers by that date.

If such contracts of the type became common, some types of emergency could involve no more than supervising the adaptation of the competitive arrangements to cope with the changing circumstances. A more extreme emergency would inevitably lead to the competitive arrangements breaking down and possibly the threat of serious disruption to the country. Individual companies could in these circumstances only take account of their shareholders' interests. If the national interest required them to take actions contrary to that, they would have to be directed. The government would have to intervene and the Secretary of State would have to exercise the emergency powers available to him.

ROLE OF THE NATIONAL GRID COMPANY

The National Grid Company would have a key role in the contingency planning and emergency management arrangements. This is recognised by their chairmanship of the Contingency Planning Review Panel, which would advise the Secretary of State who would then direct. The National Grid Company is the only body with the ability to analyse and interpret the overall implications for electricity supply of any actual or threatened emergency. Together with the government they would need the full support of the industry to be successful in keeping the lights on. It would be in no one's interest for the lights to go out or even dimmed, but the price of avoiding that might be high.

WHAT DOES IT ALL MEAN?

What does all this mean to the prospects for keeping the lights on in the 1990s and beyond? The risks that remain, from the potential emergencies considered in this analysis, are generally a result of the new market arrangements not addressing security *per se*. They include the possible lack of sufficient lead time to redress plant capacity shortage, the trend to too great a dependence on gas, with the possible loss of the present fuel diversity, and the lack of a power system development strategy or an overall energy policy. The degree of importance of these factors is difficult to judge. It should be remembered that the Regulator and the Secretary of State both have a responsibility to oversee security of supply and to take action when this is necessary.

The arrangements for contingency planning and emergency management seem adequate. The emergency powers available to the Secretary of State should enable the operation of the power system, including all its generators, to be directed in the public interest. He will be heavily dependent on the advice of the National Grid Company in managing the operation of the system in what is likely to be a completely different way from its normal form.

A public relations problem that it would be wise to take into account is that, since the customers pay, they are likely to demand an explanation of what is being done in their interests. A no-information policy, of the type that was successful in the 1984-5 miners' strike, may not be a feasible option. The difficulty of explaining power system issues to the general public should not be underestimated.

A factor not included in this analysis is the one which was the most important during the 1984–5 miners' strike. This was the public service ethic that led workers in the industry to choose to keep the lights on in the face of strong contrary pressures. It is difficult to predict the extent to which this has been preserved in the restructured privatised electricity supply industry and the effect that it would have in the event of a future emergency.

The main conclusions are that electricity supply emergencies are less likely in the future than in the past but that, should they occur, they would be more difficult to deal with.

Electricity generation: a brief history

The electricity supply industry started in the 1870s although supplies were limited to arc lamp demonstrations. The number and size of lighting and traction applications increased rapidly, backed in the 1880s and 1900s by statutes providing some sort of regulatory framework. Electricity was provided to the immediate locality by small machines set up in sheds, basements and the like.

Rapid technological developments in the period up to World War I enabled the size of generators to increase from a few kilowatts to several megawatts. Hundreds of independent privately and publicly owned undertakings established themselves and by 1914 sales of electricity for power were greater than for lighting and traction. Among the great engineering pioneers of the time were Sebastian di Ferranti, Charles Parsons and Charles Merz.

By 1907 about 20 000 people were employed wholly or mainly in electricity supply work (i.e. generation and distribution). Wages were rather above the generally prevailing level. About five per cent of employees were in trade unions – mainly craftsmen in the Electrical Trades Union – but there was no collective bargaining on pay rates and conditions.

WORLD WAR I

During World War I demand for electricity increased from 1.96 TWHs to 3.57, being greatly stimulated by munitions production. The great limitation was that the six hundred or so undertakings were unable to export their spare capacity to neighbouring supply systems because of technical differences and lack of interconnections. London alone had fifty electricity supply systems, twenty-four different voltages and ten different frequencies. Several government committees examined the problem and made recommendations; legislation followed in 1919.

During the war numbers employed in electricity supply in Great Britain rose to about 34 000. By 1917 there were a dozen or so trade unions with members in the industry with the ETU giving a strong and in London a militant lead. In January 1918 workers in the industry gained the 12.5 per cent increase earlier given to munitions workers, a reflection of the bargaining strength of the supply unions. In November 1918 a claim for London supply and tram workers led to a famous arbitration award – No. 2772 – which established a basic rate for an electrician, standardising rates and grades throughout London and providing the basis for negotiations throughout Great Britain. The Electrical Power Engineers' Association (EPEA), representing technical and scientific grades, had been established towards the end of the war and was to be a strong force in the industry. The EPEA and the ETU were at loggerheads for many years, especially in London.

ELECTRICITY IN THE POST-WAR YEARS

Under the Electricity (Supply) Act, 1919, Electricity Commissioners were established. They were to perform a regulatory role and to encourage co-ordinated regional developments through joint electricity authorities. But few were formed.

In post-war industrial conditions the government feared a workers' revolution. In February 1919 they extended the Conspiracy and Protection of Property Act 1875 to cover electricity supply. In October 1920 Parliament passed an Emergency Powers Act. In keeping with the recommendations of the war-time Whitley Committee the electricity employers, public and private, and ten manual workers' trade unions (each with one representative except the ETU, which had two) formed a National Joint Industrial Council (NJIC) in 1919. This was followed in 1920 by district joint industrial councils, covering Great Britain and making provision for works committees. From then until 1945 the district councils drew up schedules of conditions of work and scales of pay with NJIC guidelines. The unions would not accept the EPEA's application to join and in 1920 the Association and the employers set up a parallel body, the National Joint Board (NJB). With this separation the social and working demarcation lines in the industry were set for many years.

In November 1921 the NJIC trade unions managed, in spite of the recession, to negotiate a relatively generous sliding scale agreement. Nevertheless, in 1924 the unions threatened a national strike. However, they took their case to arbitration where they lost.

ELECTRICITY UNTIL WORLD WAR II

Many electricity supply workers were involved in the General Strike in the summer of 1926 (described in Chapter 2). At the time of that strike total sales of electricity were 5.8 TWH, generated by 479 power stations with a total capacity of 4422 MW. The local authorities owned 264 stations and companies owned 215. By this time the largest stations had over 100 MW of plant installed.

The industry's basic problem remained unchanged – the general lack of interconnections between the utilities and between the power stations. However, in 1926 the new Electricity Act not only provided for existing undertakings to maintain control of distribution, but also provided for the co-ordination of new power station planning and the control of power station operations to be undertaken, within the framework of a newly constructed 'grid-iron' of high voltage transmission lines, by a new publicly owned body, the Central Electricity Board (CEB).

By April 1948 the CEB, with the Electricity Commissioners, had done a sound job in developing a modern electricity system. By 1933 some 4000 miles of transmission lines had been erected and by 1935 the grid was complete with 148 of the most efficient power stations under the CEB's direction. The only real setback had been in 1934 when a power station accident and an overload triggered a complete blackout of eleven southern counties for several hours.

The savings arising from the grid were large and demand grew rapidly. In 1914 sales per head of population had been 77 kWH and by 1939 they were 486. By that year the installed capacity in Great Britain was 9712 MW, most of the new generators being of either 30 or 50 MW capacity. In 1938–9 the grid became a nationally integrated network and a National Control Centre was set up.

The General Strike (as Chapter 2 makes plain) set back relations between the electricity employees and the NJIC trade unions for some time. Nevertheless, in 1927 the unions gained a suspension of the sliding-scale agreement, although this was shortlived. In 1930 and 1931 electricity workers in some areas had to accept a pay cut. With economic improvement in the mid-1930s the pay of the industry's manual employees did not improve as rapidly as for some comparable groups elsewhere. By 1940 average weekly earnings of the industry's manual employees were below the national average and remained so until 1945 and beyond. However, conditions on matters such as holidays, hours and sick pay were better than for most. The technical and scientific staff were helped in supporting their pay standards by having them linked to the growth of plant capacity or maximum demand in a rapidly expanding industry.

WORLD WAR II AND ITS AFTERMATH

The periods of World War II and post-war reconstruction brought many difficulties not only to the industry but to the economy as a whole. Several power stations suffered bomb damage. In addition, barrage balloons that had broken from their moorings trailed their cables across overhead lines causing short-circuit faults. The National Grid Centre was moved from Bankside to two disused underground lift shafts at St Paul's as protection against the bombing.

Plant construction, repairs and maintenance had to be cut back in war time and a shortage of electricity after the war was inevitable. This was made worse by an acute coal shortage which led people to buy and use large numbers of electric fires. In the winter of 1946–7 everything went wrong: added to the coal and electricity shortage was the most terrible weather. On 7 February 1947 industrial consumers in the South East, Central and North West England grid areas were only allowed to use electricity from 9.00am to noon and from 2.00pm to 4.00pm. From 13 February these restrictions were extended to the whole country. By that time there was, on average, only one-and-a-half weeks' coal supplies left at the power stations. Supplies were not back to normal until the end of March.

NATIONALISATION: THE FIRST TEN YEARS

The 1947 Electricity Act nationalised the industry in Great Britain from April 1948. The assets of the 200 companies and 369 local authority undertakings and those of the CEB and the Electricity Commissioners were transferred to a British Electricity Authority (BEA), under the chairmanship of Lord Citrine, and 14 distribution boards (a North of Scotland Hydro-Electric Board had been established during the war and remained, being largely independent of the rest of the industry). Within the BEA a Central Authority was to run the power stations and the grid transmission system.

All told there were about 156 000 employees (April 1949) of whom about 41 000 worked for the Central Authority. There were 197 power stations with just a quarter accounting for nine-tenths of total output. Priority was given to the building of the 6000 MW of plant ordered before April 1948 and the construction of a supergrid that would operate at 275 kV. The area boards had to rationalise the different practices, supply 11 000 000 consumers and get on with rural electrification.

Gradually the industry overcame its worst problems. Larger, more efficient, generating sets were ordered and growth of sales was at a rate of 7–8 per cent a year. In 1954 the industry in the south of Scotland was hived off and the BEA became the Central Electricity Authority (CEA).

The government set up a committee under Sir Edwin Herbert to look at the industry's organisation; it made recommendations for substantial changes. A new Electricity Act applied from 1 January 1958. It provided for the abolition of the CEA and the establishment of a Central Electricity Generating Board with responsibility, in England and Wales, for generation and main transmission, together with an Electricity Council, which was to act as a central body for the whole industry in England and Wales and to carry certain specific responsibilities, for example the maintenance of the industrial relations machinery.

On or within two or three years of the vesting date the industry established or reconstructed national negotiating bodies separately covering manual workers (NJIC), technical and scientific (NJB), clerical and administrative (NJC) and managerial and higher executive grades (except for a handful of top managers and also industrial relations officers directly involved). There were district and local bodies associated with the NJIC and NJC and district bodies with the others. There was also a National Joint Advisory Council and district and local bodies for joint consultation on which all the boards and trade unions and/or staff were represented. The NJAC developed personnel policies, especially education and training, but excluded pay and employment conditions. Lord Citrine, Chairman of the BEA and CEA, put great personal effort into making this machinery a success.

In the period to 1957 progress within the negotiating bodies was limited, although it was an enormous job to assimilate employees to new conditions and relationships. It is remarkable that the only serious breach of procedures was in 1949 (in the events described in Chapter 3).

One of the basic problems in the NJIC was that pay was entirely time based and nationally determined. Many other industries, competing for the same skills at a time of skill shortage, had much more flexible pay structures. In order to hold on to NJIC employees local managers conceded heavy overtime to boost weekly earnings. This was inimical with high productivity and effective managerial control. The Herbert Committee criticised the CEA for not going for properly based incentives and for over-centralising industrial relations decision-making. The other machines made modest progress, one of the main recurrent problems being over differential pay movements between the different machines.

CEGB IN THE 1960s

The CEGB established five regions, which ran its power stations and transmission network. The power station construction programme was placed with three project groups, later reduced to one. The Board inherited a magnox nuclear power station programme. The early plans provided for new coal-and oil-fired power stations built at or near their main fuel sources, the coal mines and refineries. The Board planned and started to build 500 MW generating units in 2000 MW stations plus 6700 miles of 400 kV and 275 kV transmission lines. The commissioning programme on the big sites ran into trouble through faults in power station construction. The Board, with increased numbers of technical and scientific staff, became deeply involved with the plant contractors, in getting the new stations right. In the winter of 1962–3 the country suffered severe weather and the Board, with the distribution boards, had extreme problems to deal with and for short periods were forced to cut power supplies.

By the start of the 1970s some 75 per cent of the supergrid had been built and all 8 nuclear stations were operating, together with several 2000 MW stations. A start was being made on the advanced gas-cooled reactor nuclear power station programme, which was to create many problems for the Board. In the last year (1957) of the CEA sales of power had been 40.3 TWHs from 262 power stations with a capacity of 24.34 GW. By 1970–71 total sales were 184 TWH from 187 power stations with a maximum output of 49.28 GW. This was a remarkable rate of growth, which greatly exceeded that of the following fifteen years.

Soon after they were established the Electricity Council and the CEGB devised plans for cutting out heavy, regular overtime work, raising the status of manual workers, removing restrictive practices and identifying and establishing widely the best work practices. Proposals to these ends were put to the NJIC unions. There were serious setbacks in the negotiations and in 1964 more than a flurry of industrial action occurred. Indeed it took a Court of Inquiry to point the two sides of the NJIC in the right direction. In 1964 and 1965 an NJIC status agreement was made, which embodied most of what the employers and unions had set out to achieve.

In 1967 and 1968, with the help of the National Board for Prices and Incomes, national agreements were made in the NJIC governing the introduction of work-study-based schemes for NJIC employees, now called industrial staff. The schemes were to be introduced in each local work unit, such as a power station, only after method study and work measurement had been completed. This all took time, the boards were accused of dragging their feet and in December 1970 there was official industrial action in the industry (described in Chapter 4). In March 1971 a Court of Inquiry under Lord Wilberforce recommended a way through that was acceptable.

In March 1967 the number of industrial staff in the Board had been 53 915. By March 1973, when 77 per cent of these staff were working under incentive scheme conditions, mostly at standard performance, the number was down to 38 893, a 28.7 per cent reduction. Overtime was then no more than an hour or two a week on average and weekly earnings were among the best in the country. These changes and the impact of incomes policies affected negotiations in the other machines. Productivity agreements were made there, including a work measurement scheme for clerical staff. These agreements were not, however, as far-reaching as those for the industrial staff.

LATER CEGB DEVELOPMENTS

The 1970s and early 1980s certainly had their ups and downs for the Board. There was heavy picketing of the power stations by striking miners, especially in 1972 (see Chapter 5). The 2000 MW coal-and-oil-fired stations were coming good and the 400 kV supergrid was completed. In 1973–4 there was a serious fuel emergency associated with the Middle East War and oil embargoes, industrial action by technical and scientific staff and then a world recession. In 1975–6 the Board closed 5000 MW of plant and made the jobs of 5000 staff redundant (they were redeployed).

In the mid-1970s there was a long public debate over nuclear reactor choice. A government committee reported on the industry's future organisation, but the subsequent legislative proposals did not reach the statute book. In 1977 there was unofficial action by industrial staff in many power stations leading to interruptions of supply (see Chapter 7). The winter of 1978–9 brought severe weather, causing extreme problems for the industry's staff, whose work enabled supplies to be maintained.

The Conservative government elected in June 1979 was committed to privatise the electricity supply. In the early 1980s the Monopolies and Mergers Commission examined the Board's work and produced a generally favourable report. The 2000 MW cross-Channel power link was started, the Board made a formal application to build a pressurised water reactor at Sizewell in Suffolk and in January 1983 the public inquiry started. The pumped storage scheme at Dinorwig in North Wales was officially opened in May 1984.

Over the period 1981 to 1984, 9000 MW of generating plant were closed down with about the name number of job losses. By March 1984, the start of the miners' strike, the Board had 90 power stations with a capacity of 51 028 MW and annual sales of £7146 millions.

In the period 1971 to 1984 relations of the Board with the industrial staff and their unions were co-operative, except in 1977 (see Chapter 7). There were many changes in productivity scheme arrangements and in 1980 a complete re-structuring of the NJIC agreement provided for virtually full staff status and only five payment bands below foreman level.

In the NJC, the clerical and administrative staff machine, much time was taken up with negotiating and revising an agreement on the use by these staff of new technology. In the early 1970s the EPEA elected a new executive committee, which appointed a strong General Secretary in John Lyons. New agreements were made in the NJB where negotiations were hard-going and time-consuming, illustrated by the fact that a job evaluation scheme took ten years to negotiate and apply. However, the EPEA and the technical and scientific staff, in spite of the 1973 industrial action, had an outstanding record of helping the industry during operational crises.

In the period 1967 to 1984 the Board's staff fell from 80 189 to 50 250, a 37.32 per cent drop, the industrial staff bearing the greatest losses. There were no grounds for complacency however: the negotiation of pay and conditions was over-centralised and the existence of four separate negotiating bodies created and perpetuated restrictive practices. Reductions in numbers in the CEGB successor companies indicate that in 1984 there had remained considerable scope for improvement.

However, in spite of all these limitations, the CEGB in March 1984 was a coherent, purposeful and competent organisation by the standards of the time. The following twelve months were to put it to the test as it faced the greatest challenge in its own and the whole industry's history.

The miners' strike, 1984–5

CHRONOLOGY OF MAIN EVENTS

1981

18 February   Following the threat of a national NUM strike, agreement between Secretary of State for Energy, NCB and NUM results in withdrawal of colliery closure list, curtailment of imports and other concessions. CEGB imports restricted to 750 000 tonnes a year. CEGB coal stocks 15 000 000 tonnes.

May   Discussion with the Department of Energy on measures to protect electricity supplies in the event of future miners' strike. Increased coal delivery programme begins.

14 September   Nigel Lawson appointed Secretary of State for Energy.

8 December   Arthur Scargill elected President of the NUM. CEGB coal stocks 19 000 000 tonnes

1982

January to February   ASLEF overtime ban followed by strike reduces coal deliveries. CEGB increases oil-fired generation to protect coal stocks.

23 February   Agreements with government and NCB to fill power station stockyards to their capacity estimated at 24 000 000 tonnes, later modified to 26 000 000 tonnes. Accelerated coal delivery scheme agreed with government and NCB to cover CEGB additional costs.

1 July   Walter Marshall takes up his appointment as Chairman of CEGB. Norman Siddall appointed NCB Chairman for one year to succeed Sir Derek Ezra.

4 August   CEGB decides to increase storage of all commodities essential to power station operation to equal endurance of coal stock.

30 September	Power station coal stocks reach 26 000 000 tonnes.

1983

January	Power station coal stocks target increased to 30 000 000 tonnes.
28 March	Secretary of State for Energy announces the appointment of Ian MacGregor as Chairman of the NCB.
10 June	General Election – Conservative government returned with a majority of 144. Peter Walker becomes Secretary of State for Energy.
1 September	Ian MacGregor takes over as Chairman of NCB.
21 October	NUM delegate conference votes to reject NCB pay offer and for overtime ban starting on 31 October.
23 October	Power station coal stocks reach a peak of 30 800 000 tonnes. Increased storage facilities for all essential commodities in place.
31 October	NUM overtime ban starts.
December	CEGB arrange limited coal imports to Thames power stations over Christmas. New Year coal supply break.

1984

1 January	Power station coal stocks fall to 28 000 000 tonnes.
January and February	The effect of the NUM overtime ban on CEGB coal stocks increases. If overtime ban continues to October and then there is a strike CEGB will then only be able to maintain electricity supplies for twelve weeks.
1 March	Local coal trade union representatives in Yorkshire told of accelerated closure (effective April) of Cortonwood and Bullcliffe pits on economic grounds.
6 March	NCB tells unions about future years' plan which implies closure of 4 000 000 tonnes of capacity.
8 March	NUM Executive votes to give official support to Yorkshire and Scottish NUM who are already committed to strike action from weekend 9–12 March.
12 March	Strike begins. Flying pickets move into Nottinghamshire and other areas where the strike call is being resisted. CEGB coal stock 23 900 000 tonnes.
15 March	Yorkshire picket dies at Ollerton Colliery, Nottinghamshire.
18 March	Police mobilised to deal with mass picketing. National Reporting Centre set up to co-ordinate police reinforcements.
19 March	Four of the six main electricity industry unions advise members to continue to perform normal duties.

26 March	Despite doubt about whether strike will continue without ballot and with miners still working, CEGB decide to start major oil burn increasing to a maximum of 350 000 tonnes a week over weekly 25 per cent steps.
27 March	T&GWU advise members in power stations not to handle incoming coal supplies. Rail unions are giving strong support to NUM and are blocking coal and oil movements to power stations.
28 March	NUM pickets switch to power stations and NUM calls for a complete power stoppage. First 25 per cent increase in oil-fired generation implemented.
4 April	Oil-fired generation now at 50 per cent level.
5 April	Nottinghamshire miners reject NUM Executive's recommendation not to cross picket lines and vote overwhelmingly to work on. Ballot goes three to one against area leaders' advice to join the strike.
11 April	Oil-fired generation now up to 75 per cent of maximum. Rail-borne coal difficulties continue.
19 April	NUM delegate conference decides to reduce requirement for strike ballot to simple majority (from 55 per cent) and urge all coalfields to strike.
20 April	Arthur Scargill says CEGB has at best nine weeks of coal left. Coal deliveries by road being set up in the Midlands Region. Cottam and West Burton Power stations receive 400 lorries a day.
26 April	Full oil-fired generation now in operation and the loading regimes of coal stations now arranged to give maximum endurance with available coal. Coal stock now 17 950 000 tonnes.
30 April	Strike now establishes a record as the longest stoppage in the coal industry since the miners' strike of 1926.
13 May	Problems with rail transport continue but are now compensated for by further increases in road-borne supplies. Coal stock now 17 300 000 tonnes.
22 May	First negotiations between NUM and NCB since strike started break down after one hour.
25 May	High Court judge declares strike unconstitutional and grants injunction to 631 Nottinghamshire miners banning union from instructing them to stop work.
27 May	Output from Grain and Littlebrook oil-fired power stations increased to use overload capacity in full.
29 and 30 May	Mass picketing at Orgreave Colliery; police and pickets injured. Arthur Scargill arrested.

8 June	NUM and NCB meet for talks in Edinburgh; resume in Rotherham and fail.
10 June	Road tanker supplies of oil to power stations being set up with small tanker companies. Coal stock at power stations now 16 000 000 tonnes.
11 June	Pro-strike Left heavily defeated in Nottinghamshire Area NUM elections.
15 June	Picket killed by a lorry at the entrance to Ferrybridge Power Station. TGWU national official instructs lorry drivers not to move oil normally moved by rail.
18 June	Orgreave battle between pickets and police continues.
9 July	Talks between NUM and NCB resume in Edinburgh but break up without agreement. National dock strike called because non-registered labour is used to unload iron ore at Immingham.
15 July	Oil-burn being increased at Blyth B and Tilbury Power Stations. Coal stocks now 14 800 000 tonnes.
18 July	Another round of coal peace talks collapses after eleven hours.
19 July	Dover dockers call off strike as stranded lorry drivers threaten reprisals.
30 July	South Wales NUM fined for contempt for defying order to stop picketing Port Talbot steelworks and following refusal to pay the fine; a sequestrator appointed.
July and early August	CEGB concern about the length of the strike and the possibility of not being able to meet winter electricity demand. All means of improving the situation being investigated and when practicable implemented.
5 August	Gas turbine generators now being used and oil burn at coal-fired power stations being increased in an effort to get through the winter. The problem is road transport of the oil.
12 August	Oil burn at coal-fired stations further increased. Decommissioned stations in the South Eastern Region being returned to service.
19 August	Gas burning to half capacity now started at Hams Hall power station in the Midlands as a further step to improve winter prospects.
23 August	Another dock dispute over docking of a ship with imported coal at Hunterston without TGWU dockers.
3 September	TUC debate the miners' dispute at annual Congress; courageous speeches made by Eric Hammond and John Lyons, but massive support given to striking miners.
9 September	Greater efforts by CEGB result in coal supplies by rail

and road reaching 589 000 tonnes a week – the highest since the strike. (Normal supplies would be over 1 500 000 tonnes). The highest oil burn yet achieved – 446 000 tonnes. Considerable effort being applied to get through the winter. Further NUM-NCB peace talks over a period of several days in several locations; they eventually fail.

28 September   NACODS votes to strike. High Court rules that NUM cannot deem the strike to be official unless there is a ballot with a majority in favour of a strike.

1 October   NCB-NACODS talk to avert strike. Writ served on Scargill and NUM for continuing to call the strike official. Over the last few weeks CEGB coal stocks have been increasing slightly. Oil supplies to more coal-fired power stations reintroduced, supported by union guidelines following the TUC annual congress. Hams Hall power station is on full gas burn. Coal stocks now 14 700 000 tonnes.

7 October   Measures are being taken to ensure that cross Channel-link with Electricité de France is commissioned in time to help supplies in winter 1985–6.

10 October   Following Arthur Scargill and NUM Executive defying the High Court ruling, the NUM is fined £200 000, and Arthur Scargill £1000, for contempt.

16 October   NACODS executive call strike from 25 October. Arthur Scargill's fine paid by unidentified person.

24 October   NACODS call off the proposed stoppage on the basis of an agreement reached with NCB under ACAS help.

25 October   Judge orders seizure of NUM funds after union fails to pay £200 000 fine. NUM and NCB meet at ACAS but little optimism about talks which collapse on 31 October.

2 November   NCB makes an offer of a Christmas bonus and holiday pay for men back at work by 19 November. 10 000 miners return to work over a period of two weeks.

4 November   Although coal stocks have recently increased and improved the overall position of electricity supply, the problem of those power stations not receiving supplies is serious. They are likely to run out of coal during the winter and make some power cuts necessary over periods of high electricity demand. Coal stocks now 14 800 000 tonnes.

5 November   First large return to work; NUM funds frozen in Dublin bank. First road-borne coal deliveries to Didcot Power Station.

12 November	Pit gate battles intensify as the return to work continues. Improvements in road-borne coal deliveries and oil burn at power stations continue.
25 November	Highest oil burn to date at 534 000 tonnes a week. Coal stocks reducing with higher electricity demand; now at 14 500 000 tonnes.
30 November	A South Wales taxi driver killed when concrete is thrown from a bridge on to his taxi when carrying a miner to work. Receiver appointed to assume financial control of NUM funds.
3 December	NUM delegate conference votes to continue defiance of courts but against resisting the Receiver.
7 December	New Receiver appointed to replace the original appointee.
11 December	Nottinghamshire miners vote heavily in favour of a constitution to give area rules precedence over national NUM rules.
14 December	The TUC liaison group meets Peter Walker who confirms that it is necessary for the NUM to accept the closure of uneconomic collieries.
16 December	CEGB operational strategy is now well established and the prospects are brighter for maintaining electricity supplies through the winter. The position of the have-not power stations is improving. Coal stocks now 14 300 000 tonnes.
26 December	CEGB position has improved sufficiently for Peter Walker to announce that electricity supplies will be maintained throughout 1985.

1985

6 January	Vessels with NUS crews are now being used to take coal from Maryport to Brighton Power Station. Coal stock at power stations now 13 300 000 tonnes.
7 January	The drift back to work continues with 1200 'new faces' in one day.
13 January	New peak coal production of 640 000 tonnes.
16 and 17 January	During a spell of cold weather record levels of electricity demand met in full. Announcement of this achievement receives wide coverage in the media.
17 January	Rail unions stage one-day strike in protest against British Rail harassment of railwaymen blocking coal.
20 January	Record oil burn of 561 000 tonnes achieved. Coal supplies and their use at Didcot Power Station now fully accepted; it is no longer a have-not station. Coal stock now 12 500 000 tonnes.

27 January	Oil deliveries are becoming uncertain because HM Customs and Excise decides to apply EEC import duty regulations to some cargoes thought to be exempt. Coal stocks now 12 200 000 tonnes.
29 January	An attempt at reopening peace talks fails.
30 January	Receiver recovers NUM funds from Luxembourg.
31 January	Norman Willis, General Secretary, TUC seeks to gain resumption of peace talks.
1 February	Idea of return to work without agreement emerges as settlement seems further away.
4 February	Return to work by 2318 miners.
12 – 17 February	Norman Willis shuttles between the two sides in an attempt to get talks going. There is no common ground and the attempt fails.
17 February	Road-borne coal supplies established into Aberthaw power station in South Wales. Coal stock now 11 400 00 tonnes.
24 February	Coal supplies by sea now set up into Thames-side power stations.
25 February	Strike abandoned by 3807 miners.
27 February	NCB claims over 50 per cent working.
3 March	NUM special delegate conference votes to end strike and to return to work from 5 March. Rail unions maintain their support to the end; they lift their ban on coal flow at midnight on 4 March.
5 March	Return to work except for some small groups whose return was delayed for a few days. Coal stocks 11 100 000 tonnes.
	The strike ends.

The CEGB organisation 1984–5

The CEGB organisation at March 1984 is shown in Figure AIII.1, page 302. Those holding appointments at the end of March 1984 are shown in Table AIII.1, page 303. The members of the Board were appointed by the Secretary of State for Energy. The full-time members met weekly as the Executive and shared corporate responsibility for policy and general business control. The full Board met monthly. The Executive members held individual responsibility on behalf of their colleagues for particular parts of the business. The roles relative to the miners' strike were: Mr Bonner had responsibility for finance and the Bulk Supply Tariff; Mr Blackman had responsibility for the operation of the power stations and supply system and the development of industrial relations polices; Mr Baker had responsibility for commercial links with the National Coal Board and for public affairs.

The Board's assets were generally managed by the regions, each headed by a Director General. During the year of the strike, the organisation was being changed and Regional Directors General were being replaced by Executive Directors, who were generally the Region's Director of Production with increased delegations of authority. A typical regional organisation is shown in Figure AIII.2. It has senior representation for the specialist service functions, which were managed at Headquarters by a Board Chief Officer.

The Divisions managed three important areas of development concerned with power station construction, transmission construction and technology with research. They were general management units, each with their own supporting services.

The Board chief Officers were responsible for advising the Executive and the Board, for developing policy and for co-ordinating the general management units on matters relating to their specialist areas.

The organisation of the Operations Department that played the main co-ordinating role through the miners' strike is shown in Figure AIII.3.

Central Electricity Generating Board

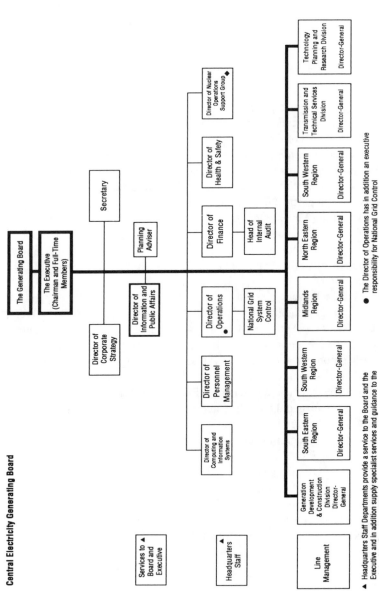

Figure AIII.1 The CEGB organisation at March 1984

Source: CEGB

Table AIII.1 CEGB March 1984

Central Electricity Generating Board at
31 March 1984

Full-time members

Chairman	Sir Walter Marshall CBE FRS
Deputy Chairman	FE Bonner CBE
	John Baker
	GAW Blackman CBE

Part-time Members	AG Derbyshire
	RV Giordano
	E Sharp CBE

Secretary	GH Hadley

Principal Officers at 31 March 1984

Adviser to the Executive	FCW Colmer OBE
Director of Computing and Information Systems	JJ Williamson
Director of Corporate Strategy	DA Davis
Director of Finance	James Smith
Director of Health and Safety	RR Matthews
Director of Information and Public Affairs	PN Vey
Director of Nuclear Operations Support Group	Dr B Edmondson
Director of Operations	F Ledger
Director of Personnel Management	JD Harrison

Regions

Director-General: South Eastern Region	GN Stone
Director-General: South Western Region	A vacancy at that time
Director-General: Midlands Region	J Porteous
Director-General: North Eastern Region	RJ Weeks
Director-General: North Western Region	JR Craig

Divisions

Director-General: Generation Development and Construction Division	JG Collier
Director-General: Transmission and Technical Services Division	Dr Peter R Howard
Director-General: Technology Planning and Research Division	Dr T Broom OBE

Director General (later Executive Director)

Personnel Manager	Scientific Services Controller	Director of Engineering	Director of Production	Director of Resource Planning	Financial Controller	Secretary
Industrial Relations	Chemistry	Workshops	Power Stations	System Operation	Revenue	Public Relations
Education & Training	Engineering	Projects	Production Services	Computing	Salaries	Estates & Wayleaves
Personnel Services	Materials	Engineering Services	Fuel Supplies	Management Services	Cash & Banking	Legal
Medical			Transmission	Planning	Capital	Security
						Purchasing

Figure AIII.2 Typical CEGB regional organisation 1984–5

Source: CEGB

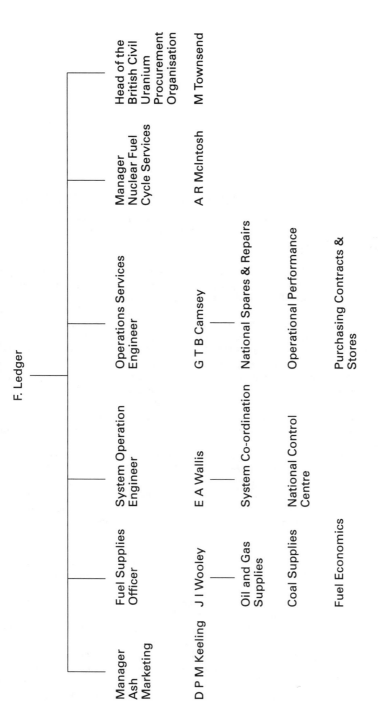

Director of Operations

F. Ledger

| Manager Ash Marketing | Fuel Supplies Officer | System Operation Engineer | Operations Services Engineer | Manager Nuclear Fuel Cycle Services | Head of the British Civil Uranium Procurement Organisation |

D P M Keeling   J I Wooley   E A Wallis   G T B Camsey   A R McIntosh   M Townsend

Oil and Gas Supplies

System Co-ordination

National Spares & Repairs

Coal Supplies

National Control Centre

Operational Performance

Fuel Economics

Purchasing Contracts & Stores

Figure AIII.3 CEGB Operations Department organisation

Source: CEGB

Notes

---

1 BRITAIN'S MOST VULNERABLE INDUSTRY IN PERSPECTIVE

1   Appendix I is derived from much fuller accounts of the industry's technological, organisational and industrial relations developments, the brief account in this chapter being in turn derived from the appendix. The fuller accounts are available at cost from the authors.

The main sources of information used are: *Annual Reports of the Electricity Council and Central Electricity Generating Board;* research by R Cochrane, ex CEGB; Sir Ronald Edwards and R D V Roberts, *Status, Productivity and Pay: A Major Experiment* (London: Macmillan, 1971); Leslie Hannah, *Electricity before Nationalisation – A Study of the Development of the Electricity Supply Industry in Britain to 1948* (London: Macmillan, 1979); Leslie Hannah, *Engineers, Managers and Politicians* (London: Macmillan, 1982); John Lloyd, *Light and Liberty: The history of the EETPU* (London: Weidenfeld and Nicholson, 1990).

2   The Conspiracy and Protection of Property Act as extended to electricity supply gave the government powers to fine or imprison strikers in a serious civil emergency. The application of the Act to electricity supply was given permanent statutory form at the end of the year in Section 31 of the Electricity (Supply) Act 1919. In fact no prosecution has ever been instituted under this section against anyone associated with electricity supply.

3   The Emergency Powers Act 1920, as amended in 1964, in effect gave the government power to deal with threatened or actual action by individuals or groups which would seriously interfere with the supply and distribution of food, water, fuel or light etc. When a proclamation has been made the government may, for one month, but extendibly, make regulations to secure the essentials of life and give the appropriate Secretary of State the powers he needs. The regulations made expire after 7 days unless extended by Parliament.

4   At the time of nationalisation the unions covering the manual workers in the industry were the Electrical Trades Union, the Amalgamated Engineering Union, the Transport and General Workers' Union and the National Union of Enginemen, Firemen and Electrical Workers. All but the last remained parties to the NJIC Agreement (reconstituted on 1 April 1948) down to the early 1990s although three of the four had changed their names although not unrecognisably so. In November 1948 an agreement was reached with the National Federation of Building Trades Operators covering building and civil engineering workers of whom there were about 3500. It closely followed decisions in the NJIC. The Electrical Power Engineers' Association represented technical and scientific staff on the National Joint Board, reconstituted on 1 April 1948. On that date a National Joint Council for clerical and administrative staff was established. There were four unions the largest of which was the National

Association of Local government Officers, which in 1952 became the National and Local Government Officers' Association. A National Joint Managerial and Higher Executive Grades Committee was established in 1951 with representatives from a number of unions of which the EPEA and NALGO were the largest.

5 *Report of the Committee of Inquiry into the Electricity Supply Industry*, January 1956. Chairman, Sir Edwin Herbert.

6 *Report of a Court of Inquiry into a dispute between the parties represented on the National Joint Industrial Council for the Electricity Supply Industry*, (February 1971).

7 Monopolies and Mergers Commission report: *The Central Electricity Generating Board: A Report on the Operation by the Board of its System for the Generation and Supply of Electricity in Bulk*, 1981.

2 1926: ELECTRICITY SUPPLY AND THE GENERAL STRIKE

1 The summary in this first section was derived from a number of sources, particularly from: Eric Wigham, *Strikes and the Government 1893–1981*, 2nd edition (London: Macmillan, 1982).

2 Keith Jeffery and Peter Hennessy, *States of Emergency*, (London: Routledge and Kegan Paul, 1983) op cit p38.

3 Lord Citrine, *Men and Work*, (London: Hutchinson, 1964) op cit pp162–176.

4 The proceedings of the STC are available in CAB 27/260 at the Public Record Office, Kew and are extensively used here, but balanced by references from the other sources quoted.

5 Op cit p177.

6 G A Phillips, *The General Strike. The Politics of Industrial Conflict*, (London: Weidenfeld and Nicholson, 1976) pp153–154.

7 According to Phillips (op cit pp218–219) the Ministry of Labour estimated that, excluding the miners, 1 580 000 workers were affected by the stoppage, while the TUC's Strike Organisation Committee claimed that 2 000 000 had stopped work by 8 May. Phillips adds that the 4 national railway companies calculated that just over 540 000 staff failed to report for duty on 5–6 May and that another 20 000 probably refused to report on the Metropolitan and Underground railway. Excluded from the total figures were men in the engineering and shipbuilding industries who, on 9 May, were called on to join the strike on 12 May, its last day.

8 Op cit p184.

9 Op cit p195.

10 The basis of the ruling that the strike was illegal and not protected by the Trade Disputes Act was that no trade dispute could exist between the TUC and the government and the nation. This ruling was strongly disputed. The TUC insisted that their sole aim was to secure for the miners a decent standard of life.

11 Op cit p196.

12 Op cit p197.

13 MT 249, the report of an STC sub-committee that met to review strike experience.

14 Plus 44 power stations owned by railway companies, 24 by tramway authorities and 23 by non-statutory authorities.

15 This was stated in a note (MT 249) of a meeting, held long after the strike, of an STC sub-committee held to review the organisation of the strike.

16 *The Electrical Power Engineer*, (May 1926) p152.

17 John Lloyd, *Light and Liberty: The History of the EETPU*, (London: Weidenfeld and Nicholson, 1990) p174.

18 Citrine (op cit p175) recorded in his diary for 3 May: 'The ETU, it appeared, had sent out instructions that they were going to stop the power stations, as they could not discriminate between lighting and power. We sent Finlay with a letter from me to try to persuade them not to do this.'

19 Op cit p175.
20 Op cit pp218–219.
21 Christopher Farman, *The General Strike: May 1926*, (London: Rupert Hart-Davis, 1972) p119.
22 Leslie Hannah, *Electricity Before Nationalisation*, (London: Macmillan, 1979) p272.
23 Undertakings where, according to the *Electrical Review*, staff remained at work included the Yorkshire and the Mersey power companies and, in the local authorities, Birmingham, Sheffield, Swansea and Manchester. There were other undertakings like Newcastle where in some stations men ceased to work. In Poplar, St Marylebone, Bristol and other places volunteers helped the technical staff. In Hammersmith, Hackney and Islington (and certainly elsewhere) naval ratings replaced striking stokers. In the North Met. Company men ceased work at different times at Brimsdown, Willesden and Hertford Power Stations. The refusal of Fulham Council to agree to cut off 54 consumers led to men stopping work and the station closing down. St Pancras Power Station closed for a while and also Wimbledon Power Station.
    Lloyd (op cit p175–176) does not entirely agree. He states that Manchester did not come out because they were not called out, that the Birmingham men were not withdrawn until two days before the strike ended and that Wolverhampton and Coventry Power Station men came out.
24 This last figure, taken in conjunction with the total figure of 1194 civilian volunteers quoted earlier, means that 457 civilian volunteers were used in the provincial power stations. But the figures of 1194 and 737 are drawn from different sources.
25 Op cit p176.
26 Op cit p119.
27 This paragraph is based on Lloyd, op cit, especially p177.
28 In more detail the build-up of help for the London stations, as reported in the proceedings of the STC, was as follows. On 4 May protection was provided for 8 power stations, at which naval ratings or civil volunteers had been introduced and 150 naval ratings had been sent to 8 power stations and 150 civilian volunteers to 7. On the next day they were informed that 'the position at all of the 74 stations excepting 5 was satisfactory and that 270 naval ratings (33 per cent of the total available) had been sent to stations'. On 8 May a further 13 calls for naval ratings were met and an indication given that there were plenty more in reserve.
29 Op cit p177.
30 Judy Slinn, *Engineers in Power: 75 years of the EPEA*, (London: Lawrence and Wishart, 1984) p99.
31 The STC Sub-Committee, reviewing the strike (MT 249) said that 'had the EPEA's co-operation been withheld the task of maintaining the stations would have been rendered far more difficult and indeed almost impossible'.
32 *Report of the Electricity Commissioners 1 April 1926 to 31 March 1927*, p34.
33 Percentage increases in electricity sales on 1921 figures

Year ending 31 March	
1921	–
1922	(–5.5)
1923	11
1924	29.3
1925	43.5
1926	57.2
1927	61.9

Source: *Report of the Electricity Commissioners*, 1927

34 CAB 27/260.
35 The ETU entered the strike with around £25 000 in assets and cash. They had 15 000 on strike at some stage and between 10 May and 1 June they paid out £18 222 in strike pay alone. (John Lloyd, op cit p180).

3 1949: REDS UNDER THE BED?

1 *Marshall Plan*: A programme of American financial aid to Europe initiated in a speech by Gen. George Marshall in June 1947. US$17 000 000 000 was expended between 1948 and 1952.
2 *Personal Incomes, Costs and Prices* (February 1948).
3 Ben Pimlott, *Harold Wilson*, (London: Harper Collins, 1992) p146.
4 Eric Wigham, *Strikes and the Government 1893–1981*, 2nd edition (London: Macmillan, 1982). On p102 Wigham states that the number of strikes fell steadily from 2293 in 1945 to 1339 in 1950, while the number of working days lost fell from 2 835 000 to 1 389 000.
5 US Senator Joe McCarthy caused a sensation in 1950 by claiming to hold a list of about 200 Communists in the US State Department. He maintained a witch hunt for Communists, especially in Hollywood, until discredited in 1954.
6 Most of the background information on government policy on industrial emergencies used in this chapter was derived from Keith Jeffery and Peter Hennessy's *States of Emergency*. However, specific references to emergency action not attributable to these authors were derived from original sources at the Public Record Office, Kew. The specific quotation from 'Fuel and Power Sub-Committee Report', 31 December 1948, T221/22 is taken from Jeffery and Hennessy (op cit p196).
7 Lord Citrine, a talented, courageous and dedicated public servant, had been General Secretary of the TUC from 1926 to 1946. He then became a full-time member of the National Coal Board, but was soon made Chairman-designate of the British Electricity Authority to prepare for nationalisation of Electricity Supply.
8 *British Electricity Authority Annual Report 1949–50*. Although the Grid system had been established for some years, it was a 132 KV network of limited capacity. That means that, although mutual support was available between power stations in a grid control area, the system did not have the capacity to give much support between grid areas. Hence if there was a problem in the South East Grid Control Area the load shedding to deal with it would largely have to be within that control area. The Super-Grid, with higher capacity 275 KV and 400 KV circuits, was in being by the late 1960s by which time large volumes of electricity could be transmitted from one part of the country to another.
9 *The Economic Survey of 1948* (Cmnd 7344).
10 Demand increased by over 100 per cent in the 10 years to March 1949. One of the main reasons was the hugely increased purchase and use of electric fires in homes at a time when domestic coal was scarce.
11 *British Electricity Authority Annual Report 1949–50*.
12 However the unions' chief negotiator, the ETU's General President, Frank Foulkes, a Communist, was much respected as a man who kept his word and delivered agreements. John Lloyd, writing many years later about Frank Foulkes as he operated in 1949, referred to him as 'circumspect to the point of anonymity'. John Lloyd, *Light and Liberty: The History of the EETPU* (London: Weidenfeld and Nicholson, 1990) p316.
13 Lord Citrine, *Two Careers*, (London: Hutchinson, 1967) p284.
14 Jeffery and Hennessy, op cit p197.
15 *Review of British Docks Strikes 1949* (Cmnd 7851), 16 December 1949.
16 *The Times* (16 December 1949). © Times Newspaper Ltd, 1949.

17 *British Electricity Authority Annual Report 1949–50.*
18 *Emergencies Committee, 2 and 12 December 1949*, CAB 134/176.
19 E W Bussey had been General Secretary of the ETU from 1941 to 1948.
20 *The Times* (15 December 1949). © Times Newspaper Ltd, 1949.
21 CAB 128/16/72.
22 On Friday 16 December George Isaacs, Minister of Labour, made a statement in the House, quoted in *The Times* (17 December), explaining that the Central Authority's 'original statement had been made to remove any possible misunderstanding in view of last minute attempts by unofficial strike leaders to impose conditions for a resumption'. This was the basis of the statement posted in the stations. © Times Newspaper Ltd, 1949.
23 Prem. 8/1290.
24 Also Prem. 8/1290.
25 Meeting of Ministers, 24 January 1950, CAB 130/58 Gen. 314/1.
26 Prem. 8/1275.
27 Jeffery and Hennessy, op cit pp217–218.
28 Cabinet meeting 16 August 1950, CAB 128/18.
29 POWE 10/462.
30 The fight against the Communist leadership of the ETU was led by Les Cannon and Frank Chapple in the late 1950s and early 1960s. Frank Foulkes had been General President from 1945 to 1962 and Chairman of the Trade Union side of the NJIC from 1948. Les Cannon was General President from 1963 until his untimely death in 1970. He had been Chairman of the Trade Union side of the NJIC. Frank Chapple, General Secretary from 1966 to his retirement in 1984, was also General President, from 1972 to 1974. He succeeded Cannon as Chairman of the Trade Union side of the NJIC.
31 Unless this is read in the context of the local application of the NJIC agreement on pay and conditions it would appear to be unfair to Citrine and his colleagues. They were pioneers in developing industry-wide and local joint consultation and continuous encouragement was given to power station managers to give an effective lead on this. But matters for joint consultation were kept separate from those relating to negotiated agreements on pay and conditions.

4 WORKING TO WHOSE RULES?

This chapter draws on: *Annual Reports of the Electricity Council and the Electricity Boards;* Sir Ronald Edwards and R D V Roberts, *Status, Productivity and Pay – A Major Experiment*, (London: Macmillan, 1971); Eric Wigham, *Strikes and the Government 1893–1981*, 2nd edition (London: Macmillan, 1982); press references; CEGB archive material and the direct experience of the authors.

1   In the 1970–1 financial year CEGB sold 184.45 TWH, an increase of 3.7 per cent over 1969–70. It had a total revenue of £1086 million (up 13.9 per cent) but made a loss of £14 million after paying interest. It owned 187 power stations with a maximum output capacity of 49 281 MW (but see note 9 below for 9 December 1970). New plant brought into operation was 3535 MW including eleven 500 MW units. The maximum load met on the system was 38 619 MW (5 January 1971). The Board consumed 68 500 000 tons (metric measurement was not introduced by CEGB until 1 April 1974) of coal, 19 700 000 tons of coal equivalent in oil and 7 000 000 tons of coal equivalent at nuclear power stations. Thermal efficiency was 28.12 per cent. In March 1971 the number of employees was 70 285, including 45 142 industrial staff, 5.2 per cent less of the latter than in the year before.
2   The number of wholly unemployed, excluding school leavers, was just over 550 000. The balance of payments on current account was just about on the credit side. The GDP had increased by about 2 per cent since June 1969.

3 *Royal Commission on Trade Unions and Employers' Associations 1965–8, Report June 1968. Chairman Lord Donovan.*

4 This analysis is succinctly summarised in Wigham, op cit p145, to the effect that the Commission rejected most proposals for legislative restrictions on trade unions and strikes. The main theme was that Britain had two systems of industrial relations, one the formal system embodied in official institutions and the other the informal system created by the actual behaviour of trade unions and employers' associations, the managers, the shop stewards and workers. The central defect in British industrial relations was the resultant disorder in factory and workshop relations and pay structures. The remedy was for factory-wide (or company) collective agreements to regulate pay systems, grievance, redundancy and disciplinary procedures and the rights of shop stewards. Only company boards of directors had the power to bring this about. Industry-wide agreements should be limited to those matters they could effectively regulate, but they could set out guidelines for factory and company agreements.

5 The electricity supply industry's sponsoring ministry to October 1970 was Technology, which was reorganised into Trade and Industry in that month. John Davies was the Secretary of State, being succeeded in November 1972 by Peter Walker.

6 Arthur Scargill, 'The New Unionism', *New Left Review*, (June 1975).

7 In the 12 months to 31 December 1970 the GDP had gone up by 2 per cent, the balance of payments on current account was £579 million in credit and the level of unemployment (GB, seasonally adjusted) was nearly 600 000 (2.6 per cent of the insured population).

8 Average weekly earnings of adult male manual workers in the industry at that time were £24 5s 6d, although they would have been higher in the Generating Board because they worked more unsocial hours than were found in the industry as a whole.

9 A typical daily plant situation during the emergency (for Wednesday 9 December) for the whole of the Generating Board was as follows: maximum output capacity 47 468 MW; net capacity readily usable 26 707 MW (56 per cent); loss of capacity (all causes) 20 747 MW; loss due to industrial action 8225 MW; loss of capacity due to sickness etc 240 MW; loss of capacity due to fuel difficulties 423 MW; loss of capacity due to other reasons, including overhauls, breakdowns etc 11 859 MW. This high unavailability was typical of the CEGB at this time when a large capacity of prototype generating units was being commissioned and experiencing the first years in service. The position improved later.

10 *Report of a Court of Inquiry into a dispute between the parties represented on the National Joint Industrial Council for the Electricity Supply Industry* (February 1971). The members of the Court were Lord Wilberforce, a High Court Judge (Chairman), Sir Raymond Brookes, Chairman and Chief Executive of Guest, Keen and Nettlefold and J E Mortimer, a member of the NBPI.

11 Op cit p425.

12 Decimal currency was introduced from 15 February 1971.

13 Op cit p441.

5 1971–2: THE EDGE OF DARKNESS

This chapter draws mainly on *Annual Reports of the Electricity Council and the Electricity Boards;* Richard Clutterbuck, *Britain in Agony. The Growth of Political Violence* (London: Faber and Faber, 1978); Joe Gormley, *Battered Cherub* (London: Hamish Hamilton, 1982); Douglas Hurd, *An End to Promises*, (London: Collins, 1979); Keith Jeffery and Peter Hennessy, *States of Emergency* (London: Routledge and Kegan Paul,

1983); Eric Wigham, *Strikes and the Government 1893–1981*, 2nd edition (London: Macmillan, 1982); press references; CEGB archive material, and personal experience.

1 Douglas Hurd, op cit p102.
2 Eric Wigham, op cit p158.
3 Joe Gormley, op cit p86.
4 *Keesing's Contemporary Archives.*
5 Joe Gormley, op cit p96.
6 Arthur Scargill interview in *New Left Review* (1975).
7 These priority categories, set out by the Department of Trade and Industry, were: (a) households dependent solely on solid fuel for cooking; (b) households in certain health risk categories normally relying on solid fuel for space and/or water heating and where no alternative was available; (c) health and social service establishments relying on solid fuel (e.g. hospitals) and essential public services (e.g. sewage works) still dependent on solid fuel.
8 Hurd, op cit p102.
9 Under the Trade Disputes Act of 1906, which remained at the time the relevant law, it was lawful for anyone or any group of people in contemplation or furtherance of a trade dispute to attend at or near a works or a house to give or receive information or to receive or peacefully persuade someone not to work. They were also protected collectively if they did nothing which would be actionable if they did it individually. If they trespassed that was a civil wrong. If they used violence or intimidation that was a crime.
10 This contrasts with the position in the 1984–5 miners' strike.
11 Hurd, op cit p103.
12 This short account is based on Clutterbuck, op cit pp65–93.
13 Article by Arthur Osman. © Times Newspapers Ltd, 1972.
14 The other members of the Court were John Garnett, Director of the Industrial Society and Professor Lawrence Hunter of Glasgow University.
15 *Keesing's Contemporary Archives.*
16 The total effect of the various measures taken to reduce coal consumption in the period 11 February to 1 March was to save 3.08 TWH of energy (22.9 per cent) and to save 1 370 000 tons of coal (37.8 per cent).
17 The Board was deeply aware that if such a system collapse occurred it would have a calamitous effect on food and water supplies and the operation of sewage systems. Even if coal supplies were then restored it would take a week or more to get back to normal.
18 The time switches had gone haywire with the stopping and starting of supplies and many were on all day, giving the public entirely the wrong impression.
19 The problem for National Control was to learn how to instruct load shedding at normal frequency. They were used to doing it with a falling frequency when there was a plant shortage. It took a few days to get it right.
20 Gormley (op cit pp115–117), states that by midnight he and his colleagues had won agreement on no less than twenty items, which included a complex concession on what was referred to as a bonus shift, an extra week's holiday and the payment of the adult rate to everyone over eighteen, phased in over five years (other commentators say three). On the other hand the two sides agreed to negotiate a productivity payment scheme by September 1972. Gormley alleged (op cit p114) that he could have swung his executive to accept the Wilberforce terms without the extra but he decided to teach the government and the Coal Board 'that they'll have to start heeding advice in future'.
21 The percentage increases on basic weekly rates were 27.8 per cent on the surface minimum and 31.6 per cent on the underground minimum and would represent 15 per cent on the national power loading agreement rate.

22 The vote was 210 039 for acceptance and 7581 against.
23 Gormley (op cit p113) makes it clear that he and his Executive were fully aware of the gravity of the power situation. John Davies's TV statement on 17 February reinforced Gormley, the following day, in his belief that 'somehow, an agreement had to be worked out that day'.
24 This information on the Prime Minister's attitude, the review of the civil planning machine and the revised machine is taken from Jeffery and Hennessy, op cit p237.
25 *Annual Reports of the Electricity Council and the Electricity Boards 1971–2.*

6 1973–4: HEATH AND THE MINERS

Main sources used in the preparation of this chapter were: William Ashworth, *1946–1982: The Nationalised Industry, The History of the British Coal Industry*, vol 5: 1946–1982 (London: Oxford University Press, 1986); Richard Clutterbuck, *Britain in Agony. the Growth of Political Violence* (London: Faber and Faber, 1978); *Electricity Council, CEGB and Area Electricity Board Annual Reports*; Stephen Fay and Hugo Young, 'The Fall of Heath' *Sunday Times Weekly Review*, (22, 29 February and 7 March 1976); *Joe Gormley, Battered Cherub* (London: Hamish Hamilton, 1982); Eric Wigham, *Strikes and the Government 1893–1981*, 2nd edition (London: Macmillan, 1982); Douglas Hurd, *An End to Promises* (London: Collins, 1979); Arthur Scargill, 'The New Unionism', *New Left Review* (June 1975); Keith Jeffery and Peter Hennessy, *States of Emergency* (London: Routledge and Kegan Paul, 1983); The Times newspaper; CEGB archive material and the authors' own diaries and recollection of events in which they were involved.

1 Op cit pp98–99.
2 Op cit pp114–115.
3 Gormley, op cit pp124–5.
4 © Times Newspaper Ltd, 1976.
5 A number of commentators have expressed surprise that the NCB should have made its maximum offer straight away, pointing out that union leaders never expect the first offer to be the last and that they have to be seen by their members to be doing a tough negotiating job. William Ashworth (op cit), on the other hand, implied that this was the inevitable product of the government's very early intervention in the dispute and its consequent increasingly political character. Joe Gormley, although he appreciated that the government had taken the hint over an unsocial hours provision in the White Paper, was annoyed because it was to apply to everyone. By this policy, he said (op cit p127) the government 'had effectively blocked a loophole by which our own position, relative to the rest of industry, could have been restored'.
6 We stated in Chapter 5, referring to Jeffery and Hennessy, that the government's principal formal weapon for dealing with the 1973–4 crisis was the Civil Contingency Unit (CCU). However Jeffery and Hennessy added (op cit p239) that the Unit's efforts had realistically to be directed at mitigating the consequences of directly applied union strength rather than by directly attempting to curb that power in a once-and-for-all manner. In this the government were helped by restrained picketing and a State of Emergency deployed in plenty of time. A senior civil servant involved in the CCU's work at this time expresses the view that it was found not to work fast enough to deal with day-to-day events and that individual departments, such as DTI, deeply involved in the dispute, needed their own set-up to deal effectively with day-to-day issues.
7 Gormley, op cit p131.
8 The concept of 'the critical coal stock level' needs to be explained. The CEGB had a conceptual model, which saw a particular level of megawatt output only being capable of being met down to a particular level of coal stock. That came from a belief that when a power station was reclaiming all its coal from stock it could only meet the

requirements of burn while its stock was over a particular size. If the stock fell below this critical level, the reclaim rate fell and the station had to reduce load. In the 1971–2 strike this level was believed to be about 4 000 000 tonnes. In the 1973–4 strike the figure was 6 000 000 tonnes. The higher figure came from the maldistribution of coal from the prolonged period of emergency that had preceded the NUM strike.

9 Policy-making on energy matters remained at the Department of Trade and Industry, where Peter Walker was Secretary of State, until early January 1974 when the Department of Energy was established with Lord Carrington as Secretary of State and Patrick Jenkin as the Minister.

Philip Jones had been Under-Secretary in charge of the Electricity Division at the DTI. He moved in that capacity to the new Department of Energy and later became Deputy Secretary. In 1983 he was appointed Chairman of the Electricity Council and was knighted in 1986. Sir Philip Jones CB remained Chairman until 1989.

As head of the Electricity Division Philip Jones advised ministers on the creation of and renewal of states of emergency, emergency orders, the three-day week etc. Dr Trevor Broom, as Director of Operations in CEGB, advised the CEGB Board on operational matters, co-ordinated the operational work of the five regions and made decisions on system and fuel supplies issues. Dr Broom advised Philip Jones on CEGB endurance and the need for reductions in energy consumption to extend endurance.

Harry Shepherd was responsible for advising Philip Jones on distribution issues and the curtailment of classes of consumers' energy use necessary to achieve government and CEGB requirements.

10 Orders issued under the emergency powers are far too detailed to be specified here. The order controlling electricity consumption to apply from 17 December covered heating, lighting, advertising and display.

11 In early January the NUM had second thoughts, produced improved figures and got Roy Mason MP to talk to the Pay Board. They told him that a proposal could be submitted only by the employer and only after it had been signed by the two sides.

12 Another Order, which was to apply from 31 December, was even more extensive. It prohibited the use of electricity supplied by an electricity board, except under a licence granted by the Secretary of State, on any industrial or commercial premises as defined or for building or engineering operations, on any day other than the three days (either Monday to Wednesday or Thursday to Saturday) specified. The days applicable to any particular premises depended on the situation of those premises within areas designated within each electricity board. The Order defined a 'day' for industrial premises and set out rules relating to the use of electricity in shops.

13 The electricity employers and the EPEA had agreed, through the NJB in November 1972, payments for stand-by and call-out but these had been frozen under the pay policy. The Pay Board had now however agreed that the payments could be backdated to 1 April 1973, the beginning of Phase Two.

14 Maurice Corina © Times Newspaper Ltd, 1974.

15 Article by Paul Routledge © Times Newspaper Ltd, 1974.

16 Gormley states (op cit p141) that he wanted to put off the strike in view of the announcement of the General Election, but the arguments which prevailed within the union were that: (i) the strike was not politically motivated; (ii) there had been an overwhelming demand for it; and (iii) to call it off would weaken the union's bargaining position.

17 Op cit p129.

18 'Firm Action for a Fair Britain', the *Conservative Party Manifesto* (1974).

19 Op cit p336 © National Coal Board 1986 by permission of the Oxford University Press. Gormley (op cit p144) expressed the view that the Prime Minister did not need to call an election. 'He had a perfectly good working majority. But he had got himself

into a fixed position from which he felt he couldn't move, and I believe that, as on the first occasion, it was due as much as anything else to his acceptance of bad advice from his Ministers.'

20 Op cit p23.

21 Op cit.

22 Op cit p143.

23 Op cit p338 © National Coal Board 1986 by permission of the Oxford University Press.

24 See note 8 of chapter 12.

7 1977: NO WORK, NO PAY

This chapter draws mainly on: *Annual Reports of the Electricity Council and the electricity boards*; CEGB archive material and the direct experience of the authors; Richard Clutterbuck, *Britain in Agony. The Growth of Political Violence*, (London: Faber and Faber, 1978); *Keesing's Contemporary Archives*; various government statistical publications; press references; Eric Wigham, *Strikes and the Government 1893–1981* (London: Macmillan, 1982);

1 The result of the 10 October 1974 General Election had been: Conservative seats 277; Liberal 13; Labour 319; and Others 26.

2 The Trade Union and Labour Relations Act 1974 put the law back in general to where it was before. The Act also abolished the Industrial Relations Court, the Commission on Industrial Relations and the Registry of Trade Unions and Employers' Associations. It extended existing statutory provisions relating to unfair dismissals and the Code of Industrial Relations Practice.

3 In 1974, compared with 1973, weekly wage rates were up 28.5 per cent, the balance of payments on current account had a deficit of £3380 million and 'growth' in the GDP was minus 1.5 per cent. The number of days lost in strikes was 14 740 000 (mostly in the February 1974 miners' strike). Unemployment, seasonally adjusted (GB), was up from less than 500 000 to 585 000. The RPI rose by 21.2 per cent in the 12 months to March 1975.

4 The guidelines also provided that priority should be given to agreements that should benefit unit costs, reform pay structures, improve job security and maintain a specified minimum rate. Continuing aims should be social improvement of various kinds. Full use should be made of ACAS.

5 The weekly earnings figure is taken from the Department of Employment's New Earnings Survey covering adult male manual workers in an April 1975 payweek.

6 'Growth' in GDP in 1975 was minus 0.8 per cent. The balance of payments deficit on current account was down to minus £1617 million. The RPI was up by 23.4 per cent and the average weekly earnings of adult male manual workers were up (April 1975 over April 1974) by 27.7 per cent. The unemployment figure was 936 000 and the number of days lost in strikes was 6 012 000.

7 Richard Clutterbuck, op cit pp191–210. The clerical workers' union APEX had a protracted dispute over union recognition at the Grunwick film processing laboratories at Willesden, North London, with a number of employees taking strike action. It came to a head on 11 July when 18 000 trade unionists demonstrated outside the factory. Thirty people were hurt and seventy arrested. A public inquiry under Lord Justice Scarman, in a report published in August, blamed both sides and recommended that the company should re-employ the strikers, which it refused to do.

8 This average earnings comparison is taken from the Department of Employment's half-yearly return, based at that time on a 100 per cent return of the earnings of adult male manual workers in all industries and services. Other earnings figures quoted are from other official sources.

9   Taking the calendar year 1977 the GDP was up by 2.6 per cent, the balance of payments on current account was only £225 million in deficit, and the RPI was at last moving into single figures. However, seasonally adjusted unemployment (GB) was well over 1 300 000 (5.9 per cent of the working population). Days lost through industrial disputes were 9 500 000.

10 The figures for all industries and CEGB are derived from the Department of Employment's half-yearly survey published in the Gazette and relate to an October pay week. The figure for coal was provided by NCB, but the breakdown for surface, underground and face workers was not readily available.

11 The work-to-rule took much the same form as in December 1970 and described in Chapter 4. Practices varied from one power station and transmission unit to another but mostly employees would no longer accept temporary transfers or temporary up- or down-grading and refused to drive vans unless they were officially designated transport drivers. They also refused to do work that was part of the flexible working arrangements. The ban on overtime meant not only that men would not work outside rostered hours but would refuse to stand by at home or undertake call-out duties and depart from strict shift rotas.

12 The full text of the letter was: 'Those staff taking unofficial industrial action are not complying with the NJIC agreement which is incorporated in their individual contracts of employment and are working to rules of their own making. They are therefore in breach of contract and will not be paid until they resume normal working.'

13 On 1 November the NUM membership voted by 110 634 to 87 901 against local wage incentives being allowed in the pits. The schemes provided for rises of £23.50 a week for face workers who completed an agreed weekly output target. It had been hoped that acceptance of these local wage incentives would head off a direct conflict with the government, but immediately the NUM put in a pay claim for £135 a week at the coal face, £114 elsewhere underground and £92 on the surface. Current rates were £70.35, £56.70 and £49.50; the claim was far beyond the current 10 per cent guideline.

14 In Tony Benn's *Diaries 1977–80* (London: Hutchinson, 1991) he gives his own account in his entry for 8 November. On pp243–244 he says:

> Jim [The Prime Minister] took me aside before the meeting [of the Cabinet Committee on Economic Strategy]. 'I hear you're saying this is not a problem for the government. You're not suggesting the power workers be paid?' 'Well, it wouldn't present a problem for the government,' I said. 'But this is unofficial action.' 'Jim, are you after winning the pay policy or grinding every shop steward's face into the mud? You must leave me with some discretion on how I handle this matter. I'm trying to improve the government's position.'

On p244 Benn referred to the telephone call from John Lyons: 'Lyons said that, if such payments were made, his members would withdraw their support. I must say that his influence throughout this dispute has been entirely unhelpful and negative.'

15 For readers wanting more technical detail, during the dispute demand was curtailed as necessary by two stages of voltage reductions of 3 per cent giving in general a joint demand relief of 6 per cent while each stage of load disconnection gave about 5 per cent of demand relief. Supplies frequency was kept within the statutory limits of 49.5 and 50.5Hz and the system demand was regulated to match the available generation. The supergrid system once again showed its ability to accommodate wide variations in power flow patterns (e.g. a power export of 1500 MW from the North Eastern region became a power import of that magnitude).

16 Henthorn and Taylor were members of the industrial staff at Fiddlers Ferry Power Station. They started actions against the CEGB in the County Court for the pay which they claimed they were entitled to receive. The Judge ruled that the defendants had not

discharged the burden of proof of showing that the plaintiffs were not ready and willing to perform their contracts of employment. The Board applied to have the award set aside and in July 1980 the Court of Appeal held that when the plaintiff claims that he is entitled to be paid money under a contract which he alleges the defendant has broken he must prove that he was ready and willing to perform the contract. It was for the plaintiffs to prove their case. The award of the County Court was set aside and remitted to the appropriate County Court for a new hearing by a different judge. The issue was not pursued further in the County Court.

8 CONFLICT IN CONTEXT

The main sources of the information used in this chapter were as follows, together with the direct experience of the authors: *Department of Employment Gazette*; *Electricity Council and Central Electricity Generating Board Annual Reports and Accounts*; *Economic Trends*; Christopher Johnson, *The Economy under Mrs Thatcher 1979–1990* (London: Penguin Books, 1991); *Keesing's Contemporary Archives*; John MacInnes, *Thatcherism at Work* (London: Open University Press, 1989); Eric Suter, *Legislation for Personnel Managers*, 3rd edition (London: IPM).

1 The 1978–9 winter of discontent was the title generally used to describe the great upsurge of strikes in that period, especially in the public sector.
2 The 1976 figure of days lost was 3 509 000. The 1977 figure was 10 378 000 and 1978 9 391 000.
3 Exceptional increases, to be made in two annual stages, resulted from independent awards for a number of public service groups (whose pay had previously been adjusted largely on comparability with outside pay) and from concessions to the lowest paid. A 'kitty' principle allowed groups to make their own arrangements within the overall limit.
4 Nicholas Ridley, *My Style of Government* (London: Fontana, 1991) p16.
5 *The Economist* (27 May 1978) pp21–22.
6 The action started on 22 January 1979 and involved stoppages, go–slows, work-to-rule, overtime bans and other restrictions. On 16 February the employers made a 9 per cent pay offer and promised a pay comparability study. On 21–22 February they made a further offer of £1 a week on account and this was accepted in early March.
7 On 14 February the unions representing workers in the water and sewage services accepted an 8.05 per cent pay increase with a 6–9 per cent 'self-financing' efficiency bonus.
8 To keep this figure for a 9-month period in perspective it may be compared with the annual average figure for 1970 to 1979 of 12 870 000.
9 The distribution of seats in the new House was: Conservatives 339, Labour 268, Liberals 11, others 16.
10 In more detail, the Chancellor of the Exchequer's spring 1979 Budget, while it cut income tax, increased VAT on many items to 15 per cent, adding 3.5 per cent to the RPI. In the 12 months to May 1980 the RPI increased by 22 per cent while the minimum lending rate increased from 12 per cent to 17 per cent and the sterling exchange rate by 30 per cent. John MacInnes (op cit p65) adds that the high RPI figure resulted from a combination of a rising underlying trend left by the Labour government, the boost from the switch to indirect taxation in the Conservative Budget and the cost of the Clegg Commission's comparability-based public sector pay awards.
11 Op cit p67.
12 The distribution of seats in the new House was: Conservatives 397, Labour 209, Liberal/Social Democratic Alliance 23, Others 21.
13 In more detail the GDP was up by 1.7 per cent in 1982 and by 3.7 per cent in 1983.

The decline in manufacturing was arrested in 1982 and a slow improvement occurred in 1983. At the end of 1982 the RPI was up by 8.6 per cent on the year and in 1983 by only 4.6 per cent. The balance of payments on current account, which had been reassuring in 1980 and 1981, remained healthy in the next two years (1980 £2927 million; 1981 £7272 million; 1982 £4934 million; 1983 £3164 million). On the other hand, according to MacInnes, op cit p67, between 1979–80 and 1982–3 the share of taxation in GDP rose from 39 per cent to 45 per cent, while the share of public expenditure in the GDP rose from 43.5 per cent to 47 per cent.

14 The grounds for objection ranged from conscience or other deeply held personal convictions to being a member of any union or a particular union.

15 There was a strongly supported Day of Action in May 1980, a march of some unemployed people from Liverpool to London in the same month, a huge demonstration in Liverpool in November and in April 1981 a TUC campaign week and, in Glasgow, a large rally.

16 The number of strikes in 1981 was 1383 and days lost in disputes totalled 4 244 000. In 1982 the corresponding figures were 1528 and 5 313 000.

17 In view of the importance of secret ballots during the miners' strike it should be explained that under the 1984 Act a union planning industrial action could only escape liability in tort for inducement to breach or interfere with a commercial contract or a contract of employment in relation to industrial or strike action by first having a secret ballot of those who would be involved with those taking part in the ballot having voted for such action by a majority.

18 Other figures are as follows: thermal efficiency increased from 31.83 per cent to 34.39 per cent; coal consumed increased by 2.3 per cent (from 75 500 000 tonnes to 77 210 000), although with the heavy fall in (costly) oil consumption, the total coal and coal equivalent consumed was down by about 8 per cent from 104 200 000 tonnes to 95 460 000. The number of staff fell from 61 709 to 50 250. The number of industrial staff fell from 35 783 to 28 397.

19 William Ashworth, '1946–1982: The Nationalised Industry', *The History of the British Coal Industry*, vol 5 (London: Oxford University Press, 1986) pp416–417.

9 PREPARATIONS FOR THE INEVITABLE?

1 The short description of the events in the NCB, NUM and government are summaries from the following three books: Martin Adeney and John Lloyd, *The Miners' Strike 1984–5, Loss Without Limit* (London: Routledge and Kegan Paul, 1985); Joe Gormley, *Battered Cherub*, (London: Hamish Hamilton, 1982); Peter Wilsher, Donald Macintyre and Michael Jones, *Strike – a Sunday Times Insight Book* (London: Hodder and Stoughton, 1985).

2 *The Times* (2 February 1981). 52 171 voted: 44 674 (85.6 per cent) in favour and 7497 against.

3 Op cit p176.

4 The first statement was reported in *The Times* of 11 February 1981. The second was reported in *The Times* of 13 February 1981 and referred to a speech made at a rally in Euston. Article by Paul Routledge © Times Newspapers Ltd, 1981.

5 Margaret Thatcher, *The Downing Street Years* (London: Harper and Collins, 1993) and © Nigel Lawson, 1993. Extract from p. 140 of *The View from No. 11*. Published by Bantam Books, all rights reserved. Permission for the world rights, except UK and Commonwealth, given by Peters, Fraser and Dunlop.

6 Contingency planning in electricity supply generally covered two aspects. One was the limitation of the effect of some emergency situation by diversity of supply, additional stocks or some other arrangements. The other was to be able to deal with

the failure to meet consumer electricity demand in full. The latter, described in earlier chapters, was co-ordinated by the Electricity Council and implemented by the area boards and involved sophisticated rota disconnection plans. These arrangements were generally coupled with government emergency measures involving declaring a state of emergency.
7   This preceded an EEC directive that required thirty days' fuel stocks and therefore CEGB policy did not have to be altered.
8   Op cit p341.

10 OVERTIME BAN

1   The two ballots were in November 1982 and March 1983. In November 1982 the membership rejected by 125 233 votes to 81 592 the executive's recommendation to take industrial action if necessary. In effect this was a vote in favour of accepting the NCB pay offer.
     In March, following strikes in South Wales and sympathetic action in other coalfields on the issue of pit closures, a national ballot rejected by 118 954 votes to 76 540 an executive recommendation for industrial action against closure or partial closure of any pit, plant or unit, other than on grounds of exhaustion (*Keesing's Contemporary Archives*).
2   The MMC inquiry started in March 1982. It had studied a number of the NCB's functions relating to the development, production and supply of coal. The Commission found that surplus production from high cost, low productivity pits was a crucial problem preventing the coal industry becoming viable. They made a number of recommendations including one proposing that areas should be made into business units.
3   Roy Ottey, *The Strike – An Insider's Story* (London: Sidgwick and Jackson, 1985) p53. Roy Ottey was General Secretary of the Power Group of the NUM and a member of the National Executive Committee in 1984.
4   *Keesing's Contemporary Archives*.
5   Roy Ottey, op cit p53.
6   The CEGB's coal imports were first delivered in bulk carriers of 100 000 tonnes to continental ports and stocked there. The imports to UK power stations were by much smaller ships, typically 10 000 tonnes, which could be accommodated at the power station jetties. Because of the government constraints on imports and the fact that import coal purchase contracts had not yet run down, there were about 3 000 000 tonnes of coal in stock on the continent. It was a relatively simple action to arrange for some of this to be shipped to the Thames.
7   Peter Wilsher, Donald Macintyre and Michael Jones, *Strike – a Sunday Times Insight Book* (London: Hodder and Stoughton, 1985) p36.
8   'Energy Trends', *Department of Energy Statistical Bulletin*, (April 1984).
9   Peter Heathfield was elected by 74 186 votes to 70 571 for John Walsh (*Keesing's Contemporary Archives*).
10   Ian MacGregor, *The Enemies Within* (London: Collins, 1986) pp146–170.
11   According to David Prendergast, Vice President, Union of Democratic Mineworkers (now, 1994) who, during the strike, was an NUM Area official in Nottinghamshire.
12   This account is from James Cowan and from Ian MacGregor (op cit pp146–170).

11 STRIKE

1   *Keesing's Contemporary Archives*.
2   MacGregor, pp167 and 168.
3   *Keesing's Contemporary Archives*.

4 There were 7285 votes in favour and 20 188 against a strike, that is a 73.5 per cent 'no' vote. No pit had a majority in favour.
5 Adeney and Lloyd, op cit p98.
6 *The Times* (12 March 1984).
7 This statement is about all power station coal stocks. It includes the power stations of the South of Scotland Electricity Board and those associated with other industries such as coal, steel and chemicals.
8 Op cit p350.
9 *The Times*, (17 April 1984).
10 During the strike Roy Lynk was an NUM area official in Nottinghamshire. He became National General Secretary of the Union of Democratic Mineworkers when it was formed in December 1985.
11 Alan Griffin, *County Under Siege* (London: Moorland, 1985) p7.
12 Jim Porteous left to become Chairman of Yorkshire Electricity Board at the end of October 1984. The post of Executive Director was created as an intermediate step to the new functional organisation that the CEGB were then setting up.

12 FACING UP TO THE LONG HAUL

1 Grain and Littlebrook Power Stations were oil-fired. Kingsnorth was designed with a capability of burning 100 per cent oil or coal or a mixture of the two. It was described as a dual-fired power station. Tilbury and West Thurrock were coal-fired power stations but the latter had been converted to burn natural gas and did that for a number of years before reverting to coal on gas becoming very expensive.
2 *Keesing's Contemporary Archives.*
3 *The Times*, 30 April 1984.
4 *The Times*, 7 May 1984.
5 *The Times*, 8 May 1984 and *The Times*, 12 May 1984.
6 *The Times*, 14 May 1984.
7 This account is based on information from: Adeney and Lloyd, op cit pp187–188; Wilsher, Macintyre and Jones, op cit pp127–128; MacGregor, op cit pp238–239; Ottey, op cit pp120–121.
8 There had been a series of documents with the title Plan for Coal over the nationalised life of the coal industry: the first one in 1950 and the fourth one, referred to frequently during the strike, in 1974. This was a plan which the Labour government, following the 1974 election, produced as a tripartite agreement between NUM, NCB and the Department of Energy. The main content relevant to the 1984–5 dispute was the high level of coal production and sales that it envisaged.
9 Cold welding is a technique that enabled satisfactory repair welds to be made without the normal preheating of the material to be welded or without heating after welding to relieve stresses. It is a simpler and quicker process than that normally used.
10 Wilsher, Macintyre and Jones, op cit pp130–131 and 188–189; MacGregor, op cit pp242–243 and 246–247.
11 *Keesing's Contemporary Archives.*
12 A 'registered' port was one defined within the National Dock Labour Scheme as one that was manned exclusively by registered dockworkers, who worked under agreed conditions of employment. The registered ports were generally the traditional ones and did not include the new ports such as Felixstowe.
13 Wilsher, Macintyre and Jones, op cit pp135–136; MacGregor, op cit pp248–250.
14 *Keesing's Contemporary Archives.*
15 Thatcher, op cit pp358–359.
16 Account from Lord Marshall.

13 CAN WE GET THROUGH THE WINTER?

1 The Electricity Supply Trade Union Council (ESTUC) covered all the trade unions recognised within the industry. It acquired this title in the first half of 1984 having previously been called the Employees' National Committee.
2 *Keesing's Contemporary Archives.*
3 Ferrybridge C Power Station was not receiving coal or oil supplies and could not use the full capacity of its plant. It was useful therefore to move plant to increase oil-fired generation where this was possible.
4 Op cit p154.
5 *The Times*, 19 July 1984.
6 *The Times*, 18 October 1984.
7 *Keesing's Contemporary Archives.*
8 The coal burn saving from gas turbine generation was later to increase to over 70 000 tonnes a week.

14 WINTER

1 *Keesing's Contemporary Archives.*
2 MacGregor, op cit pp324–330.
3 *National Coal Board Report and Accounts 1984–5.*
4 The account in this and the following section on negotiations and the return to work is based on a number of sources but particularly the NCB Report referred to in note 3.

15 BACK TO NORMAL AND COUNTING THE COST

1 Lawson, op cit pp160–161; Nicholas Ridley, *My Style of Government* (London: Fontana, 1991) p. 70; Peter Walker, *Staying Power* (London: Bloomsbury, 1991) pp165–181.
2 *Keesing's Contemporary Archives.*
3 Lawson, op cit p160. These costs included the £2020 million additional costs of the CEGB. © Nigel Lawson, 1993. Extract from p. 160 of *The View from No. 11*. Published by Bantam Books, all rights reserved. Permission for the world rights, except UK and Commonwealth, given by Peters, Fraser and Dunlop.
4 Adeney and Lloyd, op cit p202.
5 Op cit p161.
6 *British Coal: Report and Accounts 1985–6.*
7 Arthur Scargill more than once made reference to the removal of the Thatcher government as one of his objectives. He seemed to see this as part of a class struggle that at times took on revolutionary characteristics. Walker, Lawson and others refer to this. Adeney & Lloyd devote their Chapter 3 to it. It was a well understood issue at the time.
8 The generation referred to here includes gas turbine generation, small oil-fired stations, oil burn at coal-fired stations and gas-fired generation at Hams Hall Power Station in addition to that at the major oil-fired stations.
9 Sources of information include: Mr F E Bonner CBE, Deputy Chairman, CEGB 1977–1986; *Central Electricity Generating Board Annual Report and Accounts 1984–5*; *The Electricity Council Annual Report 1984–5*; Sir Philip Jones CB, Chairman, Electricity Council 1983 to 1989.
10 The bulk supply tariff was the charging arrangement for bulk supplies from the CEGB to the area electricity boards. It was set annually for the year ahead and was formulated in such a way that the costs of the CEGB were recovered together with an agreed level of profit.
11 The profits and losses quoted are after interest and extraordinary items on a current

cost accounting basis and before crediting the exceptional charge of £934 million referred to later.

12 These figures do not take account of the benefit to the Treasury of an extra £157 million of oil duty paid to HM Customs and Excise.

16 COAL ON THE MOVE

The authors have made extensive use of the CEGB archives and the recollections and notes of: Mr J Evans, Fuel Supplies Officer; Mr H L Mathews OBE, Director of Production; Mr M Rainbow, Secretary; all of the CEGB Midlands Region during the time of the 1984–5 miners' strike.

1 All imported coal was first delivered to Continental ports in 100 000 tonne bulk carriers. It was placed into stock and loaded as required on to smaller ships, 8 000 to 20 000 tonnes, which could be accommodated at the jetties of the coal-fired power stations in South East England. The effect of reducing coal imports into this country was that the contracted cargoes still arriving at the continental ports built up our stocks there.

2 The continental coal stocks were later to be used to supply some 2 750 000 tonnes of coal to the NCB's European customers during the coal strike.

3 Several chapters in Part II and in particular Chapter 11 described the strong support given by the rail unions to the striking miners, which resulted in only limited rail transport of coal throughout the strike.

17 OIL: THE £4 BILLION STORY

The authors have made extensive use of the CEGB archives and the recollections and notes of: J I Wooley OBE, CEGB Fuel Supplies Officer; D R Bridger, CEGB Oil and Gas Supplies Officer; L Jonathan of his section.

1 The government had in some previous emergencies set up the Oil Industry Emergency Committee. The committee consisted of senior members of the oil industry and performed the role of organising the allocation and flow of oil products within the UK. The committee had last operated during the 1973–4 oil and coal crisis and is referred to in Chapter 6.

2 Asphaltenes are complex hydrocarbons of high molecular weight. They are a normal part of the heavy fuel oil produced during the cracking process at a refinery. Asphaltenes are difficult to burn completely in the furnace of a boiler and may be emitted from the chimney as a smut. The limiting of asphaltenes content was to reduce the risk of smut emissions.

18 THE POWER SYSTEM: INNOVATION AND FLEXIBILITY

The authors have made extensive use of the CEGB archives and the recollections and notes of managers involved.

1 The transmission planning standards were clearly defined and formally approved by the CEGB Executive. They were the guide to those planning the development of the transmission system in support of the generation construction programme and the distribution boards' supply requirements. They included an interconnection capacity that enabled more flexible operation of the generation capacity than was normally required in many other countries. This flexibility had been of great benefit in this country on a number of occasions in the past.

2   A pump-storage power station has two lakes, one at high level and one at a lower level. At night when electricity demand is low and the marginal cost of generation is low, it pumps water to the higher level lake. During the day when electricity demand and the marginal cost of generation are high, the station generates electricity by passing water from the higher level lake through water turbines to the lower lake. During the strike that role enabled some coal-fired generation to be avoided during the day by using oil-fired generation to supply the pumping load overnight.

19 ESSENTIAL SUPPLIES: FROM HELICOPTERS TO CO$_2$

The authors have made extensive use of the CEGB archives and the recollections and notes of: G T B Camsey, CEGB Headquarters Operations Services Engineer; A Bradshaw, CEGB Operational Performance Engineer; R A West, CEGB National Spares and Repairs Engineer; and P G Willett, CEGB Purchasing Contracts and Stores Officer.

1   The emergency information room was the place where all the information necessary for monitoring the emergency from the CEGB's point of view was marshalled and displayed. It provided the central information service to support the management of CEGB's response to the strike.
2   The Nuclear Installations Inspectorate's requirement was that, in the event of failure of a CO$_2$ storage vessel, the consequential damage that could occur to other plant should be acceptable. In practice this required the vessels to be situated further from existing plant than was feasible with the limited site areas.

20 GENERATING PLANT: PROBLEMS AND OPPORTUNITIES

The authors have made extensive use of the CEGB archives and the recollections and notes of: A Bradshaw, CEGB Operational Performance Engineer; G B T Camsey, CEGB Operations Service Engineer; F Kirkby, Station Manager, Grain Power Station; T McInerney, Director of Production and later Executive Director CEGB, South Eastern Region; and R A West, CEGB National Spares and Repairs Engineer.

1   An electrical rotor is the rotating part of an electrical generator. Another word for an AC generator is alternator and this or a generator may be used interchangeably.
2   Both Hams Hall and West Thurrock Power Stations had been gas-burning stations in earlier times. A coal-fired boiler can be readily adapted to gas burning. In addition to that modification it was necessary to change electrical equipment in the boiler house to a flameproof design to avoid the risk of explosions.

21 THE MANAGERS, THE UNIONS AND THE STAFF

1   In fact in the 1970s the EPEA had become part of the Engineers' and Managers' Association with members in a number of other industries.
2   In 1968 the ETU and the plumbers' trade union had joined forces. Later the ETU-PTU extended its sphere of interest in the electronics and telecommunications business and adopted its current name of the Electrical, Electronics, Telecommunications and Plumbing Union (EETPU).

22 WHO IS MY BROTHER?

1   For an account written from a different point of view see Huw Beynon (ed.), *Digging Deeper: Issues in the Miners' Strike* (London: Verso, 1985), especially Chapter 5.
2   Arthur Scargill, 'The New Unionism', *New Left Review* (June 1975) p13.

3   Thomas and Others v. NUM (South Wales Area) and Others. Chancery Division (1986) 1 ch. 20 (1985) 2 All ERI, 11 February 1985.
4   On 28 September 1984 Nicholls J in Taylor (RH) v NUM (Yorkshire Area) made an interlocutory order against both the Yorkshire Union and the National Union to restrain them from instructing or urging any members of the Yorkshire Union to strike, or not to work or not to cross any picket lines in the Yorkshire area and from describing the strike or any picket in such an area as 'official'.
    On 10 October 1984, owing to the union's disregard of those and similar orders relating to other union areas, Nicholls J, in respect of the action brought by the plaintiffs against the Yorkshire Union, imposed a fine of £200 000 on the union and on 25 October 1984, since the union refused to pay the fine, he issued a sequestration order against all the union's property.
5   It was reported (Law Report, 19 March 1985, Richard Read (Transport) Ltd v NUM) that, when the fine in contempt of court imposed on the NUM was paid out of the sequestrated union funds, Mr Justice Scott held that, despite the absence of any apology, the contempt had been cleared. Mr Justice Scott was not troubled by the absence of a formal apology as he considered that the Court's dignity did not depend upon a required and expressed public recantation the sincerity of which, in the circumstances, might be open to question.
6   Richard Read (Transport) Ltd v NUM (South Wales Area); George M Read Ltd v NUM (South Wales Area), Queen's Bench Division (1985) IRCR 67, 134 NLJ, 30 July 1984. The union did not pay the fines and their funds were sequestrated. The Law Report 19 March 1985 reported that the High Court had ordered the discharge of the writs of sequestration.
7   Clarke and Others v Chadburn and Others, Chancery Division (Transcript: Nunnery), 25 May 1984.
8   Taylor and Others v NUM (Derbyshire Area) and Others. Chancery Division (1984) IRLR 440, 28 September 1984.
9   Kim Howells, 'The Birth of a New Kind of Politics', in Huw Beynon (ed.), *Digging Deeper: Issues in the Miners' Strike* (London: Verso, 1985), p145 of ch.7. Howells, at the time of the strike, was research officer for the South Wales Area of the NUM.
10 These two paragraphs on picketing at pits, steelworks and coke plants include factual information from Martin Adeney and John Lloyd, *The Miners' Strike 1984–5, Loss Without Limit* (London: Routledge and Kegan Paul, 1985).
11 The factual information on picketing at the power stations is based on CEGB daily records and press references.
12 Kim Howells, op cit p142, raised the question of why striking miners in so many NUM areas other than South Wales 'seemed very reluctant to stick at the daily grind of picketing power stations. We knew that it was less spectacular work than the daily round of battling with the police outside pits, but in our eyes it was much more vital in any long-term quest for victory'.

23 PARTNERS: THE DISTRIBUTION BOARDS

This chapter is based on interviews by a co-author with managers of the two distribution electricity companies most directly involved in events during the strike and also the direct experience of the authors.

1   Some of the figures quoted relating to the South Yorkshire and West Yorkshire areas were collected in December 1984 during the strike and are subject to a margin of error.
2   Alan Griffin, *County Under Siege* (London: Morland, 1985).

24 INFORMATION: HANDLE WITH CARE

The authors acknowledge the extensive help in preparing this chapter given by Peter Vey who, at the time of the 1984–5 strike, was the CEGB's Director of Public Relations and Information.

25 KEEPING THE LIGHTS ON IN THE 1990s AND BEYOND

1 *Electricity Act 1989, Part 1, Section 3, Subsection 3.*
2 *Electricity Act 1989, Part 1, Section 3 Subsection 1.*
3 *Transmission Licence, Condition 12.*
4 *Transmission Licence, Condition 10.* The generation security standard was that the supply of electricity will not be disconnected in more than 9 years in any 100 years and the voltage or frequency of electricity supplies will not be reduced below the usual operational limits in more than 30 years in any 100 years.
5 Section 34.
6 The Secretary of State directed National Power and PowerGen to hold stocks of coal that vary from month to month, reflecting the seasonal nature of electricity demand. Initially, for the year ending 31 March 1991, they varied from 22 000 000 to 27 000 000 tonnes. These stock requirements were exceeded in successive years as a result of the coal that the two companies were committed to purchase from British Coal in the contracts set up at vesting.
7 Condition 10(b) 5 of the Transmission Licence identifies the grounds on which the NGC can refuse to connect a generator. They include that it would be in breach of its duties under Section 9 of the Act which are 'to develop an efficient, coordinated and economical system of electricity transmission' and 'to facilitate competition'; in breach of regulations concerning safety; and in breach of the Grid Code.
   The Secretary of State's consent is required for all generation developments over 50 MW, under Section 36 of the 1989 Act. If he had grounds for not granting permission, he could do so and exercise a degree of control over the location of new generating plant.
8 Text of statement dated 17 October 1990 from DGES to the Secretary of State.
9 Discontinuous action is a new process written into Section 21 of the Trade Union Reform and Employment Rights Act 1993. A union intends industrial action to be 'discontinuous' if it intends it to take place only on some days on which there is an opportunity to take the action. The law provides that a union must, at least seven days before it intends official industrial action to take place, give written notice of it to the employer. If it fails to do so it will lose its protection under the statutory immunities against civil law proceedings. The notice must, among other things, describe the employees involved, indicate whether the action is to be continuous or discontinuous and, if discontinuous, the days on which the action is intended to take place.

Index

Aberthaw Power Stations 79, 161, 162, 163, 167, 169, 191, 206, 236
Admiralty: Marshal arrests oil tanker at Kingsnorth jetty 168, 203–4; Registrar 204; repair facilities, requests for 239
Advisory Conciliation and Arbitration Service (ACAS): NACODS dispute 156; statutory powers 75, 89
Agecroft Power Station 253
Aire Valley Power Stations 208
Allen, Jim 144, 151
Amalgamated Society of Locomotive Engineers and Firemen's Union (ASLEF) overtime ban (1973-4) 59, 64, 65, 68, 68, 70, 72, 186; support for NUM 206, 207
Amereda Hess 200
Area Electricity boards: Code of Practice for payment of debts 258–60; East Midland Electricity Board in (1984-5) miners' strike 259–60; emergencies management 272; fuel crisis (1973) 64, 67; fuel price adjustment consultation on (1984-5) 177; independent sources of generation investigation into 257; miners' strikes (1972) 43, 51, 52, 57–8, (1974) 72, (1984-5) 256–60; system control arrangements 256; system reserve reduction option 151–2; transmission problems 218; Yorkshire Electricity Board in (1984-5) miners' strike 257–8
Army: consideration in (1984-5) miners' strike 142; soldiers used in power strike (1949) 28, 30–1, 32–3
Ashworth, William 69, 72
Astbury, Mr Justice 14
Attlee, Clement 19, 23, 24, 30, 31

AUEW 147, 242
Australia: coal exports to CEGB 182

Baker, John 301
Baldwin, Stanley 11, 13
Banks, John 158
Barber, Anthony 36, 67
Barking Power Station 15, 26, 27, 28
Battersea Power Station 18, 28
BBC: General strike news coverage 13; unsheeted coal vehicle filmed 193
Beatt, Roy 162, 163
Beaumont, Tim 133
Beckett, Sir Terence 149
Belvedere Power Station 153, 237
Benn, Tony 80, 253
Bermondsey Power Station 18
Bevercotes pit 116
Bevin, Ernest 14
Bilsthorpe pit 116
Blackman, Gil 97, 100, 102, 103, 133, 161, 166, 168, 172, 301
Blake, Mike 198
Blyth Power Station 150, 154, 161, (B) 206, 235, 249, 251, 252
Bold Power Station 139, 156, 253
Bonner, Fred 102, 301
bonus payments 26, 27, 30, 33
BP: drivers' attitude to picketing 250; Kent refinery 198; Shipping 227
Bradshaw, Alan 224, 238
Bridger, David 127, 198, 206
Bridges, Sir Edward 30
Brighton Power Station 163, 191, 216, 251, 252
Brimsdown Power Station 27, 30
Bristows' helicopters service 227
British Airways Helicopters Ltd 227

British Association of Colliery Managers (BACM) 105, 132, 156
British Coal: future coal needs 279; name change from NCB 172
British Electricity Authority: power strike (1949) 27–9, 31, 32, 33; set up 6, 25, 290; subversion fears 31; unofficial strikes 30
British Gas Corporation 145, 152
British Gazette: General Strike issue 14
British Oxygen Company (BOC): deliveries to power station 228, 250; drivers' refusal to cross picket line 249
British Productivity Council set up 23
British Rail *see* railways
British Steel: electricity generation 257
British Worker: TUC General Strike issue 14
Broom, Dr Trevor 65
Brunswick Wharf Power Station 235
Budgets: (1970) 36–7; (1972) 59; (1973) 66, (1976) 75
Bulk Supply Tariff 99
Bulls Bridge Power Station 155, 208
Bussey, E. W. 27

Callaghan, James 75
Camsey, Granville 98, 101, 133, 151, 224, 238
Canadian Seamen's Union 27
carbon dioxide: for generators cooling 222; for nuclear power stations 100, 131, 137, 155, 222–3, 224, 225, 226, 228, 250; privatised industry supply 280; seaborne delivery investigation 227–8
Caribbean oil deliveries 168, 200, 203, 204–5
Carr, Robert 35, 40, 47
Carrington, Lord 68
Carrington Power Station 253
Central Electricity Authority (CEA): 6, 290, 291
Central Electricity Board (CEB): 'grid iron' control 5, 32; set up 5, 289; undertakings transfer to BEA 290
Central Electricity Generating Board: Bulk Supply Tariff 99; chairmanship 102–3; coal *see* coal; Commercial Branch 144; computer programs predictions (1984) 108, 123, 133, 141, 153, 211; computerised management

information ViewData 262–3; contingency planning 88, 95, 96–102, 105–7, 110, 125, 129, 175, 199, 213, 218, 226, 230, 256, 271, 272; development 6–7, 45, 60, 75–6, 90–2; electricity supply *see* electricity supply; employees *see* employees; endurance capability 108, 114, 123,130, 133, 134, 135, 136, 138, 141, 142, 145, 150–3, 159, 166, 172, 175, 176, 264–6; endurance strategy 191, 195, 212, 213–14, 219, 223, 230; energy modelling 211, 212, 213–14; essential commodities supply safeguard 100–1, 103; established 6, 290; external financing limit (EFL) 178; financial cost of miners' strike (1984-5) 168, 170, 176–8, 262–3; fuel crisis (1973) 60-1, 64; gas turbine *see* gas turbine power stations; industrial action (1969-70) 37, 38, 39, (1977) 79, 81–2; job losses 7, 45, 75, 91, 126, 292, 293 legal action against miners' strike (1984-5) consideration of 247–8; legal case Henthorn and Taylor v CEGB 82; legal case oil tanker arrested 203–4; load shedding instructions 39; managing the power system 210–12, 271; members' list 303; miners' overtime bans and strikes *see under* miners; monitoring 133, 211; Monopolies and Mergers Commission report 7, 104, 292; National Control 72, 266; NCB attitude to 181–3, 189–90; NCB cash flow with 189; nuclear *see* nuclear power stations; oil purchasing *see* oil; operational planning 216–20; Operations Department 98, 133, 174, 210–13, 301–2, 305; Operations General Management 133; Operations Services Branch 101; organisation development 291–3, 301 plant closure *see* power stations; political implications 99, 265, 266, 267; privatisation 3, 267, 271, 272–3; public relations 134, 154, 171, 261–7, 286; regional organisation (1984-5) 304; road tankers, acquisition of 101, 103, 227, 250; sales in strike (1984-5) 257; statutory responsibilities 98–9, 160, 171, 178, 266; statutory responsibilities, release from (1972) 52,

56, (1973-4) 66; strategy success
174–6; Systems Operation Branch 98,
123, 133, 143, 152–3, 161, 219;
systems preparation for strike 211–20;
see also electricity supplies, employees
of CEGB, industrial staff *and* power
stations
Channel 4 News 263
chemicals for water treatment plant for
power stations 222, 225, 226
Citizens Advice Bureaux 259
Citrine, Walter (later Lord) 13, 14, 25, 26,
27, 29–30, 31, 290
Civil Commissioner 19
Civil Contingencies Unit: establishment
56; miners' overtime ban (1973) 63
Civil Service: Pay Research Unit 90
Clegg, Hugh 88
Cliff Quay Power Station 153
Clutterbuck, Richard 61
Coal: accelerated delivery scheme (1982)
182; Battle of Saltley coke depot 47,
51–2, 55: computer program
predictions 108, 212; consumption
(1926–7) 20, (1950) 25, (1971-2) 45,
(1984-5) 130, 175, 177; costs of
miners' strike (1984-5) 177; deliveries
weekly (1984-5) table 188–9;
endurance potential (1984) 108, 114;
fuel crisis (1973) 60, 67; (1979-84) 91;
General strike year consumption 20;
imports from Australia 182; imports in
nineties 279; imports limit 91–2, 96,
106, 107, 182; miners' strike (1972)
shortage 50–5, 57; miners' strikes *see*
miners' strikes; oil-based generation
saving in strike 175; oil burn power
stations save 208; over-production
(1984) 99, 104, 107; overtime bans by
NUM (1973) 59, 62, 63, 67; (1983-4)
101, 103, 105–7, 108, 109, 113, 175;
picketing *see* picketing; pit closures
strike threat (1981-4) 90, 91, 96, 99,
104, 107, 108, 109; price increases 91,
182; production during strike (1984-5)
175, 187, 213; production resumption
after strike (1985) 172; quality
standards 185–6, 191; shortage after
World War Two 6, 24; ship delivery
163; spontaneous combustion 183;
stocks (1971-2) 54, 55, 57, (1981–4)
181–6;(1984-5) 98, 99, 102, 105–6,

107–9, 113, 114, 115, 125, 128–31,
133–4, 135, 136, 139, 141, 143, 153–4,
157–8, 161, 164, 174, 175, 212, 213,
216, 264; stocks following strike 172;
supplies to 'have not' stations 125,
158, 159, 161–4, 165–6, 167–8, 174,
176, 187, 191, 213, 214–16; technical
and scientific staff industrial action
effect on distribution of 62; transport of
see railways *and* road transport; wet
coal problem 152 *see also* miners,
National Coal Board *and* pit closures
Coal Board *see* National Coal Board
coal industry *see* mining industry
Coal Industry Act (1980) 95
Coal Industry National Consultative
Council 109, 111
Cold War 24–5. 33
collieries closure *see* pit closures
Combined Works Committee 26, 28, 29
Commission on Pay Comparability 88
Communism: Attlee administration fear
of subversion 24–5; dock strikes 26–7;
ETU leaders 26, 33; *Morning Star*
advertisements 252; power stations 26,
27, 29–30, 31, 33
Communist Party of GB 24
computer: ICI terminal at CEGB 224;
management information system
ViewData 262–3; program predictions
of fuel requirements 108, 123–4, 133,
141 153, 211
Conditions of Employment and National
Arbitration Order, 1305 (1940) 23
Confederation of British Industry (CBI):
save electricity request in miners' strike
(1984) 149; three day working week 68
Conspiracy and Protection of Property
Act 1875: 5, 31, 33, 288
consumers: information on crisis to 3
Contingency Planning Review Panel
(CPRP) 274, 277, 278, 280, 285
Cortonwood pit, South Yorkshire 109, 111
Cottam Power Station 79, 80, 116, 138,
146, 154, 191, 193, 251
Counter-Inflation Act (1973) 60
Cowan, James 108, 109, 136
Craig, Jim 156
Creswell pit 116
Cripps, Sir Stafford 24
crisis management: future threats 4; what
it means 2–3

cross-Channel power link 7, 92, 166, 168
Customs and Excise, HM 168, 204–5

Daily Herald, General Strike *British Worker* 14
Daily Mail, printers' action (1926) 13
Daly, Lawrence 103, 107
Dartford Power Station 26
Davies, John 53
Davis, Jack, Hams Hall Power Station 152
Department of Energy: accelerated coal delivery scheme 182; contingency planning 96, 97, 98 102; established 68; media response to miners' strike 262, 264, 265; miners' strike (1974) 71; miners' strike (1984-5) 133, 138, 178; oil import duty 204; oil supplies views on 209; oil tanker arrest discussions 204
Department of Trade and Industry (DTI): miners' overtime bans (1970) 46, (1973) 65; miners' strike (1972) 47, 55–6
Deptford Power Station 28
Didcot Power Station 161, 162, 164, 166, 167, 191–2, 207, 216, 227, 235, 239, 249, 252–3, 261
Dinorwig pumped storage power station 7, 92, 145, 218, 293
Director General of Electricity Supplies (DGES) 273–4, 278, 279
District Joint Industrial Councils: electricity companies leave in General Strike 21; formed 288
Dock Labour Board 24
dock strikes (1949) 24, 26–7, 31; (1970) 35; (1984) 138, 139–40, 174, 197
Donovan, Lord 35
Drakelow Power Station 79, 80, 119, 249
Drax Power Station 79, 80, 81, 91, 158, 161, 207, 249, 261
Dungeness Power Station 253

Eastham oil terminal 207
economic situation: before miners' strike (1984-5) 87–9; crisis conditions in the nineties 284; leading to 1949 power workers' strike 24; miners' strike (1984-5) effect 170; recession consequences 281–2; state of (1979-84) 88–9
Economist, The: nationalised industries, Conservative policy group 87

Edwards, Sir Ronald 41,42
EETPU 146, 241, 242
Eggborough Power Station 79, 80, 156, 161, 251
Electrical Power Engineers' Association (EPEA): appointment of John Lyons 293; conflict with ETU 5, 15–16, 20; formed 5, 288; General Strike role 15–19, 20, 21; industrial action (1973) 34, 59, 61–2, 64, 67, 72; membership 241; miners' strike (1984-5) 242; power station picketing (1984) 131; power workers' industrial action (1977) 77; power workers' strike (1969-70) 39; running power stations 77, 78–9, 80, 82, 293 *see also* Engineers and Managers Association
Electrical Review, General Strike articles 17, 19
Electrical Trades Union (ETU): arbitration award (No. 2772) 288; Communist leaders 26, 33; conflict with EPEA 5, 15, 20; General Strike (1926) 5, 15, 16–19, 20; membership before World War One 4, 287
Electricite de France (EDF) 166
Electricity Act (1926) 288
Electricity Act (1947) 290
Electricity Act (1957) 98, 290
Electricity Act (1989) 272, 274, 275, 279
Electricity Commissioners: established 5; General Strike year annual report 20
Electricity Council: annual report and accounts (1984-5) 176, 177; Contingency Review Panel 52; established 6, 290; emergencies management 272; fuel crisis (1973) 64; fuel price (1984-5) adjustment consultation 177; media response to strike 264; miners' strikes (1972) 47, 56, 57, (1974) 71, (1984-5) 178, 260; power workers' industrial action (1977) 79, 81; power workers' strike (1969-70) 40, 42; prices co-ordination of area boards 262; system reserve reduction option 152; work practices 291
electricity generation: before World War One 4
electricity supply: cost of purchases in miners' strike (1984-5) 177; crisis (1947) 23; cross-Channel power link 7,

92, 166, 168; dangers to 3, 4; endurance capability 108, 114, 123, 130, 133, 134, 135, 138, 141, 142, 145, 150–3, 159, 166, 172, 175, 176; endurance strategy 191, 195, 212, 213–15, 219, 223, 230; essential access 3; essential services list (1972) 53; fuel crisis (1973) 59, 64; generation from NCB coal 279; generation output control 128; General Strike 15–20; imports from France 166; importance of 1, 97–8, 99; independent generation 257; legislation 5–7, 98; load reductions 51, 62, 71 (1977) 79; load shedding 39; load spreading (1949) 25–6; miners' strikes see miners' strike; nuclear see nuclear power stations; operational planning 123, 211–13; over-capacity 91; power flows (1984-5) 126, 128, 212, 216–18; power transfer from Scotland 129–30, 174, 176,199, 211, 218; power transfers 212, 220; power workers' strike (1969-70) 39–42; prices not passed to consumers in miners' strike 176–8; private generators 144, 151; privatisation 3, 4, 267, 271, 272–8, 280–6; rationing (1972) 52, 55, (1973-4) 65, 66–7, 70, (1977) 81; rota disconnections (1948-51) 25–6, 29, (1970) 39–40, 42, (1972) 52–3, 54–5, 57–8, 65, (1973) 62, 63, 64-5, 66, (1977) 79, 80, 81–2(1984-5) 159, 256, (1990s) 272, 274; restrictions 3; safeguarding 3, 99; sales (1974-5) 75; (1979-84) 91; security in privatised industry 273–4; shortages (1949-50) 25, 28, 29; strike threats 3, 30–1; system collapse 23, 24, 210–11, 218; three-day working week (1974) 65, 67, 72; transmission problems 218–19; unofficial strikes 29, 30–1; voltage reductions (1970) 40, 41, (1971-2) 51, (1973-4) 62, 71 (1977) 77–8, 81, (1984-5) 144, 151, 152; winter crisis (1946-47) 24, 289-90; winter peak (1984-5) demands 159–64, 167–8, 265, 266 see also Central Electricity Generating Board ((CEGB), nuclear power stations, oil fired power stations and power stations
Electricity (Supply) Act (1919) 288;

Electricity Supply Emergency Code 274–5
Electricity Supply Industry (ESI): history of 4–7, 287–93; trade unions in see trade unions and named unions
Electricity Supply Trade Union Council (ESTUC) 131, 147, 241, 242, 244, 249
Electricity Supply Union 76
emergencies: civil emergencies cost 279; essential supplies 280; in privatised electricity industry 274–8, 285–6 see also States of Emergency
Emergencies Committee of the Cabinet 25
Emergency Powers Act 1920: 5
employees of CEGB: electricity industry before World War One 4; Honours recognition after miners' strike 172, 198, 266; incentive schemes 7; joint consultation 6; job losses 7, 91, 126, 293; living in mining communities 3, 99, 118, 120, 148, 159–60, 243, 250, 258, 259, 261; miners' strike (1984-5) advice from CEGB 118–19, 120, 126–7, 160; miners' strike (1984-5) attitudes of staff 243–5; non-unionism post-war 26; nuclear stations' craftsmen grading dispute 137; pay and conditions machinery set up 6; statistics 6, 45; transport to remote power stations 76; see also industrial staff, manual workers, pay, power workers' strikes and technical/scientific staff
Employment Acts (1980-84) 221, 246, 247
employment protection legislation 75, 89, 90, 95
endurance: capability of CEGB 108, 114, 123,130, 133, 134, 135, 136, 138, 141, 142, 145, 150–3, 159, 166, 172, 175, 176, 264–6; strategy 191, 195, 212, 213–15, 219, 223, 230
energy modelling 211, 212, 213–14
Energy Act (1976) 274, 279
Engineers and Managers Association 146
England, Glyn 102
Esso private electricity generation 144; oil for power stations 155, 197
European Economic Community: oil duty 168, 204–5; treaty signed 44
Evans, Jack 122, 153, 162, 187
Ezra, Derek 45, 73, 95, 96

Factories Acts 136, 237–8

Factories Inspectorate, HM 137, 238
Fairclough, John 167
Farman, Christopher. 17, 18
Fawley Power Station 127, 197, 233, 249
Fawley Refinery 197
Feather, Vic 40
Ferranti, Sebastian di 4, 287
Ferrybridge Power Station 79, 81, 137,
    138, 150, 161, 166, 207, 208, 218, 230,
    232, 249, 250
Fiddlers Ferry Power Station 116, 161,
    164, 207, 219, 249
flying pickets 36, 42, 44, 47, 89, 112
Foot, Michael 72
Ford Motor Co private electricity
    generation 144
Foulkes, Frank 28, 29
France: cross-Channel power link 7, 92,
    166, 168; power system collapse 210
free collective bargaining: return to
    (1977) 75, 77, 87; (1978) 88
fuel: crisis (1947) 23, 24, 25; (1973) 59,
    60-1, 64, 67; computer program
    predictions (1984) 108
Fuel Security Code 275, 279, 280
fuel supply emergency in the future 276,
    279-80

Gaitskell, Hugh 26, 29-30, 31
gas: costs of miners' strike (1984-5) 177;
    industrial gases essential 13, 222 see
    also carbon dioxide and hydrogen
gas-cooled reactors see nuclear power
gas turbine generators 143-4, 150-1, 157,
    164, 238-9, 279
gas turbine power stations 144, 145, 152,
    155, 206, 207, 231, 234, 280
General Elections: Conservative victory
    (1983) 89, 90; Labour Government
    (1974) 73, 75-6; miners' strike (1974)
    and 69, 71, 72; winter of discontent
    consequence (1979) 87
General Strike 1926: Civil Commissioner
    19; electricity industry, state of 5, 288,
    289; events leading to 11-13; govern-
    ment arrangements 12-13: miners' lock
    out 12, 13; miners' strike 15, 20; power
    supplies 15-20; progress of 13-15;
    State of Emergency 13; TUC role 12-13;
    summing up 21; work, return to 20-1
Generating Board see Central Electricity
    Generating Board

GMBATU 147, 241, 242
Gormley, Joe 44, 45, 46, 47, 56, 62, 63,
    68, 71, 73, 95, 96, 97
Grain Power Station 76, 92, 126, 127,
    135, 150, 168, 198, 201, 202, 204, 233
Green, Joe: killed on picket line 138
grid see national grid and supergrid
'grid-iron' of high voltage transmission
    lines 5, 32, 289
Grunwick film processing laboratory
    strike 75
Gulf oil deliveries to power station 197,
    200, 204

Haigh pit 116
Hammond, Eric 146, 147
Hams Hall Power Station 145, 152, 237
Hannah, Leslie 17
Hardman Committee 44
Hartlepool Nuclear Power Station 219,
    249, 251, 252
hauliers see road transport
Hawkins, Arthur (later Sir) 67
Healey, Denis (later Lord) 75
Heath, Edward (later Sir) 35, 43, 47, 59,
    65, 66, 69, 71, 72
Heathfield, Peter 36, 107, 131, 136
helicopter deliveries of essential supplies
    101, 103, 146, 165, 225, 226-7
Henthorn and Taylor v CEGB 82
Herbert Committee 6, 290, 291
Heysham Nuclear Power Station 92
High Marnham Power Station 116, 134,
    219, 251
Hinkley Point Power Station 131, 137
history of the electricity supply industry
    4-7, 287-93
Holland, Norman 162
Hollis, R,H, (later Sir Roger) 31
Holmes, Maurice 119, 120
Home Office: miners' strike (1974) 71
Houghton, Roy 156
Howell, David 92, 95
Howells, Kim 248
Huncoat Power Station 156
Hurd, Douglas 43, 51, 56, 62, 69
hydrogen: generator cooling supplies 100,
    222, 225; miners' strike (1972)
    shortage 48, 50; storage problems 226

ICI, carbon dioxide deliveries to nuclear
    power stations 100, 137, 155, 224, 228;

computer terminal placed in CEGB
224; picketing, drivers' response 249,
250; private electricity generation 144;
tanker drivers' industrial action 137,
155, 228
Ince Power Station 127, 137, 150, 156,
197, 230, 232, 233
incomes policy *see* prices and incomes
policy
industrial action *see* General Strike *and*
strikes
industrial relations: Commission on 35;
guidelines for negotiators from TUC
74; legal framework 34, 89;
management of 3; miners' strike
(1984-5) 159-60, 241-5; nationalised
industry 271; non-unionism post-war
26; pay refused to staff not working
normally (1977) 82; privatised
electricity supply industry 280-6;
progress 6, 7; restoring after crisis 3,
176; Royal Commission 35;
Wilberforce Inquiry report 41-2 *see
also* trade unions *and* named unions
Industrial Relations Act (1971): repealed
74
Industrial Relations Bill (1970) 37, 44
industrial staff: concessionary electricity
sought 77, 82; electricity bills payment
in strike (1984-5) 257-8, 259, 260;
incentive schemes 7; job losses 7, 45,
91, 126; living in mining communities
3, 99, 118, 120, 148, 159-60, 243. 250,
258, 259, 261; redeployment during
miners' strike (1984-5) 244; staff status
7, 83, 291; statistics 7; unofficial shop
stewards 243-4 *see also* employees of
CEGB, pay *and* power workers' strikes
industry: output collapse (1979-82) 89;
three-day working week (1974) 65-6,
67, 72
International Energy Agency (IEA) 195
Inverkip Power Station 128, 199
Iron and Steel Trades Confederation
(ISTC) 90, 115
Ironbridge Power Station 193
Isaacs, George 26
Isle of Grain Power Station *see* Grain
Power Station

Jonathan, Les 204
Jones, Aubrey 34

Jones, Philip (later Sir) 65, 66, 114, 177

Kellingley pit 138
Kingsnorth Power Station 126, 127, 135,
137, 143, 150, 168, 198, 201, 202, 203,
204, 235
Kirk, Geoff 263
Kirkby, Fred 127
Knapp, Jimmy 147, 253
'Knee' curve monitor 213-14

Lawson, Nigel (later Lord) 96, 97, 103,
104, 171, 203, 170
Leason, Dennis 151
Ledger, Frank 98, 133
Leicester Power Station 208
Lewis, John, West Thurrock Power
Station Manager 150, 165
lighting-up oil *see* oil
Littlebrook Power Stations, 26, 27, 126,
135, 150, 200, 201, 202, 205, 233, 249,
252
Littlebrook Workshops 151, 238-9
Lloyd, John 17, 18
Lloyd George, David 12
load reductions *see* electricity supply
load shedding *see* electricity supply
local authorities: claims for road damage
193
local government manual workers' strike 36
London Electricity Shop Stewards'
Committee 26
London: power supplies in General Strike
17, 18-19
London Electric Power Scheme (1926)
12, 18
London Power Companies 15
lorries *see* road transport
Lynk, Roy 121, 138
Lyons, John 80, 131, 146, 147, 293

McGahey, Mick 36, 63, 97, 108, 136
MacGregor, Ian 104-5, 107, 109, 136,
148, 263
McInerney, Tom 126, 143, 153, 163
McKie, Robert 262
Magnox nuclear power stations 6
management information: importance of
2, 3, 134
Manchester power stations 15
Manley, Ivor 97
manual workers: average earnings (1977)

76; General Strike effect on 20; negotiating machinery *see* National Joint Industrial Council; overtime 6, 7, 291; pay in thirties 5; renamed industrial staff 7, 291; wage increase (1949) 27 *see also* industrial staff and named industries

Marshall, Sir Walter (later Lord) 102, 114, 133, 141, 142, 166, 171, 204, 261–2, 266

Marshall Plan (from USA) 23

Maryport pit 116

Mathews, Hugh 122, 126, 153, 172

media: presentation of electricity crisis to 3, 261–7, 286

Middle East: oil crisis 7, 60-1, 72, 272, 292; Yom Kippur War 61

Middleton, Neil 133

military *see* Army, RAF *and* Royal Navy

Miners' Federation of Great Britain: wage agreement ended (1924) 11, 21

miners' overtime bans: (1973) 63; (1983) 101, 103, 105–7, 108, 109;

miners' strike 1926 *see* General Strike

miners' strike (1969-70): Yorkshire 36

miners' strike (1972): economic background 43–4; lessons learnt from 55–8; NUR refusal to move coal 46; power station picketing 43, 45, 46, 47–50, 52, 100; progress of 46-55; Wilberforce Court of Inquiry 43, 52, 54, 55, 56

miners' strike (1974); CEGB staff attitudes to 243; economic background 62–9; progress of 69–73;

miners' strike (1984-5): background to 87–92, 95–110, 241–5; ballots by NUM for strike action 130, 243; chronology of main events 294–300; coal *see* coal; cost of 168, 170, 176–8, 262; electricity use encouragement by NUM 149; ending of 169, 253; Government policy 166, 171–2; Government reaction to Tebbit letter 141–2; importance of 85; legal cases 246–8; Northumberland Miners' Strike Bulletin 252; NUM internal differences 122; official, attempts to make 138, 148–9; peace talks NUM/NCB 132, 135–6, 140, 148, 155, 164, 168–9; picketing *see* picketing; political objectives 243; progress of 109-10,

111–42; railwaymen support *see* railways; refusal to join 112–13, 129, 130, 132, 138, 178, 246; return to work campaign by NCB 122, 165, 167, 168–9, 253; significance of 170–2; South Wales legal judgement 246–7; strategic and tactical failures 173–4; tenth anniversary 1–2; TGWU support 118, 119, 131, 139, 140, 147, 174, 242; timing of 110, 173, 174; trade unions' attitude to 241–3; Triple Alliance with transport and steel theory 108; winter 159–64, 167–8; working days loss 170 *see also* National Union of Mineworkers

mining industry: concessionary coal and travel 77; Conservative nationalisation policy group 87–8; electricity generation from NCB coal 279; laying off due to overtime ban 106; Monopolies and Mergers Commission report 7, 104; Notts miners and others vote against strike (1984) 112-13, 120–1, 123, 138; Notts miners withdrawal from MFGB 15,21; over-production (1984) 99, 104, 107; overtime ban by NUM (1973) 63-4, 67; (1983-4) 101, 103, 105–7, 108, 109, 113; pit closures *see* pit closures; recession (1925) 11; railwaymen support 119; Royal Commission report (1926) 11; wage agreements (1924)11, 21, (1973) 60, (1974) 72; wage claims (1971) 44–5, 46 (1973) 60, 62-3, 66, 67–8, 71, 72, (1983) 104-5 *see also* coal *and* National Coal Board

Ministry of Defence Fleetlands repair facility 150, 238, 239

Monopolies and Mergers Commission CEGB: report 7, 104, 292

Morning Star 252

motor workers' strikes: British Leyland (1977) 75; (1979) 89; Ford's (1971) 44; (1978-9) 88

Murray, Len 66, 67–8, 131, 146

NALGO 241, 242

National Association of Colliery Overmen, Deputies and Shotfirers (NACODS) 105, 132, 156–7, 168–9

National Board for Prices and Incomes 34, 35, 292

National Coal Board (NCB): accelerated

coal delivery scheme 182; budget
(1984-5) 109, 111; cash flow with
CEGB 189; CEGB, attitude to 181–3;
chairman appointment (1983) 104;
contingency planning 97, 108–9;
deferred payments scheme of CEGB
99; external financing limits 91; legal
injunction against picketing 247;
management influenced by NUM 181;
miners' strikes see miners' strikes;
name change to British Coal 172;
over-production (1984) 99, 104, 107,
122; overtime ban by NUM (1973)
63-4, 67; (1983-4) 101, 103,105–7,
108, 109, 113; NACODS dispute
156–7; Pay Board report 72; peace
talks with NUM (1984) 132, 135–6,
140, 148, 155, 164, 168–9; pit closures
see pit closures; productivity incentive
scheme 172; public relations 263, 264;
return to work campaign 122; stocks
see coal stocks; 'Support for Coal'
agreements with CEGB 60, 91–2; wage
awards (1972) 54, (1973) 60; wage
claims (1971) 44–45, 46; (1973) 60,
62–3, 66, 67–8, 71, 72; (1983) 104–5;
Wilberforce Court of Inquiry 43, 52,
54, 55 see also British Coal, coal, and
mining industry
National Control Centre: nationally
integrated network 5
National Dock Labour Board 139
National Economic Development Council
67, 89
National Enterprise Board 89
national grid: Control Centre 211 289;
miners' strike (1972) difficulties 56–7;
power workers' industrial action
(1977) 82–3; statistics (1949–50) 25,
32; supergrid 6, 7, 56–7, 220;
transmission constraints 216, 218;
transmission equipment maintenance
218
National Grid Company (NGC):
contingency planning and emergency
planning 275–7, 285–6; Electricity
Supply Emergency Committee chairing
274; established 272; fuel supply
emergency advice 279; industrial
relations 281–6; Pool Executive
Committee representation 273; Seven
Year Statement 277–8; strike action

scenario 282; telecommunication
business 273; trade union agreements
281; transmission system development
276–7
National Industrial Relations Court 46
National Joint Advisory Council 290
National Joint Board: agreements 292;
established 5, 288; General Strike 16
National Joint Council 290, 293
National Joint Council of the Port
Transport Industry 140
National Joint Industrial Council (NJIC)
manual workers' negotiating
machinery): agreement reconstruction
(1980) 83, 293; electricity companies
leave 21; electricity industry
agreements 291–2; miners' strike
(1972) 46; miners' strike (1984-5) 243;
national agreements 7; pay refused to
staff not working normally (1977) 82;
power strike (1949) 28, 29, 30;
reconstituted 26, 290; set up 5, 23, 288;
settlement of differences 21; suspended
in General Strike 15, 21; travelling
allowances claim 76, 78; wage
agreements industrial staff (1969-70)
37, 38, (1971) 50; wage claim
industrial staff (1977) 78, 79, 82–3
National Power (NP) diversification 273;
Electricity Supply Emergency Code
274; essential supplies in an emergency
280; established 272; industrial
relations 281–6; shareholders' interests
279; trade union agreements 281
National Power Loading Agreement 54,
60
National Union of Mineworkers (NUM):
alliance with ISTC and NUR 90, 115;
assets frozen 149; ballots for strike
action 130, 173, 247; basic wage call
(1970) 36; branch elections, legal action
138, 173, 247; coal imports limit, 96,
106, 181–2; coal stocks see coal
stocks; constitution change 36;
contingency planning for strike 103,
174; flying pickets see picketing; funds
problem 254; General Secretary election
(1984) 107; legal judgements during
strike (1984-5) 246–7; NCB (1984-5)
budget meeting 109, 111; NCB management influenced 181; Nottinghamshire
miners see Nottinghamshire; official,

attempts to make 138; overtime ban (1973) 59, 62, 63; (1983) 101, 103, 105–7, 108, 109, 113, 175, 182; Pay Board report (1974) 72; peace talks with NCB (1984) 132, 135–6, 140, 148, 155, 164, 168–9; picketing *see* picketing; presidency 44, 95, 96, 97; relations with supervisory and management unions 105–6; return to work order 169; return to work, pay inducements 164–5; Scottish NUM support strike (1984) 111; sequestration of assets 149, 173, 247; split 169, 173, 229, 229; strike domino theory 108, 109, 112, 113, 173; support of other unions in (1984-5) strike 241–3; strikes *see* miners; strikes; wage awards (1972) 54, (1973) 60; wage claims (1971) 44–5, (1973) 60, 62-3, 66, 67–8, 72; Wilberforce Court of Inquiry 43, 52, 54 *see also* coal, miners' strikes, mining industry *and* picketing
National Union of Railwaymen (NUR): alliance with ISTC and NUM 90, 115; coal imports prevention pledge (1984) 107; miners' strike (1972) coal movement 46; miners' strike (1984-5) support 115, 147, 206
National Union of Seamen (NUS) 251
nationalised electricity: assets 6, 25; industrial action during 34, 271–2; organisation 4, 272; statutory obligation to maintain public supplies 1
nationalised industries: contingency planning 97; Conservative policy group 87–8; external financing limits 91; public service ethic 286
NATO agreement to use of RN spares by CEGB 239
natural gas: power stations 45, 63
Nechells Power Station, Birmingham 52
NEI-Parsons turbine manufacturers 135, 137, 230
Newcastle-upon-Tyne power stations 15
Nicholls, Mr Justice 149
Noel-Baker, Philip 31
North of Scotland Hydro-Electric Board 6, 25, 129, 290
Northfleet Power Station 153, 237
Northumberland Miners' Strike Bulletin 252
Nottinghamshire: coal production during

strike 175; divorce from NUM 169, 173; electricity payment problems 259; legal action against NUM 138, 247; miners withdrawal from MFGB (1926) 15, 21; picketing 248, 254, 259; vote against strike (1984) 112–13, 120–1, 123, 130, 132, 138, 148
Nottinghamshire County Council roads damage claims 193
Nuclear Electric (NE) 272
nuclear power stations: carbon dioxide for coolant systems 100, 131, 155, 222–3, 224, 225, 226, 227–8, 250; CEGB strategy 91; costs of miners' strike (1984-5) 177; endurance objective contribution 134; future under privatised electricity 272, 279; gas-cooled reactor, Heysham 92; Magnox 6, 291; miners' strike (1974) 70; output fall in EPEA industrial action 62, 67; output increase in miners' strike 174, 211; public relations 263; shift from coal to 45; shut-down times 134; Sizewell pressurised water-reactor 7, 92; statutory requirements 134, 237; strategy of CEGB 92, 291

Observer, The 262
Ocker Hill Power Station 208
oil: Caribbean supplies 168, 200, 203, 204; consumption in power station (1926) 20, 21–2; (1979-84) 91, 101; costs of miners' strike (1984-5) 177, 208; duty payable from non-EEC sources 168, 203–5; essential commodities stock build-up 100–1, 103, 221–5; gas oil supplies 151, 208; Gulf supplies 197, 203–204; lighting-up delivery problems (1984-5) 117–18, 128, 130, 135, 140, 148, 161, 168, 206, 212, 213; lighting up essential commodity 221; lighting-up shortage in miners' strike (1972) 48, 50; Middle East crisis 7, 59-61, 64, 67, 72; miners' overtime ban (1973) effect 64, 67; miners' strike (1974) 70; (1984-5) 125, 127–8; miscellaneous oils purchases 206–7; national strategic stock 195; pipeline supplies to power stations 196–7, 207; power stations many uses of 61, 100; power stations policy 45, 92, 101, 107, 113-14, 125–8;

prices 59, 61, 91, 107, 127, 168, 172,
    195, 196, 198–200, 208–9, 232; procure-
    ment programme 195–206; rail strike
    reduces coal stocks effect 102;
    stockpiling impossible 198; supplies
    (1984-5) 101–2, 114, 123, 125, 127–8,
    133, 135,137, 139–40, 148, 155,
    160–1, 164, 165, 167, 168, 195–209,
    (1990s) 279; supplies reduction after
    strike 172; tankers discharge 127, 165,
    168, 207; traction oil for diesel loco-
    motives 120; USA supplies 203–4
oil-fired power stations: coal replacement
    45, 128, 154, 230, 232, 234–7; coal-
    fired with oil burn capability 203–6;
    231, 234; commissioning 92, 116, 123,
    124, 125–7, 135, 195, 232, 233; cost of
    114; future of 279; history of 232–3;
    oil burn capability table 231; oil burn
    consumption tables 201–2; oil burn
    generation table 234, 237; reduction
    after strike 172; Scotland 129, 198,
    199, 200, 201; statistics during strike
    175, 201–2; storage space limited 198;
    switch to policy 101, 107, 113–14,
    125–9, 130, 133, 135, 139, 143, 150,
    154–5, 157–8, 165, 167, 168, 174, 175,
    195–202, 211, 230–3
Oil Industries Emergency Committee
    (OIEC) 61, 64, 195
oil industry: miners' strike (1984-5)
    deliveries 118, 200–5; oil-burn power
    station increase 195–202; supplies for
    CEGB 101–2, 195–209
oil tankers: arrest at Kingsnorth jetty
    blocks unloading 168, 203–4; docked
    without tugs 197; power station
    supplies 201–2, 203–7; Sten delivery
    165; USSR oil tanker to Kingsnorth
    power station 137, 203
Oldbury Power Station 137, 232
Ollerton pit 116
operational unit: flexibility 3
Organisation for the Maintenance of
    Supplies (OMS) 12, 14
Organisation of Petroleum Exporting
    Countries (OPEC) 61, 127, 272
Orgreave coke plant picketing (1984)
    131–2, 248
Osborne, P.A. 31

Padiham Power Station 164, 253

Parsons, Charles. 4, 287
Parsons works 232
pay in ESI: bonus payments 26, 27, 30,
    33; Commission on Pay Comparability
    88, 89; differentials 71; electricians'
    standard rate established 5; flat rate
    limit (1975) 75; free collective
    bargaining (1977) 75, 77, 87; (1978)
    88; manual workers in thirties 5;
    overtime dependence 6, 291; overtime
    levels during miners' strike (1984) 127,
    148, 243; performance related 281,
    283; refused to staff not working
    normally (1977) 82; relativities 60, 68,
    69, 71; Royal Commission on the
    Redistribution of Incomes and Wealth
    89; striking miners, inducement (1984)
    164–5; travelling allowances claim 76,
    78, 79, 80; voluntary wage restraint
    (1966-9) 24; wage claims (1977) 78;
    wage control legislation 34; wage
    increase (1927-45) 289, (1971) 50,
    (1977) 76; wage settlement norm
    (1969) 34; (1980-1) 89; White Paper
    (1973) 60-1, 62; Wilberforce Inquiry
    recommendations 41–2, 292 see also
    employees, industrial staff and
    technical/scientific staff
Pay Board: established 60; miners' pay
    (1973) 63, 66, 71; miners' pay dispute
    (1974) 72; relativities report 60, 68, 71
Pay Research Unit of Civil Service 90
Pearson, Lord 35
Pembroke Power Station 127, 133, 135,
    137, 150, 197, 230, 232, 233
Peterhead Power Station 128, 129, 199
Phillips, G.A. 14, 17
picketing: accident kills picket at
    Ferrybridge 138, 250; area electricity
    boards 256; Battle of Saltley coke
    depot 47, 51–2, 55, 152; Code of
    Practice 89, 247; essential commodities
    224, 228, 229; financing of 254; flying
    pickets 36, 42, 44, 47, 89, 112, 206,
    254, 259; helicopter delivery to overfly
    101, 103, 146, 165, 225, 226–7; leaflet
    distribution 252, 253; legal cases
    246–7; legislation 89, 95, 246; miners'
    strike (1972) 43, 45, 46, 47–50, 52, 55,
    100, 221; miners' strike (1974) 71;
    miners' strike (1984-5) 112, 122, 123,
    131, 138, 145–6, 248; nuclear power

stations 137, 155, 228, 242, 249; oil
deliveries to power stations 197, 249;
pit closures strike threat (1981-4) 96,
99, 103, 104, 107, 108, 109–10; Port
Talbot steelworks fine 149; power
stations 131, 138, 145–6, 173, 248–55;
privatised industry agreements 281;
road tankers 227, 249; road transport to
power stations (1971-2) 43, 46;
(1973-4) 71; (1984-5)129, 130–1, 146,
153–4, 155–6, 163, 165, 167, 190, 192,
248–55; secondary 44, 47, 89, 95, 113,
148-9, 221, 248, 250, 254, 255, 280,
282; steel industry Orgreave coke plant
(1984) 131–2, 248; taxi driver killed
165; TUC guidelines 242–3
pit closures: Cortonwood pit, South
Yorkshire 109, 111; miners' strike
(1984-5) peace talks 132, 136, 140,
148; NCB policy 170–1; Polmaise pit
closure 111; proposed 90, 91, 96, 99,
104, 105, 107, 108, 109–10;
unprofitable closure 172, 181;
Yorkshire decision 111
plant shortage: winter (1949-50) 25, 27
Point of Ayr pit 116
police: casualty 253; charges against
demonstrators 251; electricity supplies
disruption attempts 253; miners' strike
(1972) picketing 49–50, 55; miners'
strike (1984-5) picketing deployment
113, 122, 146, 153, 156, 163, 167, 178,
250, 251, 252, 255, 259; National
Police Intelligence Unit 253; National
Reporting Centre, New Scotland Yard
113, 253; nuclear power stations
deliveries 131; Orgreave coke plant
picketing 248; role in miners' strike
253–4
Polmaise pit closure 111
Pool Executive Committee 273, 278
Poplar Power Station 18
Port Talbot steelworks 149
Porteous, Jim 122
Portsmouth Evening News 239
postal strike (1971) 44
power cuts *see* electricity supply: rota
disconnections
power stations: closure 7, 75, 91, 119,
126; coal-fired 45, 91, 127, 211, 212;
coal fired with oil burn capability table
203; coal stocks *see* coal; coal supplies

to 'have not' stations 125, 158, 159,
161–4, 165–6, 167–8, 174, 176, 187,
191, 213, 214–16; Dinorwig pumped
storage 7, 92, 145, 218, 293; essential
commodities other than coal for 100–1,
103, 122, 221–9; General Strike 5,
15-20; high efficiency 71; installed
capacity 5, 6, 91; linking 5; location
map (1984-5) 93; London Electric
Power Scheme (1926) 12; gas for flame
stabilisation 145; gas turbine generators
143–4, 150–1, 157, 206; Middle East
oil crisis 7, 59-61, 64; miners' strikes
see under miners; oil, lighting-up
shortage in miners' strike (1972) 48,
50; plant breakdown 152, 197, 218–19;
plant closure 126; plant construction
272, 274; plant modifications 218;
plant overhaul statutory requirements
136–7; plant shortage (1949–50) 25,
272; repair technology 135; servicemen
use in 12, 17, 18, 20, 28, 30–1, 32-3;
security 149; statistics 6–7, 15, 25, 45,
91; statutory inspections 237; storage
capacity for essential commodities
224–6; subversion inquiry 31; system
control room practices 211; system
reserve 145, 151-3; system security
211; technical staff running 77, 78–9;
trade union membership *see* trade
unions; transmission network (1984-5)
94, 144; unlinked 5, 15; water industry
strike effect (1983) 101; winter peak
demands; 159–64, 167–8, 213–14;
water treatment plant chemicals 222;
water tube boilers technology 237–8;
World War Two damage 6 *see also*
coal, electricity supply, natural gas,
nuclear *and* oil fired power stations
power supplies: statutory obligation to
maintain 1
power system description 210–13
Power Worker, The 26
power workers' industrial action l969-70;
legislative restraints lacking 283;
progress 34, 37–42; Wilberforce Court
of Inquiry 41–2
power workers' industrial action 1977:
background to 74–7; legislative
restraints lacking 283; progress 77–81;
travel allowances 76; unofficial shop
steward committee 77, 78, 80–1, 83

power workers' strike (1949): Bridges
    report 30; Cabinet sub-committee to
    prepare for (1947) 25; communist
    influence 26, 27, 33; economic
    background to 23–6; government
    involvement 26–31; progress of 27–9,
    32; servicemen use 28, 20–1, 32–3
Powergen: diversification 273; Electricity
    Supply Emergency Code 274; essential
    supplies in an emergency 280;
    established 272; fuel supplies officer
    198; industrial relations 281–6;
    shareholders' interests 279; trade union
    agreements 281
Prain, Bob. ETU official in General Strike
    16, 18
Prendergast, David 112, 121, 138
Prices and Incomes Acts (1966), (1967)
    34
prices and incomes policies: (1966-7) 34,
    35, 37, 38; (1972-3) 60, 62, 66;
    (1974-7) 74–5, 87
Prices Commission: established 60
privatised electricity industry: completion
    date 285; emergencies and
    contingencies 274–8, 285; increasing
    number of independent generating
    companies 273, 281; generation Seven
    Year Statement 277–8; industrial
    relations 280–6; plant capacity surplus
    277; public relations 279–80; security
    of supply 273–4; 285; shareholders'
    interests 285; structure change 3, 267,
    271, 272–3; vulnerability to assaults 4,
    285
Public Electricity Supply Licence 274
public expenditure cuts (1970) 37
Public Record Office: material used 3
public relations: CEGB134, 154, 171,
    261–7; privatised electricity 279
Public Sector Borrowing Requirement 170

RAF: power strike (1949) men used 28,
    30–1, 32–3
railways: ASLEF/NUR support for
    miners' strike (1984-5) 115, 116;
    ASLEF overtime ban (1972-3) 64, 65,
    68, 70, 72; coal imports prevention by
    NUR 107; coal stocks level for CEGB
    98, 102; coal transport to power
    stations 115, 121–2, 123, 133–4, 139,
    141, 175, 186, 187; contingency

planning 120; diesel locomotives
    traction oil 120; General Strike trains
    run 13, 14, 15; industrial action
    (1976-83) 102, 186; miners' strike
    (1972) 53, 58; miners' strike (1984-5)
    support 97, 115-18, 119–20, 121–2,
    123, 129, 140–1, 248, 255; mining
    industry traditional support 119, 174,
    175, 193; oil for lighting up delivery
    problems 117-18, 128, 206–7; power
    stations connection map 117; services
    resumption after strike 172; strikes
    (1919) 12; strike threats (1983) 101,
    102; tripartite meetings BR, NCB and
    CEGB 186; winter of discontent
    (1978-9) 87
Ratcliffe Power Station 76, 79, 80, 116,
    134, 138, 146, 192, 251
Read Brothers, Forest of Dean hauliers
    247
Regional Electricity Companies 273, 274,
    277
regulation: Electricity Commissioners
    established 5
Relativities Board: report (1973) 60, 68,
    71
Richardson, Derek 137, 232
Richardson, Ronald 66
Richborough Power Station 153, 237,
    249, 251, 253
Ridley, Nicholas 87
road tankers: acquisition by CEGB 101,
    103, 227, 250; independent used in
    miners' strike (1984-5) 118, 154, 162;
road transport: ash removal from power
    stations 187; coal to power stations
    (1984) 115–18, 121–2, 123, 129, 130,
    133, 139, 140, 153–4, 156, 157–8, 162,
    164, 175, 187–90; cost (1984-5) 189,
    193–4; drivers' of coal lorries 178,
    186–7; drivers' attitudes to picketing
    249–50; environmental factors 192,
    193; fraudulent practice 192; garage
    burnt down 154; haulage companies'
    negotiations 187, 189–91, 192, 193;
    industrial gases delivery problems 131;
    legal injunction granted to haulier 247;
    lorries protection 154, 190; lorry
    drivers' frustration in dock strike 140;
    oil, miscellaneous types delivery
    problem 205–7; organisation of
    additional movements 191–3; TGWU

support *see* Transport and General Workers Union; use after strike 194; Yorkshire pits coal delivery 192, 255

roads damage by coal lorries 192–3

Robens, Alf (later Lord) 29, 44

Roberts, R.D.V. 40, 41, 42

Rolls Royce overhaul facility 150, 151, 238–9

rota disconnections *see* electricity supply

Rowan, Jimmy: ETU General Secretary in General Strike 18

Royal Commissions: Redistribution of Incomes and Wealth 89; Trade Unions and Employers' Associations 35

Royal Navy: engines loan for gas turbine generating (1984-5) 239; naval ratings used in some power stations in General Strike 12, 17, 18, 20; power strike (1949) 28, 30–1, 32–3;

Rufford pit 116

Rugeley Power Station 79, 80, 138

St Helens: power station union dispute in General Strike 18, 19

Saltley, Battle of (coke depot) 47, 51–2, 55, 152

Samuel Sir Herbert 11, 14

Scamp, Sir Jack 36

Scargill, Arthur 36, 44, 47, 52, 71, 96, 103, 104, 107, 112, 113, 131, 135–6, 138, 139, 146, 147, 149, 166, 170, 173, 186, 205, 245, 246, 264

Scotland: electricity industry structure 290; electricity transfer in miners' strike (1984-5) 129–30, 174, 199, 211, 218; miners' strike (1984-5) 112, 113; oil-burn power stations 129, 198, 199, 200, 201–2

seamen support for miners' strike (1984-5) 27, 251, 252

Secretary of State: role in electricity supply emergency 273–5, 278

Shell: drivers' attitude to picketing 250; private electricity generation 144

Shepherd, Harry 65

Sherwood pit 116

ship *Kindrance* coal delivery 163; oil tankers *see* oil tankers

Shipbuilding and Engineering Unions 14–15

shop stewards: Combined Works Committee 26, 28, 29

Siddall, Norman 63

Sizewell nuclear power station 7, 92, 222, 249, 262, 263

Skelton Grange Power Station 81, 256

Slater, Jim 139, 163

Smith, Ned 136

social contract: Labour Party/TUC commitment 74–5

South Denes Power Station 153, 191, 237

South of Scotland Electricity Board 129, 174, 176

Spencer, George 15

States of Emergency: dock strikes 24; fuel crisis (1973-4) 66, 72; General Strike 13; miners' overtime ban (1973) 63; miners' strike (1972) 43, 51, 52, 55, 56, 57; miners' strike (1974) 72; power workers' industrial action (1970) 35, 40

steel industry: Orgreave coke plant picketing (1984) 131–2, 248 *see also* Iron and Steel Trades Confederation (ISTC)

Stepney Borough Council: power supplies in General Strike 18-19

sterling: crisis (1947) 24; devaluation (1949) 24

Stevens, Alan 163

Stone, Geoffrey 126

strikes: associated industries to electricity under privatisation 283–4; Conspiracy and Protection of Property Act 1875: 5, 31; days lost (1970) 35; (1971-2) 44; (1972-3) 59; (1977-8) 87; (1978-9) 88, 89; (1980) 89; (1981) 90; (1982) 90 (1984-5) 170; domino theory of NUM 108, 109–10, 112, 113, 173; Government policy in World War One 12; nationalised industries 271–2; pay-freeze (1972-3) 60; picketing *see* picketing; privatised electricity industry 282–3; prohibited in World War Two 23; unofficial 24, 29–30; winter of discontent (1978-9) 88 *see also* General Strike, specific industries *and* States of Emergency *Sunday Times*: electricity price rise story 262; NUM pay claim (1973-4) 62, 71

supergrid: building of 6, 7, 220; miners' strike (1972) use 56–7

supplies *see* electricity supplies

Supply and Transport Committee (STC) 12, 13, 15, 17, 19, 20

Supply and Transport Organisation (STO)
12, 25

Taylor (RH) v NUM (Yorkshire Area) 247
Taylors Lane Power Station 208, 252, 253
technical and scientific staff: industrial
    action (1973) 34, 59, 61–2, 64, 65, 67,
    72; negotiating machinery set up 5;
    running power stations 77, 78–9, 80, 82
Tebbit, Norman 141, 142
Television News 263, 264
Texaco oil supplies 197, 207
Thatcher, Margaret (later Baroness) 2, 88,
    95, 96, 103, 114, 141, 168. 170, 171, 266
Thoresby pit 116
Thorpe Marsh Power Station 48, 79, 81,
    166, 208, 251, 252
Tilbury Power Station 126, 127, 139, 150,
    154, 235, 249, 252, 253
Times, The : fuel crisis (1973) 67; miners'
    overtime ban (1973-4) 68; miners'
    strike (l972) 52; miners' strike
    (1984-5) 113, 114–15, 131, 138; pit
    closures (1981) 96; power strike (1949)
    28; power workers' industrial action
    (1977) 82; printed in General Strike 13
Tir John Power Station, Swansea 27
trade dispute definition 90
Trade Disputes Act (1927) 20
Trade Union and Industrial Relations Act
    (1974) 89
trade unions: actions in tort 90; associated
    industries to electricity 283–4; ballots
    costs 89; closed shop 89, 90 collective
    bargaining 5, 75, 87, 88; Combined
    Works Committee of shop stewards 26,
    28, 29; consultative papers (1983) 90;
    decline of 170–1; electricity supply
    industry 46, 118–19, 126–7, 133, 160,
    173, 241–5, 271, 281–4; Employment
    Acts (1980-84) 221, 246, 247; General
    Strike effect on 20; Industrial Relations
    Bill (1970) demonstrations 37; manual
    workers' negotiating machinery 5;
    membership, changes in law relating to
    90; membership social composition in
    the nineties 284; miners' strike
    (1984-5) CEGB employees and
    118–19, 126–7, 241–3; non-unionism
    post-war 26; picketing *see* picketing;
    power curbing legislation 88, 89, 95;
    power stations single agreements 281;

privatised electricity 281–4; Royal
    Commission on 35;
Trades Union Congress (TUC):
    Conservative economic policy (1970)
    37; economic crisis scenario 284;
    events leading to General Strike (1926)
    12–13; free collective bargaining 75,
    87, 88; guidelines for negotiators 74;
    incomes policy relaxed for miners
    (1973-4) 67–8; miners' strike (1974)
    picket lines 68–9; miners' strike
    (1984–5) Congress debate 184–6, 160,
    242; miners' strike (1984–5) settlement
    168-9; picketing guidelines 242–3;
    progress of General Strike 13–16, 21;
    secret ballots 89, 90; social contract
    (1977) 74; union-labour only contracts
    void 90; wage control legislation 34;
    White Paper *In Place of Strife* 35
transmission *see* electricity supplies,
    national grid, National Grid Company
    and super-grid
Transmission Licence 273
transport: crisis management 3
    see also railways *and* road transport
Transport and General Workers Union
    (TGWU) 118, 119, 131, 139, 140, 147,
    163, 174, 242, 248, 250
Transport Development Group 227
Trawsfynydd Nuclear Power Station 134,
    228, 263
travelling allowances claim: industrial
    staff 76, 78, 79, 80
Trent Valley power stations 77
Tynemouth oil terminal 206

USA: New York blackout 210; oil
    supplies 203–4
Uskmouth Power Station 162, 163, 191,
    212
USSR: Ministry of Power and
    Electrification 135; oil tanker to
    Kingsnorth power station 137, 203

Vey, Peter 262, 264
Vickers, Brian 150
Virgin Island refinery contract 200
voltage reductions *see* electricity supplies

wages *see* pay
Walker, Peter 66, 109, 114, 133, 141,
    166, 171, 205, 262, 265

Wallis, Ed 98, 123, 129, 133, 161, 174, 210, 219
Walsh, John 107
water: CEGB supplies safeguards 101; industry strike (1983) 101; treatment plant chemicals 222, 225, 226
Webb, Bill. ETU official in General Strike 16, 17–18
Weeks, Bob 158
Welbeck pit 116
West, Roy 151, 224
West Burton Power Station 79, 81, 116, 138, 193, 251
West Ham Power Station 18
West Thurrock Power Station 126, 127, 139, 150, 154, 165, 235–6, 249, 252
Westwood Power Station 253
Wharton, Jim 198

Whitakers shipping 206
White, John 122
White Papers: dock strikes (1949) 27; *In Place of Strife* 35; pay policy (1973) 60, 62
Whitelaw, William 66, 68, 69
Wilberforce Courts of Inquiry: power workers (1970) 41–2, 292; miners' strike (1972) 43, 52, 54, 55, 56
Willesden Power Station 27
Willet, Phil 224
Wilson, Harold (later Lord) 71, 72, 75
'winter of discontent' (1978-9) 87
Wooley, John 98, 127, 133, 198
Wylfa Nuclear Power Station 137

Yom Kippur War 61